The Inner Adversary

The Inner Adversary

The Struggle Against Philistinism as the Moral Mission of the Russian Intelligentsia

Timo Vihavainen

New Academia Publishing, LLC
Washington, DC

Library of Congress Control Number: 2006925146
ISBN 0-9777908-2-7 paperback (alk. paper)

New Academia Publishing, LLC
P.O. Box 27420, Washington, DC 20038-7420
www.newacademia.com - info@newacademia.com

To the memory of my parents.

Contents

About This Book

This book is not a history of the Russian intelligentsia. Rather, its subject is the intellectual tradition of the Russian intelligentsia, with special attention being given to the topics "the spirit of the bourgeoisie," "philistinism" and its opposites, "human divinity" and "heroism," as they are reflected in the changing discourses of the Russian intelligentsia. However, this volume is not just a book about "text." I have also tried to put these discourses into the context of political and social history. Especially during the Soviet period, the political "subtext" often became a matter of life and death.

Rather than trace the origins and course of ideas, although attention has been paid to that, I have tried to trace the sequence of these changing and intertwined discourses, which over and over again seem to have been concentrated around ideas about philistinism and its opposites. It seems to me that in this intellectual tradition we can, perhaps, trace the heart of the Russian intellectual tradition, which adopted Western ideas, but gave them special Russian meanings. In a way, this reminds one of Oswald Spengler's famous concept "Russian pseudomorphosis."

In Russia, as in many other countries, anti-bourgeois sentiments were largely concentrated in the intelligentsia. The intelligentsia attained a quite special weight in Russian society where this social group wanted to represent the popular masses, and where the bourgeoisie proper always remained quite small.

The anti-bourgeois tradition has also been an important phenomenon in Western Europe. Its Western proponents have included influential representatives of labor movements, aristocrats and bohemian artists, literary geniuses and social prophets and nonconformists of various calibers. In Russia, however, the role, and consequences, of the anti-bourgeois movement have been even more remarkable.

The Bourgeoisie proper never played a major part in Russian society. This fact by no means hindered the growth of anti-bourgeois sentiments in Russia, but it probably played some role in making the anti-bourgeois movement specifically Russian. For the Russian intelligentsia, the infamous bourgeois spirit was represented first and foremost in petty bourgeois philistinism. This alleged intellectual, aesthetic, and moral defect was not restricted to its original source, the petty bourgeoisie, but could appear anywhere. From the middle of the nineteenth century, the idea that Western Europe—and even more so, the USA—were severely contaminated by philistinism, while Russia was not, gained widespread acceptance in Russia. Both the conservative and radical intelligentsia regarded the salvation of Russia from the philistine danger, as one of their central tasks. The issue of philistinism was at the center of the discourse of the Russian Silver Age.

The Marxists—especially the Leninists among them—defined the issues of bourgeois conscience and philistinism in their own way. After the Bolshevik revolution, the Russian intelligentsia, which had regarded itself as the main task force in the battle against philistinism, was now dismissed for being itself part of the petty bourgeoisie.

However, at this point the Bolsheviks were faced with an ideological problem, because their party was utterly dependent on representatives of the intelligentsia. The Bolsheviks resolved this problem by defining philistinism in a new way. This, to some extent, separated their ideology from both the Russian and the Western European anti-bourgeois traditions.

During the 1920s, the Bolsheviks considered the intelligentsia to be, a priori, an unreliable petty bourgeois element with philistine views and a philistine psychology. By the mid-1930s, however, a new Soviet intelligentsia had been created. New cultural ideas, including a novel way of understanding the meaning of "philistinism" now served the needs of the new totalitarian state. However, the Russian tradition still played a role. Maxim Gorky, who greatly influenced the ideas and practices of the then evolving Stalinist culture, considered the problems of philistinism and the intelligentsia to be central to the Soviet society.

During the second half of the 1930s, the Soviet cultural world was increasingly influenced by "middle class values," to use Vera Dunham's words. The norms and values of the ideal new intelligentsia very much resembled those of the pre-revolutionary petty bourgeoisie. From the point of view of totalitarianism, however, the new system was flawed. The homage paid to classical culture in general and the Russian classics in particular, undermined the new norms. The new Soviet intelligentsia imbibed not only the Stalinist dogmas, but also the heritage of the Russian anti-bourgeois tradition and was never able to extinguish totally its critical attitude towards official Soviet institutions, including the "new classes" and their philistine ways of life.

The approach of this book is essentially a traditional one. The main idea has been to give a new reading to texts, which, as such, are mostly well-known and also to bring together various texts where the topic has been discussed. This is a narrative, which uses the standard materials of the history of ideas and also of political history. The main sources are published texts including ideological documents, news in the daily press, discussions and feuilletons in literary and other journals, manifestoes, memoirs, diaries, literature and literary criticism and the like. Some archival material has also been used, especially the results of the surveillance of people's opinions by the secret police during the 1920s and 1930s. The author has had access to several Soviet archives, including that of the secret police, the OGPU (now FSB). It must be underlined that masses of hitherto secret sources have also been published recently and they greatly further our understanding of the realities of the 1920s and 1930s.

This book is not just a translation of my earlier volume *Vnutrennii vrag*, which was published in Russian. The materials in both books are essentially the same, but the analysis in the present volume has been somewhat developed and the conclusions have been substantiated with new material.

It goes without saying that on many points the author has been able to lean heavily on the work and ideas of other researchers. In this respect, I could mention literally dozens of people, but I particularly want to recognize my indebtedness to those, who have read the manuscript or parts of it: Natalia Baschmakoff, Liisa Byckling, Ekaterina Gerasimova, A.V. Golubev, Jukka Gronow, Elena Hellberg-Hirn, Paula Kaipainen, Marja Leinonen, Pekka Pesonen, Johannes Remy, Richard Stites, Sofia Tchouikina, Irina Takala, Marina Vituhnovskaia and Mikko Ylikangas. I am most grateful for all their criticism and suggestions, which I have tried to utilize to the best of my understanding.

Very special thanks is due to Marina Vituhnovskaia, who worked as my research assistant in 2000-2001 doing all kinds of invaluable work from surveying newspaper material and doing bibliographical searches to planning interviews and criticizing the central ideas of the research. Ekaterina Gerasimova and Sofia Tchouikina, sociologists from The European University of Saint Petersburg, also rendered invaluable service by conducting interviews in Saint Petersburg and collecting newspaper material. They also translated this book into Russian and checked a considerable amount of bibliographical data. I am also glad to recognize the contribution of my colleagues from the Finnish Academy project "Popular Opinion in the Soviet Union during the 1920s and1930s," Jeremy Smith and Iain Lauchlan. Among the Russian partners of our project, the role of professor Andrei N. Sakharov, director of the Institute of Russian History of the Russian Academy of Sciences in Moscow and Dr.Ludmila P. Kolodnikova have been especially important. The services of the FSB archive, its director V.K. Vinogradov, and scholarly secretary N.M. Peremyshlennikova have also been useful. Visits to several centers of Russian studies have been most rewarding, and I want to thank the librarians and colleagues of several institutions in Berlin, Birmingham, Florence, Helsinki, Joensuu, London, Moscow, Paris, Pisa, Saint Petersburg and Tuebingen for their help. Mr Godfrey Weldhen has rendered valuable services in correcting my English.

Financially, this work was made possible by a Finnish Academy grant for a Senior Research Fellow for the years 2000-2002. The Renvall Institute of the University of Helsinki has granted me the best possible surroundings for this kind of work, both mentally and physically. Last but not least, I thank my family.

Timo Vihavainen, Helsinki 2005

1
The Petty Bourgeoisie and its Enemies
"Philistinism" and the "Intelligentsia" in the Nineteenth Century

The concept of the intelligentsia

The concept of the intelligentsia has been defined in a number of ways, which often sharply differ from each other. There is no general agreement as to an adequate definition of the concept, nor is there any unanimity about the historical role of the group, which is denoted by that concept. In fact, the various conflicting definitions of the intelligentsia have often had the practical purpose of serving some political or group interest rather than of elucidating the phenomenon in question. Defining certain social elements or concrete persons as members or non-members of the intelligentsia has been, and is, a very value-laden act. Instead of trying to give an all-encompassing definition of the concept, I will present some examples of the usage of the term, which has varied considerably during the nineteenth and twentieth centuries.

The social group, which has been denoted by the term, has changed in composition over the course of time. Rather than try to extract the sociological essence of the group, which called itself the intelligentsia, I will pick out some moments of fundamental change in the social situation of this group. One red thread that runs through the story is the attention given to the tradition of estrangement among the intelligentsia, its opposition to mainstream culture, state and society. The objects of resistance, the conditions of opposition, and the moods of the intelligentsia changed many times due to state politics, the development of society, revolutions, and the introduction of new ideas. However, certain traditional attitudes seem to have persisted, and I try to chart this development by paying attention to judgments about "philistinism". The term "intelligentsia" was introduced into the Russian language during the 1860s.[1] Hardly anybody, however, thinks that the social group, which has been denoted by the term, appeared as late as that. Some scholars have traced the beginning of the history of the Russian intelligentsia as far back as the Time of Troubles at the beginning of the seventeenth century. Some have pointed to the men of the Enlightenment in the latter part of the eighteenth century, and still others have concluded that the first Russian *intelligent* (the Russian term denoting a member of the intelligentsia) was Peter the Great.[2]

As regards the essence, social role and attributes of the group called the intelligentsia, there have been a number of conflicting views. For some populists (in Russian *narodniks*—friends of the people), like N.K. Mikhailovsky, the term intelligentsia meant the progressive part of the educated classes. For Peter Lavrov, it meant all critically thinking people. For some Marxists, the intelligentsia was a class, but for both Lenin and Stalin, as well as for post-Stalinist Soviet official ideology, it was a social layer (*prosloika*), which had no independent class-character, but which reflected the interests of the ruling class. Non-Marxists, like Nicholas Berdiaev, often considered, and even emphasized, that the intelligentsia lacked class-character. This was also the view of the Socialist Revolutionary Party.[3]

In Brezhnev's time, the official Dictionary of the Russian Language published by the Academy of Sciences defined the intelligentsia as a "social group, which consists of people, who have got education and special knowledge in the fields of science, technology and culture and who are professionally doing mental work."[4] Post-communist dictionaries have more or less returned to the pre-Revolutionary understanding of the term. A definition from the year 2000 defines the intelligentsia as a

> social layer of people, who are professionally engaged in mental, mostly complicated work and with the development and distribution of culture. The concept of intelligentsia is often given also a moral meaning and the group is considered to represent high standards of morality.[5]

The intelligentsia has also been defined by its supposed role of serving the "people" (in Russian *narod*), by being its "brain" and/or by being the conscience of society.

The intelligentsia has traditionally been considered to consist of individual intellectuals (*intelligent* in Russian), who are educated, or, more expressly, who share the quality of *intelligentnost'*,[6] which is something else, and something more than mere education. On the other hand, there have are those who explicitly deny that either education or *intelligentnost'*, which refer to personal qualities of individuals, can be the main criterion of the intelligentsia as a group. Rather, the word "intelligentsia" has been reserved to denote the collective name of that politically active and enlightened group, which, collectively, has a progressive social role and promotes progressive ideas. - Clearly, in this case, there could be members of the intelligentsia, who are not intelligents at all.[7]

It has been thought that the intelligentsia, collectively, felt guilty be-fore the people and was, therefore, obliged to serve it through its knowl-edge, conscience, and behavior.[8] In the traditional sense, an intelligent is not just a specialist doing mental work, but also member of a socially ac-tive group, almost a lay order, whose members are deeply engaged in the struggle for ethical principles.

The origins

Marc Raeff has maintained that "two major themes have dominated the history of Imperial Russia from the reign of Peter the Great to the Revo-lution of 1917: westernization (or modernization) and revolutionary fer-ment." These developments have been brought about, he considers, by the partly overlapping groups of the nobility and the intelligentsia.[9] Raeff's view is well-founded and must be given its due. Here, however, the begin-ning of the story will be put back to a later date. In the modern sense of the word, the intelligentsia, as a social group, was formed in Russia during the first half of the nineteenth century. The first generation, known as "the men of the forties", were mostly of noble origin and well-to-do, whereas the next generation, which emerged in the 1860s and were known as "the sons" (and daughters), came from diverse groups within society (the Rus-sian word "*raznochintsy*" refers to this fact). The birth of the Russian intel-ligentsia is connected with the flow of Western ideas to Russia, especially German romanticism, which gave rise to the renowned Slavophile contro-versy. Sometimes the birth of the Russian intelligentsia is dated to the de-bate, started by the famous "Philosophical Letter," which was published by Peter Chaadaev in 1836 where he presented the blasphemous idea that Russia had not up to then created a culture of its own, but had merely copied Western European culture.[10] The ensuing debate divided the intel-lectually active public into two parts, the Slavophiles and the Westerners. Both were armed with Hegelian philosophy, which purported to be the scientific method in philosophy and was to put an end to the intellectual vagaries of romanticism. It soon proved to be the case that Hegel was as well-suited to promoting the extravagant nationalism of the founders of Slavophilism, the Aksakovs and the Kireevskys as he was the totalitarian anarchism of Mikhail Bakunin and the libertarian socialism of Alexander Herzen.

Along with Slavophilism, the other great anti-Western political and intellectual movement of nineteenth century Russia was a nationally colored Russian form of socialism, which, in its later phase, became known as *narodnichestvo* (populism). Its founding father was Alexander Herzen, who emigrated to Western Europe as an avowed westerner, but once there soon became convinced of the superiority of Russian popular traditions vis-à-vis the Western European social institutions. Both Slavophilism and populism bore the hallmarks of romanticism and both stressed the uniqueness of Russia and the necessity of escaping the fate of being turned into a capitalist (bourgeois) society, as had happened in Western Europe.[11] For the Slavophiles, Western Europe was understood to have become old and barren, and its creative energies were believed to have been spent, whereas the future would belong to Russia, which was young. Russian socialists too began to believe that their society was not simply backward. Russia, which seemed to lag behind Western Europe, was in fact ahead of it. The West had attained maturity, which was reflected in the birth of the middle class. Maturity, however, was just a step away from stagnation, Herzen concluded. Russia, for its part, could be spared the phase of capitalist development, and socialism could be introduced there on the basis of the traditional village commune (in Russian *mir* or *obshchina*).[12] Herzen congratulated the Russians for the fact that the question about socialism, which so deeply divided Western society, was not such a divisive issue in Russia: even the Slavophiles supported it. Russian society was undeveloped, but this just meant that it was free from the ballast of history. A radical transformation was a more realistic prospect in Russia than it was in Western Europe. Russia would never choose the golden mean, *juste milieu*,[13] but stage a revolution with thoroughgoing social consequences.[14]

It was not, however, true that all the intellectuals, "the people with principles," as they were then called would have supported some form of socialism. There were also the liberal Westerners, whose outstanding representative, Ivan Turgenev, inveighed against Herzen's views. However, even the liberals could not avoid being in radical opposition towards the powers that be, for the tsarist state with its program of "official nationality" did not recognize the idea of independent political thinking and public opinion. The famous triad of "orthodoxy, autocracy, and nationality," which Count Uvarov, the minister of education, presented in 1833, was answered by the adoption of the slogan of the French revolution "Liberty, equality, fraternity" by the educated public.[15]

The new-born Russian intelligentsia of the 1840s unanimously supported the idea that there was a substantial cleavage between Russia and "Europe." The main difference amongst them was about the desirable direction of development. The Slavophiles and the Russian socialists supported the idea that the difference between Russian and Europe should persist and even be widened, whereas the Westerners thought that Russian society should become more and more like its Western counterpart.[16]

A new social group and political force

It has often been considered that the phenomenon of the intelligentsia is (or has been) something specifically, even uniquely, Russian. This was already a popular view in the nineteenth century. It was assumed that this specificity was caused by unique Russian circumstances, that is, by the absence of the "parental environment of an established bourgeoisie," by a relative "overproduction" of intellectuals, and most of all, by the policies of an oppressive absolutism, which in other civilized countries had already given way to a more popular rule.[17] Overproduction would be a "rational" explanation for the alienation of a whole social group, which constituted the intellectual elite of the country. However, it is also true that the deep personal alienation of intellectuals was not just a typically Russian phenomenon in the nineteenth century. Although it is not possible to measure the effect of this factor, its existence is no less real for that. It is well-known that many leading intellectuals also experienced this kind of problem in Western Europe at the beginning of the nineteenth century. In the aftermath of the Napoleonic wars, it was called the "*maladie du siécle,*" and the chief concerns of the alienated individuals had an existential rather than a social character, but quite often the problem was also projected onto society. For Herzen and Bakunin, as well as for Thomas Carlyle or Comte de Saint-Simon, social issues were closely intertwined with the problem of alienation (although they hardly used the word) and also quite expressly with personal concerns. In the new post-war cultural context, the individual's life for many men of letters seemed to be hopelessly devoid of meaning. In order to solve the dilemma, the lonely individual had to be "reconciled with the reality." In practice this often meant merging with the community. As a member of a greater whole one could attain a meaningful, even eternal, life. Capitalism, which had made "payment in cash" the sole liaison between human beings, as both Karl Marx and Thomas Carlyle defined the new spirit of the age, not only deprived people of the material goods, to which they were entitled, but also of their souls.[18] In fact, social activity often became a way of dealing with personal problems, which had arisen from deeply personal longings. Accordingly, political discourse, even when it was pursued in a most rationalistic, dry-as-dust way, was laden with passions, which stemmed from the inner depths of the human soul.

Alienation, which was caused by the new impersonal order in society, certainly existed in Europe and not only among literary men. Social unrest, which swept across Europe from England to Silesia, very probably had its roots in the newly-established capitalist mode of production.

In Russia the toiling masses had not yet experienced either the vices or the virtues of a modern capitalist economy. Nevertheless, in Russian literature and society during the first half of the nineteenth century the "superfluous man" figure also loomed large, from Griboedov, Pushkin, and Lermontov to Turgenev and Chekhov. It was not just a literary loan from the West. To some extent it clearly reflected endemic social processes. A whole new group of people, the *raznochintsy*, which belonged to none of the old estates, had now emerged and continued to grow rapidly during the second half of the nineteenth century.

Eventually, the group which called itself the intelligentsia became more and more alienated from both the state and high society. The social activism of the "people with principles" and "critically thinking people" increased in the 1860s. Clandestine political organizations were born. Both the Land and Freedom (*Zemlia i volia*) of the 1860s and its follower the People's Will (*Narodnaia volia*) of the 1870s adopted a Manichean position, where the tsarist government was demonized and the simple people, the *narod*, became an object of uncritical adoration. The student youth adopted the new radical ideas en masse and the new word "intelligentsia" was introduced to denote all those who were politically active and took the side of the "people." Being a member of the intelligentsia attained a specific meaning. Ivan Turgenev, who did not use the word, depicted a "nihilist" type in his novel "Fathers and sons" (1862). Although the literary type of "nihilist," represented by Turgenev clearly did not apply to all members of the intelligentsia, it certainly gave its stamp to the new generation. The "superfluous man," or alienated and noble individual, that Pushkin, Lermontov and Turgenev had described- had already been a model for the old generation. The "sons" now developed the alienation still further by adopting an irreconcilable attitude towards the tsarist state and society, which they wanted to remold in a most radical way.

Along with existential and socio-psychological problems, remarkable changes in the social position of the educated classes also took place in Europe. Naturally this happened also in Russia. It would appear that to some extent, one can explain the radicalism of the Russian intelligentsia by the relative overproduction of educated people and the ever-growing mass of the *raznochintsy*.

The expansion of higher education in Russia was rather rapid. During the nineteenth century the government for some time even artificially retarded the process, in order to keep radicalism in check. But the process could not be stopped; indeed, it accelerated, particularly from 1900 onwards.

The pace of growth was quite impressive. The number of university students, which had been 4125 in 1865, had doubled by 1880. In 1899 the number was 16295.[19] As the number of students increased, more and more representatives of non-gentry elements began to have access to education. However, this "democratization" must not be exaggerated. The nobles preserved their position in the universities remarkably well: in 1880 they accounted for 46, 6 percent of the students at 8 Russian universities, and in 1900 the number was 51,8 percent![20] In 1906 48,4 percent of the university students were still of gentry origin "or scions of civil servants."[21]

It is true that the social origins of the students in absolute terms does not tell us very much about the group known as the intelligentsia. If we look at the statistics of those who were mixed up in political trials, the following picture emerges:

During the period 1884-1890, 30,6 percent of the people accused in political trials had been of gentry origin. In 1901-1903 the figure was 10,7 percent. At the same time, the figure for offspring of the clergy fell from 6, 4 to 1,6 percent and for honorary citizens and merchants from 12,1 to 4,1 percent. The proportion of people who were of petty bourgeois (in Russian *meshchanstvo*) origin rose from 27, 5 percent to 43,9 percent and that of "countryside estates" rose from 19,1 to 37,0 percent.[22] In fact, it seems that the much-abused petty bourgeoisie (as an official estate) was rather the backbone of the political movement in Russia during the second half of the nineteenth century. The official classification used in Russia in those days does not give a clear idea of the social background of the elements concerned. Some representatives of the "petty bourgeoisie" could well have been, in fact, workers and many "nobles" were in fact starving outcasts of society. However, when we are told that in 1884-1890, 34, 2 percent of the accused in political trials had higher education and 33, 2 percent intermediary education, it is clear that political radicalism in the nineteenth century was an elitist occupation. It was also concentrated in educational institutions. During the 1860s, no less than 60 percent of those who took part in the "social movement" (political activity), were students and in the 1870s their share was 52 percent. Thereafter their share fell and at the beginning of the twentieth century it was somewhat less than 10 percent.[23] The numerical strength of the educated classes grew rapidly.

By the middle of the First World War there were 125,000 higher-education students, of which 30,000 were women. The number of schoolteachers, for instance, grew even faster. In 1900 there were about 60,000 teachers in elementary schools. By 1914 their number had increased to 135,000. The educated classes were also becoming more "democratic," while a substantial gentry element still survived. The proportion of hereditary nobles among the educated classes had been 23,2 percent in 1880, whilst in 1914 it was 7,6 percent. Adding the offspring of the personal nobility[24] would seriously inflate the numbers.[25]

It goes without saying that not all of those who received higher or intermediary education identified themselves with the politically active intelligentsia. The number of scholars and literary men, who, rightly or wrongly, could, a priori, be conceived as the vanguard of independent thinking, was still very small. At the end of the nineteenth century there were 3,296 professional scholars and litterateurs in Russia, while there were no less than 151,346 civil servants, 204,623 clerks of private industry, and 52,471 representatives of the "military intelligentsia."[26] Clearly, among the cultured classes, representatives of the loyal bureaucracy far outnumbered those inclined to opposition. Among the educated classes of Russia, active fighters against the autocracy must have been in a minority.

The moral dimension

The intelligentsia proper was, however, understood to be an opposition group, which was fighting the autocracy. The influence of this element also far exceeded its numerical strength. Being in irreconcilable opposition to the autocracy and selflessly fighting for the rights of the martyred people, to which the *intelligenty* were not supposed to really belong, was an integral part of the myth of the intelligentsia, the key to its self-understanding. It has been stressed that the Russian intelligents did not have the same role in society as, for instance, their French counterparts.[27] A Russian *intelligent* was not just a critic of the powers that be or of mainstream culture and society. Still less was he or she merely an educated or learned individual. As a rule, he or she had to fulfill all these criteria, but this alone was not enough. A Manichean picture of the martyred "people" on the one hand and the oppressive state and its supporters on the other, ruled out the prospect of peaceful coexistence and the building of a civil society on a basis of mutual tolerance and compromise.

The underlying moving force of the *intelligent*, who dedicated his life to the people, was guilt. Only the first generation of the intelligentsia had been preponderantly of gentry origin, but even the later representatives of this group, who were separated from the people by virtue of being educated and freed from the physical toil and brutishness of popular life, retained a feeling of guilt. It is also true that the gentry element among the intelligentsia always remained large. Paradoxically, becoming educated lifted the individual out of the ranks of the "people," into the ranks of the intelligentsia, which, for its part, unselfishly dedicated its life to the service of the people. It goes without saying that this model of life had religious overtones and counterparts. The guilt-complex of the Russian intelligentsia and its "obsession with the ideas of collective sin and social redemption engendered a general outlook which can only be described as eschatological," writes Tibor Szamuely.[28]

The image of the classical Russian *intelligent* became, in the "ideal" case, that of a martyr, like Alexander Radishchev, Pavel Pestel, or Nikolai Chernyshevsky, who paid for their opinions with their own freedom and lives. It was not only the champions of freedom of speech and conscience who attracted sympathy. People who had undertaken the task of killing the tsar also received the admiration and sympathy of the mainstream intelligentsia. The People's Will's terrorists were hanged by the tsarist state, and subsequently the "official savagery" of the state claimed the lives of many others. The views and convictions of these people could not be overcome by violence; indeed, the effect may very possibly have been the opposite. The example of the martyrs attracted thousands of followers in the second half of the nineteenth century. The students of St. Petersburg University, which, incidentally, was exceptionally aristocratic,[29] had shown the way in the early 1860s and soon the students of many other institutions of higher learning became fervent fighters for the freedom of the "people."

On the mythological level, the idealized self-image of an *intelligent* can be found in literature. Nikolai Chernyshevsky's novel *What Is To Be Done?* became holy writ for the Russian radical intelligentsia and the "new people" which it described. The character of Rakhmetov, whose life belonged to the people, and who was also an awe-inspiring man of iron will, was, for many, the ideal intelligent.

The moderate intelligentsia

But not all educated Russians were, or wanted to be, members of this militant intelligentsia. There were always people who were lukewarm, skeptical or inimical towards the radicals. There was always sharp intellectual criticism of the excesses of the radicals. The most devastating critique of the radical tradition was presented by Fedor Dostoevsky, who, in his novel *Memoirs from Underground*, attacked Chernyshevsky's magnum opus with murderous irony.[30] His novel *The Possessed* (*Besy*) in fact described the notorious case of Sergei Nechaev, who had made his followers murder a member of the group. The main reason for this collective crime may have been to further the radical cause by welding the culprits still more tightly together in their service of the organization.[31] Many other luminaries of Russian cultural life, even people considered to be leading progressive intellectuals, were equally unsympathetic to the excesses of the radicals. Ivan Turgenev described how the liberal generation (the "Fathers") had to give way to the radical nihilists (the "Sons"), in whose hands the noble ideas of the intelligentsia degenerated into vulgar blasphemy and hooliganism. Later, Anton Chekhov who had also experienced his own period of social activism became disappointed with the realities of the Russian intelligentsia of his day.[32] Leo Tolstoy, whose ethical maximalism and anarchism were extremely radical and served as an inspiration for a part of the radical intelligentsia, at the same time preached non-violence and even non-resistance to evil, which was a far cry from the ideals and practices of the men of action. Tolstoy was not only an enemy of the state, but also of the hierarchies and hypocrisies of civil society. With some justification, he has even been considered a predecessor of the Bolshevik revolution, even though he preached a religion of love.[33]

Consequently, the educated, politically conscious classes in nineteenth century Russia were by no means a united tightly-knit revolutionary order, as one might think from reading some anti-intelligentsia pamphlets and treatises. Writers like Tolstoy, Turgenev and Chekhov described intellectual types, who were conscious of the great social issues ("accursed questions") of the day without being militant radicals. One example is Levin in Tolstoy's *Anna Karenina*, a man, who deeply felt the wrongs of society, but instead of joining the political struggle, preferred to restrict his activity to his immediate surroundings. For many, self-perfection was a more vital issue than politics. Chekhov's characters rather typically represented those traits of personality which were understood to constitute so called *intelligentnost'* namely, perceptive and compassionate attitudes towards fellow human beings. Checkhov is important in this respect, because his characters[34] are also considered to be typical *intelligenty*, even though their differed considerably from that of Turgenev's Bazarov or Chernyshevsky's Rakhmetov, who were the other archetypal intelligents.[35]

It would appear that a kind of mainstream political correctness among the intelligentsia wanted to reserve the term "intelligentsia" for the active militants, who accepted even the most radical means if they served the struggle against absolutism. Therefore, people like Chekhov, who considered universal human values absolute and inviolable, sometimes even refused to consider themselves members of the intelligentsia at all.[36] It can be assumed that there were always two intelligentsia traditions; one radical and even extremist and another moderate and soft-minded, although the former always seemed to prevail.[37] The former gave its stamp to the word "intelligentsia," while the latter represented the values of *intelligentnost'* with its overtones of refined sense of morality, and an empathy and respect for human dignity.

Since the beginning of the 1860s, being a member of the intelligentsia had more or less become the equivalent of being in uncompromising opposition to the regime and entertaining a tendency for self-sacrifice. Politics was for the militants, the all-encompassing element of life, and revolution was understood to be the panacea for all problems. After the abortive 1905-07 revolution, a group of *intelligenty* came into second thoughts about the clearly self-contradictory nature of the myth of the intelligentsia. They challenged the mainstream and self-complimentary views of the intelligentsia, maintaining that the intelligentsia's social role had been fruitless and even detrimental and that its philosophy was superficial. They published a pamphlet called *Vekhi* (*Signposts*), which was devoted to criticizing the radical Russian intelligentsia and its moral and intellectual condition. In the opinion of the *Vekhi* group, the staunch, caste-like opposition and rigid articles of faith of the intelligentsia had deprived it of a real role in building society and had instead led it into a futile struggle for a revolution, which would supposedly work miracles and solve all society's problems once and for all. This faith, however, had no foundation in reality.[38]

The *Vekhi* critique of the intelligentsia after the revolution of 1905 was a major symbolic watershed in the history of the intelligentsia, but it did not have a decisive effect on future developments. The February revolution in 1917 was, once again, largely a creation of the radical intelligentsia. Even though it seems to be the case that the majority of the intelligentsia was inimical to the October coup of 1917 (or "The Great October Socialist Revolution," as it was officially called in the Soviet Union), many authors have expressed the idea that the intelligentsia also has to bear a lot of responsibility for the totalitarian regime, which subsequently condemned Russia to captivity for a period of three generations.[39] Tibor Szamuely, the son of a famous Hungarian revolutionary, has concluded that an essential element of Russian totalitarian thinking originated and persisted in the tradition of the intelligentsia.[40]

According to Szamuely, one of the elements of Russian totalitarianism, which gave rise to the Soviet Union, was the Russian state tradition, from the Mongols to Alexander I and Nicholas I, whilst the other was the revolutionary tradition, born of the intelligentsia, from the Decembrists to the Marxists. Indeed, as Szamuely shows, the Russian intelligentsia does offer an imposing array of revolutionary fanatics with a totalitarian approach; such as, the nihilists of the Young Russia, the conspiratorial principle of Nechaev, and the proto-Leninist idea of a ruling minority-party of Petr Tkachev.[41] Many of the tenets of Russian revolutionaries had been invented by the Jacobins of the French Revolution, or by the utopian socialists of the mid-nineteenth century. According to Szamuely, the important point is that politically the Russian intelligentsia was anti-liberal and hypnotized by the prospect of a miracle-working revolution. It was alienated from society and the state and lived in a world of its own.

It never cared about legal forms and guarantees of personal freedom and other liberal institutions. On the other hand, Szamuely points out that the Russian intelligentsia also always believed that the interests of the individual must be subordinated to those of society.[42] With the exception of the minor current of Bakunin's anarchism, the Russian ideological and social beliefs of the intelligentsia were statist and authoritarian. This was true of Slavophiles and Westerners alike, Szamuely asserts.[43]

This is a truly devastating critique, but many other authors have, more or less, shared Szamuely's verdict. The *Vekhi*-almanac in 1909 had already made, essentially, the same analysis. Several critics have subsequently pointed to the unconstructive and alienated attitudes of the intelligentsia. For example, Alexander Solzhenitsyn, who, with some other dissidents, published an almanach called *Iz-pod glyb* (*From Under the Rubble*) in the 1970s, considered himself an heir to the Vekhi-tradition and condemned what he perceived to be the barren radicalism of the intelligentsia.[44] Solzhenitsyn's massive multi-volume novel *The Red Wheel* (*Krasnoe koleso*) is obviously written from the point of view of a liberal-conservative critic of the intelligentsia. The sympathies of the author are with the Octobrist Party, who wanted to co-operate with the authorities in order to survive the First World War. The radicals, from the SRs and the Bolsheviks through to the Kadets, who were preaching liberalism, and whose policies in any Western country would have been ordinary liberalism, were represented as destructive forces in Russian society, which had a specific nature.[45] Not all authors, however, have shared the harsh verdict on the intelligentsia of a Szamuely or a Solzhenitsyn. Isaiah Berlin, a staunch critic of totalitarianism and authoritarianism, has expressed his great admiration for the Russian intelligentsia: "The phenomenon itself, with its historical and literally revolutionary consequences, is, I suppose, the largest single Russian contribution to social change in the world."[46] Berlin conceded the totalitarian character of such a self-professed champion of liberty as Mikhail Bakunin, but noted that Alexander Herzen, a socialist and hence a collectivist, always remained a champion of the liberty of the individual and a "sworn enemy of all systems and of all claims to suppress liberties in their name."[47]

The political and social role of the intelligentsia apart, the representatives of this group have been ascribed a mass of specific positive attributes, which have been denoted by the word *"intelligentnost'."* In the opinion of Soviet dissidents during the post- WW2 period, "intelligents" were thought to embody such qualities as morality, honor, pity, conscientious work, decency (*poriadochnost'*) and honesty. It has also been said that an (ideal) intelligent is lacking in aggressiveness and suspiciousness, suffers from an inferiority complex, and has gentle manners.[48] In short, at least since the perestroika period, it is being commonly believed that the intelligents also represent the quality of *intelligentnost'*. This may, however, be a Soviet and post-Soviet, rather than pre-Soviet idea. Certainly, literary heroes like Dostoevsky's Verkhovensky and Turgenev's Bazarov or real-life *intelligenty* like Sergei Nechaev and the People's Will's terrorists were not obvious champions of humane and moderate *intelligentnost'* values.

The enemies of the intelligentsia

The intelligentsia, understood politically as a fighting order against absolutism, was, naturally, resisted and detested by large segments of educated society. High society for its part hated those who detested it and disturbed its peace of mind, even though many of its members had relatives among the militant intelligentsia. Respectable people of whatever social origin who were happy to adapt their lives to the framework of the existing order did not like troublemakers. Among educated society, however, the rebellious "friends of the people" became more and more respectable. Even such people who did not share the revolutionary views of the activists, often considered it to be their duty to defend them against the brutality of the regime. A *cause célèbre*, where this attitude was demonstrated, was the trial of Vera Zasulich, whom the jury declared not guilty of attempted murder, although the evidence against her was clear.[49] The pressure towards conformism among the educated classes of the nineteenth century Russian society was enormous, as Dostoevsky, among others also testified. He told his publisher Suvorin, that nobody, including himself, would inform the police about a planned terrorist act. Everybody would fear the stigma of being an "informer" more than death.

> The liberals would never forgive me. They would torment me, drive me to despair. Is this normal? Everything is abnormal in our society: That is why all these things happen, and nobody knows how to act –not only in the most difficult situations, but even in the simplest. I would have written about this... but one can't do so. In our society one is not allowed to speak about the most important things.[50]

But enemies of the intelligentsia were always present, not only among the well off, but also among the "people" itself, which the intelligentsia wanted to defend. The case of the peasants, who, in the 1870s, had handed over rebellious students, who had tried to preach their revolutionary gospel to them, to the police, is well known. But it was not just the "unenlightened" peasants, who resented the intelligents. Even workers were malevolent an suspicious towards their self-appointed friends. For instance, it would appear that the self-righteousness of some of the *intelligenty* aroused the ire of the more mundane representatives of the people. The huge void between the intelligentsia and the other sections of society even survived the revolution due to such distinctive traits as their way of thinking, which seemed perverse and incomprehensible to outsiders. Their manners were different, as was their mindset, which could be suspected of being patronizing, along with their pretensions to superiority. Ivan Turgenev described in a piece of fiction, how workers (in 1878) did not care a bit about the hanging of an intellectual, who was suffering for their cause, but were only interested in getting a fiber of the hanging rope, because it was supposed to bring good luck.[51]

Well-educated people of the older generation resented the arrogance of the new intelligentsia, which it considered half-baked. M. Zheltov wrote in 1890:

> We used to have 'learned people' as well as 'educated people' and besides also such people, who were not 'learned' people and not 'educated' ones, but in any case 'wise' people. But 'Intelligentsia' and *'intelligentnost'* do not refer to the first group, nor the second or either the third one. Any dropout, who has picked up some new-styled sayings and words, often even one, who is a complete blockhead, but uses such words, is considered to be an *'intelligent'* and the whole group of them is being called the *'intelligentsiia.'*[52]

During the Soviet period the word *"intelligent"* at first was a term of abuse, and up to the end of the Soviet period the concept bore at least some potentially negative connotations. The negative traits of the *"intelligenty"* were attached to certain traditions of the intelligentsia way of life.

In a dictionary of the Russian language, published in 1935, the term *"intelligent"* was explained as follows:

> *Intelligent*...(contemptuous): One, whose social conduct is characterized by lack of will, wavering and doubts; *Intelligentstvo* (cont.) -pattern of thinking, customs (*privychki*), typical of an I.; *Intelligenshchina* -the same as *intelligentstvo* (but still more despising)."[53]

More recently V.B. Kataev has presented several other derogatory forms of the word *"intelligent"*: *"intelliagushka"* (intelfrog), *"antiligent,"* *"zatykannyi intelligent"* (full-stuffed intelligent); *"intelligusiia"* (intel-gooses).[54]

During the Soviet period the term "*intelligentnyi*" denoting the virtues of the social group of the intelligentsia, also received pejorative counterpart, "*intelligentskii*," which denoted the vices of that group, especially as it had been before the revolution. The Dictionary of Russian Language of the Academy of Sciences elucidated the term in the 1980s, citing Lenin: "Solving controversial issues by much shouting, swearing and with unfounded declarations is the typical manner of intelligent (*intelligentskie*) circles."[55] A citation from Maxim Gorky puts it in the following way: "It seems to be that in an intelligent-like (*intelligentskii*) way you are busy with yourself." One of Nikolai Ostrovsky's heroes assured "I tell you, that derives from her intelligent-like (*intelligentskii*) soft-mindedness."[56]

Iu. S. Stepanov, who has studied the contemporary intelligentsia, refers to a term, which bystanders used about the people (intelligents), who marched in Moscow in 1991 to demonstrate against the, ultimately, abortive putsch. For the mob, the intelligents were *ochkariki*—people, who wore spectacles. In fact, said Stepanov, they did not wear spectacles any more so than the bystanders, but they were the kind of people who "in principle" wore spectacles.[57]

As contemporary authors observed, in the 1920s the epithet "*intelligent*" could be used as a word of abuse by proletarian-minded youths who despised the over-refined manners or ways of other youths. In this context, its meaning was more or less equal to "petty bourgeois."[58] This was the approach of the masses, of those who did not regard themselves as intelligents. The lower ranks of Soviet society did not like being considered inferior by those, who were more educated, well-bred, and quite often got better salary for an occupation, which was rarely physically exhausting and was mostly done in comfortable and tidy surroundings.[59]

This resentment may have something in common with Lenin's critique of the intelligents: they were whining and wavering, they were upset by the spectacle of the (deserved) slaughter of some thousands of bourgeois bloodsuckers, whereas the proletarians had a more straight-forward attitude: when trees are felled, splinters fly.[60] It was, to say the least, awkward that the whole top layer of the party and state apparatus, Lenin himself included, was not proletarian. A few officials did have proletarian origin, but now they were doing desk-work. They were proletarians only "by conviction."[61] The opinion surveillance of the secret police made it plain to those in power that despite their wish to be regarded as the "responsible workers," the masses regarded them as were "the others" along with "the new bourgeoisie, the "Jews," the "academics," the "rotten intelligentsia" and the "little tsars."[62]

The negative image of the intelligent in many respects resembled that of his/her counterparts in France and Germany. As Dietz Bering says, *"ein Intellektueller"* was almost always a derogatory word in the German language. In the Weimar Republic the conservative nationalists and Nazis associated the intellectual with abstract reasoning that is someone devoid of instinct, prone to "negative analytical thinking" (dismissed as "dissection"). An intellectual smelt of rootlessness, decadence, city-life, and Jewishness.[63] In France, where the term *"les intellectuels"* attained notoriety during the Dreyfus-scandal, the same attributes were used.[64] For the Nazis, the most serious defect of intellectuals was their lacking the capability for action.[65]

The age of Marxist newspeak

The "responsible functionaries (*rabotniki*)" of the Soviet era were officially considered to be part of the new "working" intelligentsia, which was officially recognized in the 1930s. Actually, the common people did not see a substantial difference between this privileged caste and the "bourgeoisie." According to some intelligence reports, this view was widespread. It was even called the "people's truth."[66] In other words, the official justification for the privileges of the administrative caste as opposed to the toilers was well-known, but perceptions about everyday practices determined the assessments of the common people.

In the Soviet Union, some remnants of the culture of the pre-revolutionary educated classes seem to have survived. The intelligents retained some of their old traditions in the private sphere and continued to meet each other at certain concerts and libraries. In the Soviet period, this element came to be called the "hereditary" (*nasledstvennaia*) intelligentsia and its members probably did not really consider themselves as belonging to the same group as the masses of "party-nominated" intelligentsia. In this context, the term "intelligentsia" obviously obtained a new meaning: to belong to the intelligentsia meant to be cultured and was not a synonym for political engagement –rather the contrary.

For some educated radicals, who did not want to be *intelligenty* at all, but adopted a "proletarian" identity, the *intelligenty* were considered inferior, because of their softness and lack of resolution. In 1937 Stalin stressed that the inevitable, and probably innocent, victims were not the main consideration in social engineering. They were probably unavoidable, but the main point was that revolutionary violence had to hit all the right targets. Not a single "wrecker" was to survive.[67] It was the humanitarian scruples of the intelligentsia, which were most despised by top Bolshevik luminaries. Lenin had this in mind, when he said that the *intelligenty* were not the brain of the people, but its shit.[68]

For Lenin, who always liked to use Marxist terminology, the intelligents were, first of all, representatives of their "class," although they were not a class in themselves. Their consciousness was determined by the class they served. Accordingly, the engineers and scientists were, first of all, bourgeois. They might not have been capitalists themselves in any sense, but they had been serving that system and been remunerated by it. They were part of the old society, which had to be turned upside down. In his writings from the early days of the Bolshevik revolution, Lenin considered the bourgeois specialists, who were obviously part of the intelligentsia, as part of the old order, which had to be kept in check and repressed: its property might be partly confiscated, and the masses would be instigated against it to get the spoils, but, on the other hand, the specialists would, in the short term, be paid a better salary than the average worker. This was to be temporary, for full equality was the natural goal of socialism.[69]

However, apart from the specialists, there were also politically active intelligents outside the ranks of the Bolshevik party. As the Bolsheviks, by definition, were the only party which expressed the interests of the proletarians, all the other parties were dubbed "petty bourgeois." In the case of the SRs, for instance, this had a certain Marxist logic, because the SRs purported to represent the peasants, who, as petty producers, were also "petty bourgeois," according to Marxist theory. The Mensheviks, Anarchists and other socialist parties, which appealed to the proletariat, were regarded as petty bourgeois by virtue of their "opportunism." In the case of the Mensheviks, this referred to their unwillingness to take power in a situation, where, according to their Marxist analysis, the conditions for a proletarian revolution had not been satisfied.[70] In the case of the anarchists, their "opportunism" referred to their propensity to go too far to the left, thus endangering the revolution.[71]

"*Intelligent*" became a term of abuse in the young Soviet country that was the USSR and was more or less fused with the term "petty bourgeois." This liaison persisted, to some extent, up to the end of the Soviet period. Even though the petty bourgeoisie was annihilated in the Soviet Union as a class, it always existed abroad. The image of the petty-bourgeois political *intelligent* (the Trotskyites, the SRs, the Mensheviks, and the Kadets) in the Soviet press was repulsive: small men with spectacles and mustaches, often with an umbrella, looked like rats and always had a cowardly air. Incidentally, the image of the bureaucrat, who always had a briefcase with him, was almost identical.[72]

German Marxists between the world wars considered the vices of intellectuals in much the same way as their Russian brethren: the intellectuals were unruly individualists, who lacked (class) instinct, they were feeble in their revolutionary faith, and were wavering opportunists, proud of their education and learning. Worst of all, they were petty bourgeois and it was from amongst them that fascism obtained its ideologues.[73]

The petty bourgeois mind: philistinism

The English word "philistinism," which I have chosen to denote its Russian equivalents, is somewhat problematic. In Russian there are several words, which can be used interchangeably, which have approximately the same meaning as philistine. One of them is *meshchanstvo*, which originally referred to a social estate of urban kleinbuerger, who were neither peasants nor gentry, nor members of a merchants' guild. As a rule, the *meshchane* were extremely poor, often subsisting on the verge of starvation. In 1897 there were 7, 449, 300 members of this estate in Russia and they comprised 44,3 percent of Russian townspeople.[74] The adjective *"meshchanskii"* means traits that are typical of the petty bourgeois. The small Soviet encyclopedia in 1930 defined the term as follows:

> Restrictedness of views, narrowness of opinions, philistine (*obyvatel'-skoe*) striving for personal well-being, separateness from the common interests of the collective. The basic cell of the '*meshchanskii*' way of life is the family.[75]

The Dictionary of Russian language defined the term *"meshchanskii"* in 1983 as: "restrictedness caused by the interests of the petty proprietor, philistine (*obyvatel'skii*)." A citation from Chekhov's letter elucidated the meaning: "There is nothing nastier than the *meshchanskaia* life with its coins and meals, its absurd discussions and senseless conditional virtues."[76] The term *"obyvatel'"* and the adjectival form *"obyvatel'skii,"* which originally referred just to a permanent resident of a place, has almost exactly the same meaning and can be used interchangeably with, *"meshchanin."*[77]

The adjective *"melkoburzhuaznyi"* refers to the same layer of citizens and the psychology attached to it, but also has also a "scientific" use and a scholarly connotation, while *"meshchanskii"* is reserved almost exclusively for moral purposes. There is also the word *"filister,"* which is a synonym of *"meshchanin"* and *"obyvatel',"*[78] but is rarely used and belongs to a literary or high style.

The English word "philistine" is probably the best equivalent of both *"meshchanin,"* *"obyvatel',"* and *"filister,"* but sometimes it may be better to translate the term as "petty bourgeois," keeping in mind that the meanings are not always exactly equivalent.

In the Russian language, there is also a special adjective, *"poshlyi,"* which refers to the mental world and values of the philistine. The Dictionary of Russian language defines it as "something that is low or trivial in a spiritual or moral sense... unoriginal, banal... contains something indecent, unworthy." A second meaning refers to something that is "unoriginal, sickening, worn-out, banal... tastelessly rude, vulgar."[79] The concept of *poshlost'* has been made famous in the West by Vladimir Nabokov, who maintained that it is a uniquely Russian category of understanding. As defined and described by Nabokov, *poshlost'* is pretentious sham: "not only the obviously trashy, but also the falsely important, the falsely beautiful, the falsely clever, the falsely attractive."[80] A modern scholar, Svetlana Boym is skeptical of the supposed Russian uniqueness of the concept and refers to it as "Russian version of banality, with a characteristic national flavoring of metaphysics and high morality, and a peculiar conjunction of the sexual and the spiritual. This one word encompasses triviality, vulgarity, sexual promiscuity and lack of spirituality."[81] Nabokov holds that pre-revolutionary Russians were especially averse to *poshlost'*, whereas some nations, like the Germans, were very prone to it, not to mention America, which was just concentrated *poshlost'*. Boym points out that Nabokov has in mind the criteria of good taste of the Russian aristocracy, which were more or less taken over by the intelligentsia in the second half of the nineteenth Century.[82] "Ashamed of being too common and unable to be *comme il faut* in the traditional aristocratic sense,"[83] the intelligentsia and especially its radical vanguard, the nihilists, adopted looks that made them look different: short hair for women and long hair for men, untidiness and so on. "Awkwardness and a lack of social grace were turned into signs of authenticity and were cultivated as part of the new revolutionary self-fashioning," as Boym explains.[84] Boym thinks that the intelligentsia had "peculiar inferiority-superiority complex" and saw itself as the spiritual heir of the aristocratic tradition. The petty bourgeoisie (*meshchanstvo*) for its part, which was part of neither the aristocracy nor peasantry, did not fit to the intelligentsia's romanticized ideal of the common people. Paradoxically, then, the petty bourgeoisie, which was a very normal phenomenon, was considered "perversion and profanation of true Russian folk."[85]

Boym's criticism may be quite correct as deconstruction, but at the same time it unavoidably reflects the point of view of a de-moralized world, where the high and the low in society are no longer strictly separated from each other, and where making value judgments has become a sign of unabashed arrogance, whereas it used to be a *conditio sine qua non* for any civilized person.[86] This was not the world of nineteenth century Russia. The moralist approach has always been a matter of course for the Russian intelligentsia. It was so already with Herzen, whose *My Past and Thoughts* is a highly moralistic verdict of Nicholas I and the Russian bureaucracy of his time. Emigrants like Nicholas Berdiaev wrote prolifically on moral matters, including the topic of *poshlost'*, in emigration.[87] Moreover, the moralistic approach persisted among the Russian intelligentsia throughout the entire Soviet period. The Soviet intelligents were quite shocked, when they met a morally complacent West during and after perestroika.[88]

The way of life of the petty bourgeoisie is determined by the necessities of private life (*byt*).[89] Having no higher aspirations than comfort and success for himself and his family, so it was claimed, the philistine indulges in things that may be described by the words *"poshlost'"* and *"kitsch."* In any culture, concepts have their specific contents, which cannot be translated into another culture by using just one word or two. *Byt* or private life has been considered to be one of these. It is the time one takes for oneself, one's family and friends. For obvious reasons *byt* was demonized by the radical intelligentsia. In the 1920s Vladimir Mayakovsky envisioned Karl Marx resurrected, shouting anathema on the philistine *byt*:

> The revolution is strangled up in philistine threads
> More terrible than Wrangel is philistine *byt*
> Better
> To twist off canaries' heads, So communism
> Won't be struck down by canaries.[90]

It may be noted that S. Smidovich, using the authoritative forum of the Small Soviet Encyclopedia, proclaimed expressly that it was not canary-birds or curtains, which made a person philistine as such, but the psychology, which placed home and its cares above those of the collective.[91] The family, as an institution, was the root of philistinism (*meshchanstvo*), but in the Soviet Union, family was already fading away (in 1930) and giving way to other varieties of human community.[92]

In the nineteenth Century the concept of *byt* also had another usage. The Slavophiles even assumed that the Russian peasant in his land-commune was living not just for his own sake, but that his *byt* meant communion with the whole community, unselfishly taking care of the common interest.[93]

Since time immemorial, or at least since the beginning of the nineteenth century, it was the bourgeois, atomized family, and its bourgeois way of life which was despised by the Russian intelligentsia. Indeed, private life and the idea that one's home was one's castle where one lives just for oneself were despised by Russian travelers to Western Europe already as early as the eighteenth Century. A renowned observer of Russia of the beginning of the nineteenth century the Marquis de Custine related that the private sphere was underdeveloped in Russia. Herzen later answered in kind repeating the Russian critique of the isolated way of life and illustrating it with examples of the life of the French bourgeoisie.[94] It would be rather risky to maintain that the Russian's private life was especially underdeveloped. The great mass of the peasantry lived in much the same way as their colleagues in neighboring countries, or anywhere in the world, as Maxim Gorky used to point out. As modern research has shown, the idea of the Russian peasant's supposedly altruistic, communal way of life was no more than a myth.[95] Certainly, it seems plausible that, among the educated classes, private life and its "philistine" charms were despised by the Russian intelligentsia more than by its counterparts in many other countries, at least so far as this is reflected in its ideological pronouncements.

As was mentioned above, all segments of the Russian intelligentsia loathed philistinism, as a matter of course. Moreover, the Russian intelligentsia, or at least a substantial part of it, also shared an aversion towards the bourgeoisie in general and was appalled by the prospect of Russia adopting capitalism and developing a sizable class of bourgeoisie.[96] Very often the words "bourgeois" and "petty bourgeois" were used interchangeably. On the Slavophile side, and not only there, the idea of an innate "anti-bourgeois" nature of the Russian people[97] had remarkable support from the first half of the nineteenth century down to the revolution and beyond.

It is also true that being anti-philistine was by no means an exclusively Russian characteristic, even though many Russian intellectuals liked to think so.[98]

Anti-bourgeois traditions

There had been several anti-bourgeois currents in Western Europe since the eighteenth century. For the most part they were not exactly political but were content to just criticize and despise the bourgeoisie. Some, however, did have a program for building a better world. The heritage of such currents of thought was instrumental in creating the psychological basis for what has been called "political religions:" communism, Nazism, fascism, anarchism. The "sacralization of politics"[99] is an age-old phenomenon. To give just a couple of examples, we may refer to the Jesuits in Paraguay, Calvin in Geneve or the Taleban in Afghanistan. It would appear that in every age in the history of humankind there have been people who have been excessively obsessed with existential problems, and others, for whom daily life has been almost their sole concern. Since biblical days, zealots have loathed the lukewarm and imagined a better world purged of blasphemers and the feeble-in faith, preferably by God himself.

Sacral politics with immanent, worldly contents appeared with the French revolution. Jacobinism and its followers from Robespierre to Saint-Just, Babeuf, and Buonarroti developed radical constructions, which J.L.Talmon has called by the oxymoronic name "totalitarian democracy."[100] It would be wrong to equate such different phenomena as Russian messianism represented by Dostoevsky of Solzhenitsyn, and Russian totalitarianism represented by Lenin or Stalin. Yet all of them are critical of the profane bourgeois way of life and yearn for a higher purpose of existence.

The bourgeois way of life began to be represented as a problem at the beginning of the nineteenth century. Within the upper, enlightened layers of society, the Enlightenment destroyed the naïve faith in religion, and it became clear that man's eternal existential needs would, thereafter have to be satisfied by other means.

Isaiah Berlin has stressed that the idea of the "artist as a sacred vessel" was exceedingly widespread in the first half of the nineteenth century. It was a new phenomenon and artists like Mozart and Haydn would have been very surprised if they had been told that as artists they were "particularly sacred, lifted far over other men, priests uniquely dedicated to the worship of some transcendent reality, to betray which is mortal sin."[101] Berlin believes that this idea came largely from Germany. I would risk saying that Johann Gottlieb Fichte's influence was important here. Fichte's famous works *Ueber das Wesen des Gelehrten* and *Anweisung zum seeligen Leben* explicitly demonstrated the sacred nature of the vocation of the man of letters as the middleman between divinity and the popular masses.[102] Fichte also stressed the importance of turning the divine vision into action: only in action does man became "real." In fact, people, who lived outside the divine sphere, did not actually exist at all. Their deeds were doomed to perish in history. This also made the idea that a righteous man was stronger than a hundred mean ones understandable.[103]

As we know, Fichte was very popular among the Stankevich circle, which brought together such luminaries of the newly-born Russian intelligentsia like Bakunin, Belinsky, Granovsky, Herzen and Konstantin Aksakov. Bakunin even translated some of Fichte's works.[104] It was Fichte, who created the idea of the "hero as the man of letters" to use the formulation of Thomas Carlyle, another of Fichte's pupils.

Fichte's starting point was individualism, even solipsism, which, in a mental tour de force, was turned into a kind of proto-totalitarian thinking in terms of the greater entity (*Gattung*). The people became the enlarged "me," which was to serve under quasi-divine leadership in order to be "free."[105]

True, in Russia, Fichte's popularity was not long-lived; he was soon overshadowed by Hegel, Feuerbach, Schopenhauer, and others. However, the fundamental idea of the divinity of the immanent world, and especially of the people, was to stay in Russian discourse. It may be that its roots were in the orthodox idea of *"bogochelovechestvo,"* the deification (*theosis*) of human beings.[106]

When the radical political religion of the French revolution and its diluted Napoleonic continuation resulted in political bankruptcy, the restless souls looked for immanent salvation elsewhere. The subsequent wave of psychological alienation, which was typical for the era of romanticism, has been mentioned above. One should probably stress that the psychology of Europeans of the first half of the nineteenth century had many dissimilarities with that of the 21 century. The human mind was not understood in terms of psychoanalysis, and the individual was not seen as an end in himself, but rather as an incarnation of certain collectively approved vices and virtues, good or ill.[107] As a result of the new intellectual and political situation, a spirit of forsakenness overcame many youthful souls. This was the renowned syndrome of the superfluous man, estranged and forsaken, not just in society, but in the universe. Lord Byron, Stendhal, Mikhail Lermontov, Giacomo Leopardi, Alfred de Musset, Alfred de Vigny, Thomas Carlyle and countless others suffered from the so-called *maladie du siécle*, or paralyzing depression, which offered the prospect of an empty eternity and a senseless world, which offered no possibility of a higher existence.[108]

While the bourgeoisie went on living more comfortably than ever and seemed to be happy with its earthly concerns, and insensitive to the sufferings of the proletariat, on whose exploitation its opulence was being built, poetical souls had to find other solutions. On the one hand, they had to solve the existential problem of being forsaken in an empty universe, revealed to humanity by the progress of science. On the other hand, there was the emptiness caused by the erosion of the old society. Capitalist development destroyed the old patriarchal *Gemeinschaft* and substituted for it the new impersonal capitalist *Gesellschaft*, to use Ferdinand Tönnies' famous concepts.

The novel nature of bourgeois society aroused reactions on the part of intellectuals on various levels. A satanic rebellion against God, a cynical play with life and death were the answers given by romantics such as Byron and Lermontov. Others, like Carlyle, or the "prophets of Paris," Saint-Simon, Fourier, and Comte invented solutions, where the isolation, shallowness, and hypocrisy of the prevailing society was overcome and a return to "community" was achieved in the mutual warmth of communes. Each of the latter authors also developed a kind of immanent religion, where the supposedly true talents and propensities of man were emancipated and which was supposed to quench the metaphysical thirst of man and reconcile both the emotional and rational elements of the human soul.[109] Each of them was destined to recognize that the great majority of their fellow citizens were not interested in their prophecy.

Saint-Simon, Fourier, and Comte, each of whom seems, at least from a twenty-first century perspective, to have been eccentric, and each of whom, indeed, spent some time in lunatic asylum at some point in their life, were, nevertheless, immensely popular across the whole of Europe in their day. If we are to believe Herzen, among the most cogent reasons for their popularity was the fact that they presented an idea of a better, more caring community and, in the case of Saint-Simon in particular, that meant recognizing the importance of the carnal instincts of man, which the hypocritical and suffocating nature of bourgeois society was not prepared to do.[110]

If we look at nineteenth-century France, we can conclude that there was a lively anti-bourgeois tradition from the Great Revolution of 1789 up to the fin de siècle modernists and beyond. A representative of the 1850s, Gustave Flaubert, described, how bourgeois "grocers" with their frocks and false respectability made him feel physically sick. Flaubert, who occasionally called himself Gustavus Flaubertus Bourgeoisophobus, characteristically wrote to Gorge Sand: "Axiom: Hatred of Bourgeois is the beginning of all virtue".[111]

Flaubert's aversion towards the bourgeoisie does not, however, approximate the kind of psychology, which was typical for the Russian intelligentsia, Isaiah Berlin asserts. He believes that, unlike French intellectuals, the Russian intelligentsia was convinced of the need for a total commitment to the cause of truth: their attitude to life and to art was identical. The French, by contrast, were happy to think that art was for art's sake and hardly expected that an intellectual to be a moral example.[112]

Thomas Carlyle was truly representative of the anti-bourgeois reaction in the Anglo-Saxon world. In a ruggedly Scotch manner he applied the ideas of German romanticism to British realities, pointing out, how unfavorably the profane practices of British society compared with the divine nature of existence. He loathed the "respectability" of the "gentleman" and the "respectable" cant, which also prevented the common man from seeing the grandiose, metaphysical meaning of the world around him. This lack of "reason" was, incidentally, not at all connected with a lack of education, which, in any case, did not offer "reason" to anyone, but, instead, just inculcated intelligence, which only had an instrumental use. True understanding depended on the mindset of the individual, not on learning or education, which did not necessarily provide anything of importance. Thoroughly honest people could always recognize the truth of things delivered to them by great men: the heroes. While the truth always prospered and untruth perished in history, the righteous were also given an eternal life, for their deeds never perished.[113]

It was cleat, then, that people, who lived in the superficial world of appearances and hearsay and did not dedicate their life to the serving the truth, however austere that might be, were not to have eternal life. In fact they did not even have a temporal life, Carlyle reasoned. From the point of view of God, which transcended time and place, those gentlemen (and ladies, the philistines of either sex, we could say) did not exist at all.[114]

Carlyle's views contained elements of many contemporary continental, especially German romantic doctrines from Kant, Fichte, Goethe, and Novalis, to mention a few. It has even been said that Carlyle's thinking was no more than a *"resumé de tous les doctrines contemporaines."*[115] Carlyle did not create a system of socialized politics, but his thinking is pervaded by the idea that all of life, including politics, should retain contact with the mystical essence of reality, and that a person's everyday life should not be allowed to fall to the level of the profane material concerns of the individual. In Carlyle, conquering "happiness" was definitely not possible by material means, if it was possible at all. He reasoned that even if all the bankers, upholsterers and confectioners of Europe would found a joint-stock company to make a shoeblack happy, they would not succeed. Or, they could succeed only for a couple of hours. This was because the shoe-black has a "soul, which is not the same as his stomach."[116]

Carlyle was cultivating the heritage of Fichte, who, for some time, was very popular both in Germany and in Russia. Carlyle's doctrine, as regards practical politics, was very unclear and its corollaries were hardly compelling for anybody inclined not to believe in it. In this respect, Hegel, who soon became enormously popular on the European continent, was different and was believed to signal the dawn of a new epoch. Hegel's philosophy was greeted as a scientific method, which would render romanticism obsolete.[117] Of course, this proved to be wrong. In a certain and very real sense different thinkers like Mikhail Bakunin, and Ludwig Feuerbach, Vissarion Belinsky, Ivan Aksakov, and Alexander Herzen can hardly be denied the honor of being called romantics, even if most of them did not think of themselves in this way. For all of them, politics was not just a case of pragmatic production and distribution plus administration. Hegel, like his followers, endeavored to explain the essence of the whole world, no less. Accordingly, the absolute justification of any political conclusions, including extreme measures, could, in principle be demonstrated. The Hegelian understanding of the world as a process of progressive history, which was proceeding through revolutions, where different "principles" stood in antagonistic conflict, also easily enabled ideas about the "creative" nature of annihilation, as is the case with Bakunin's thinking.

Among the Hegelians, Marx and Engels, as well as many of their followers, also retained the spirit of sacral politics in their early writings and, in effect, continued to do so until the end of their lives. Knowing the secret of history armed man with divine understanding and even gave him license to do anything, which could be proved right from this higher point of view. Eternal life was also within reach for people, who fused their personal life with the service of great causes, serving their class or national spirit, which had a mission in the progressive course of history.[118]

I believe that the modern reader is likely to miss the emotional impact which the most dry-as-dust philosophical systems often had on the readers of the nineteenth century, whom it released from the fetters of conventional morality and metaphysical uncertainty. Ludwig Feuerbach, for instance, did not just show that religion had been invented by men, he also rediscovered the inherent divinity in things immanent, which the human mind had projected to the transcendent world. This is how Feuerbach ends his book *Das Wesen des Christentums*:

> So remember God... the man, at every moment, when you eat your bread...But don't forget...gratitude to the holy nature....So one must just interrupt the usual, banal succession of things in order to bring back the unusual meaning of the usual and the religious meaning of life in general. Sacred be, therefore, for us the bread. Sacred be the wine but sacred also the water! Amen."[119]

The psychology of the author reminds one of the religious experience as understood by William James or, by that matter, the zen-buddhists.[120] Although becoming conscious of the mystical or transcendental nature of this world did not always lead to political chiliasm, it often did. Feuerbach's most famous pupil in Russia was Nikolai Chernyshevsky.

Unlike his mentor, Chernyshevsky always wrote in a restrained manner. His very influential novel *Chto delat'? (What to Do?)* is written in an almost mockingly matter-of fact manner. However, its influence among the youth of the day was immense. In fact, the author's serene style probably just helped give more impact to the radical message of his book. The book, which to later generations seems quite dull, spoke about "new" people, who had begun to behave in a rational way and had organized their mutual relations according to the rules of rational egoism. From Feuerbach, Chernyshevsky had got the idea that only individuals are real, and it is not difficult to deduce that if there is something divine in the world, it must reside in the individual. Chernyshevsky, who spent years in prison and banishment for his ideas, became the archetypal intelligent. He was a martyr, one of those "new men," whom he had depicted in his novel. It is well-known that Chernyshevsky's *Chto delat'?* was V.I. Lenin's favorite book.[121]

Political extremists and the problem of quietism

The enemy, for all of the representatives of sacral politics, was the petty-bourgeois mind, which could neither grasp anything great nor sacrifice its personal comfort for the promotion of larger-than-life ideas.

Sergei Nechaev, Peter Tkachev and Mikhail Bakunin were representative men of the Russian intelligentsia, who drew the logical conclusions of the philosophical doctrines of the day and did not stop at half-measures. Nechaev and Bakunin wrote jointly the Revolutionary Catechism, where the ends and means of political struggle were exposed. "The revolutionary", the programme said

...is a lost man. He has no interests of his own, no affairs of his own, no feelings, no attachments, no belongings, not even a name of his own. Everything in him is absorbed by a single, exclusive interest, a single thought, a single passion –the revolution. In the very depths of his being, not just in words but in deeds he has broken every tie with the civil order and the whole educated world, with all laws, conventions, generally accepted conditions and morals of this world. He will be an implacable enemy of this world, and if he continues to live in it, that will only be so as to destroy it more effectively... He despises public opinion; he despises and hates existing social morality in all its demands and expressions. For him moral means everything that facilitates the triumph of the triumph of the revolution; everything that hinders it is immoral and criminal... Day and night he must have only one thought, one purpose –merciless destruction. Working tirelessly and cold-bloodedly towards this aim, he must always be prepared to die and to destroy with his own hands anything that stands in the way of this achievement...[122]

The authors of the catechism divided Russian society into six categories, each of which had to treated differently –exterminated at once or later, ensnared and blackmailed, provoked into savagery and so on. The mindset of the authors could hardly be called Machiavellian, rather, it was, in many ways similar to Ignatius Loyola and his followers. As the final goal represented something of infinite value, it was impossible to consider anything commensurable with it. "Wrongs" were not wrongs at all, if they eventually brought about infinite happiness. As the catechism put it:

> The association has no other aim but the fullest emancipation and happiness of people, i.e. the toiling masses. As we are convinced that this emancipation and happiness can only be achieved through an all-destroying popular revolution, the association will use every means in its power to foster and spread those wrongs and those evils which will finally break the patience of our people and force them to general revolt....[123]

Nechaev committed murder, was caught, tried, and sentenced to jail. Although he became the anti-hero of Dostoevsky's *The Possessed* and even while the conspiratorial principle proved a failure in practical politics, the spirit of extremism survived. As Tibor Szamuely concludes: "The revolutionary amorality he practiced and preached was hardly different in essence from the principles generally, if tacitly, accepted by the radical intelligentsia".[124] It could be said that from the point of view of the authors of the Catechism, "amorality" was something, which philistines and those, who were feeble in faith, ascribed to the revolutionaries. They, in turn, considered themselves to be serving a sacred cause and proved their faith by sacrificing human beings, including themselves.

Dostoevsky's *Possessed* is an influential, although not necessarily accurate, description of the social psychology of the period and the reactions towards revolutionary extremism. As such it deserves closer examination. In his novel, Dostoevsky describes the generations of the "fathers" and the "sons" in glaring colors, often turning them into caricatures. The "fathers" are superficial nonentities: Karmazinov (evidently representing Turgenev)[125] is a shallow, conceited windbag, and Stepan Trofimovich Verkhovensky is a depraved good for nothing, a sentimental crank. The "sons" for their part are more serious characters. Pyotr Stepanovich Verkhovensky, whose character Stepan Trofimovich has spoiled by his own irresponsibility, and Nikolai Vsevolodovich Stavrogin are both engaged in crime. The "sons" have received their program from the "fathers" which Stepan Trofimovich Verkhovensky Sr. (whose model was T.N. Granovsky)[126] understands, but the point is that they take it seriously, which the older generation did not. Stavrogin's fascination with crime does not arise from lack of will, which was typical for the "fathers." For him, the inability to find God is the central problem, indeed, the matter of life and death, not just a subject for idle talk as it was for the "fathers." Petr Stepanovich Verkhovensky is a serious person and does not lack character. Criminal acts are natural for him and they are fully in accordance with his view of the world. The socialist ideals they profess, in fact, mean nothing for the young heroes. The superficial and mediocre nature of their nihilist following is greeted with open contempt by them. However, one understands, it is Stavrogin and Pyotr Stepanovich Verkhovensky, who deserve to be taken seriously. The writer chose a passage from the gospel of Luke as the motto of the book: there the evil spirits, which have gone to a man, are driven away by Christ and go to swine, which go mad and perish.

This somewhat cryptic motto obviously points to the importance attached to the deep concern over the existential dilemma and to the idea that genuine spiritual experience is the only salvation from the evils, which have come into the world with the disappearance of God. In Dostoevsky's book, even the ridiculous and depraved Stepan Trofimovich Verkhovensky finally finds his way to God after forsaking his philistine way of life.

But do the masses of philistine nihilists and their fashionable supporters in high society have any salvation? Dostoevsky twice cites the Apocalypse, where the divine spirit tells:

> I know your deeds, that you are neither cold not hot. I wish you were either one or the other! So, because you are lukewarm, neither hot nor cold, I am about to spit you out of my mouth. You say, 'I am rich; I have acquired wealth and do not need a thing.' But you do not realize that you are wretched, pitiful, poor, blind and naked.

Although Dostoevsky does not use the word "philistine" in its modern sense, it is clear that he too thinks that the lukewarm do not belong in the kingdom of God. The people, for whom personal riches, spiritual or material, are enough, are nonentities, the inferior part of humanity.

But there was still hope. Stepan Trofimovich Verkhovensky was a perfect scoundrel. He had spiritually killed his son; he had made an innocent man a criminal in order to cover his gambling debts; and his life was not only despicable but also ridiculous (and being ridiculous was something many of Dostoevsky's heroes feared more than death). However, this representative of the "fathers'" generation succeeded in rationalizing his pettiness by means of the shallowest arguments. His life was a complete lie. Almost right to the end of the book, it seems to the reader that this person was organically incapable of anything higher, and will never even recognize a need for it. However, at the end of his life he miraculously understands that everybody needs "an idea of something, which is immeasurably better and greater than himself. If that is taken away from people, they do not live, but die out of desperation." Paradoxically, then, this representative of the "fathers" generation lives an empty life and is a curse to his environment, yet miraculously seems to be saved at the very moment of his death.

The "sons" for their part, although apparently concerned with great ideas do not find an idea that is "immeasurably better and greater than themselves". It is not possible to create a human God.

The book ends with the death of Stavrogin, the candidate for human divinity. He dies of desperation, but, one is led to believe that this was not necessary. He was neither one of the lukewarm, nor an irredeemable philistine, but he had gone astray and had not found the path to truth.[127]

The social perils of philistinism

Unlike heroes and philosophers, for Carlyle the hero and the great thinker were likely to be the same person, the petty bourgeoisie and their mindset, philistinism, was obviously too dull to warrant much discussion among the philosophers of the nineteenth century

Probably the most influential contribution to the theory of the petty bourgeoisie was that of John Stuart Mill, who himself would hardly have been denied the status of a petty bourgeois thinker by many of the more romantic souls of the nineteenth century.

John Stuart Mill was the son of James Mill, who, along with Jeremy Bentham, was one of the founders of utilitarianism. Utilitarianism, which made pretensions to being the one and only scientific ethical system, had developed the idea of a pleasure calculus as the unerring criterion of good and evil. John Stuart Mill had been taught in his childhood to analyze everything from the point of view of maximal residual pleasure. As a bright young thing, he had succeeded very well in learning this method. However, it turned out that not all psychological problems could be solved for good by using this "scientific" device. Mill underwent a psychological crisis, where he felt like a "lifeless stock or stone, without feelings."[128] At this time he became acquainted with Carlyle, whom he considered a poet. The latter, for his part saw in Mill a mystic and a close friendship was born which lasted several years. The political views of the two thinkers did not actually coincide and Carlyle's *Latter Day Pamphlets* finally led to a parting of ways.[129] This experience of psychological emptiness in bourgeois society and his ensuing flirtation with romantic ideas, however, probably made Mill more open to the importance of the problem of the fateful psychological stagnation of bourgeois society and the need for a plurality, and free competition of ideas.

Mill formulated his ideas on the danger which philistinism, this "conglomerated mediocrity," caused to society, in his famous essay "On

Liberty." He purported to show that society must be open to new ideas, otherwise it would become stationary. There was "a warning example" – China. China had remained as it was for thousands of years. It had succeeded in making all people alike. "If they are ever to be farther improved, it must be by foreigners," Mill concluded, without actually presenting evidence about the actual state of things in China.[130] In Europe, Mill claimed, public opinion represented a yoke, against which individuality had to assert itself. Otherwise Europe ran the risk of becoming another China. So far, it was diversity that had saved Europe.[131]

In his classical treatise, Mill pointed to the eternal *bête noire* of the intelligentsia of any country: conformism. Public opinion, however "democratic," did not foster innovation or any deviation from mainstream ideas or norms whatsoever, but suffocated it. In fact, the democratic majority was always mediocre and, thus, petty bourgeois by definition. But it had to be forced to develop by clever individuals, who had the courage to defy it.

In Russia, the most remarkable critic of the petty bourgeoisie and the petty bourgeois way of life (meshchanstvo) was probably Alexander Herzen, who had emigrated to Western Europe as a Westerner, but soon became a critic of Western society and was especially appalled by the spiritless materialism of Western society. France, England, Italy, and Germany were all petty bourgeois, Herzen concluded, but America was even more so, its society having only the middle class. Philistinism had only two virtues, moderation and punctuality (*umerennost' i akkuratnost'*). Philistinism, the last word of civilization, was based on the absolute rule of property and was rapidly expanding.[132] Herzen also noted John Stuart Mill's warnings about the perils of stagnation, which collective mediocrity was causing.[133]

For the Russian intelligentsia, philistinism meant, of course, more a state of mind than a social category. People who excessively cared about themselves were not respectable from the intelligentsia's point of view. To avoid being suspected of philistinism, it was advisable to use worn-out clothes, to ignore one's own personal hygiene and look unconventional: boys could have long hair, while girls cut theirs short This was a way of distinguishing oneself from the petty-bourgeois mass.

Needless to say, anti-bourgeois *épatage* and deviation from the petty-bourgeois norms has later become a major phenomenon everywhere in the modern world. It may well be that, as an institution, it was born among the Russian intelligentsia in the sixties of the nineteenth century. It also persisted throughout the Soviet period. Occasionally the aversion to philistinism in the Soviet period came to mean a rejection of all kinds of material niceties. According to some memoirs, some intelligents, in order to avoid philistine contamination, possessed no dishes, no real furniture, and held no ceremonies like weddings or birthday parties. For some reason even traditional Russian felt boots (*valenki*) were considered philistine.[134]

This testifies to the longevity of the heritage of the literary figure of Evgeny Bazarov, the nihilist in Turgenev's Fathers and Sons. He also forsook everything that was not rational and useful, including polite manners. Rationality, including the commonplaces of natural science, was something for which the nihilists had a pseudo-religious respect, but rationality was for them nothing more than what they were able to understand in scientific terms with their own reason.[135] It has been pointed out that the Bazarov model was, in fact, already intellectually outdated at the beginning of the twentieth century.[136] But this did not change the radicals' contempt for the "useless" adornments of life. Usefulness, for that matter, was not exactly an intelligent but a philistine quality, but in some instances it could be used in order to "*épater le bourgeois.*"

The real difference between an *intelligent* and a philistine was in their value orientation. The philistine's "usefulness" was just senseless concentration on the agenda of daily life, for the *intelligent*, for whom life always had a higher meaning, be it altruistic dedication to the cause of liberating the "people," bringing them the light of understanding (intellectual or artistic or moral), or religious or pseudo-religious, moral-political salvation in the land commune or through Marxist socialism.

Soviet Russia inherited its educated class from tsarist Russia. The generation of the intelligentsia which experienced the Russian revolution was very conscious of its responsibility for the fate of Russian culture and society and of the spiritual heritage of the intelligentsia tradition. The Russian "Silver Age" developed a whole body of original ideology, where Western ideas were fused with domestic ones and often attained a totally novel form and essence. This was especially true concerning ideas about the intelligentsia, philistinism, the people, and the revolution. Therefore, it is necessary to look closer at the pre-1917 situation. This will be done in the next chapter.

2
The Discourse of the Silver Age

The general setting

The epoch, which has been called the Silver Age of Russian culture comprises roughly the reign of Nicholas II (1894-1917). This period produced an impressive quantity of interesting thinkers and excellent artists. By now, Russia had become one of the great European cultural centers, where new ideas originated and old ones were fruitfully developed. This was the time of the "*Belle époque*" of Western Europe, of Epicureanism, of the opulence and frivolous pastimes of the well-to-do as well as of angry threats and demands from the masses, of political tension and a growing need for social reforms and democratic institutions.

The same tendencies could be seen in Russia, which by now was more closely connected with Western Europe than ever before. Steamships, railways, telegraph, and even the telephone cut the distance between Western Europe and the vast plains of Russia, which until recently had been almost like a foreign continent, hard both to reach and leave. Now the contacts were lively and the number of Russians who visited Western Europe was steadily growing. The popular press spread news and ideas on an unprecedented scale. While the famous "thick" journals of the Golden Age had sold in hundreds, modern newspapers had a readership of hundreds of thousands.[1] It is true that the literacy rate still was rather low in Russia, but it must be born in mind that most representatives of the young generation could already read, including practically all the young men, who had served in the army. This was also the politically most active element. The development of Russian society lagged behind Western Europe as regards the pace of popular education, for instance, but it was also a comparatively new institution elsewhere. Here, the difference was hardly qualitative, but rather quantitative. Russia was making progress all the time and the pace of that progress was fast.

At the same time, the Russian way of development showed its specific traits. Many of the social issues were the same as in Europe, but there were also differences, which were not only quantitative but even qualitative. In Russia, the uneven pace of social change and industrial development had caused exceptionally strong tensions, which revealed the backwardness and vulnerability of certain parts of the society. The famine of 1891-92, which exposed the ineffectiveness and corruption of the tsarist system, was a major milestone in the history of Russian civil society, whose collective memory recorded the vices of the bureaucracy and the virtues of intelligents like Korolenko, Tolstoy, Chekhov, and others, who actively struggled for the relief of the people.[2]

Now, a new generation of the intelligentsia, "the grandsons" emerged. Unlike its predecessors, it largely shared a liberal outlook, or, at least, paid lip-service to it.[3] But this was not the liberalism of the so called "small deeds," which had prevailed earlier among the gentry, but one of so called "senseless dreams," that is, a radical variety, which met hard-headed opposition from the tsar. Marxism also began to be increasingly popular in Russia. To some extent, the growing professional middle class cherished the traditions of the old Russian intelligentsia. The business middle class was underdeveloped in Russia and the politically active civil society did not exactly look very "petty bourgeois," as regards its outlook. On the contrary, its unofficial groups, the "circles," which became very popular since the 1890s, and even the professional unions often nurtured radical ideas and, on some occasions, defiantly presented them to the autocracy.[4]

As a new political force, the workers also entered the political stage. As a more educated and politically more active element than the peasants, the workers soon became the new symbol for "the people" for many intelligents. The workers were lionized, adored, and envied for their class-instinct but the love was not always mutual. However, the workers represented a new element, which was not only politically active, but even shared "intelligent" ideas, which the peasants had never had.[5]

Some have concluded that the ills of Russian society stemmed from the "developing country" syndrome, whose basic ingredients included very rapid growth of population and an inability by the emerging industry to employ "surplus people," whom the small land holdings of the village communes could not feed.[6] At the same time, industrial growth was very rapid, with French capital boosting industrial enterprise and railway construction. The industrial output of the empire, as well as the number of factory workers, who often worked in huge production units, multiplied in a couple of decades. But the increased wealth was not evenly distributed. One of the most threatening results of these developments was the growing gap between the well-to-do layers of society and the rural and urban proletariat, which lived at a subsistence level. Things were not made any better by the inflexibility and narrow-mindedness of the new monarch. Only after the revolutionary turmoil of 1905 did Nicholas re-luctantly consent to make certain concessions to civic society, although he soon succeeded in restoring much of his powers. After the brief epoch of Stolypin, a supreme power was once again in the hands of second-rate tal-ents. On the eve of the First World War, the issue of defending the people from the violence of the tyrannical state, had lost none of its potency since the days of Nicholas I. Moreover, this struggle had by now developed much fiercer methods than had ever been seen before. By the early twen-tieth century, politics was no longer the exclusive occupation of the elite. Popular masses became more and more active, which, in the turmoil of the 1905 revolution, often took the form of callous violence, where the "red rooster" (arson) was let loose, and representatives of the higher classes and their agents were brutally murdered. Almost 3000 manor houses, that is, 15 per cent of the total, were destroyed in 1905-06.[7]

At the beginning of the twentieth century the issue of violence also came increasingly to the fore in intelligentsia circles. It was not only the neo-populists, the SR party and its fighting organization that began to or-ganize assassinations. Other political movements did so with remarkable success and the government answered in kind. Once again the intelligen-tsia approved the terror. The views of the terrorists were now considered so compelling that even parts of high society approved of them.[8] This may be considered a novelty, even if Dostoevsky had already complained about such sentiments as we mentioned in the previous chapter.

After the 1905-07 revolution, the terrorists were effectively destroyed by a state conducted counter terror, which was initiated by Stolypin. Ca-sualties were now counted in thousands. Compared with the nineteenth century, the new epoch already seemed more cruel and destructive.

As noted above, politics now became a popular occupation in many senses of the word. During, and after, the 1905-07 revolution, the popular masses became the decisive factor in political life. The "mass society," which had been a distant possibility for the contemporaries of Tocqueville and Herzen, had also become a reality in Europe. It was no longer enough to speak for the people and in the name of the people, the popular masses themselves had a say, and the intellectuals, who wanted to work for them, had to convince them and canvass their support. Doing propaganda work among the popular masses was no novelty in Russia, where leaflets had abounded as early as in the 1860s, and where the intelligents had tried to "go to the people" in the 1870s, but now it became a genuinely real business, where great successes could be had. The issues of the day had to be explained to and inculcated by, a semiliterate or even literate mass audience, which was not always without its own ideas.

It has been noted that Slavophilism, which had begun as an idealistic current more or less critical of the powers that be, had, by the beginning of the twentieth century, become a xenophobic, proto-fascist movement, which supported autocracy and reaction. Rabid anti-Semitism, spurred by false accusations and forgeries, culminated in pogroms. Some scholars have considered the "malign" progress of slavophile ideology to be something specifically Russian.[9] However, this kind of process did not take place just in Russia. Among European intellectuals, racism had its heyday in the decades of high imperialism.[10] Chamberlain and Gobineau in their time were not considered to be just eccentric cranks. Racial science was a respectable occupation. The adoration of one's own nationality, on racial or other grounds, was the order of the day throughout Europe. In mass society politicians had to flatter their clientele. General categories as class, race and nationality were well suited for this purpose. In Germany, the "*völkisch*" ideas, which praised the innate merits of the German people, were already well-developed by the beginning of the twentieth Century.[11] Russia was, in fact, the first country to create the institution of organized xenophobic political hooliganism, but after the First Word War it was rapidly adopted by Italian, German and other comparable mass movements. It should also be kept in mind that the renowned Russian "Black hundreds" were by no means a respectable part of the educated community. They were mostly supported by peasants and clergymen whilst in the Duma, their outstanding representatives Purishkevich, Markov, and Dubrovin were constantly censured and castigated for hooliganism and unruly behaviour.[12] Political correctness prevented any decent representative of the intelligentsia from cooperating with the "black hundreds" and the political forces behind them.[13]

As regards the renowned "accursed questions" of the Russian intelligentsia, its relation to the popular masses was put into the test by the new social situation. Especially during, and after, the 1905-07 revolution, the issues of "serving" the people, fighting "for the people" and going "with" the people, which had been more or less abstract in past decades, had been filled with a quite new content. Paradoxically, the revolution had given rise to repulsive scenes, which hardly even the staunchest idolaters of popular virtues could hardly approve. Vandalism and the spilling of innocent blood was no longer seen only as the preserve of the powers that be. When representatives of the tsarist establishment spoke about "Pugachevs with university diplomas," they did not need to go to the eighteenth century to find examples of popular savagery. Moreover, in some cases mob violence, allegedly inspired by the extreme right and the police, had also been directed against students and other representatives of the intelligentsia.[14] Finally, the establishment of the Duma and freedom of the press in 1905 totally changed the situation for the intelligentsia. Now it became possible, even realistic for it to try to affect the state's policies and discuss political issues of almost any kind. The change was, in principle, a qualitative one. As the possibility of taking part in the political process was now open, estrangement from the establishment was no longer predetermined, but became an optional stance for the intelligentsia.

The question of nihilism. The Nietzschean dilemma in turn of the century Russian thinking

What one might call the Nietzschean dilemma of the human predicament was not a brand-new phenomenon in Western intellectual history at the beginning of the twentieth century. The idea of the Death of God, or, at any rate, man's troubled relationship with God had been the subject of a mass of romantic literature and philosophizing ever since the early nineteenth century. In philosophy, German romanticism had concentrated on questions of immanent salvation in a world where belief in a transcendent God was waning. During the second half of the nineteenth century, Marxism, a hybrid of Hegelianism and materialism, proved to be the most persistent variety of Hegelianism, but even Marxism was soon divided into several orthodoxies and split by revisionism. In the second half of the nineteenth century an irrational strain, with an oriental emphasis on the primacy of will, also emerged. From Schopenhauer to Max Stirner to Nietzsche, a new emphasis was put on the reality and importance of the individual. Neo-Kantianism, which made a considerable impact on the Russian intellectual atmosphere, worked in the same direction. In France, Henri Bergson's thinking considerably undermined the credibility of straightforward rationalism. In fact, the very development of the natural sciences cast simplistic materialism in doubt. Ernst Mach and Richard Avenarius developed empiriocriticism, which for some, seemed to restore the spirit to its rightful place. This infuriated orthodox materialists of the old school, such as Lenin for instance.

In the Anglo-Saxon world, in particular, it had been "the Sage of Chelsea," Thomas Carlyle and his not too numerous followers, who had been obsessed by questions of a meaningful life in a world where once self-evident and eternal truths had given way to an unending search amidst the competing pretensions of various philosophical systems. Carlyle influenced Ruskin and Emerson, but towards the end of the nineteenth century his influence had waned.[15] The conventional wisdom, which deserves certain respect, considers that by the end of the nineteenth century, Anglo-Saxon intellectuals had largely remained content with the common sense, and pedestrian ideas of utilitarianism and positivism, while their continental colleagues continued to look for more drastic and/or aristocratic solutions to the ultimate questions of human existence. Russian social discourse preserved a very different tone, although even there consciousness of the simplistic tenets of Nineteenth century rationalism, which had contributed to the fanaticism of the militant intelligentsia, had begun to be cast into doubt.[16]

Ironically, the Russian debate on philistinism, nihilism, and the role of the intelligentsia at the beginning of the twentieth century, took some of its central romantic theses from Alexander Herzen, who in turn, had got them from John Stuart Mill.[17] Mill, of course, had not been a romantic at all. Friedrich Nietzsche, who understood this, had been particularly venomous about him.[18] Now, however, Mill's critique of the mass society, which he had presented in the 1860s, was being used by Russian romantics as an argument against the philistine way of life.

The Russian intellectual community at the turn of century was very well aware of the new continental currents of thought, and this caused a crisis for the old, well-nigh monolithic, ideology of the intelligentsia.[19] The mindset of the intelligentsia did not necessarily change, but there was a need for new arguments; mere Darwinism and materialism were no longer adequate substitutes for religion, as they had been for Turgenev's Bazarov. The new solutions could be either romantic or rationalist.

A new romantic solution par excellence for the cultural crisis, which had been created by the "death of God," was Nietzsche's idea of the "Superman" as the new purpose of Man in the universe.[20] The idea of anthropotheism was not exactly new and the popularity of Nietzsche's ideas at the turn of the century in Russia and elsewhere in Europe must, no doubt, be seen in the context of the new importance of the ever growing middle-class. In general, the influence of the popular masses in society and culture also became very relevant on the political level. In Russia this happened spectacularly after the Russian Revolution of 1905-1907. The ideas that were the philosophical starting point for Nietzsche, had been forcefully posed in Russia by Dostoevsky. If there was no God, could, then, a Raskolnikov, Pyotr Verkhovensky, Sergei Nechaev, or, indeed, anybody else be blamed for anything? Their radicalism was simply proof of the seriousness of their moral convictions. This, at least, was something which favorably separated them from the philistine middle classes. Dostoevsky's works reflected the intellectual scene of late nineteenth-century Russia, where he himself represented the conservative side.

Another great intellectual authority, who had undertaken a reappraisal of both the existential problem and its consequences for life and society, was Leo Tolstoy. Tolstoy's solution was totally different from that of the other intellectual luminaries of the period. However, together with most of them, Tolstoy also condemned most severely philistine consciousness. As for the writer of the Apocalypse, for Tolstoy too, the lukewarm ones were the most unworthy of human beings.

For Tolstoy, human dignity and the foundations of a worthy life were being hampered first of all by institutions, such as the state, religion, and other creations of man. The philistine "idolaters" worshipped these empty forms, not letting reality enter their conscience. In his famous short story *The Death of Ivan Ilich* Tolstoy very typically tells that the life of the protagonist was "most common and, accordingly, most appalling."[21] But the ultimate evil for Tolstoy resided not in institutions, but in passions. The original sin of the petty bourgeois, the worship of mammon, did not loom conspicuously large in Tolstoy's works, but it was quite obvious that Tolstoy loathed all the values of petty bourgeois society, where, he believed, greed and lust were praised, and the soulless and the arrogant prevailed. In his vitriolic invective "What is Art" Tolstoy also includes the worship of beauty in the same gallery of vices as greed and dissoluteness. Art, in its present form, was nothing else than lust and decadence, Tolstoy preached, for it had lost its genuine religious essence.[22]

Tolstoy's solution to the great dilemma of the disappearance of God (who was not dead, but did survive in a secret way) was a truly oriental extinction of will and non-resistance to evil.[23] This was completely in line with the teaching of eminent philosophers like Schopenhauer, who had influenced Tolstoy. Moreover, Tolstoy believed that knowledge of God had been lost only by the educated classes (the intelligentsia as well as the upper layers of the society). Common people, who were doing physical work, still understood God and holiness very clearly.[24] Tolstoy's individualistic and anarchist gospel did have its supporters both among the representatives of the intelligentsia and popular masses, but it remained a minor current among the former. Tolstoy's pathos was not only anti-bourgeois but also anti-intellectual. In any case Tolstoy, together with Dostoevsky, did a great deal to keep the issue of a worthy life present in a world where God had disappeared or was hidden.

Vladimir Soloviev, who has often been called the most remarkable of Russian philosophers, died in 1900, but the impact of his metaphysical idealism only increased after his death. Like Nietzsche, he became in vogue after his death, and his ideas about "divinization of man" (*bogochelovechestvo*) and the future synthesis of the real and the ideal became the source of inspiration for many Russian symbolists, from Andrei Belyi to Dmitry Merezhkovsky to Alexander Blok, who could simultaneously include elements from Nietzsche, Rudolf Steiner and even Marx in their thinking.[25] Soloviev's intellectual development was contradictory, and in old age he forsook many of the ideas of his youth, including the idea of a theocratic state.[26] However, Soloviev left behind a vigorous intellectual heritage, in which questions of religion and politics existed side by side. The disciples of Soloviev included the symbolists and the authors of the Vekhi, which will be discussed more thoroughly below.

Nietzsche's ideas penetrated Russia with new vitality at the turn of century, when several of Nietzsche's books were translated into Russian.[27] His thoughts unleashed a lively and lengthy discussion in Russia. It was discovered that Nietzsche had, in fact, been working with the same problems, which had tormented many of the foremost Russian thinkers, although they had not known about each other.[28] For obvious reasons, Nietzsche has been called "the most Russian of the Western philosophers," and even "the most Christian" of them.[29] While both of these characteristics may be exaggerated, they are not entirely groundless.

It is commonplace to say that Nietzsche's contempt for the masses was aristocratic in character. For Nietzsche, the masses embodied the "last man," who had "invented happiness."[30] His style left no room for doubt:

> Causes of nihilism... the lower species ("herd", "mass", "society") unlearns modesty and blows up its needs into cosmic and metaphysical values. In this way the whole of existence is vulgarized: in so far as the mass is dominant it bullies the exceptions, so they lose their faith in themselves and become nihilists...."[31]

At the same time, the idea of the good life as simply a materially secured existence and procreation with no higher aspirations whatever was understood to be a middle-class phenomenon, which was rapidly growing. However, the prospects were still modest. Petty bourgeois happiness just a hundred years ago was still understood to mean just being content with having a full stomach, clothes, and respectable standing in society.[32]

It was the prospect that this ignoble satisfaction of the average human being might be the future norm and ideal for all, which tormented intellectuals. The proletarian masses, from this point of view, had the virtue of not being consumerists. Karl Marx clearly supposed that they had even forsaken the "illusion" of ever reaching an opulent life under capitalism and would, therefore, have some quite distinct values of their own.[33] For romantic souls, the proletarians could, thus, be thought to represent another, purer, and higher world (in being or in becoming). For most nineteenth or early twentieth century intellectuals, it would have been blasphemous to think that socialism was desirable just because it would help to give the blessings of consumerism to the workers.

The danger of the future "age of the masses" was, however, appreciated. The USA was the warning example par excellence. America was widely believed to be the most developed capitalist country and thus, perhaps, the unavoidable mirror of the future for all. Tocqueville, who popularized the idea that Europe would be Americanized, also saw that Russia would have a great role in the future world, even if it avoided developing in the same direction as America.[34] Herzen, in the middle of the nineteenth century, had voiced his dislike of America, which he believed to be thoroughly petty-bourgeois. As we know, a sizable contingent of Russian intelligents (the neo-narodniks, or the SRs) at the beginning of the twentieth century still cherished the idea that Russia could avoid the fate of becoming a capitalist country.[35] The American model was not attractive to most Russian *intelligenty*, because of its notorious lack of spiritual values. For Maxim Gorky, who even had personal experience of America it was a "country of teenagers, where nobody mentally developed over the level of a 13-15 year-old." The blasphemous reduction of life to mere consumption was appalling for Gorky: his observation of American culture made him mostly feel nauseous and he said that he often "laughed like a madman" at it.[36]

Among the political radicals, Gorky, along with the future people's commissar of enlightenment, Anatoly Lunacharsky, and the philosopher and writer Aleksandr Bogdanov, formed the nucleus of the movement of so-called God-builders, which strived for a new intellectual synthesis at the beginning of the twentieth century.[37] The "God-building" of Lunacharsky and Gorky was a variety of the Nietzschean enterprise for filling the vacuum which the death of God had created and which the philistine values of the petty bourgeois masses threatened to occupy.[38] In the vein of Ludwig Feuerbach, Lunacharsky inferred that if the idea of God were purified of its transcendental guise, there would remain nothing more than an idealized humanity with all the good human attributes. Echoing Chernyshevsky, Lunacharsky argued that Truth, Goodness and Beauty should be understood from the point of view of life: all that promoted life was truth, goodness and beauty; everything that undermined it was falsehood, evil, and ugliness.[39] Anything which impoverished and diminished life was sin, even if it brought enjoyment. In the vein of the oriental tradition, resembling the thinking of Leo Tolstoy, Lunacharsky believed that sin could also be formulated as the lack of unity of humankind. The Fall of Man was, in effect, identical with the introduction of private property. Fortunately, there was Salvation and that was Labor incarnated in its international classless organization. Indeed, the Proletariat as the incarnation of labor would become the true Messiah of the World. For Lunacharsky, there was also immortality: it consisted of changing the center of gravity from the individual "me" to the great "we," which consisted of a creative, struggling, progressive humanity.[40] It has been suggested that Gorky was

Lunacharsky's pupil, but it seems more plausible that both developed the elements of their thinking independently. Both were built on the standard elements of the intellectual environment of the Russian fin-de siècle.[41]

Quite naturally, the actual condition of the working classes and their attitude to the intelligents was a crucial question for the ideologues. Some experiments with live proletarians were made by Gorky and Lunacharsky in the Capri and Bologna "party schools."[42] The cleavage between the workers and the intelligentsia persisted, although both elements were well represented in the Russian Social Democratic Party. It seemed logical that the hoped for unification of these elements would take place first in a future socialist society.[43]

The impact of Nietzsche on Russian culture in the Silver Age was also reflected in other ways. For instance, the symbolists, in general shared certain Nietzschean approaches, but gave them their own formulation, which reflected the specificity of the Russian intellectual agenda. One of the specific issues concerned the relationship between the "people" and the intelligentsia. The case of Alexander Blok is illustrative of this. In his early works, Nietzsche had postulated a dichotomy between the Dionysian and Apollonian principles in culture. Blok, in turn, wrote about "intoxication," which was represented by the "people" (narodnaia stikhiia) and about the "dream," which was represented by the intelligentsia. For Blok, as for Nietzsche, the West had lost its innocence with the Renaissance, which had given birth to the individual and, consequently, to the bifurcation of "culture" and "civilization," and eventually to the atomization of society.[44]

For Blok, strange, as it may seem, it was the "people," which preserved the true treasures of culture, and still possessed "the spirit of music," even if it expressed its aspirations in a language, which was "wild and incomprehensible for the humanists, in the barbaric language of uprisings and bloody retaliations."[45] In a truly romantic way Blok believed that the "people" was to be differentiated from the "rabble" (chern). The "rabble" was people who were philistine in spirit, and expected utility, and the service of external goals from a poet. The common people, however, even though they did not understand poetry, did not belong to the rabble. They just lacked the necessary education.[46]

It was not only some poets and writers who were great admirers of the popular masses. In the thinking of the Silver Age there was also another romantic current in the guise of materialism, whose proximity to the ideas of Nietzsche may deserve some attention. The belief in the exemplary (if not always discernible) virtues of the common people was typical not only for Tolstoy and some other men of letters. It was also shared by certain political movements. Not only the SRs but, strangely enough, even an ultra-rationalist and pragmatic movement such as Bolshevism took it completely seriously. As a thinker, V.I. Lenin was certainly a philosophical enemy of Nietzsche and other "idealists" and apparently he really did believe that his dogmatic political thinking could be given and had a thoroughly "scientific," materialist foundation.[47] But even though Lenin was very critical of God-building, this was, first and foremost, because he sensed hidden there the ontological "idealism" of empiriocriticism, derived from Ernst Mach's thinking. Approaching the problems of the world from the wrong angle could amount to a kind of "competing truth," which was intolerable for a political movement like the Bolsheviks, whose ideology was built in the form of a closed and infallible system.[48]

This, however, did not mean that Lenin was totally indifferent to the romantic gospel of the epoch, for which Nietzsche was just one of the foremost purveyors. Lenin's blatantly utopian plans for proletarian rule and his apparently unflinching belief in the inevitability of a communist society in the near future also contained a romantic, even aesthetic element.[49] The ideal proletarian, for Lenin, was a higher figure than the bourgeois and, thus, destined to become a full-fledged man, emancipated from the crippling hold of capitalism. This certainly meant that, for Lenin, there was a way out of Nietzsche's dilemma and that in a future society, and with the coming to an end of man's prehistory, there was the prospect of a new Man[50] –who would be a Superman, what else?

It may be objected that Lenin was no romantic, but above all a pragmatic politician, who was always flexible in matters of ideology, whenever practical considerations deemed it necessary. But it may be noted that his thinking fitted very well into the common framework of the epoch, with its emphasis on the existential level, and this, doubtless, also contributed to its success amongst the intelligentsia.

In still another sense, it may be argued that overtly Nietzschean figures such as Lunacharsky and Gorky (in theory, at least), as well as practical politicians like Lenin and Trotsky and a legion of others were romantics: they approved of the thesis that if God was dead, then Christian morals, let alone the practical philistine moralizing of the petty bourgeois, were just a sham. A higher type of man stood above this petty bourgeois prejudice, as Lenin repeatedly stated, since he found the bearers of the new morality in the ruthless representatives of the proletariat. True, the Russian intelligentsia did not need Nietzsche in order to reach this conclusion: it had been shared by several radicals ever since the 1860s.[51]

As a parallel consequence of fin-de siècle romanticism, German Nazism deserves some attention. Nazism was a typically romantic ideology and, hence, it possessed an anti-bourgeois bias. This fact has often been obscured by the conventional Marxist thesis that emphasizes the supposedly petty-bourgeois character of Nazism.[52] It is true that the

National-Socialistic German Workers' Party had a much more "bourgeois" electorate than the communists. But its ethos was also anti-philistine, it despised the pedestrian aspirations of the "*Spiessbuerger*" or "*korpulente Bierphilister*"; it called for heroism and sacrifice, and it also gave morals a new foundation in a loathing for to the "petty bourgeois" prejudice of common decency.[53]

Nazism built much of its intellectually dubious ideology on an eclectic collection of questionable pseudo sciences and popular prejudices, but it was also a revolutionary political religion –very far from any kind of conservatism.[54] It also professed an ill-founded belief in the dormant, but inherent, virtues of the common people (Volk), and wanted to build a "New Man," and it also radically rejected conventional morals. But which, of these two ideologies could really claim to be the true heirs of Nietzsche? Representatives of both Bolshevism and Nazism readily proved their superiority over the philistine by having the courage and resolution to kill those who, according to the professed faith, deserved to be killed. To say that Nietzsche was one of the ancestors of Nazism is a commonplace, but to think that it was Nietzsche's idea that the Germans were better than their neighbors, which was a central point of the Nazi program, would be absurd. For both the Nazis and the Bolsheviks, it was, in effect, the popular masses, which counted, not the fictitious "proletarians" or the "*Volk*." The task of the epoch was to mobilize the masses to get political influence. The ideas of Gustave Le Bon and Georges Sorel were eagerly studied throughout Europe by socialist, anarchist, and fascist thinkers alike. The new importance of the popular masses seemed to contain both the prospect of ultimate salvation, through a radical change of system, and of ruin, through decadence and degeneration.

Besides Nietzscheanism, several other continental currents in turn of the century thinking also reinforced the traditional anti-philistine ethos of the Russian intelligentsia.[55] Many Western European intellectuals strongly disliked philistines.[56] Gustave Flaubert had given his contribution for European culture already in the 1850s and his ideas were still popular. He had been succeeded by Charles Baudelaire, Théophile Gautier, Paul Verlaine, Emile Zola, and others. Many of these figures divided the opinions amongst the educated classes, but were generally considered remarkable and even great enough to warrant a monument. The plays of Henrik Ibsen, which became enormously popular in Russia, savagely attacked the petty bourgeois way of life.[57] There were also the books of the briefly popular Max Nordau[58], who had acquired his inspiration from the books of Cesare Lombroso and who saw contemporary Western culture as a spectacle of decadence in the literal sense of the word.[59] In Wilhelmine Germany the idea that there was a new illness of the age, neurasthenia, became popular. This mental disorder, which was sometimes also considered to be a symptom of degeneration, was found to ail the bourgeoisie as a whole. At the same time, a new, more vigorous and aggressive ideal of masculinity spread across Western Europe.[60] The culture of a strong will became the fashion of the day. The philistines were, of course, lacking in this respect.[61]

In short, the omnipresent inferiority of the petty bourgeoisie as a cultural danger was the slogan of the day in European intellectual life. These ideas also quickly penetrated Russia, where a fertile soil awaited them. Peter Gay argues that there was something new in the intellectual climate of the period. Now, in fact, the whole of European civilization began to criticize itself instead of its external adversaries as had earlier been the case. There was also something new in the vehemence of the anti bourgeois ethos. Earlier, even the satirists had worked, as it were, "within the system," now they conceived themselves to be outside it.[62] The alternative to this abominable mediocre mass was the nonconformist intellectual, and even the "people" in its ideal, if not actual, form.

Ivanov-Razumnik. The intelligentsia vs. philistinism

Ivanov-Razumnik,[63] who was a remarkable intelligent of his epoch and a left SR, published two weighty volumes on the *History of Russian Social Thought* (*Istoria russkoi obshchestvennoi mysli*), where the topic of the intelligentsia was central. Clearly, the book was aimed more or less at the "neo-idealists" such as Berdiaev, Bulgakov, Struve etc., who had already published a book called *Problems of Idealism* and were to publish the famous volume *Vekhi*.[64] Razumnik's book aroused angry criticism, especially on the part of Marxists, like Georgy Plekhanov and Trotsky, who accused him of ignoring the importance of social classes and making the intelligentsia the navel of the world.[65] Plekhanov even called Razumnik's thinking "the ideology of the philistine of our age."[66] The emotions, which Razumnik's work aroused, testify to the impact of his work, which "made a resumé of the experience of a whole historical period" now, as populism was giving way to Marxism.[67] The struggle of the intelligentsia against philistinism was the red thread running through the entire work. To use the author's own words: "The struggle against philistinism (meshchanstvo) and for individualism ... this is a point of view, which is general enough to give us the opportunity to examine the whole two-hundred year history of Russian consciousness."[68] What then for Ivanov-Razumnik was philistinism, the enemy formidable and vicious enough to determine the entire mission of the intelligentsia?

For Ivanov-Razumnik a negative way of defining philistines was to say that intelligents were not philistines, but, rather, anti-philistines.[69] The philistines were devoid of activity, of new ideals, of new forms and were not involved in the active promotion of such ideals and forms. Philistinism meant narrowness (*uzkost'*), flatness (*ploskost'*) and facelessness (*bezlichnost'*). Philistinism had no content at all and could only be defined by its form. It meant a certain relation to things. It was philistinism that transformed the most profound things into platitudes, the largest things into the smallest, the most individual into the faceless and the dull. Echoing Herzen, Ivanov-Razumnik asserted that individuals were dissolved in philistinism. It had just two talents: moderation and punctuality. It expressed itself in formalism and its symbol of faith was to be "like all the others". Referring to John Stuart Mill, the author also used the English term "conglomerated mediocrity."[70]

A person could be a professor, or even an academician, but he could still be a philistine and, accordingly, would not be admitted into the order of the intellectuals.[71] The intelligents, for their part, were always actively promoting new forms and ideals, whose aim was the emancipation of the individual. In so doing, they constantly had to fight the resistance of the philistines. Clearly, then, it was the intelligents who were the moving force of society and the source of all progress.

Sociologically, Ivanov-Razumnik concluded, the intelligentsia was a non-estate, non-class group with a history of its own, which, from the ethical point of view was anti-philistine.[72] What kind of individuality were the intelligents trying to achieve? Ivanov-Razumnik refers to N. Mikhailovsky's "Platonic" idea of individuality: individuality was not something which was distinctive for some personality but "the complex of all the traits, which are typical for the human being in general."[73] The ideal for which the human being was to strive was to become more human, a more general representative of the species homo sapiens.

Individualism meant, first, the primacy of the individual: a human being is an end in itself, the author stated, echoing Kant. This principle had also been preached by Dostoevsky and Tolstoy. On the other hand, individualism meant the primacy of individuality, the opposite of philistinism. On a third level, individualism meant primacy of the individual over society.

The plight of the Russian intelligentsia was to be engaged in a constant series of struggles against philistinism and for individuality, for the breadth and depth and intensity (*iarkost'*) of the human "I"; against the state and against the pressure of the society (*obshchestvennost'*). The struggle was also to be waged for the human personality (*chelovecheskaia lichnost'*) as an end in itself and against theories and practices that saw in the human being just an instrument for some other ends.[74]

Needless to say, Ivanov-Razumnik's lofty vision of the intelligentsia's mission was not shared by all its members. Plekhanov and Lunacharsky chided him for the lack of a class-position.[75] A remarkable socialist intellectual using the pen-name of Leon Trotsky, dismissed Razumnik's ideas as too self-centered and self-complimentary, and for substituting the intelligentsia for the masses (the fallacy of "substitutionalism").[76] In fact, this was a dilemma not just for Ivanov-Razumnik, but also for Marxist "vanguards," including the Bolsheviks, whom Trotsky joined in 1917.

Indeed, the most crucial issue, dividing the intelligentsia was that of individualism versus collectivism. Although Ivanov-Razumnik was convinced that only individualism, represented by the intelligentsia, could act as the antidote of philistinism, others claimed that individualism itself was nothing other than philistinism. But to what extent should an *intelligent* express solidarity with the masses? Shouldn't he condemn any crimes even if they were committed by the people? Was the only way to avoid the Scylla of philistinism to resign one's critical faculties? Did engagement in the people's cause mean becoming its apologist? Was there not the Charybdis of uncritical, self-serving submission to irrational forces?

Leon Trotsky probably found a grain of truth, when he pointed out that the unabashedly self-centered and belligerently anti-philistine world-view of the Russian intelligentsia, which Razumnik displayed, could be explained by the fact that the petty bourgeoisie had, in fact, been non-existent in Russian history. The Russian people as a whole were existing on the level of pauperism and were not, therefore, "petty bourgeois," but primitive. The intelligentsia was like the antennae of the Russian nation, touching foreign European culture. The intelligentsia by praising the Russian people for its lack of philistinism, was wrong in thinking that this was something laudable and progressive. It was just retrograde. It was due to the physical and cultural pauperism of the Russian people. The intelligentsia, for its part, was playing the part of the people. It was taking the role of parties, of the classes, and the people – but all this only happened in the imagination of the intelligentsia.[77]

Merezhkovsky and the "coming barbarian"

One of the severest critics of the Russian revolutionary intelligentsia was Dmitri Merezhkovsky. He belonged to a group, which had had its Nietzschean apprenticeship in the 1890s and early 1900s, and which since 1905 had began to advocate a religious revolution, "which would solve all personal and social problems by inaugurating, literally, the Millennium."[78] As with *Vekhi*, which would appear a few years later, the core of Merezhkovsky"s critique had a religious character.

In his pamphlet *Griadushchii kham* (*The Coming Barbarian*), Merezh-kovsky saw the task of the intelligentsia first of all as the struggle with philistinism. Citing Herzen and John Stuart Mill, Merezhkovsky stressed the latter's fear that, in the long run, this process would make England, and not only England, a new China.[79] China was a metaphor for the "crys-tallization of philistinism" (*meshchanskaia kristallizatsiia*) for Merezhkovsky (and, at least according to him, this was also the case for Mill). In China, religion had already been transformed into a non-transcendental, godless "positivism" (Lao Che, Confucius). In the West, the same process was, although unfinished, nevertheless on the march. Forsaking God (and the "hunger for God") inevitably led to "absolute philistinism," so the argu-ment continued. The Europeans had already advanced quite far along this path and the Americans even further.[80] In fact, Merezhkovsky pondered, the renowned "yellow peril" might not mean that there was a danger that the Chinese (and Japanese) might come to Europe, but that the Europeans might go spiritually to Asia.[81]

For Merezhkovsky, the prospect of universal philistinism was appall-ing. However, for the urban proletariat, becoming petty bourgeois seemed to be the only possible way out of their distress. Merezhkovsky considered that mentally the "proletarians" and the petty bourgeois were very near each other, and that between a sensible, replete philistinism and a sense-less, hungry bestiality there was but a step. If not today, then tomorrow both would attack each other and an unprecedented war would begin.[82] For Merezhkovsky, the imminent liberation of the proletariat would not lead to the creation of a good society, but would unleash the proletariat's inferior, philistine nature. The only way out of the dilemma was a reli-gious rebirth: only the Coming of Christ could conquer the Coming of the Barbarian.[83]

Merezhkovsky's prophecy was drastic, but not necessarily convincing for the broad masses. In the eyes of the narodniks it was blasphemous, of course. In any event, Merezhkovsky's political solutions, which included destroying the state and turning the Orthodox church into a revolutionary body, were not at all practical and could hardly compete with the other political currents.[84]

The aristocratically minded Konstantin Leontiev seems to have been the first to use the concept of *kham* (barbarian, bully, insolent person) about representatives of contemporary educated Russians.[85] For him, the *kham* was a person, who was deeply inimical to culture, a new type who despite having an education was spiritually mediocre. The equality the Russian intelligentsia was striving for, was merely the equality of barbarians.[86] Leontiev's critique of the *intelligenty* resembled the critique of the philistines as presented by the "intelligent" tradition. That Leontiev's ethos was aristocratic and anti-democratic did not make much difference, for so was, in essence, the *intelligent* tradition in general, as many critics had pointed out.[87]

It was Dmitri Merezhkovsky, however, who had the nerve to use the word *kham* to denote the idealized, uneducated, Russian people, the adored *narod* itself.

Merezhkovsky's view of the intelligentsia was obviously not as optimistic as that of, say, Ivanov-Razumnik. For the former, the enemy was not just the conformist and oppressive philistine, whom the *intelligent* was supposed to bravely defy. The innovative artist, who, for Ivanov-Razumnik, was the champion of progress and individualism could, for Merezhkovsky, be a *kham*—a barbarian, as was the case with the futurists. But the danger of *"khamstvo* in its ugliest form" came from below: hooligans had impeccably popular origins, but this did not make them any better. They were also philistine.[88] Here, philistinism was once again the ultimate evil, which could spoil all that had, at first, been good.

In fact, the *khams* already had their staunch defenders, whose influence would last for generations. Maxim Gorky had, at the end of 1905, published his "Remarks on the Philistine" ("*Zametki o meshchanine*"), which will be discussed later. As defined by Gorky, the fundamentals of philistinism were a hypertrophied sense of property, an incessant striving for tranquility both within and without the self, and a blind fear of everything which could disturb this state of mind. At the root of all this was a terrible fear of life and a fear of the people, at whose expense the petty bourgeois had built his well-being.[89]

Clearly, Gorky's approach here was preponderantly socio-political in nature. His analysis had pretensions to understanding the causal mechanism of things. The philistines were now to be understood, first of all, as those petty bourgeois who owned property, which had been acquired at the expense of the "people."

In the opinion of many contemporary analysts, the spectacle of the rising barbarian had already become a reality in the 1905 revolution. The Moscow uprising, which should be seen as providing the background for Gorky's essay on the philistines and for the ensuing polemics, was a vivid example of the excesses, of which the once idealized "people" were capable. A cardinal question for the Russian intelligentsia had now become crucial: should it act as a servant of the people even when the latter were committing barbaric acts? Or should the intelligentsia try to reconcile the opposing sides and find a civilized outcome to the crisis?

In 1905, Gorky adopted the former of these positions. The intellectual should unconditionally be on the side of the people and not try to "reconcile, what cannot be reconciled," in his view, echoing the Hegelian heritage of

Marxism. For Gorky, philistinism meant an individualism which had had the impudence to part ways with the "people."

Nicholas Berdiaev answered Gorky, asserting that praising and supporting the ugly sides of the revolution was nothing else than hooliganism: "In the world, there are sacred things and only a barbarian variety of philistinism (*meshchanstvo-khamstvo*) can raise its hand against them".[90] If we approved of Gorky's definition of philistinism, Berdiaev concluded, our thinking would amount to a mere cult of force, to a worship of the working people as it happens to be, to an enmity against individual creation, to a rejection of cultural values and we would reach an approach towards human beings, which understands them as means for some other ends.[91]

In fact, this was almost exactly the definition of philistinism that Ivanov-Razumnik would present a little later. Interestingly, Berdiaev went as far as to assert that the masses themselves were not fresh, creative, and youthful, but "decadent." There was no reason to believe in the elevated nature of the masses: the mere number of heads was no guarantee of a higher level of humanity. On the contrary, the "amalgamation of self-conceit and low-mindedness made a terrible mixture." Also the self-sacrifice of the *intelligenty*, if it resulted only in the promotion of the vulgar greed of the masses, did not justify anything. The ideas of Nietzsche had now been vulgarized, and the whole phenomenon of Nietzscheanism in Russia was emitting a bad smell, which was becoming worse and worse every day, Berdiaev wrote. The idea of a democratized superman was just a contradictio in adiecto.[92]

Evidently, the terms "philistine" and "*intelligent*" could be defined and assessed in various, even directly opposite, ways. A constant, which persisted, was that nobody wanted to be identified as a philistine.

Vladimir Ilyich Lenin, who was already a rather well-known political figure, also took part in this discussion in his article "About Party Literature,"[93] which Merezhkovsky had taken into account.

For Lenin, of course, truth had a "class" character, and the most important factor about any intellectual activity was that it was always in the service of a certain class. It was an axiom for Gorky, and even more so for Lenin, that any intellectual had to be a servant of the proletariat (more precisely of its vanguard, the party), otherwise he was serving its enemies. Of course, Lenin understood this "service" in a specific way and he granted an enormous role in the making of history to that part of the intelligentsia that would bring the proletariat its "consciousness."[94]

In 1909, Gorky published another treatise on the topic of philistinism. In a volume called *Essays on the Philosophy of Collectivism*,[95] whose name revealed the main idea, he justified the summary mob violence of the hooligans in a way which resembled psychoanalytic interpretation. The philistines, Gorky wrote, were sinning against every aspect of their own moral code: The philistine filled his days with filth, with mean stupidity (*poshlost'*), and kept committing his little, mischievous sins against the human body and soul, and relishing it.[96] The world of the philistine was full of pornography and the neurasthenic philistine made his toothache a problem of world importance.[97] Philistinism, this wretched curse of the world, was, in essence, the revenge of the dead material world against the living, creative human soul. This phenomenon was especially acute today, he wrote. The human personality was contaminated by the poison of nihilist individualism, which transformed a human being into a hooligan, the philistine was a dissolute monster, whose brain was in pieces, whose nerves were shattered, who was deaf to anything but the call of instincts and the malign whisper of unhealthy passions. Because of philistinism, man was transformed from Prometheus into hooligan. But the hooligan was the child of the philistine, the fruit of its womb. History had reserved for it the role of Oedipus. It would kill its father.[98]

It is worth noticing that, oddly enough, Gorky seems to presage here the summary mob-violence which took place in Petrograd in 1917-1918 and which he, in fact, then fiercely condemned. It is also interesting to note a couple of other dimensions in Gorky's thinking. Gorky was preaching collectivism, and this readily linked him with Bolshevism,[99] despite the fact that his thinking had very little in common with any form of Marxism. Another, is that Gorky's terminology strongly suggests that he considered the "perversion" of philistinism to have a sexual basis. Incidentally, the term *poshlost'*, which denotes things dear to the philistine, also has a subsidiary sexual meaning: sexual pleasure also belonged to the category of "base" or "cheap" things.

The *Vekhi* group

A devastating critique of the radical Russian intelligentsia was presented by the renowned *Vekhi* (Signposts) group in 1909. The intellectual history of perhaps the most influential figure of this group, Petr Struve, originated in the populist group Black Repartition (*Chernyi peredel*), whose members later became known as "The Legal Marxists" and subsequently turned into a form of conservative liberalism with Christian overtones.[100] Many of the authors of Vekhi had already taken part in another volume *Problems of Idealism*, which had led to major polemics.[101] *Vekhi* has been regarded as an exercise in self-criticism by repentant intelligents, who were appalled at the experience of the 1905-07 Revolution. Despite the warnings of these conservative liberals,[102] the 1917 February revolution took place, with the enthusiastic support of many *intelligenty*. After the Bolshevik revolution, the conservative liberal critics published a new volume called *Iz glubiny* (*From the depths*), which continued the analysis of the Russian revolution in the same vein. As is generally known, the ideology of the *Vekhi* group was later shared by Alexander Solzhenitsyn, who, with his friends in the 1970s published another volume called *Iz-pod glyb* (*From under the Rubble*) which consciously continued the same tradition.[103]

The authors of *Vekhi*, N.A. Berdiaev, S.N. Bulgakov, M.O. Gershenzon, A.S. Izgoev, B.A. Kistiakovski, P.B. Struve and S.L. Frank were representatives of different backgrounds, from Marxism and economics to law and divinity studies, and their critique approached its subject from various angles, from philosophy to jurisprudence. But, their critique had at least one common denominator: all agreed that the Russian intelligentsia lacked religious consciousness and that this constituted its innermost, and most fatal, flaw. The Russian intelligentsia prided itself on its high moral standards: its "principles," its uncompromising stance against the oppressive regime, its unselfishness, its love of liberty and its intellectual superiority over those who served the autocracy. In different ways, morally as well as intellectually, the *intelligenty* raised themselves above the bourgeois rabble and served the "people" and suffered for it.

For many observers, this heroic stance of the Russian *intelligenty* seemed like a religious dedication, which often amounted to true martyrdom, given that the tsarist state incarcerated and even killed its opponents. *Vekhi* attacked the foundations of the intellectuals' edifice of self-esteem. Each author in turn attempted to show that the intelligentsia was both morally and intellectually deficient, and that from the point of view of Russian society and its prospects for development it had had a positively detrimental role. With religion, which the *Vekhi*'s authors respected, the intelligentsia had nothing in common, they claimed.

The philosopher Nicholas Berdiaev analyzed the mutual relation of the philosophical and *intelligent* varieties of truth (*Filosofskaia istina i intelligentskaia pravda*). The Russian words which the author uses are *istina*, denoting a higher order of truthfulness and *pravda*, which has a more practical character, being the opposite of an untruth, and also refers to justness. Bulgakov tried to point out that the Russian intelligentsia, a caste-like, closed group, had ceased to be interested in truth as such and had exchanged the love for truth for a love of making people happy by leveling their income.[104] In fact, this amounted to the maxim of Dostoevsky's Grand Inquisitor: let truth perish, if people live better without it.[105] Bulgakov also analyzed the striving for heroism, which was typical of the intelligentsia which despised, so he argued, the "petty bourgeois" way of life of Western Europeans, with its "everyday virtuousness," and its hard-working, intensive economy, which was accompanied by pedestrian narrow-mindedness. This "anti-bourgeois" cast of mind had its origins in Herzen, Bulgakov asserted. In his opinion, this psychology had several sources, including the habits of the gentry, which was accustomed to living without the problems of "petty bourgeois" everyday life. There was also an element of insolence. A central tenet of the intelligentsia was its faith in the natural goodness of man and in unending progress. In fact, this faith bore the traits of the cultural conceit of a parvenu. Both socialism and individualism were examples of the self-adoration (*samoobozhestvlenie*) of the European petty bourgeoisie (*meshchanstvo*), Bulgakov wrote, which amounted to hitting the intelligentsia with its own favorite weapons.[106]

Heroism was something that the intelligentsia strove for, Bulgakov wrote, but even this one could find clear symptoms of a syndrome of self-adoration. The pretension to heroism was a kind of spiritual aristocratism. Russian youth had been rapidly transformed from the philistine (*obyvatel'*) into a heroic type and very little had been needed to achieve this transformation—just some dogmas about the divinity of the human being (*chelovekobozhestvo*), some quasi-scientific programs of political parties and there it was; a new consciousness had been born.[107]

A hero was understood to be something of a superman (*sverkhchelovek*), who had the proud and defiant air of a savior towards his fellowmen. Despite all its democratism, the intelligentsia was just a special form of aristocracy, which considered itself as the opposite of the philistine (*obyvatel'*). Faith in one's own impeccability, and condescension and contempt towards those who had different ideas were typical for it.[108] In fact, the most mediocre philistine, who was in no way better than his fellowmen, every now and then just put on the uniform of an *intelligent* and began to despise others.[109]

Mikhail Gershenzon considered the intelligentsia's chief defect to be its neglect of the development of the individual. This was based on the belief that all evil in the world was the result of objective circumstances.[110] As regards the relationship between the intelligentsia and the people, the latter considered the intelligentsia even more alien than the Turks or the French. There was no understanding of the intelligents among the people and, in fact, the *intelligenty* had the bayonets and the gaols of the state to thank for saving them from the wrath of the people.[111]

A. S. Izgoev, who wrote about Russian students, pointed to the low professional standards of the intelligents and their contempt for erudition and regular work. Everything that was too bourgeois was dismissed as unworthy of serious attention, and the *intelligenty* competed to be radical, dismissing all political currents to their right as "bourgeois."[112]

Boris Kistiakovsky, who wrote about the intelligentsia's relation to law and jurisprudence, pointed out that since the Slavophiles, there had been a tradition of enmity towards formal law and its institutions in Russia. An "outer right" had been opposed to an "inner right," which was deemed to be more true and worthy of attention, while the "outer," formal guarantees of social relations were considered not only inferior, but even obnoxious.[113] In the diagnosis of Petr Struve, the constant condition of the Russian intelligentsia had been its separateness from the state and, indeed, enmity towards it.[114]

Finally, Semen Frank defined the ideology of the intelligentsia as "nihilist moralism," his point being that the intelligentsia thought only in moral terms and neglected or denied theoretical, aesthetic, and religious values.

The spiritual condition of the intelligentsia could not be called religious, it was just fanaticism. While the intelligentsia did not recognize any other kind of values than immanent, human values, it necessarily remained nihilistic in character. "Nihilist moralism" might sound paradoxical, but what else was nihilism than a rejection of absolute values?

The message of the *Vekhi* was met with hostility from all sides. Not only radicals like Lenin but also liberal critics dismissed it as odious. Maxim Gorky cursed it in a private letter and called it "the vilest little book in the whole history of Russian literature. Hell knows what it is! A cemetery, corpses and the dissolution of an organism".[115] Lenin called it "the encyclopedia of liberal apostasy" and thought that the book "revealed the real essence of today's Kadetism."[116] But the Bolsheviks were just a minor fraction of the critics. No less than two hundred comments on it were published.[117]

A volume called *The Intelligentsia in Russia* (*Intelligentsiia v Rossii*) was published in 1910 as an answer to *Vekhi*. Its authors, K.K. Arsenev, M.M. Kovalevski, P.N. Miliukov, D.N. Ovsianiko-Kulikovski, I.I. Petrunkevich, M.A. Slavinski and M.I. Tugan-Baranovski were illustrious liberal politicians and thinkers. Miliukov was the leader of the Kadet party and Ovsianiko-Kulikovski was the author of a major history of the Russian intelligentsia.[118] The general tenor of the volume was a vindication of the radical history and present of the Russian intelligentsia in general and of the Kadets in particular. It had a clear function for the politics of the day.

The introduction of the volume was written by Petrunkevich, another remarkable liberal politician. The author wrote rather arrogantly, in the name of "Russian society." He defended the radical heritage of Belinski and Chernyshevski and accused the authors of *Vekhi* of simplification.[119]

Miliukov, who wrote about the intelligentsia and historical tradition, defined intelligentsia as the inner circle of the educated layer, which generated initiative and creativity. The intelligentsia was the opposite of the philistines (*meshchanstvo*). In fact, *intelligentnost'* and philistinism were principles which were not clearly separated from each other, but were present in every individual to a greater or lesser extent. *Intelligentnost'* was not the same thing as refinement (*kulturnost'*). So, people could have a lot of *intelligentnost'*, but little *kulturnost'* and on the other hand, there were people, who were very cultured, but lacked *intelligentnost'*. Such people were especially common among the middle classes of France and England.[120]

As for philistinism, Miliukov maintained that it meant, in fact, "the concept of culture, which has been organically rooted in the consciousness of the educated European." The Russians, the "boys without trousers" resented the ways of the educated. The authors of the *Vekhi* were, in fact, following the Russian tradition in this respect.[121]

Miliukov criticized *Vekhi* rather unsparingly, but recognized that the accusation of maximalism was not unfounded. But Miliukov's main conlusion was clear: it was not inner perfection and the "heroic deed of repentance" that was needed. In practical politics one had to do the opposite of what the *Vekhi* authors advised. Miliukov said sarcastically that denying generally known truths was, of course, interesting, but it was necessary to put the record right, even though this would look like an act of philistinism to those, who loved romantic irony. The Russian intelligentsia had to continue its work with resolution. The present generation was just a link in the chain of tradition, which was a worthy one and whose goals had not been invented by idle reasoning, but created by the laws of life.[122]

Another eminent author of the *Intelligentsiia v Rossii* volume was M.I. Tugan-Baranovsky, Russia's leading economist and a member of the Kadet party. Tugan-Baranovsky explained the specific traits of the Russian intelligentsia by using social history. Russia had not given birth to a bourgeoisie, which was the bearer of the philistine values that had so much impressed Herzen in France. The mass of Russian society had lived outside political life. In Western Europe, there were already socialist institutions in society and they were an organic part of that society. The Russian intelligentsia was not petty bourgeois (*meshchanstvo*), Struve had said, although he believed that it should become so. This, indeed, was the central question for the future of the intelligentsia, Tugan-Baranovsky wrote. The mindset of the intelligentsia had to change, and this change would happen because of changes which were taking place in the structure of Russian society and not because of the spontaneous creative processes of the personality. In fact, many Russian intelligents, especially Marxists, believed that the intelligentsia would be remolded into a bourgeois element. In Western Europe this had been the case, many *intelligenty* thought. This was an oversimplification, the author wrote. In Western Europe an increasingly important layer of critical *intelligenty* was being born and it was supported by certain new structures, like the cooperative movement, the socialist press and so on. The philistine nature of Western society, which had so shocked Herzen and which had been caused by the nature of that society, was changing. This was giving rise to the birth of a Western European intelligentsia, in the Russian sense of the word.[123]

The *Vekhi* debate became very widespread and most of the important Russian intelligents took part in it. Many authors accused *Vekhi* of escapism, which equaled desertion on the field of battle. One of them was professor Robert Vipper, a historian, who wrote a treatise about the phenomenon of the bifurcation of the intelligentsia. In his view, this phenomenon had had a precedent in ancient Greece and had been repeating itself every now and then ever since.[124] Vipper's idea was that one group of the intelligentsia did care about the wider public, whereas the other one was interested only in its own self-perfection. The latter always rose to the surface after the first one had been defeated and began to ridicule it and blame it for godlessness.

Vipper's intention was, of course, to attack *Vekhi*. Some years later, in the 1918 *Iz glubiny* album one of its authors, P. Novgorodtsev, with the hindsight of the Bolshevik revolution snatched the weapon from Vipper and used it for the defense of the *Vekhi*-tradition.[125]

Yes, there was a bifurcation, Novgorodtsev recognized. There was the tradition of Chaadaev, Dostoevsky, and Vl. Soloviev, but there was also the tradition of Bakunin, Chernyshevsky, Lavrov, and Mikhailovsky. The latter was a calamity both for the intelligentsia and for the fatherland. Really, the ideas of *Vekhi* had been unanimously denounced and, subsequently, in 1917 Russia had been thrown into a new Time of Troubles. The intelligentsia had been incapable of thinking constructively, and, fatally isolated from reality, it had preached a rationalist utopianism and enshrined the people. The fallacy of the intelligentsia did, indeed, have its counterpart in ancient Greece: the Sophists who had also been preaching relativism and skepticism, and in their case reason had also lost its universal foundation. It was Socrates and Plato, who had criticized the Sophists for their godless and destructive activity. Now, the Russian intelligentsia was playing the part of the Sophists.[126]

Novgorodtsev believed that the crisis of the Russian intelligentsia was not an isolated phenomenon: in France there a book had been published which criticized the intellectuals for their hollow rationalism and proposed a turn away from Descartes to Pascal.[127]

Merezhkovsky also joined the critics of *Vekhi*. In his article "Seven Humble Ones" he pointed out that while the authors were pretending to be religious, they had broken away from Russian messianism and from revolution, which, after all, had to be looked upon not only from a scientific (evolutionary) point of view, but also from the point of view of mysticism and eschatology.[128]

Vekhi was a major moment in the history of the Russian intelligentsia, but it could not change the basic characteristics of the radical "order," which met its challenge with sneers and indignation. It seems that only a handful of more remarkable intellectuals, like Andrei Belyi, were converted by the *Vekhi*.[129] The issue of philistinism also loomed large in the *Vekhi* discussion. Although nobody was prepared to be called a philistine, there was some genuine criticism of the radical use of the term as an insult, and also some social analysis, which attempted to explain the extravagant aversion of the Russian intelligentsia to things bourgeois. *Vekhi* and the very lively discussion it caused[130] did not alter the course of history, but was a clear sign that the Russian intelligentsia was not just a monolithic, fanatic order, dedicated to political struggle. There was also a humane, spiritual tradition, which stressed that no political goals whatsoever can ever be an alternative to spiritual values, which were, it was claimed, the essence of true *intelligentnost'*. Politically, many of the members of the *Vekhi* group were former legal Marxists and thereafter active members of the Kadet party. This may sound strange, given that we know how severely their leading party comrades, like Miliukov and Petrunkevich, attacked their views. It is well-known that some analysts have considered that the Kadet party was not actually a liberal political factor in Russia, even though its political views were near those of, say, English liberals. In the Russian political milieu, however, the Kadets became a radical party, which promoted a total break with the Russian past and refused to cooperate with the autocracy staying true to the intelligentsia tradition.[131] As the *Vekhi* case demonstrates, the crisis of the Russian intelligentsia was not so much a matter of party politics, but, rather metaphysical and moral. Inside the Kadet party, there were both moderates and unwavering radicals.

The accusation of futile radicalism among the Kadets receives some support from the surveys of the political attitudes of St. Petersburg students. Students were a very radical element, who took an active part in all major actions against the government. However, the strongest party among the students was the Kadets. It has been established that the Kadets had the support of about 30-50 per cent of the students and in some institutes of higher learning they had an absolute majority. After the February revolution of 1917, the students of Petrograd university elected their own soviet, where the Social Democrats got 26,5 per cent of the votes, the SRs also 26,5, the Kadets 40 per cent, and non-party people 7 per cent.[132]

The Russian intelligentsia began to be divided into two parts more clearly than ever. As Aileen Kelly has noticed, there was a very strong tradition of self-censorship among the intelligentsia. It complemented the official censorship and, as a result, not too much room for free-thinking was left. It has even been said that it was "a very real question," which of the two censorships was worse.[133]

The locus classicus of the intelligentsia's heritage was the "positive hero." It was taken for granted that the ideal heroes of the progressive movement had to be presented as flawless persons, worthy of emulation. At the beginning of the twentieth century, this tradition suffered a crisis. Boris Savinkov, an active organizer of terrorist acts for the SR fighting organization, published books, where he described the heroes/martyrs in a realistic way: terrorism involved "not only sacrifice, but also blood, deceit and shame."[134] The books provoked a major outcry among the radical intelligentsia. Another example of the new spirit was the fate of Maxim Gorky's appeal that a play *Nikolai Stavrogin*, which was based on Dostoevsky's *The Possessed* should not be staged in the Moscow Art Theatre. In Gorky's opinion, "Karamazovism" and "Karataevism" (allusions to Dostoevsky's and Tolstoy's personages) were unworthy remnants of Russia's Eastern past and should not be reinforced. "The Stavrogins" should not be shown to the public.[135] The ensuing polemics showed, Kelly argues, that the overwhelming majority of the intelligentsia was already against this kind of (anti)intellectual approach. Gorky, the future founder of Socialist realism, was, for his part, already applying the principles of "party-mindedness" before it was necessary. Gorky was not without his supporters. The tradition of "progressive" censorship and the urge to idealize and educate people was later continued in the Soviet Union.

Nikolai Berdiaev

Nikolai Berdiaev continued to uphold the intellectual tradition of *Vekhi* in Russia until 1922, when he was expelled from the country. He was, perhaps, the most prominent Russian émigré philosopher up to the 1940s. In his writings, both the anti-philistine tradition of the Russian intelligentsia and the liberal-conservative critique of the intelligentsia are intertwined.

Berdiaev was already a prolific publicist before *Vekhi* and often his views were uncongenial to the radical intelligentsia. He was also one of those figures, who saw decadence, decadence of the soul, not just decadence of the arts, as a major symptom of the ills of the epoch.[136] During the First World War, Berdiaev wrote several essays in which he analyzed the national characteristics of the Russians as well as those of several other European nations.[137]

As regards the Russians, Berdiaev presented his famous diagnosis about the feminine character of the Russian nation. In fact, the Russians have both a feminine and a masculine character, which exist separately from each other, Berdiaev argued. This gives rise to important consequences and makes the Russian soul appear contradictory. On the one hand, Russia is the most non-bourgeois country in the world. In Russia, there is not a trace of the powerful philistinism, which is so uncongenial for Russians visiting the West. Russia is a country with a liberty of lifestyles (*strana bytovoi svobody*) to a degree unknown among the leading nations of the West. The latter are enserfed by petty bourgeois norms. For Russians, the wanderer figure (*strannik*) is characteristic. The *strannik* is the freest human being in the world. He symbolizes the greatness of the Russian people and its craving for the pure life. The *strannik* is not only typical of the people's life, but also for the best part of the intelligentsia. In literature, Raskolnikov and Myshkin, Stavrogin and Versilov, Prince Andrei Bolkonsky and Pierre Bezukhov are all *stranniks*. Russia is a fantastic country of pious intoxication, of *khlysty*, of *dukhobory* and other such figures from Kondrati Selivanov (the founder of the *skoptsy* or self-immolators) to Rasputin. The Russian mind does not sit in a certain place, it is not a philistine mind, not a parochial mind (*ne siditsia na meste, eto ne meshchanskaia dusha, ne mestnaia dusha*). It wants to go further and further away, until the ends of the earth in order to find an outlet from the world, from everything that is restricted and philistine (*mestnoe, meshchanskoe*). Russia is a country of endless freedom and spiritual vastness.[138] On the other hand, Russia is also the antithesis of these elevated virtues. It is a country of servility, fat merchants, and conservative bureaucrats, inert, lazy, soulless and materialistic. The point of the mystery is in the separate existence of the masculine and feminine principles in the Russian mind. The Russian national principle (*stikhiia*) is feminine and it always looks for the masculine principle outside. The solution for the dilemma is to find the masculine principle in Russia itself.[139] As an example of philistinism, Berdiaev takes an ally of the Russian nation in the First World War, the French. France and especially Paris were terribly philistine, in Berdiaev's opinion. The cardinal element, the closed cell of philistinism was the self-conceited bourgeois family. Philistinism was the other side of an unquenchable thirst for enjoyment. Petty-bourgeois norms are, in fact, fruits of a disbelief in the possibility of voluntary moderation. Real freedom, freedom from mendacious conventions and hypocritical norms reigns only among the Russians. Nowhere in the world outside Paris is there such a competition for success in life, such a cult of affluence and such contempt for the poor. Philistine France had elevated personal and family egoism into a virtue. France was not at all frivolous. The Russians were wrong in believing thus.

Philistinism is a metaphysical and not a social category, Berdiaev wrote. It is atheistic, non-religious in character. The philistine life is a life of external appearances which are mistaken for the nucleus, depth, and essence of life. The French had already lost their national virtues and philistinism had gradually killed their soul. Only great catastrophes and ordeals could purify and liberate a human being from philistinism. Now that war had come, Berdiaev felt that it could heal France by forcing it to solve new kinds of problems. In fact, the war itself had been called forth by the inner disease of humanity, its petty bourgeois self-conceit and narrowness.[140]

Although he was a representative of that part of the intelligentsia which was criticizing the credulity and simplistic tenets of the mainstream intelligentsia, Berdiaev evidently also shared some of its general beliefs. Like any other Russian intelligent worthy of the name, Berdiaev not only despised the petty bourgeois, but even thought that this wretched creature should be destroyed, even if it required a drastic event like a world war.

Maxim Gorky

Maxim Gorky was already at the beginning of the twentieth century one of the great names of Russian literature. He was also genuinely popular and famous for his revolutionary feats. According to a contemporary survey, even workers widely read Gorky. Tolstoy and Gorky were the two most popular writers several years before the Bolshevik revolution.[141] For Maxim Gorky, philistinism was always a major theme, if not the main one. His early play *The Philistines* (*Meshchane*) was a major success. Before the Bolshevik revolution, Gorky had also written essays on this topic and engaged in a major polemics a couple of times, in 1905 and 1908-09. They warrant a closer examination.

In his essay "Notes on Philistinism" ("*Zametki o meshchanstve*") of 1905 Gorky defined and described the philistine in several ways, and gave some concrete examples of representatives of this principle. Philistinism, he wrote "is the cast of mind of a representative of the contemporary commanding classes." The main characteristic traits of the philistines were "a morbidly developed sense of property, an intense craving for inward and outward tranquility, a gloomy fear of everything that in one way or another could disturb that tranquility, and a constant urge to explain away, for oneself, everything that could disturb one's precious balance of mind. This 'explaining away' was necessary in order to rationalize one's own ways, one's passivity in the struggle of life."[142]

Gorky's concepts were somewhat unorthodox from a Marxist point of view: for him the petty bourgeois was not just a would-be big bourgeois but a representative of the "commanding classes" and he also had property. He had created the state in order to guard his property, yet, on the other hand, property could guard him against the state.[143] In fact, it seems that Gorky is here using the word petty bourgeois (*meshchanin*) here as a synonym of both of the spiritual qualities of the philistine and of the bourgeoisie as a social group, which comprises both small holders and big proprietors.

Life is, "as is generally known," a struggle of the masters for power and of the slaves for liberation, Gorky wrote.[144] The philistines were not willing to take an active part in this struggle. The conflict between the "people" and the commanding classes was irreconcilable, but the philistine tried to reconcile the two. The philistine's incessant attempts to do the impossible had given rise to a "disease", which he had christened conscience. In effect, conscience was nothing more than fear of retaliation. Humanism also stemmed from the same source and was in effect just a disguised form of philistinism.[145]

Given this general picture, one would have expected that Gorky was happy that the mass of those who had property and power were not willing to fight for them. It seems, however, that for Gorky, the oppressor was not so much the inert bourgeois class as such, but the sinister force of philistinism, which kept the "people" itself in its grip and diverted it from the revolutionary struggle.

For Gorky, two outstanding representatives of philistinism were Tolstoy and Dostoevsky. Dostoevsky preached the gospel of humility, while Tolstoy concentrated on self-perfection. Both were philistines even though they were geniuses. The decisive flaw in their thinking was that they wanted to reconcile the irreconcilable: the torturer and the tortured.[146]

In fact, then, the philistines were Lilliputians and the people were Gulliver, tied down with threads of lies and deception. When the giant awakened in 1905, the philistines ran to the forefront and declared themselves the victors, as representatives of the people.

Gorky's extremism and his apparently unwavering faith in the necessity of a drastic final solution to the philistine question, pleased Lenin, who gave a positive appraisal of Gorky's views. Gorky's thesis on the origin of conscience was blunt, and for many, outrageous. The characterization of conscience as a "disease" had probably been taken from Nietzsche. Gorky admired Nietzsche and deplored that also the philistines used his thinking for their own purposes.[147]

The philistine, in this instance, was no longer seen as a lukewarm and inert creature, but as a totally politicized being. It stemmed from the nature of things that there should be no scruples in the political struggle, which inevitably was leading to a just and truthful world. For some reason, however, a merciless struggle was not constantly taking place. This hardly happened just because of the detrimental influence of the philistine intelligents. Rather in the society the people themselves remained to some extent unconscious and consequently philistine even though they represented a potentially anti-philistine force.

In short, the philistine, for the early Gorky, is a person, who lacks radicalism and is afraid of the ultimate doomsday which was to settle the scores between tortured and torturers.

To complete the picture it is useful to look at another, somewhat earlier, image of the philistine in Gorky's works. Here the philistine is not just a representative of the "commanding classes," and not even just a political being. For Gorky, the philistine was apparently an eternal principle: the philistine represented and was the inferior part of man. Only by overcoming philistinism was it possible to discover Man, who, when liberated from philistinism, embodied all that was brave and great in a human being.[148]

"Man (chelovek), the conqueror of the earth, wrote Gorky, burns in the darkness of life like a lighthouse, like a flower of fire, born of thought. "Man" (with capital letter) burns bright and walks in front of the people, and shows them the way to perfection. But far from him, carefully looking for his every step... comes after him the real lord of the whole earth, the sensible and respectable philistine". The hands and feet of the philistine are bound with the chains of property and he is all the time trying to bind himself still more tightly. The philistine is sensible, he does not know what inner freedom is, and his small heart is full of yearning for comfort, rest, nourishment and respect. He wants to fill his stomach and his soul, and in this he sees his happiness. The philistine follows "Man" from afar and utilizes his accomplishments. When "Man" conquers fire from the skies the philistine lights his bedroom lamp with this fire. If "Man" explores the essence of sound, the philistine uses his work for making a gramophone for his entertainment. The cryptic x-rays, which "Man" has discovered, he uses for guarding his property. In everything, the philistine makes the existence of "Man" useful or entertaining for himself. He himself likes stable truths, behind which he can hide from new currents of Thought.

As we can see, for Gorky, "Man", with a capital M was very much the same as the conglomerate intellectual. He was the bold explorer and generator of new thoughts. He was not enslaved by considerations of practical usefulness or the opinion of the masses. The Man, intellectual, did not want peace for himself but was going forward, towards perfection, not caring for the difficulties and dangers he had to face. The parallel between Ivanov-Razumnik"s intelligentsia and Gorky's Man, as the innovative force in society, is obvious. The philistine, on the other hand, is more or less representative of the broad masses whose interests are always practical and narrow and who are afraid of change. It is easy to see that even in this framework; radicals of all kinds could be considered representatives of the Man, while moderates would be philistines, and the more moderate, the more philistine.

When Gorky spoke about Man with a capital M in 1904; it was evident for the audience that he had in mind Nietzsche's superman.[149] Gorky's anti-degeneration pathos was no less understandable for the literary audience of the time. It seems that Gorky, like Lunacharsky and some others, believed that the new man would be a collective phenomenon. Gorky's novel *Mother* (1906), for instance, depicts conscious proletarians as the intelligents of a new era, as non-philistine heroes, who have forsaken the petty-bourgeois life and dedicated everything to the great cause of the liberation of man. Overcoming degeneration in literature meant, for Gorky, forsaking the "formalist" decadence, of someone like Paul Verlaine, for example. Being antibourgeois was not enough for Gorky. Any kind of excessive or queer sexuality was also sign of decadence, for Gorky, as for perhaps, the majority of his contemporaries even among the intellectuals.[150] The real salvation of humanity, however, was not a matter for literature or the work of a small group of intellectuals. It was the work of the working class, which was going to destroy everything old and rotten and build a new and vigorous culture. In his novel *Mother*, Gorky presented a fancy picture of this process, which supposedly was already taking place.

Gorky's ideal revolutionaries and the rationality of violence. *Mother*

Gorky's early works attained immense renown when the concept of "socialist realism" was launched. In the autumn of 1934, the First Congress of Soviet Writers took place with great pomp and formulated the contours of the past and present of "socialist realism," which was seen as the continuation of everything worthy in the culture of humanity so far. The idea took shape that every social formation consisted of a progressive and a reactionary component. The progressive element produced a progressive culture, which retained its worth over time, whereas reactionary culture was always barren and doomed to oblivion.[151]

The masterpieces of the new method had, of course, still to be found. It was not unnatural that a novel by Gorky, which had been published as early as 1906 was elected as a model for the authors of socialist society. The novel was an inheritance from a past epoch, but in its time it had represented a progressive workers" culture, which had now triumphed in Russia. Everything progressive in history, and that meant the best examples of the culture of each epoch, was treated with honor in the socialist Soviet Union, which continued the progressive tradition of humanity. Now the task of guarding this humanistic heritage rested totally on the shoulders of the working class, for the bourgeoisie was no longer a "cultural force."[152]

The sacralization of Gorky's novel *Mother* took place in a Russia which was totally different from the one in which it had been created. At that time it had presented a picture of the collective new man: the worker, who had been liberated from philistinism and become a kind of intelligent. In the discussion of the day it had been a bold comment on behalf of a workers' revolution. In 1917 Gorky had reason to remember, what he had written for more than ten years before.

Gorky's novel *Mother*, when it was published in 1906, was not a success. On the contrary, it was unanimously slated by the critics.[153] Plekhanov, the doyen of Russian Marxists, considered it "thoroughly false" and concluded that Gorky wanted to teach, but that was of no value, because he himself had not yet learnt.[154] Even Gorky himself was quite unhappy with the novel; he confessed that it was too openly didactic.[155] Lenin, however, who was not enthusiastic about the novel as such, nevertheless considered it "useful."[156]

It was not, therefore, self-evident that in the early 1930s, when socialist realism was taking its first steps, that *Mother* would be canonized as its *chef d'oeuvre*. In fact the book belonged to the discourse of the post-1906 period.

The book was, indeed, rather clumsy, but in any case its message was readily accessible even to the less advanced student. Its plot is rather clear-cut: the protagonist is a widowed working-class woman, whose son becomes an activist of the workers" movement. Before "the awakening" of the son and a small, but growing, group of his comrades, the whole workers' community had lacked consciousness and enlightenment. Earlier, before the good message had begun to take effect, all the workers had been crude in their manners. The mother's husband had always beaten her and sworn at her. Life had been full of stupidity and cruelty, any spare leisure time and surplus money went to the husband's drinking bouts.

When the son begins to participate in politics, everything changes: he begins to behave more modestly, does not drink, speaks politely, begins to pay attention to cleanliness, helps his mother in her daily work, which nobody else did in the neighborhood, and so on.[157]

Both the son, Pavel, and his comrades, who included also women, are, in most respects, like the ideal intelligents of that time. They have dedicated their life to a great cause. Some of them, like the daughter of a nobleman (*pomeshchik*), Sashenka, have left their families, and others consider that marriage between two revolutionaries would be wrong, because it would be detrimental to the great cause. Everybody is ready to suffer for the cause: jail and exile is unavoidable and accepted as such.

The new way of life, which the revolutionaries follow, arouses the admiration of the mother. Slowly her consciousness is developed and she understands that real purity and righteousness are found, not in religion, but in politics. The mother herself then becomes an active member of the revolutionary movement, and smuggles forbidden literature. At the end of the book, the son and his comrades leave for exile and the mother is arrested.

As for the different groups of society, the workers clearly have the leading part. There are also dropouts of the upper classes and peasants, who also serve the cause, but are not flawless. In fact, the peasants' rising, for instance, will make the land a desert, if the workers do not prevent it.[158] But the workers are different; the main heroes, Pavel and Andrei, are described no less hagiographically described than the mother.

In many places, there are useful maxims for communists (although the book was published in 1906). It made clear that, not only is it right to kill a traitor, but actually wrong not to kill him, as that would mean complicity in treason.[159]

The book also contained other prophecies concerning the socialist society: people would "walk on the earth free and be great in their freedom. They all will have open hearts, pure from envy and nobody will know anger or malice. Then life will be mere service of man, his portrait will be raised high; free people can reach the highest of peaks! Then, people will live in truth and freedom for beauty…."[160]

The message of the book is that it is now the workers, who have taken the baton from the intelligentsia, and who will, in fact, create a new and better society. Politics seems to accomplish the same metamorphosis in man that had, traditionally, been accomplished by culture: the workers who take part in political work become intellectuals, and begin to behave in a cultured way and adopt a quasi-Christian codex of values. Like Christ himself and his disciples, the worker activists leave everything petty-bourgeois behind and everything that could tie them down: parents, family, sexual relations. *Mother* sums up the tradition, which began with Chernyshevsky's *What is to be done?* It signifes that the birth of "new men" as a mass phenomenon, which Chernyshevsky had predicted had now, at the time of publishing of *Mother*, become a reality. God might be dead, but this just emphasized the grandeur of the new masses, who were realizing a new and higher order of values on earth.

In the 1930s this message was even more relevant and attained prestige and credibility from the fact that the phenomenon had been prophesied long ago by the well-renowned masters of culture, one of whom even now gave all his support to the cause, which was promoted by the general line of the Bolshevik party, led by Stalin.

In the 1930s critics stressed that, contrary to the earlier hostile criticism, Gorky was no petty bourgeois, but had really known the milieu he had described in *Mother,* and that the hostile criticism, which had slated this "first socialist novel in the strict sense of the word," had been ideologically biased.[161]

Gorky was not the only one, who had written deeply erroneous forecasts about the behavior of the workers and other revolutionary elements in the proletarian revolution and in post-capitalist society. His case was, however, different from that of most other Nietzscheans. Unlike the futurists and the symbolists, Gorky reveled in violence only in fiction. Real killings appalled him.[162] In 1905, however, violence was still kept within certain limits and could be interpreted as not necessarily senseless. In 1917 the general situation would be different.

"Man—it sounds proud" is one of Gorky's most famous phrases and it, indeed, contains the clue to his thinking. But here Gorky means the ideal Man, purified from philistinism. In fact the real man of Gorky's lifetime, was quite obviously far from the ideal type. As for Nietzsche, man was something, which had to be overcome. The liberation of Man also gave a meaning to humanity. To struggle for this cause was something higher than a mere senseless "philistine" existence. This was what Gorky had preached at the beginning of the twentieth century and this red thread in his work can be traced right up to the 1930s.

Gorky's ideas about the relationship between the toilers and the leisured classes, as found in his works, in fact, resembled those of Leo Tolstoy. While Tolstoy, in many of his works, represented the role of the state as monstrous and amoral, he often pointed to representatives of the humble people, the *narod,* as paragons of wisdom and virtue (e.g. Platon Karataev in *War and Peace*). Simple, physical work was something sacred for Tolstoy and in some of his works he described the almost religious satisfaction, which a representative of the leisure classes could get from physical work (e.g. Levin in *Anna Karenina*). In his personal life Tolstoy also sought the bliss of physical work and simple manners.

Gorky, who was a friend of Tolstoy for a long time, had somewhat similar views about the virtues of physical toil and the viciousness of leisure. For Gorky, however, physical toil had often become an unbearable burden. His toilers were often depicted as martyrs, whose sufferings the wealthy had to thank for their fortune. In *Foma Gordeyev* (1899) the protagonist is the son of a rich merchant. He is not, however, happy with his lot and the unjustness of his situation. He would like to be one of the toilers, whose work he admires, but he cannot. Instead, he becomes kind of a "holy fool"(in Russian, *iurodivyi*), who reveals all the unjustness and terrible personal corruption of the merchants. Foma's friend, a reporter, goes somewhat further and maintains that the existence of the educated classes has been bought by the blood and tears of tens of generations of Russians. What then had they done in turn?[163] For Gorky, as for a large section of the Russian intelligentsia, the shadow of guilt before the people was always a factor that could be found in his life and writing. On the other hand, the toilers, who, by definition, were no intelligents, were free from guilt and, quite naturally, would think and act differently. Quite often, Gorky's heroes exhibit appalling cruelty and there is often violence, which seems to have no reasonable justification.[164] As Dmitri Merezhkovsky stated, Gorky's *bosiaki*[165] had the spirit of an aristocrat and it even seemed as if they had read Nietzsche.[166]

In many of Gorky's works, especially in "In America" fantasies of destruction play a central role. In this work the reader is presented with a young man, who wants to grind the whole city of New York into one huge miasma of garbage and human blood. This terrible urge in the young man's brain is "as natural as a rankling sore in a beggar's body," Gorky explains. Where there is a lot of "slave work," there is no room for free, creative thought. In this case only ideas of destruction, "poisonous flowers of retaliation," a furious protest of an animal can flourish. It is understandable, Gorky argues, that when human beings spoil a man's soul, they cannot expect mercy from him for themselves. "Man has the right to seek revenge, this right is given to him by other human beings," Gorky writes.[167]

American workers, unlike their Russian colleagues, were, however, not respectable for Gorky. It seemed that American culture had somehow made even the workers inhuman by transforming them into petty bourgeois. Even when they are entertaining themselves, they remain somehow beastly and artificial at the same time. Unlike in Russia, in the streets of New York it is even impossible to find people, who are happily drunk and open their hearts in public.[168] In America, Gorky sees another kind of people: the mob, a repulsive many-headed beast, which wants to lynch an innocent man, who by accident had hit a drunk with his tram. This kind of violence seems to Gorky to be unpardonable and, apparently, very American.[169]

Violence, for Gorky, seems to have a class-nature. The violence of the petty bourgeois (including the hooligan) is just destructive. The idiocy of rural life, the greed of the merchant, and the consumerist society breed a senseless violence, which has a purely destructive nature. This, however, does not mean that one should abstain from violence. Paradoxical though it may seem, also abstinence from violence, when it is needed in class struggle, is also a crime. We can infer that, for Gorky, in the final analysis, the essence of philistinism is violence. For violence will continue as long as society breeds petty bourgeois relations between human beings and philistinism will prevent revolution from taking place.

Gorky's national and international reputation at the beginning of the twentieth century was immense, and had been ever since he had come into conflict with the tsarist autocracy and been thrown in jail for his anti-tsarist activities. Even the Academy of Sciences had elected him an honorary member. He was not exactly a Marxist in the conventional sense. In fact, Gorky was something of a mystic, in the modern, immanent sense of the word, as the Marxist professor, Mikhail Reisner, has concluded.[170] At the same time, Gorky had a social approach. The Man with a capital M, or the superman, was not a separate individual for him. Gorky angrily dismissed the oriental, meditative way of self-perfection as a method for attaining the lofty goals of Man.[171] The way to a better world had to be cleared by violence. This was something the philistine could not accept because it disturbed his peace.

The Russian intelligentsia of the Silver Age consisted of several elements, even though its critics usually spoke of it as if was a single monolith. This kind of criticism seems to have been, first of all, a rhetorical device which was used in order to make one's point more compelling. The authors of Vekhi must have known perfectly well that not "all" the Russian intelligentsia was fanatical, half-baked, ignorant and susceptible to extremism. There certainly were quite a lot of supporters of the extremist tradition. The statistics of terrorism and underground activity gave ample proof of this. But, on the other hand, there were also those soft-minded souls, who often appear in Chekhov's plays and short stories. Unimpressed by Nietzsche, they sometimes played with radical ideas, but lacked the ruthlessness of men of action (who are also present in Chekhov's works). Their respect for fellow-human beings and their lack of fanaticism made many intelligents doubt the idea that all ills could be cured by great social convulsions. Almost all the political parties wanted to get the whole of the intelligentsia on their side and tried to use as compelling arguments as possible. The adversary could always be stigmatized as "petty bourgeois." For Lenin, Trotsky and Gorky, and, indeed, for most of the symbolists and futurists, it was gentle people, those who excelled by their "intelligentnost'" or moral scruples and who lacked of resolution, who were "petty bourgeois," unlike the "masses," who somehow represented a higher, uncorrupted level of humanity. Merezhkovsky, the Vekhi, Ivanov-Razumnik, and others returned the accusation, each defining the essence of the ultimate source of evil, philistinism, in their own way. *Vekhi* was a heroic effort to condemn both futile radicalism and philistinism.

Instead of a political religion or sacralized politics, *Vekhi* preached the need for a "non-philistine" religious conscience and constructive political work at the same time. However, overcoming the estrangement of the intelligents from the state and its emotional fixation to radicalism was an insuperable task for anyone in society.

In spite of the challenge of *Vekhi*, it was the radical wing of the intelligentsia, which defined the intelligentsia's mainstream values up to the 1917 revolutions. The intelligentsia as a whole remained antibourgeois, anti philistine, and anti authoritarian, but not constructive, moderate, or prosaic. In literary circles any kind of maximalism prospered. Chiliastic movements from futurism to "Scythism" recruited new adepts. Drastic measures, instead of gradual evolution, were the slogan of the day. In poetry, Nietzschean strongmen conquered the sun. The decadence of the old order and the inertia of the bourgeois way or life were in vogue.[172] In politics, the Octobrists[173] and some elements of the Kadets,[174] formed a minor exception to the rule. As a whole, however, the Russian intelligentsia still looked forward to an all-embracing revolution, which would cure all the ills of society at a single blow.

3
The Revolution and the Revolutionaries. Theory and Practice

Lenin's ideas

V. I. Ulianov, who was writing under several pseudonyms, had been developing his own version of Marxism since the last years of the nineteenth century. It was in bitter struggles against other Marxists, such as Petr Struve, Iulii Martov, and others that Lenin created the idea of a party led by professional revolutionaries, who, in practice, were intellectuals, of course, which did not matter at all, so Lenin argued.[1] The hard nucleus of professional revolutionaries was an elite which would bring a socialist class-consciousness to the working class, which on its own was only capable of attaining a "trade-unionist" conscience.

Lenin was no less inimical towards the narodniks whom he branded "petty bourgeois" and retrograde, because they considered the development of capitalism in Russia as detrimental, postulated a specifically Russian path of economic development with the peasant economy as its basic unit, and ignored the fact that the intelligentsia unavoidably represented certain social classes.[2] The *narodniki* were "sentimental romantics and ideologues of petty bourgeoisie," Lenin argued, basing his faith on the "scientific" nature of Marxism, which proved the inevitability of capitalism.[3]

At the beginning of the twentieth century Lenin was just one of numerous estranged Russian intelligents, whose thoughts had little practical consequence. In the course of 1917, however, the Bolsheviks gained enormous success among the unruly masses. This was possible thanks to the genuinely "popular" character of Bolshevik politics, which would support any rebellious activities detrimental to the old social order. Seemingly opportunist, but, in fact, wholly practical, their politics were based on a formidable theoretical construction, which combined utopian goals with practical flexibility and a fanatical faith in the ultimate truth of their ideology. Sentimentalism and philistinism were the main enemies of this secular sectarianism.

The Bolsheviks wanted to remake both society and human nature. This might sound like a formidable task, but the dogmatic logic of Bolshevism made it seem simple. If it was true that human society and personality were determined by relations of production and those in turn, by proprietorship of the means of production, then the equation could be solved. The solution was just a technical matter, which to Lenin seemed simple.

He sketched out his ideas in what became a well-known pamphlet *State and Revolution*, which was written shortly before the October coup.[4] As Marx had argued, the proletariat, by its nature, was a force which could only lose from the existence of the bourgeois state with its capitalist economy. Therefore, once it had become conscious, it would inevitably strive for the annihilation of the very bases of bourgeois society, the existence of which meant it had only its shackles to lose.[5]

After the coup, the revolutionary Soviet state would have at its disposal an armed proletariat, which, due to its class instinct, was not likely to pursue half-hearted policies. Unlike the "sentimental little intellectuals" (*intelligentiki*), they would always be ready to punish severely representatives of the old order who were not quick enough to implement the will of the masses.[6] What stimulated the proletariat was its natural and uninhibited class-hatred towards the oppressors. By its nature, Lenin seemed to believe, the proletariat was 100 per cent ready to take part in expropriating the expropriators. Quite obviously it, by its nature, strove for equality for all, excluding the oppressors.

Not all "working people" were proletarians. The proletariat was the vanguard of the toiling masses and its psychology, due to its position in society, bore no traces of the petty-bourgeois prejudices and strivings, which still affected the psychology of many, who belonged to other working strata, including peasants and intellectuals. The latter group might even be the main stronghold of the petty bourgeoisie, because in bourgeois society it, en masse, served the autocracy. Numerically, at least, this was the case. For Lenin, a future socialist society would impossible if it was to be run by the petty bourgeoisie; for the philistines, it seemed utopian, and utopian it was for their kind of people. The truly scientific thinker, on the other hand, knew that the masses, in a proletarian society, would not be petty bourgeois. Moreover, he knew that ultimately people would easily become accustomed to behaving in a new way, sharing new values which were socialist in character.[7]

How did Lenin know this and why was he so sure about the prospects of remaking what seemed to be human nature?

It would appear that the father of the greatest social movement of the twentieth century had nothing but the vaguest of Hegelian shibboleths to support his cause. Marx had sketched out how typical social classes behaved in a revolution, using the Paris disorders of 1848 as his model, but these musings could claim no scientific respectability whatsoever. Wholesale characterizations of tens of thousands of people had a purely impressionistic character.[8] Apart from the mob's readiness to loot and its scorn for the achievements of bourgeois culture, there was not much to build on. True, the demonstrators in the streets of Petrograd in 1917 bore a variety of banners with egalitarian slogans. But this was no more than verbal radicalism. Lenin also spoke about "democratism" of the masses. This did not mean democracy, but "exclusion from democracy of the exploiters and the oppressors of the people."[9]

For Lenin, the most prominent proletarian virtues were class-hatred and the readiness to act unscrupulously. The Soviet state exploited this to the full. The imagery of Soviet cartoons, from the very beginning up to Gorbachev's perestroika, was designed to foster hatred to the greatest degree. The external as well as the internal enemy was depicted as inhuman, well fed, pretentious, bloodthirsty, cruel, and despicable, indeed, so polluted that it should not be even touched.[10]

During the revolution and civil war, the resistance of and sabotage by the bourgeoisie especially the petty bourgeoisie, in the form of the peasantry, could be represented as the cause of all the people's misery. This would later be continued in the official descriptions of the show trials, beginning in 1922. The enemy, it was claimed, was the direct cause of the many sufferings of the Soviet people: war, famine, misery, explosions, railway and mine catastrophes, poor remuneration, and so on. The solution was always simple: hitting the enemy still harder and purging its agents from the ranks of the proletariat. This was all part of a psychology of war: revenge and annihilation of the enemy also presupposed endurance and sacrifice. After 1917, the options were either final victory or total defeat. Faith in final victory justified all sacrifices. On the other hand, any wavering in that faith was one of the most unpardonable of vices. In fact, it was truly bourgeois. All in all, the general line of the party presupposed real proletarian virtues in its purveyors: they had to believe in the goals of the party and serve it selflessly. They had to fulfil their duty before the party and their class unflinchingly, letting no personal or other considerations shake their convictions.

In retrospect, the ideas of Lenin, as regards both the future socialist man and the methods used in his creation, seem terribly simplistic. Lenin's last apologies concerning the advantages which proletarian takeover had created for cultural construction seem pathetic enough. To some historians, Lenin has come to appear more respectable than he actually was, and the stress shifted to the pragmatic side of his policies. Yet, what really remains, when his aims are critically studied, is his quasi-Napoleonic utterance:

"*On s'engage et puis—on voit....*"[11] The real test of the October coup and the ensuing Bolshevik dictatorship was the struggle against "petty bourgeois" human nature, which Lenin had dismissed as a trifle in his "State and Revolution." Hatred, coined class-hatred, and inclination to struggle for the spoils, dubbed as class-struggle, proved to be working tools for the engineers of human society, although they proved to be not nearly as efficient, as had been thought.

The myth of the conscious proletarian

As the famous Marxist maxim puts it, it was man's (social) being, which determined consciousness, not the other way round.[12] The consciousness of the proletariat was supposedly dictated by its class-standing. Deprived of the means of production, to which the labor of the proletariat was attached, it had nothing to lose from a thoroughgoing social revolution, but everything to gain. The proletariat's consciousness was forged by its daily labor and life, and this meant, and made obvious that the salvation of the working class could only be achieved by the expropriation of the capitalists. In the Marxist vision, the workers were not only the direct victims of capitalist exploitation but also those who suffered most. Their class-position, however, gave them a kind of ultimate wisdom, which stemmed directly from the logic of things. It was not skewed by a "false consciousness." Having become "a class for itself," that is, having attained a consciousness of itself, and once organized for class struggle, the proletariat was bound to struggle for the ultimate liberation and progress of the human race.

Perhaps for this reason, the proletariat also showed admirable qualities, as if already reflecting the real essence of liberated humanity. For instance, Marx described with exaltation, how virtuous (in an old-fashioned sense of the word) the proletarian revolutionaries were.[13] If some workers were not virtuous, this was because they were misguided, and thus not really representative of their class. One reason for lacking class-orientation, this could happen, was that an individual might not have been "enough boiled in the kettle of the workshop." It was also possible to be of proletarian origins, but to have lost its psychology. In such cases the person was declassed, most likely becoming a "lumpenproletarian."[14]

It was work, then, which gave the proletariat its readiness to adopt the most progressive stand in society. It was not any type of work that could do this, only waged labor for the capitalist, ideally.

There were, however, some awkward questions: which values and properties of the existing proletariat adequately reflected its essence; that is, which of them were truly proletarian? If it really was the case that anything that served proletarian class interests was good, then it also had to be inferred that a value, which served the proletariat badly was bad and not proletarian at all, even if all proletarians shared it. In principle, the door was open for an interpretation, according to which the proletariat was not necessarily wholly proletarian, and that it might have to be forced to become such (perhaps by its most conscious part, as Leninist logic had it). This would be no more and no less foolish than insisting that human beings were, as yet, not really and thoroughly human, because they had not been liberated from the slavery of structures, which had created inhumanity. The question of universal values in the framework of Marxist analysis also becomes awkward. If exploitation of the proletariat is wrong, is it wrong just from the point of view of the proletariat? The bourgeoisie explains to itself, and tries to prove to others too, the necessity of capitalist exploitation, but is it a universal evil, or is it really right from the point of view of the bourgeoisie? Is anything, which best serves the proletariat, already good by virtue of its utility in the class-struggle? Is any kind of cruelty in fact virtuous, if it works well in the service of the grandiose cause of human liberation, the creation of a higher human type? Clearly, Nietzschean-proletarian romantics at the beginning of the century should have answered this question positively.

As we have seen, for Lenin too the transcending of "petty bourgeois" values was admirable as such. On the other hand, if there were universal values, then even the proletariat was bound by them and even its struggle for liberation should not offend them, unless we approve of principle, according to which a lesser evil may always be justified by the fact that it helps to avoid a greater evil. It is clear that, for Lenin, proletariat, as it was then was no more than a frame of reference, on which he projected his own image of the genuine, ideal proletariat. The Bolsheviks, as the vanguard, had the right, and even a duty, to do this, according to their theory.

According to Lenin's writings, during the revolutionary period it seems that, compassion for the exploiters, for instance, could not be proletarian, while class-hate clearly was. A thirst for culture and enlightenment probably was truly proletarian, while vandalism was not. A propensity to work conscientiously should have been proletarian, while an inclination for gluttony, drunkenness and excessive leisure could not possibly have been proletarian. The main objective of genuine proletarian consciousness was the urge to remake the whole structure of society, not to strive for immediate individual satisfaction. The latter was typical of the petty-bourgeoisie and the "lumpenproletariat." Altruism and egoism were, perhaps, not universal values, but, clearly, Marx and Engels believed that the proletariat was inclined to the former, while the bourgeoisie cherished the latter.[15] The case of collectivism and individualism was analogous, and probably derived from the same daily practice of class struggle, the logic of which proved the necessity of organization for the proletariat.

The necessity of proletarian discipline was also believed to be readily understandable for a class which could only defend its rights against the capitalist by means of concerted action, never by individual means. This is the case despite the existence of a layer of patronized labor aristocracy, which no more was a part of the proletariat for the very reason that (like the lumpenproletariat in Paris 1849) it had been bribed by the capitalists with special favors, which could not be granted to the class *en masse*.[16]

One of the problems with the Marxists ideas about the class-psychology was that they were not based on research. Studies that do not have a Marxist bias tend to point out that the actual value-orientation of the Russian proletariat differed considerably from the Marxist ideal. Mark D. Steinberg, studying workers in the printing industry, surely not the least "developed" group, came to the conclusion that the "vanguard workers" always built their critique of contemporary society and its ills on the concept of universal values. They also preferred the Mensheviks to the Bolsheviks. For the activists, violations of the workers' human dignity on the part of the employers were the grounds of their moral indignation. A common yardstick, with which both fellow workers and their superiors could be measured, was culture. It was the lack of culture that explained excessive drinking, swearing, and debauchery. The bad employers treated the workers like slaves, but many workers also behaved like slaves. To attain class-consciousness also meant raising cultural and moral self-consciousness.[17]

The more conscious workers, those who organized the demonstrations, laid great stress on the rights of man and the respect that workers also deserved. The workers (and soldiers) demanded to be addressed politely. The labor movement paid homage to the values of *kulturnost'* and it was also the case that for demonstrations workers put on their best Sunday clothes in order to stress their dignity as cultured citizens.[18] A well-known example, which probably reflected a short-lived upsurge of revolutionary mentality from the euphoric months of 1917, was that of the waiters, who demanded not to be tipped by customers, because it hurt their human dignity.[19]

The "lumpenproletariat." A variety of petty bourgeoisie?

As has often been pointed out, the Bolsheviks in Russia were in an awkward situation from a Marxist point of view, since the industrial proletariat formed just a small minority of the population, while the "petty bourgeois" peasantry was the overwhelming majority. Therefore, an extensive exploitation of what was called "petty bourgeois" elements was a required. However, not only were there proletarians and different kinds of bourgeois, there was also, according to Marx and Engels, the "lumpenproletariat." For Marx and Engels, the petty bourgeoisie had a detrimental class psychology due to its social position. The petty bourgeoisie were restaurant owners, artisans, peddlers, and the like, who did not sell their labor to the capitalist and who, apart from their chains, owned other things too.[20] The petty bourgeoisie did not want a thoroughgoing social revolution, as had been proved in Paris 1849; it wanted to stop the revolution as soon as it began to endanger private ownership. The class-nature of the petty bourgeoisie dictated its attitude to the revolution: it was bound to be cowardly, its goals and measures were as petty as its everyday business.[21]

The champion of the petty bourgeoisie, among socialists was Proudhon, who became a favorite *bête noire* of Marx and Engels. Proudhon did not see a difference of interests in principle between the proletariat and the petty bourgeoisie or the ensuing need to subordinate the latter to the former.[22]

While the petty bourgeoisie was an extremely unreliable ally of the proletariat, even if it also included some good elements, the "lumpenproletariat" was seen as scum, which consisted of the depraved elements from all classes and was, thus, the worst of all possible allies. It was "absolutely for sale and absolutely pretentious." It differed radically from the industrial proletariat and was the layer, from which thieves and all kinds of criminals were recruited. It was the lumpenproletariat, which helped smash the Paris uprising of 1849: they were "depraved adventurers of bourgeois origins, former soldiers, ex-convicts and runaways, swindlers, buffoons, *lazzaroni*, pickpockets, jugglers, gamblers, pimps, harbor hands, scribblers, organ grinders, knife grinders, tinkers, common beggars."[23] The "lumpenproletariat" was bought by Louis Napoleon for uniforms and sausages and this was enough to satisfy its ambitions.

The borderlines, which separated the lumpenproletariat from the petty bourgeoisie, on the one hand, and from the proletariat on the other, seem enigmatic. Clearly, one could not rise, socially speaking, to become a member of the "lumpenproletariat," because this layer was obviously on the bottom of society. However, it is clear that the representatives of the professions, which Marx explained to be lumpenproletariat, would in Russia have been considered typical representatives of the *meshchanstvo*. The Russian *bosiak*, or tramp, which was Maxim Gorky's favorite hero, was also to be found in the ranks of this class: the "common beggars." Later, it was sometimes argued that the whole Bolshevik revolution was essentially a revolution of the "lumpeproletarians" (*bosiaki*).[24] In reality, however, the actual psychological qualities of revolutionary activists scarcely had much to do with their social origins. Marx and Engels had no more sociological data worthy of the name than Lenin to support their views about the "necessary" behavior of revolutionary elements. The Bolsheviks' strategies, which they used in order to stay in power, had to be found by trial and error. One of the main flaws of Lenin's *State and Revolution* proved to be its image of the psychology of the conscious proletarian (as opposed to the petty bourgeois). In fact, the Bolsheviks, as well as Gorky and many others, had ample reason for revising their views about the qualities of various segments of society; workers as well as intelligents and peasants. After the revolution, concepts like "philistinism" or "petty bourgeois" soon lost all reasonable contact to their original ideological sources.

The "lumpenproletarians" and other progressive forces. Lenin's crusade against the petty bourgeois *"intelligenty"*

In "State and Revolution," Lenin argued that a proletarian dictatorship would necessarily be infinitely more democratic than a democratic bourgeois republic.[25] The new state would be a state of armed workers who would control the formerly bourgeois bureaucrats and ensure that the state was only used in the interests of the formerly oppressed classes. The task of administration, as Lenin saw it, was very simple, for it presupposed only the elementary skills of the three R's.[26] The salaries of the bureaucrats, now under proletarian surveillance, would be lowered to the level of ordinary workers, and bureaucrats would be elected and could be sacked at any moment. These principles were, according to Lenin, "self-evident" and democratic and "wholly in line with the common interests of the majority of the workers and peasants."[76]

The workers, even the now "armed people" at large, readily understood their interests and would jealously guard them, Lenin concluded. If "good-for-nothings, dandies, swindlers and similar pursuers of the heritage of capitalism" tried to violate those interests, they would be punished promptly and severely "for armed workers are practical people and not sentimental little intellectuals, and they hardly will allow any playing with themselves" so that the necessity to observe the elementary rules of all human cohabitation would very soon be transformed into a habit.[28] Communist society, Lenin stated, presupposed a higher productivity of work than had actually been achieved in Russia before 1917 and also a different kind of human being than was the contemporary philistine (*obyvatel'*). Anyway, the base for a communist society was rapidly being made and it was made by people who were not philistines: the workers.[29]

The workers were also naturally inclined to behave in a way that best served their class-interests. But how should this be organized in practice? Lenin gave a direct answer to this question in his booklet *Can the Bolsheviks Retain State Power?*[30] The article was written shortly before the October takeover and published immediately after it. The task was simple. The servants of the bourgeois state, and of the banks, had to be made to work under proletarian surveillance. Other policies, which would be used against all well-to-do people, included the institution of a grain monopoly, bread rationing, and a universal duty to work. Now, the formerly oppressed would use this system against the well-to-do, who also had to keep a work-book, which would prove every week that they had worked conscientiously for the new regime. Some specialists would, in the beginning, receive a higher salary than ordinary workers, but this would only be temporary.[31]

But there was a still more potent device which would enable the proletarian state to multiply its state machinery tenfold, a device, which no capitalist state had ever had or could have. This "excellent device" was the expropriation of the well-to-do. To explain "how easy it was to use this excellent device and to show how surely it works," Lenin took a simple case as an example: The state had to throw a family out of its apartment and give it to another. This was something the capitalist state had done all the time and was also what the proletarian state would do. As for the capitalist state, it would oust a working family, which had lost a work hand and could not pay its rent. There would be policemen, Cossacks and infantry, maybe several regiments.

As for the proletarian state, it would settle a family in great need in the apartment of a rich person. Here the detachment of the workers' militia would consist of, say 15 persons: two sailors, two conscious workers (of which only one would be a party member or sympathetic), one intellectual and eight people from among the toiling poor, necessarily no less than five women among them, servants, unskilled workers, and so on. They would come to an apartment of five rooms, thrust the rich in to two rooms and settle two families in the remaining ones. The detachment would also give the members of the well-to-do family some tasks of public service to be rendered under proletarian surveillance.[32]

According to Lenin, this was an example of revolutionary policy and similar processes should be organized everywhere, both in cities and in the countryside, and should be used when distributing foodstuffs, clothes, footwear, land, and so on. This kind of "administrative work" could at once attract ten -if not twenty- million volunteers. It was the workers, who should lead the process, but they could attract toiling the masses and the oppressed into the task of administration.[33]

The workers' psychology, in Lenin's opinion, was admirable. The proletarian discerned the essentials of politics with "astonishing clarity, which for our intellectuals is as remote as the stars in the sky." All the world is divided into two camps: "we," the toiling people, and "they," the exploiters. If the reactionaries dared to resist the proletariat, then the proletariat was ready to do, on a large scale, to them, what it had done to the "Kornilovites" in Vyborg—to kill them.[34]

The oppression of the well-to-do was essential for the popularity of the regime, Lenin saw: "When every unskilled worker, every unemployed, every housemaid and every ruined peasant sees with his own eyes that proletarian power did not serve wealth but the poor ones, that it would take surplus foodstuffs from the rich and give them to the poor, that it would place homeless in the apartments of the rich, that it would force the rich to pay for milk, but would not give to them a drop of it, before all the children of the poor families had got it enough, that lad would be given to the toiling people and factories and banks put under workers surveillance, that the millionaires would get a prompt and effective punishment for the hiding of their riches, then nothing could win the people's revolution."

What, then, in short, was the secret of proletarian rule? In Lenin's example, it was the workers, who took the lead in the new "administration," but only a few were needed. The workers were "practical" and unscrupulous, and, accordingly, effective. But the masses were less conscious, consisting to a large extent of petty bourgeoisie and the lumpenproletariat, which were also poor. What the proletarian state had to do to in order to get them on its side was to gratify their greed and their instinct for retaliation. What they wanted was to be given a chance personally to oppress the rich. Clearly, it was the petty expropriation of bourgeois property that motivated the detachment, which went to the five-room flat of the bourgeoisie. The prospect of loot was even more palpable, when it came to redistributing land in the countryside, and even foodstuffs, clothes, and shoes. This was not exactly the kind of "conscious," enlightened self-interest, which the proletariat supposedly displayed in its willingness to abolish private property in general. In Lenin's opinion this was also something natural, instinctive, and righteous and understandable for all, from the class-point of view. Clearly it was understandable also for the lumpenproletariat.

In the final analysis, self-interest was, for Lenin, what determined people's behavior. How else could he have been so sure about the undivided popularity of his "device." Evidently, the "conscious" people's idea of their real self-interest was rational and enlightened. It was rational for the workers to want to abolish capitalism and private property wholesale; for them this was clear from their everyday experience. For the petty bourgeoisie to attain this level of consciousness, transgressing petty class-limits was required. But what about the lumpenproletariat? It seemed that they always served whoever paid best. In 1917 nobody could compete with the Bolsheviks, who declared that all the wealth was for the poor.

In the beginning of January 1918, Lenin was still euphoric about his new "device." In a programmatic article "How competition should be organized."[35] he, in effect, called for a competition of soviets in oppressing the bourgeoisie. Only mass cooperation, voluntary and conscientious, implemented with revolutionary zeal in keeping in check the "rich, the swindlers, the *flâneurs* and the hooligans" could overcome these "outcasts of the society, these helplessly depraved and gangrened members, this scum, plague and rankling sore, which socialism had inherited from capitalism."

The task was a practical one; the enemy had to be smashed not only in the political but also in the economic sphere. There would be

no mercy for those enemies of the people, enemies of socialism and enemies of the toilers. A war of life and death against the rich and their bootlickers, the bourgeois intelligentsia, a war against the swindlers, the *flâneurs* and the hooligans. Both these and those, the former and the latter are brethren, children of capitalism, children of the society of the lords, pampered children of bourgeois society....[36]

Lenin, thus, decided that not only the rich but also some other elements, who clearly were not actually rich, but "objectively" odious, including representatives of the intelligentsia, were the main enemy of socialism and should be "mercilessly punished, if they violated in the slightest the rules and laws of then socialist society." Any feebleness, vacillation and sentimentality in this respect would be a "most serious crime against socialism."[37] There was even to be a competition in the practical organization of socialist administration, which, first of all, meant surveillance and the "annihilation and neutralization of the parasites ...the hysterical intellectuals etc."

The goal of this accounting and surveillance was simple and clear and understandable for everyone: "that there be bread for everybody ... that not one swindler (including those shying away from work) would stroll free, but would sit in gaol or serve out his punishment with the hardest kind of forced labor. That not one rich person could avoid the fate of a swindler (starvation)." In order to be as explicit as possible, Lenin gave a concrete example of the methods, which should be used: "Somewhere, ten rich people, a dozen swindlers and half a dozen workers, shirking from work, will be thrown into gaol, in another place they will be put to tidy the lavatories, in a third one after incarceration they will be given a yellow (prostitutes') certificate so that all the people would keep an eye on them, the harmful people until they mend their ways. In a fourth place each tenth of those caught idling will be shot on the spot. In the fifth place combinations of different methods will be invented...." There was work enough to be done everywhere, in this respect; there was ample space for "competition:" in every commune, or quarter of a city, factory, and hamlet there were "the hungry, the unemployed" and also "the rich good-for nothings, the bootlicking scoundrels of the bourgeoisie, the saboteurs, who called themselves *intelligenty*."[38]

Lenin noticed that the intelligents were consoling themselves by saying "Without us they cannot get along." This insolent consideration had proved false, Lenin wrote, as there were intellectuals, who were ready to serve the people and the people itself had great resources of various talents. The "old, absurd, wild, mean, and disgusting prejudice," according to which only the representatives of the higher classes or people schooled by them could run the state should be abandoned.[39]

It is striking that Lenin did not give much thoughts to the lumpenproletariat. A call for looting was certainly something, which would attract this group as the sausages of Louis Bonaparte had attracted their colleagues in France. We have no analysis from Lenin on the lumpenproletariat in Russia, but at this moment he was obviously convinced that his "sausages" were sure to win over the lumpenproletarians to the side of the proletariat. Lenin showed no concern about distracting or isolating certain elements (e.g. criminals or other insufficiently "proletarian" groups) from amongst the "reigning" proletariat. The only *bête noire* was the petty bourgeoisie, especially the intelligents. In his article "The Next Tasks of Soviet Power"[40] published in April 1918 Lenin nevertheless had to confess that the implementation of the elementary task of control and oversight had not made much progress. There were not many results even in "arresting and shooting swindlers." An iron hand was needed, for now, more and more. The enemy was petty bourgeois, anarchist instinct. It was necessary to fight it with violent methods. Lack of discipline was now the greatest of problems. It had to be understood that anybody, who violated work discipline in any factory or economical unit, was guilty of the calamities caused by starvation and unemployment. The culprits should be found and punished mercilessly. The problem reflected the petty bourgeois psychology of the small proprietor, who did not care about anything except the opportunity of getting more for himself. In order to solve the problem, dictatorial powers were necessary. There could still be "democratism" in meetings, but at work, there should be "iron discipline and unconditional surrender to one person, the Soviet leader." It was "not hysterical bouts of enthusiasm that we need. We need a rhythmical march of the iron battalions of the proletariat," envisioned Lenin in April 1918. Lenin, the intelligent, was thus demanding harsh punishment for representatives of the Russian proletariat, whom he accused of having a petty bourgeois psychology. What had seemed so simple and natural proved to be possible only through coercion.[41]

Another novelty in Lenin's thinking was the urge to attract bourgeois intellectuals into the service of the proletarian state. A great number of bourgeois intelligents had to be attracted into cooperating with Soviet power.[42] The specialists would have to be paid much better than rank and file. This would be impermissible later, in a developed socialist society, but for now it was necessary. The threat of a capitalist restoration came now from "petty bourgeois anarchism and dissolution." This took the form of daily petty, but frequent, attacks on proletarian discipline. This "petty bourgeois" anarchism had to be overcome and it would be.[43] The *intelligenty*, whose help Lenin now considered necessary, were, of course, not the impractical dreamers of St. Petersburg's garrets, but the captains of industry, who would hardly have called themselves *intelligents* at all. The main enemy at the moment was labelled "petty bourgeois," but it was not exactly that layer of society, which was making a livelihood through services, the intellectual professions or the retail trade. This time the epithet noticeable number of workers and their leaders, even some, who were members of the Bolshevik party.

In the session of the All-Russian Executive Committee (VTsIK) at the end of April 1918, Lenin chided both the Mensheviks and the so called "Left Communists" in the Bolshevik party, who were criticizing Taylorism, one-man management, the employment of bourgeois specialists, and the introduction of work discipline in general as un-socialistic. It was the petty bourgeois, Lenin explained, who feared discipline, organization, and control like the Devil feared holy water. The "conscious" worker did not fear the capitalist, who had been put in to supervise him, for he knew that Soviet power was his power and would defend him, Lenin asserted.[44] In his article "About the 'leftist' infantilism and petty 'philistinism'" Lenin explained practically, what he meant by these terms.

For Lenin, communists who did not share his views regarding the necessity of peace with Germany and the introduction of discipline and well-paid capitalist employees were "déclassé, intellectual party bosses" (*deklassirovannye, intelligentskie partiinye "vershki"*).[45] What strikes one about the intellectual progress of Lenin over a couple of revolutionary months, is a shift from the praise of spontaneity to a stress on the importance of discipline of the masses themselves. While it had seemed self-evident to Lenin on the eve of the revolution, that iron discipline could be enforced without particular difficulty by an "armed people" and that it was only the rich who needed to be repressed, now this image was rapidly changing. It was not only that "whining" intellectuals did not realize self-evident proletarian truths regarding the repression of the class-enemy, but also that the petty-bourgeois masses, including workers, needed to be subject to violent repression and surveillance as well. Lenin had instigated the masses to loot, but it was not that easy to get them to stop looting. Clearly, it was thought that everyone would be content with the organized looting of the Soviets and the commissions, but they were not. What had seemed to Lenin to be the natural yearning of the proletariat had in practice to be enforced by gunpoint.

Russia was exceptionally petty bourgeois, sighed Lenin in April 1918, but he must have known this before. Violent methods of punishment, which Lenin relished, were non-philistine by definition and were indeed introduced. Lenin's arrogant redefinition of the concept of "petty bourgeois," did not go unchallenged. The left communist opposition claimed that introducing harsh work discipline and reinstating former capitalist leaders meant the enslavement of the workers (which was bourgeois). Lenin was delighted to show that the Mensheviks, who were, a priori, petty bourgeois, agreed with this criticism, while the "most conscious" workers approved of discipline, or so he seemed to believe.[46] In fact, it was the most conscious and, therefore, most active workers, who mostly organized the strikes and the *volynki* (Italian strikes). This was just explained away, by defining workers who presented demands to the Bolsheviks as "bourgeois."[47] The bourgeois specialists were irreplaceable, Lenin declared, and the workers, the best workers in Russia, understood this, as they were not petty bourgeois, while the déclassé and, therefore, thoroughly petty bourgeois intelligents did not understand this. The ideas, he had expressed in *State and Revolution* before the revolution were in principle correct, but no longer relevant, Lenin explained.[48]

Drawing together what Lenin meant by philistinism, we can conclude that anything that endangered or challenged the power of the Bolshevik party, was philistine (petty bourgeois), for him. Lenin had hardly any reliable information about the degree of support his ideas enjoyed among the workers or about changes in this support. As regards the intelligents, Lenin clearly considered them to be an inferior element. At first he seemed to think they were superfluous for the new society but he soon became convinced of their indispensability.

The revolutionary intellectuals' reaction to the 1917 revolutions

Vekhi did not attract the majority of the Russian intelligentsia to its ideas, but it was a well-noted phenomenon and it affected the atmosphere.

As is well-known, the February Revolution of 1917 was a surprise to almost everybody, not least to Lenin, whom its waves would bring to the top of the Russian political scene. But there was no denying that the intelligentsia at large enthusiastically greeted the revolution. The revolution happened amidst a world war, but even this did not make the intelligentsia waver. After all, the imperial family had been deeply compromised in the eyes of the whole of society and the abdication of Nicholas II seemed to brighten the prospects even in this respect. Arguably, the decisive force in the revolution was the intelligentsia, which actively sought to establish democracy in the midst of the war. But who were the intelligents who supported the February Revolution (and, partly also the ensuing October revolution)? Were they the same people, whose romantic preconceptions had been severely shaken in 1905-07? By 1917 those days were just a decade away and the third generation ("the Grandsons") was still active part on the political scene. But there was also a younger element. Among the young ones, there were many, who experienced their first revolution and who were to live their whole lives in a "revolutionary" state.

The third generation of the Russian intelligentsia was preponderantly radical both in politics and culture, even though there were now also the truly liberal, moderate, and conservative contingents, as represented by the parties in the Duma.[49] *Vekhi* was a symptom of the bifurcation of the political views of this generation, and although the Bolsheviks well represented the extremist intelligentsia tradition and its faith in the "people," they clearly formed a minority even in 1917. The majority also opposed absolutism but supported "democracy," which was understood in different ways.[50]

The ruling generation of the Russian intelligentsia in 1917-18, who sat in the Provisional Government and in the Duma, was already in its fifties and sixties[51] and already yielding its position to younger people, whose conscious life had been formed after 1905 or in the abnormal conditions after 1914.[52] The youth of the 1917 revolution, which became the first generation of the Soviet intelligentsia proper, was born during the first decade of the twentieth century.[53] At the same time, it was the "fourth generation" of the Russian intelligentsia. Its social origins were now largely worker and peasant, while its predecessors had been raznochinets and noble. This generation which grew up in the new "socialist" society became the beneficiary of the new regime on various occasions: in the purges and campaigns of the first five-year plan period and later in the great terror of

1936-38, which opened the way to the top of society for this generation at a young age. It was also this "Brezhnev generation,"[54] which had to pay a heavy toll in the Second World War, but which also staunchly defended the Soviet regime to the end, which coincided with perestroika. The Brezhnev generation was, perhaps, the only one to consist, mostly, of true believers. It was challenged by the "men of the sixties," [55] but it only gave way only during perestroika, when it was already physically disappearing.

The orthodox Soviet view from the days of "developed socialism"[56] has a somewhat different approach. It distinguishes five "Soviet generations": the first generation, which had been born in the 1870s and was the generation of the first Russian revolution of 1905-07; the second generation which had been born between 1890-1910 and was the generation of industrialization and collectivization; the third generation which had been born between 1910 and 1929 and formed the generation of the Great Fatherland War and postwar reconstruction; the fourth generation born in the 1930s and 1940s was the generation of the cultivation of the Virgin lands, the first space flights and the criticism of the Stalinist cult of personality. The 1980s saw the emergence of the fifth Soviet generation. Whatever the relative weight of the generations, the February revolution was at first greeted enthusiastically by almost the entire intelligentsia. After the February revolution the intelligentsia was "in power," whatever this might mean in a situation where the imperatives of war and the challenge of the Soviets made governing virtually impossible.[57] Remarkably enough, even members of the *Vekhi*-group greeted the revolution.[58]

But the honeymoon was soon over. The long-awaited great liberation from the yoke of absolutism also brought with it severe disorder and economic ruin, which was appalling for most *intelligenty*. The revolution was also no answer to the deadlocked situation in the World War, and the idea of defending the newly-won civil liberties at the front won no support among the masses. In less than a year the revolution had totally ruined both the economy and the military machine of Russia.[59] The revolutionary "democracy," which the intelligentsia had greeted with such enthusiasm in February 1917, contained a built-in flaw, which ruined the coercive mechanisms of the state including the army. With the people rebelling against all authority, it was impossible to establish a free society and the rule of law. It turned out that the Russian masses were even indifferent to the fate of their own state in the war. The intelligentsia had to face the bitter fact that "the coming barbarian," which Merezhkovsky had presaged, had arrived. Faced with this situation, a number of *intelligenty* became indifferent and left political life, apart from those, who identified with the lower classes and were leading the mass parties.[60]

But the latter element was also quite numerous. All the party leaders were intelligents. At a meeting of the Menshevik Party in August 1917, 46 per cent of the delegates were *intelligenty*, while 27 per cent were workers and the rest consisted of civil servants and other elements.[61] No less than 30,000-35,000 or 10 per cent of the members of the Bolshevik party seem to have been intelligents on the eve of the October revolution.[62]

However, by the autumn of 1917 the majority of the intelligentsia was clearly ready to accept a military dictatorship in order to save what could be saved. But the strong man of the Provisional Government, Kerensky, did not support Kornilov. By October it was evident that the Provisional Government was going to share the fate of its predecessor: it no longer had pathos, trust, or power. It had "just become merely ridiculous."[63]

The Bolsheviks, who finally took power without any serious resistance, were insolent enough to trample under foot even the most sacred tenets of the intelligentsia: civic liberties, universal suffrage and freedom of the press and the inviolability of the individual.[64] It seems safe to say that the Bolsheviks did not enjoy the support of the main body of the intelligentsia after their *coup d'état* in October 1917.[65] They never gained back the trust of the old intelligentsia and, knowing this, the Bolsheviks ultimately resorted to the annihilation of this element as a group (though not every individual) and its substitution with a creation of their own. In the spring of 1918 the Bolshevik were losing their position in local Soviet elections everywhere to the Mensheviks, which indicated that it was not only intellectuals, but also proletarians who were leaving them.[66] They would not allow this to happen. However, the Bolshevik regime did not have the nerve to liquidate all "bourgeois" rights and liberties immediately: at first the Bolsheviks formed a coalition government with the left SRs, and a number of opposition-minded papers continued to appear – albeit under constant threat and persecution. After the abortive SR-putsch in the summer of 1918, the dictatorship of the Bolsheviks threw away the last fig leaf of democracy. All remnants of the opposition were suppressed and summary violence was perpetrated on the representatives of the former governing classes. In 1918 the civil war was fought between the Bolsheviks and the other revolutionaries of the *Komuch*—the supporters of the dispersed Constituent Assembly. Since the autumn of 1918, when admiral Kolchak became the "supreme governor" of non Bolshevik Russia, the counterrevolution lost much of its democratic hue. Forced by the fortunes of war and politics to fight the common enemy; namely the Kolchak government, part of the "petty bourgeois" intelligentsia once again supported the Bolsheviks and was, to some extent- tolerated by them. Every now and then, the Bolsheviks even allowed the Mensheviks to publish their own newspapers.[67]

The old radicalism of the non-Bolshevik intelligentsia died hard, and the Bolsheviks were supported as representatives of a "leftist" cause, which the rightists threatened, and which, perhaps, the democratic left would soon be put in charge of. This seems to have been the logic of the Bolsheviks' rivals on the left. Before long, an opportunity seemed to present itself. At the same time, however, Lenin decided to get rid of his political rivals for good.

The New Economic Policy (NEP) had been introduced, in the spring of 1921, in disastrous circumstances. The adoption of the new policy was, in effect, a declaration of political bankruptcy of the government, and it was considered necessary to squelch the voice of the opposition as completely as possible. A show trial was staged in the spring of 1922 to show that the SRs had been deliberately starving the Russian people. The capital sentences, meted out to the culprits, were not put into effect, but the trial showed that political opposition was no longer possible.[68]

The *intelligenty*, who had considered themselves the champions of truth and justice had come to see that the very "people," which had been brutalized by misery and violence, put all the intelligents alike in the common category of the "bourgeoisie." The *intelligenty* complained that they were being treated as parasites just because they did not have calloused hands.[69] Tens, even hundreds of thousands preferred to emigrate. There were, however, many, who would have liked to stay, at almost any cost. A sizable number of *intelligenty* had survived several years of brutality on part of the regime, which had fought the representatives of the former "commanding classes" with starvation and insults. In 1922 several hundred leading *intelligenty* were rounded up and sent out of Russia in the famous "philosophers' ship."

The Kadet party and its leaders, which had been proclaimed as the immediate class enemies and whose politics had been demonized during the reign of the Provisional Government, had no room in which to exist politically or even physically in post-October Russia.

Up to 1922, representatives of the old intelligentsia in revolutionary Russia included many different elements; the old Bolsheviks; political neophytes like Trotsky; the Mensheviks and the SRs; conservatives like Berdiaev; radical writers who praised the revolution like Mayakovsky, Blok, and Esenin; and nonconformist, original, literary men like Mandelshtam, Pilnyak, and Babel. Despite their difference of opinions, they had much in common: their knowledge of the old, pre-Revolutionary Russia, of the traditions of the old intelligentsia, of the liberal values which they had all been defending against the autocracy and its henchmen.

Gorky drew a larger-than-life picture of this group in his novel *The Life of Klim Samgin*. Alexei Tolstoy described its fate in his novel *The Road to Calvary (Khozhdenie po mukam).* Maxim Gorky's own development is also very ineresting. Although he always preserved the heritage of his pre-Revolutionary ideas, he ultimately also showed remarkable ability in adapting to the new totalitarian practices shortly after the October Revolution. Most representatives of the old intelligentsia could not approve of dictatorial measures, although they had often been collectively accused of having a totalitarian mentality and "petrograndism," that is, a mindset, which preferred rapid, total and violent measures by the state as the ideal method for transforming Russia.[70]

Romantic anticapitalists in post-capitalist society

It had been an axiom not only for the SRs, but also for the Slavophiles, that the Russian peasant's mind was devoid of the bourgeois owner's psychology. This was already clear from the fact that the peasant did not himself own the land which he tilled.[71] It was also believed that the Russian spirit was opposed to luxury: the Russian respected the rags of the weak-minded man of God more than the golden brocade of a courtier, according to Ivan Aksakov. Luxury was something imported to Russia from neighboring peoples, and Russians apologized for it and considered it sinful.[72] For Berdiaev, it was in Western Europe that people respected money and worldly success, in France for instance. In principle, the goal of the Russian revolution was not just material prosperity for the people. The anti-bourgeois Russians, from the Populists to the Marxists had always had an especially negative view of the materially prosperous, but spiritually empty, United States, which was branded "the Land of Humbug." The USA symbolized bourgeois greed and nihilism, which left human beings at the mercy of impersonal economic forces.[73] In fact, Pushkin himself, who knew America from Alexis de Tocqueville's book, had been highly critical of what he considered to be mob rule and sham culture.[74] But even Russia, of course, was not free of bourgeois pollution, even if it was less polluted than other countries.

Apart from philosophers and men of letters, there were also a considerable number of artists, who considered themselves as the anti-bourgeois force par excellence. On the eve of 1917, the avantgardists in particular dedicated their energies to the great cause of anti-bourgeois épatage and were eager to use the virtues of a new to bring the people up to a higher spiritual level.

The icon of the profane, for artists too, was the small merchant, the "lavochnik," whose world consisted of the mundane cares of everyday life and who could not understand the language of art at all. On the other hand, there was the sphere of culture, which for many artists came to mean a sacred world, a kind of ersatz religion, as Katerina Clark has called it.[75] Clark has used the term "romantic anticapitalism" to denote the world-view of a group of creative artists who preserved the traditions of the pre-revolutionary years and nurtured them in Soviet times.

For Clark, the term "romantic anticapitalism" can be used to describe the views of those who emphasized the following three points in the critique of capitalism: alienation, individualism, and the commoditization, or the market model of culture.[76] This could have been said of various groups of the Russian intelligentsia, from Tolstoy and Gorky to Berdiaev and Bulgakov, but it was certainly also true of the St. Petersburg avant-gardes, on whom Clark concentrates in her study of revolutionary culture. This was a group, which, to a great extent, suffered from what Clark called the "Hermes complex." This was a kind of megalomania, which made the members of esoteric groups consider themselves messengers from heaven, whose task it was to mediate between the world of truth and the present world, where people were afflicted by blindness.[77] Revolution, for this category of intellectuals, meant the possibility of accomplishing their sacred task: to unbind man and to give it the power of vision (as if to enfranchise the prisoners of Plato's cave).[78]

How influential these artists were on the masses is difficult to determine. However, the organizers of mass spectacles like Evreinov, Kerzhentsev, Annenkov, Piotrovsky and others were able to draw to their experiments masses of living people, with the support of the government, which would not have been possible in pre-Revolutionary Russia.[79]

While the avant-garde intelligentsia was impeccably anti philistine, the people, much to their disgust, was not. It turned out that even the Russian representative of the supposedly revolutionary people was full of philistine vices: the peasants had rushed to take their share of the property of their better-off neighbors promised to them by the Bolsheviks. Material goods in general were not despised by the working classes, whereas spiritual ones and their proponents, the intelligents, were.

The post-capitalist reality was utterly somber both from the material point of view. The whole country was utterly ravaged until, by the beginning of 1921, its economy was driven into a complete standstill. A few indicators are enough to give an idea of the scale of destruction: the production of pig iron in 1921 was no more than 100,000 tons, while it had been 4,2 million tons in 1913.[80] The population of Saint Petersburg had dropped to a mere third of its pre-war level. The rest had escaped cold and hunger by moving to the countryside or abroad. Needless to say, huge numbers of fences, walls, furniture, and books were burned just to survive the cold. Last but not least, millions of people had died or were dying of hunger, mostly in the countryside along the Volga. Cannibalism reached appalling levels.[81]

This reality of devastation could not have been very encouraging for utopians. No new houses could be built, the affluence of Fourier's phalansteries (where the best wine was always drunk) was nowhere in sight. This notwithstanding, utopianism blossomed among the artists.

Remarkably enough, the calamitous results of the revolution did not prevent some avant-garde artists like Kazimir Malevich from thinking that, in the artistic realm, Russia had a lesson to teach the West.[82] The romantic anti-capitalists had at least attained one of their essential goals: there was no longer capitalism. This, however, was just the first precondition for the revolutionary transformation of the human mind.

Several methods for the promotion of this final goal were introduced: the old symbols of power were crushed and new ones introduced. Mighty rituals and carnivals were held, and the cities were adorned with artifacts and ad hoc monuments, which manifested the new ideas of the world.[83] Almost nothing permanent in the material world could be created with the miserable resources available during the hungry years of war communism, but the anti-capitalists could have their "happenings," exhibit their concrete and papier-maché sculptures and wooden monuments. The artists could draw their posters and sketch communal houses. Even grandiose buildings, like Tatlin's famous Tower of the III International could be sketched on paper.

However, even publishing books and printing newspapers had become extremely difficult. Even the party's central organ Pravda had to resort to second, and third class paper and ink, and to cut the paper's format and circulation.[84] This utterly dire material situation must be kept in mind, when we look at the fate of the intelligentsia and the petty bourgeoisie during the revolutionary period. The threat of starvation compelled practically all the creative intelligentsia to collaborate with the regime. The threshold for doing so was lowered by the fact that the money (in practice foodstuffs and firewood) allocated to the top layers of the creative intelligentsia was distributed by Lunacharsky, who had the reputation of a very soft-minded person[85] and Gorky, who enjoyed considerable prestige among the intelligents. As a result a curious company met at Gorky's table: there was Alexander Blok, the apocalyptic revolutionary; Nikolai Gumilev, the active counterrevolutionary and former white officer; Evgeny Zamiatin, the future author of the antiutopia We; Dmitri Merezhkovsky, Kornei Chukovsky, Alexander Kuprin, and many others.[86] Enemies of the Bolsheviks such as Dmitri Merezhkovsky and his wife Zinaida Hippius also sought the company of Lunacharsky.[87] Hunger forced the masters of culture into submission.

For many intellectuals, however defined, experiencing revolution was a period of repression and hunger. More often than not, the principal task even for anti-bourgeois artists was to survive. The supposedly anti-philistine Russian "people" were hostile towards the *intelligenty* (who could easily be spotted from amongst the masses). They were considered "parasites."[88] The very people, who had considered themselves the champions of the people and had expected to be given the leadership of the country after the revolution as their right, were, in effect, abused, mugged and cast as *boorzhoi* and bloodsuckers just because they belonged to the educated classes who did mental work.[89]

This was no accident. For Lenin, the masses, who did not identify with the intellectuals, had to be attracted to their great world historical revolutionary task by showing them that they were always served first and that the former bosses (not only the capitalists, but gentlemen in general) were now being oppressed. The intellectuals as a social category were officially classified as "petty bourgeois." In practice, this meant that they were given third category bread-cards. The worst, fourth category bread cards were reserved for the bourgeoisie proper, who got "just enough bread so as not to forget the smell of it," to use Zinoviev's words.[90] True, parts of the intelligentsia were better-off: some academics were given extra rations, some got help from abroad, some through Maxim Gorky's help organization and so on. All this does not alter the fact that life for the intellectuals, who were largely considered to be not even second- but third class citizens, was extremely dire.[91]

The Symbolists and the Futurists

The period between 1900 and 1912 has been called the period of symbolism in Russian literary history.[92] It has been said that symbolism was more than just a literary school: it was not just a matter of literary technique but also of outlook. In this respect it was connected with a general crisis within the Russian intelligentsia; individualism and idealism were challenging the old tenets of materialism and the cult of civic duty.[93] As was mentioned above, the symbolists were strongly influenced by Nietzsche, especially by his idea of Apollonic and Dionysian elements in culture.

By 1917 the symbolists were being challenged by several other literary schools, including the futurists, who were no less obsessed with the problems of philistinism and the individual. The age of symbolism seemed for many having been eclipsed. However, arguably the most interesting literary work of the revolutionary period was now being created by symbolist poets, who were non-Marxist, non-Bolshevik chiliasts, who spoke of an ultimate battle of Armageddon with the philistine and "listened to the revolution," with fascination.[94] The movement known as Scythism (*Skif-stvo*) comprised Ivanov-Razumnik as its ideologue, the poets Alexander Blok and Valeri Briusov, as well as Andrei Belyi, who although a poet, was better known for his novel *Peterburg*. Also Mikhail Prishvin, Nikolai Kliuev, Vera Figner, and Sergei Esenin all published in its almanachs during 1917-1918.[95]

As regards their relation to the Bolshevik revolution, the Scythians made a distinction between themselves and the "mass" of intellectuals. Ivanov-Razumnik explained the difference: "Yes, 'Russia perished' –but what kind of Russia? This is the question! And if the 'Russia' of the tousle-headed, spectacled intelligentsia and long-haired writers perished, so in the travails, a Russia of Blok, Belyi, and Esenin was born!"[96]

It has been said, that Scythism was a kind of "everlasting spiritual maximalism and rebellion against any system and any outer order (*vnesh-nii poriadok*)."[97] This was well expressed in the foreword of the almanach "The Scythians" in 1917. The canon of life for the Scythian, it was said, had "no *skoptsy*[98]-like prohibitions of the choirboys of the truth of Sole Salvation nor were there those triply hypocritical prohibitions preached byt the politicians who understand the truth as justice...." The idealized Scythian was able to see his Truth through the loud mob of the Philistines. The Scythians had felt lonely, but all of a sudden, with the February revolution, they felt that their day had come. This proved to be temporary, however: once more the "eunuchs of Truth,"[99] were speaking from the tribunes, once more the philistine mob was continuing its smatter at the cross roads. It so happened that "the truth" of the Scythians was not wanted by the public. However, the situation *"ante revolutionis"* had not been restored: the call of the Scythians had been answered and a new revolution was ripening.[100]

"The Scythian" was a poetic label for the idealized Eastern barbarian, and his mission was supposedly to revitalize old Western ("Hellenic") civilization. But the issue was not just geographical:

> For it is not the Hellene, who is the antipode of the Scythian, but the Philistine –almighty, 'international,' everlasting. In a real 'Hellene' there is always the holy craze of the 'Scythian' and in the frenzied Scythian there is the light and clear reason of the 'Hellene.' But the Philistine clads himself in the garment of the Hellene in order to fight the Scythian, but he despises both of them. His word does not correspond with his deed, his personal moral does not correspond with that of party, society or state...it is he, the wingless and grey one, who bows to the spirit of compromise, it is he, who abominably laughs to the 'mad' words of Brand: 'hear, the spirit of Compromise, it's Satan itself.'[101]

The apocalyptic mood of the Scythians did not mean that they welcomed the First World War. In the opinion of Ivanov-Razumnik, the war was also a product of the philistines of all countries, including the Social Democrats, who had voted for the war-budgets of their respective countries. In Russia, representatives of *Vekhi* also belonged to this group.[102] However, the sins of the philistines were also bringing about their own ruin. For the symbolists, the revolutions of 1917 were primarily both a promise and a symptom of a "real" inner revolution, a spiritual one, which would annihilate philistinism. As Andrei Belyi wrote, the real revolutionaries were Ibsen, Stirner, and Nietzsche and not Engels and Marx at all. In the depths of the works of the former, "vast revolutionary explosions could be heard."[103]

The reality of life in Bolshevik Russia was not exactly what the Scythians had expected from the revolution, but some of them al least still looked forward to a world revolution.[104] Clearly, though, there would not be a final solution of the philistine question, because the enemy was eternal. But, in any event, a qualitative change in the intellectual climate could be hoped for. It was Russia's mission to deliver the antidote to philistinism to old Europe, which once had "philistinized" Christianity. This would bring about the ultimate liberation of humanity, which Christianity had failed to accomplish. This did not mean that Europe was alien, or hopelessly lost (a "cemetery" as Dostoevsky had put it). The spiritual revolution would save Europeans as well as Russians.[105]

The Scythians did not adapt very well to Bolshevik reality and they did not produce many remarkable works after the revolution. The distinction, which they made between themselves and the rest of intelligentsia was real. But so was the distinction between themselves and the new regime. The crowd may have unlearned the language of Gods, as Vyacheslav Ivanov, one of the symbolists exclaimed,[106] but the language the new barbarians developed, was not that of the symbolists. For some time it seemed at least that the future in the Soviet state belonged to the futurists.

Russian futurism has been defined as, "a post-symbolist movement in Russian poetry 1910-1930, which, roughly, put under the same roof all avant-garde forces."[107] The futurists were generally born in the mid-1880s, with the exception of Vladimir Mayakovsky, who was born in 1893; that is, they were old enough to remember 1905 and the *Vekhi*-debate. The futurists were even more thorough radicals and revolutionaries than the symbolists; some of them wanted to revolutionize language. In the case of Velimir Khlebnikov this would happen by creating a new, trans-rational language (*zaum*).[108]

Like the symbolists, the futurists were sworn enemies of philistinism and good disciples of Nietzsche. Their epoch began on the eve of the First

World War. A *Gesamtkunstwerk* opera *Victory over the Sun* in 1913 has been considered the central myth of the Futurists. In this opera futurist strongmen conquer the sun, which causes a veritable re-evaluation of all values: people feel free and experience an "extraordinary lightness," for they have been liberated from the weight of the earth's gravitation (an allusion to Nietzsche's "spirit of heaviness"). In this new world the philistine is the odd man, he (the "fat man") is totally confused. "His head lags two steps behind his body. He would like to wind his watch, but does not know which way it is going...." and so on.[109]

The futurists, in Russia as in Italy, are also bold (which the philistines will never be). The coward's song in the opera consists of mere vowels, while the aviator[110] speaks with mere consonants.[111]

The renowned manifestoes of the futurists tried to frighten even the "radical" philistines. The manifesto "Slap in the Face of Public Taste" in 1912 cursed contemporary writers from Andreev to Gorky to Blok ("wash Your hands which have touched the filthy slime of the books written by those countless Leonid Andreyevs...") and exhorted people to "throw Pushkin, Dostoevsky, Tolstoy, etc. etc. overboard from the Ship of Modernity."[112] Other manifestoes were no less modest. The titles "Go to Hell!" (1914) and "We, Too, Want Meat!" are indicative of the tone.[113] As will be evident, the circle of non-philistines was very narrow indeed, for the futurists, who, like the symbolists, were looking forward to a better era, where everything would be more worthy and more profound.[114]

Mayakovsky's role in the service of the Bolshevik revolution is well-known. In fact, he had already joined the Bolshevik faction of the Russian Social Democratic Workers' Party while at school.[115] Despite his enthusiasm, however, Mayakovsky was not the ideal candidate for a Bolshevik literary hero. The masses appreciated his ditties (*chastushki*) and graphics and he assumed the role of the "drummer of the revolution." However, as has been said, Mayakovsky's poems were "all about himself."[116] Futurism was in fact an utterly esoteric movement, which made a distinction between itself and the rest of the world. The idea that it would be understood by the broad masses was a romantic illusion par excellence. Lunacharsky, the peoples' commissar for education eagerly accepted the services of the futurists, but their bid for a Futurist dictatorship in the realm of art[117] had little chance of success in a state where only one dictatorship existed, that of the party.

The October Revolution and the "petty bourgeois intelligents"

Official Bolshevik mythology subsequently depicted the October revolution as a mighty revolutionary popular upsurge. In fact it was a small but decisive coup d'état, a final thrust, which caused the complete collapse of an inert state. Outwardly, life in Petrograd seemed almost normal. Trams kept running, high society watched Boris Godunov at the Marinsky theater and the great majority of citizens was busy with their everyday problems, paying little attention to a "revolution", which had been advertised in *Novaia zhizn'* some time beforehand. But fateful things happened: groups of armed men seized the Winter Palace, the site of the Provisional Government. This unruly shooting exercise in the middle of the city claimed some casualties and later even more were to follow in the skirmishes between the insurgents and the junkers. The Petrograd garrison remained mainly neutral.[118]

The Bolshevik takeover was met with disbelief by the intelligentsia. The Bolsheviks did not give their consent to a "homogenous socialist government," even though they admitted the left SRs to their government. The Bolsheviks did not even try to defend the fatherland but deliberately instigated the dissolution of the army even further. The Bolsheviks showed no respect for the ideas of freedom of speech or the rule of law, but acted totally at will, violating all the traditional ideals of the intelligentsia. Crushing the resistance of workers and intellectuals, who tried to stage strikes, was something unheard of and reminiscent of the methods of the tsarist autocracy. The Bolsheviks' old comrades in the RSDWP, the Mensheviks were at first taken by surprise, but had consolidated their resistance by the beginning of 1918.[119]

The disbandment of the Constituent Assembly whose election had been one of the major points of the Bolshevik program, was one of the landmarks of the Bolsheviks' progress towards totalitarian rule. In general, the Mensheviks did not take the idea of the socialist nature of the Bolshevik revolution seriously. Iuliy Martov spoke of the Bolsheviks' "senseless utopia" and "quasi-socialism," where the most reprehensible philistinism (meshchanstvo) was let loose under the guise of "proletarian power."[120]

The Menshevik dissenters, Plekhanov, Potresov and Zasulich were even more vitriolic. For Potresov, the defensist, the Bolsheviks" defeatism was treachery, but he held the left intelligentsia in general responsible for the catastrophe.[121] For Lenin's old teacher, Plekhanov, the Bolshevik revolution was premature and would necessarily end in catastrophe. For Zasulich, the Bolsheviks, by dissolving the Constituent Assembly were committing a "counterrevolutionary coup."[122]

The SRs were no more positive towards the Bolsheviks. For Viktor Chernov, the leader of the SR party, Bolshevik rule meant "The Dictatorship of the City over the Country." The Bolsheviks accused the SRs of staging an armed coup in the summer of 1918, but this may have been a provocation. The SR's most remarkable effort to resist the Bolshevik rule, the so called "Directory" in Ufa was not long-lived.[123]

The liberals, who for the Bolsheviks became the scapegoats, and who were to answer for the imperialist aspirations of the Provisional Government ("Miliukov-Dardanellskii") and for the war and its discontents in general, were most harshly persecuted by the Bolsheviks. Two members of the provisional Government, Shingarev and Kokoshkin were murdered by rebellious sailors, whilst some, like Struve, joined the White armies. Some, like Vernadsky, the famous physicist, left politics and remained safe.

For Struve, the Bolshevik revolution was an "experimental refutation of socialism," it did not deserve the name of a revolution, but was rather an "All-Russian pogrom." There revolution brought about nothing, except death and destruction.[124]

The mood of the scholarly community was probably well summed up in a document approved by the general assembly of the Russian Academy of Sciences on the 27 October 1917: "A great calamity has hit Russia: under the yoke of the violators, who have usurped power, the Russian people is losing the conscience of its own personality and its worth (dostoinstvo); it is selling its soul and at the price of a shameful and unstable separate peace it is ready to betray its allies and surrender itself at the mercy of its enemies. What do those people bring to Russia who ignore its mission and the honor of its people? — They will bring about paralysis of society, bitter disappointment and contempt on part of both our allies and foes."[125]

This reaction on the part of the academicians was due to the famous decree on peace, which was a substantial and fateful act of the new government. But, some intelligenty, like Berdiaev, at first refused to take the Bolsheviks seriously. In November 1917, Berdiaev still asked if there had been a revolution in Russia and answered negatively that what was being called the Russian revolution was only the force of inertia: "All of the past is repeating itself and acts only behind new masks. Turbulent processes occur only on the surface. These processes are only the rotting of the ragged clothes of unregenerate Russia. We are living out the consequences of our old sins: we suffer from our moral illnesses. In Russia there has been no revolution."[126]

As a rule, the general consensus was that the Bolshevik revolution could not, in any event, last for long.

From the Depths (Iz glubiny)

By the middle of 1918 it was clear that Bolshevik power was not going to fade away overnight, however perverse it might be. Petr Struve, who had been with the Volunteer Army in Southern Russia, but had returned illegally to Moscow, organized a new manifesto of the Vekhi group. The book's title *From the Dephts* (*Iz glubiny*) was a biblical allusion to the apocalyptic dimensions of the Russian catastrophe.

The hard core of the *Vekhi* group had survived. Along with Struve, the contributors included Berdyaev, Bulgakov, Frank, and Izgoev. New names were S.A. Askoldov, Viacheslav Ivanov, S.A. Kotliarevskii, V. Muraviev, P. Novgorodtsev, and I. Pokrovskii.[127] The spirit of the Vekhi tradition also survived. It was with some justification, but hardly any satisfaction, that Struve could state in the foreword of the book, "The volume '*Vekhi*,' which was published in 1909 was an appeal and a warning...."[128] In spite of the furious polemics, which Vekhi had generated, it had, in fact, been a feeble presentiment of the political and moral catastrophe, which had arrived in 1917. A historian was obliged to see that the educated classes of Russia had not heeded the warning.[129]

The Russian people and the Russian intelligentsia, their specific traits and mutual relations were assessed in the articles. As for the Russian people, recent history had witnessed that it had a predatory nature. But, it also had a human nature and a holy nature, so S.A. Askoldov maintained.[130] It was the predatory and holy nature, which were most developed in the Russian people. In the revolution, the beast had prevailed. The revolution was not about "society," but a rebellion against it.[131]

Berdiaev made the same point: a Russian was either apocalyptic or a nihilist.[132] In his article, Berdiaev analyzed the relationship of Russian classics' relation with the revolution. Gogol was no realist or humorist, Berdiaev maintained, but a describer of evil. In the revolution as in Gogol's books the spirit of fraud, which was so specific for the Russian people, was triumphant. The revolution was a tragicomedy and the finale of the Gogolean epoch.[133] Dostoevsky was another author, who had understood the depth of Russian nihilism. Even Soloviev had made fun of it and had quipped that "because man is a descendant of the apes, we are to love each other."[134] But Dostoevsky's prophecy had been fulfilled: now there was Shigalev, the cynical nihilist of the "Possessed," who had sketched out a tyrannical state of forced equality; there was the God-fighting sentimentalist, Ivan Karamazov, who forsook God for the sake of a child's tears; there was Petr Verkhovensky, for whom anything ontological was alien; and there was Fedka, the runaway prisoner, whose hands were constructing the Shigalevian dystopia. Ivan Karamazov, the *intelligent*, was there, but he had created the revolution (parricide) only in his brain. There was another nihilist, Smerdiakov, who realized in practice, what Ivan had only dreamed of. Smerdiakovism was the ultimate state of barbarism (*khamstvo*) and Smerdiakov hated Ivan, who had taught him atheism and nihilism.[135] An author, whose moral sermon had contributed to the revolution, was Leo Tolstoy, Berdiaev maintained. Tolstoy had absorbed the moral constitution of a great segment of the Russian intelligentsia. He was a sentimentalist, a maximalist, and an anarchist. Tolstoy's moralism was nihilist and demonic, Berdiaev wrote. At the same time, Tolstoy idealized the common people and despised all culture. Tolstoy's sermon amounted to a justification of the anti-governmental instincts of the Russian people. His was the moral of a nihilist; there was not even a remnant of spiritualism in Tolstoy. Unlike Paul the Apostle, Tolstoy had not understood the danger that Christianity might turn into an apocalyptic sect. In order to recover morally, Russia had to forsake Tolstoy as a moral teacher.[136] In practice, Berdiaev, who in previous years had written a lot about the extremism of the Russian soul, recommended a more practical orientation instead of apocalyptic extremism. His religiosity, even here, did not amount to advocating sacralized politics, but to a conservative and practical apology of the conventional forms of human society.

S.L. Frank also deplored the fact that the Russian intelligentsia had missed the practical life and been deaf to the prophecies of great writers. Instead, it had applauded Gorky's *bosiaki*, who had now, at last, come to power.[137]

Peter Struve also had a very practical approach to the issue of the Russian revolution and his conclusions were not without a measure of optimism. His contribution to the volume was entitled "The Historical Meaning of the Russian Revolution and National Tasks."[138] "The Russian revolution is a national bankruptcy and a world-wide shame," Struve wrote.[139] He also saw a "Gogol's" Russia emerging. The intelligentsia was responsible, to a great extent, for it had been blind to the anti-cultural and beastly forces, which had been dormant in the people. The tradition and psychology of estrangement from the state had been pernicious.[140] To speak about "classes" in this revolution was just a sham. There were just the haves and the have-nots. Antagonisms divided people into all kinds of fancy "classes" such as senior and junior university teachers.[141] A paradox of the revolution was that the popular masses had joined it, for material profit. But socialism presupposed moderation. In this sense any bourgeois society was more socialist than Bolshevist anarchy, which was deeply impregnated with materialism and individualism (atomism).[142] However, the revolution had also provided a service: it had destroyed the charm, which socialism had had on the thinking of the Russian educated classes.[143] As regards the concept of philistinism, the authors of the volume did not give much thought to it. The Bolsheviks, who assiduously used the term "petty bourgeois," were sneered at: clearly, for them, the whole population of Russia consisted of petty bourgeois, with the exception of a bunch of party- and Red Army potentates.[144]

When the volume had been written and printed, Russia had not, in fact, reached the utmost depths of the abyss. It was just after its printing that Fania Kaplan tried to kill Lenin, which triggered a ferocious "red terror," where representatives of the ruling classes were summarily executed. The instructions, which the Cheka (State terror apparatus) boss M. Lacis gave to his "chekists" at that time, meant that being an intelligent was enough to warrant a death sentence: spectacles, hat, and a goatee beard were a very dangerous combination.[145] In these circumstances, it was impossible to distribute the book. In fact, only a tiny number of copies of this edition were distributed in Russia in 1921. The next time, it was published in Paris in 1967.[146]

Gorky's "Untimely Thoughts"

After the February 1917 revolution, Gorky was the editor of *Novaia zhizn'*, which was resurrected in May (April). This Social-Democratic newspaper became for some time the most popular paper in Russia. It took up a position between the Bolsheviks and Mensheviks and sharply criticized the excesses of the masses and the extremism of some political movements, especially the Bolsheviks. *Novaia zhizn'* was radical enough even to become the forum for Zinoviev and Kamenev, the future Bolshevik luminaries, who revealed the preparations for the October coup in it. Gorky wrote a bitter criticism of unenlightened people, who committed all kinds of barbaric acts. Popular attitudes toward the past achievements of civilized society were such that Gorky repeatedly exclaimed that culture was in danger.[147] What was especially appalling for him was that the masses and the intelligentsia were drawing apart from each other. The unenlightened people were skeptical and even inimical towards the intelligents, who, in turn, were distancing themselves from the unruly mob. Even the "laboring intelligentsia" was increasingly concentrating on its own affairs. All this meant that the masses were being left without "their brain."[148]

Gorky was disgusted by the Bolsheviks' way of "organizing the revolution," that is, exhorting the masses to loot ("take back what has been robbed"). Lenin was making a revolution according to Nechaev's methods, he said. Like Nechaev, Lenin also had clearly realized that the easiest way to get Russians to follow one was to offer them the right to act in a shameful way. Lenin had the qualities of a leader, he said, but at the same time, he lacked morals. He had a nobleman's indifference towards the life and death of the masses.[149]

This way of speaking naturally aroused the anger of the Bolsheviks, and *Pravda* hinted that Gorky had become like one of the petty bourgeois he had described in his books.[150] *Novaia zhizn'*, like some other newspapers of the opposition, was published more or less regularly until the summer of 1918. In the spring of 1918 Gorky and some others founded a new organization called Culture and Freedom, which published leaflets including Gorky's "Revolution and Culture" (*"Revolutsiia i kul'tura"*). The idea was to unite the forces of intellectuals from different political currents. As Gorky saw it, the intelligentsia now had to heal the people, which was spiritually ill. There should be no party-political sectarianism, and the proletarian intelligentsia should take part in the work.[151]

Gorky's reaction to the 1917 October revolution, when it finally came, was negative. In fact, he was clearly behaving in a way which he had branded as "petty bourgeois" in 1905. Gorky had preached the necessity of going "together with the people." Now, the "revolutionary people" was no longer attractive for him. It seemed that all kinds of scoundrels had taken the most conspicuous role in the revolutionary movement, from top to bottom. This quite clearly was not something Gorky had expected. He tried to solve the dilemma in 1918 by sketching out a theory of two kinds of revolutionaries: first, the eternal revolutionary and, second, the revolutionary for a day (or for an hour). The first was an incarnation of a Promethean principle of rebellion, the spiritual heir of the whole treasury of ideas which was bringing humanity towards self-perfection. These ideas were incarnate not only in the intellect, but also in feelings, and even on the subconscious level. In any social system the eternal revolutionary felt uneasy and felt the need to make things better. The eternal revolutionary also had no personal aversion towards other people, but could always rise above the personal level. The eternal revolutionary was the yeast, which kept the brain of humanity in an everlasting process of fermentation. The "Short-time revolutionary" was a person who sorely felt social injustices. By virtue of his intellect he joined the revolutionary movement, but on the level of his feelings he remained a conservative. First of all, he reacted to the injustices, which had been done to him, personally. He had imbibed feelings of hate and would return a hundredfold. He had also lost contact with history and felt totally emancipated. In fact he was a prisoner of his base biological instincts. In the depths of his soul he was not a socialist at all, but an individualist. In fact he despised those for whose sake he had suffered, people were for him just guinea-pigs. He was a cold-blooded fanatic.[152]

This picture of the temporary revolutionary is somewhat puzzling. In many respects it could apply to V.I. Lenin, although it sounds strange to call Lenin a "conservative" and an "individualist." This kind of juggling with words had, however, been typical for Gorky as early as 1905, when he had dismissed Tolstoy and Dostoyevsky as "philistines."[153] In this instance Gorky has probably fused the image of Lenin with that of the larger group, which had transformed the revolution into an orgy of violence and destruction. In his play *Mother*, Gorky had created the literary image of a worker, who had become an intellectual. Looking at the actual behavior of the masses, Gorky was forced to ask whether they would not, once in power, just strive for the maximum satisfaction of their needs and the minimal amount of work in return.[154] Gorky's accusation of individualism, which, of course, was a deadly sin for many radicals, even though Ivanov-Razumnik had made it the cornerstone of his definition of an *intelligent*, was rather unconvincing. Now, when Gorky was criticizing both the masses and their leader, he perhaps had in mind that the leader should be a true intelligent, who would direct the energies of the masses to more elevated (non-philistine) goals instead of applauding their hooliganism. Gorky had, remarkably, been true to the idea of "going together with the people" even in the days of the 1905-07 revolution.

The destructive anarchy of revolutionary Russia in 1917-18 was, arguably, qualitatively new for Gorky. His complaints acquired a desperate and resigned tone:

> The Russian who now has full freedom cannot use its great possibilities, but uses freedom to the detriment of himself and of his fellow men. By so doing he risks losing all that has been built by the labor of centuries. Little by little all the great achievements of his forefathers are being destroyed, national wealth and the possibility of augmenting common good on earth are disappearing. Industry, transport and mail have been ruined, towns are breaking down, drowning in filth, where lurk the germs of the epidemics, which already kill half-starving children in the thousands....[155]

How could this have happened? Had the Russian intelligentsia been wrong in placing its faith in revolution as the panacea for all ills in society? Not exactly, Gorky answered, but there was one big problem, namely the inferior cultural standard of the Russian people: "If only the Russian were more educated, if he could respect the power of knowledge, he would not let this shameful ruin to happen. If our feelings and our thoughts were more well-bred, more cultured, we would have done many good things during the last year."[156]

For Gorky it was absolutism, which was still to blame for this sad state of the Russian people. In fact, he was almost arguing that the revolution had not liberated positive traits of people, but unleashed the negative ones: all that was vile in man had been liberated. All that had been foolish or filthy remained so. People robbed and deceived each other as ever and the new civil servants were no more untouchable or polite than they used to be but had become worse. A revolution without culture was just a "wild insurrection" (*dikii bunt*) without sense or usefulness. An insurrection would not help people to become better, wiser or more honest, it would just finally destroy and cripple the human being.[157]

This was a far cry from the idea of "the people" as the residence of the higher being, the Man with capital letter, which would replace the odious philistine, whose main vices, after all, were his passivity and good nature.

What, then, was the way out of the calamity? The fundamental task was to re-educate (*perevospitat'*) oneself. Spiritual (*dukhovnaia*) culture meant "respect for the great deeds of past generations. After all, a cultured human being was one whose will was strictly disciplined and whose feeling embraced all that was best in the past and the present, whose reason was softened out of pity for the suffering in the world and out of respect for the great deeds of humanity."[158]

For Gorky, the main task was to civilize people, to make them *intelligenty*. This would be achieved eventually, when the natural sciences liberated the common man, who would then have time for culture and would finally create his own culture, as the former leisure classes had created theirs.

There is no denying that, in a fundamental sense, Gorky echoed the criticism, which had been presented by the *Vekhi* group in 1909: a political revolution was an outward thing, which did not solve the fundamental problem for man, of becoming better, that is, more cultured.

At this time, Gorky seems to have wavered in his faith in the desirability of unscrupulous methods and of "going together with the people." Gorky's idea of the *intelligent* now shows traits of "softness," which he had formerly reserved for philistines. Gorky's psyche, however, was clearly divided. In the long run, it was the tough-minded trait in his character, which would prevail over the compassionate trait. Senseless revolutionary violence appalled him, but the ultimate cure, for him, was not just to be found in self-education and in preaching of love. We may conclude that ruthless measures were not, in principle, undesirable for him, but that they should not be senseless as he clearly thought they were in 1918. In the 1930s Gorky would be enthusiastic about ruthless measures, worthy of his heroes, who had been dubbed "Nietzsches of the Steppe" by the critics.[159] In 1918 Gorky began to cooperate with the Bolsheviks.

Modus vivendi. Gorky and Lenin after 1918

Lenin certainly disapproved of Gorky's articles in *Novaia zhizn'*, but he also clearly thought that Gorky's stance was temporary, and that he would eventually return to the Bolsheviks.[160] This did happen. Gorky was drawn into cooperating with the Bolsheviks by Lenin, who, in 1918, offered to him the role of being the savior of Russian culture and the Russian intelligentsia.[161] Gorky now became the chairman of a Commission for the Improvement of the Life of Intellectuals and Scholars.[162] He also began publishing articles in Bolshevik organs such as the Komintern organ *Kommunisticheskii Internatsional*, where he even spoke for the Bolshevik cause –justifying it in a personal way of his own. The pathos of Gorky's articles had very little to do with Marxism, but was also in sharp contrast to the anti-intellectual atmosphere of the epoch. It was not only some notorious Machajski and the anarchists, but Lenin as well, who had incited people against "the bourgeoisie", which actually included the intellectuals, or, indeed, anybody with spectacles or a black coat.[163]

Now Gorky realized that the fundamental problem, from where all ills stemmed, was the petty-bourgeois peasant. The peasant, Gorky wrote, was a being enslaved by nature; he did not fight it, but only adapted to it. The dark instinct of property was exceedingly strong in a peasant, who earned his living through hard work that was barely productive. When people spoke about "bourgeois culture," Gorky confessed, he was thinking about peasant culture, if these two concepts (peasants and culture) could be united at all. In fact the countryside produced no cultural goods whatever. This state of things could only be changed with the help of science and a great socialist economy. The intellectuals of the whole word, Gorky declaimed, had the same task: to give their energies to the class whose mental qualities guaranteed the further development of culture. This class was the proletariat, not the peasantry.[164]

In another issue of *Kommunisticheskii Internatsional*, Gorky urged the founding of an International of intellectuals. He deplored the fact that most Russian intellectuals had not joined the Bolsheviks long ago. The Russian working class had a gigantic task to accomplish: it had to re-educate a hundred million peasants. The peasants had a great talent for destruction, but were they able, with their psychology of a small proprietor, to create?

Now the Russian intelligentsia had begun to realize that those in power in Russia had the same interests as they had. As for the West, its intellectuals, who now were having a joint meeting in Bern, should do their best to prevent the struggle currently being waged against Russia, which was only bringing starvation to innocent children, Gorky noted.[165] Gorky also published articles in honor of Lenin's birthday in *Kommunisticheskii Internatsional*, but paradoxically he this time aroused Lenin's anger. The reason for this was perhaps, that Gorky, in a flagrant contradiction of Marxism, as it was then understood, explained that a single man, namely Lenin, like Peter the Great in his time, had the levers of history in his hands.[166] The symbiosis between Gorky and Lenin continued until 1921 when several atrocities committed by the Bolsheviks, from the crushing of the Kronstadt mutiny to the execution of Nikolai Gumilev aroused Gorky's anger. In October 1921, Gorky left Soviet Russia, although he continued to cooperate, more of less actively, with the Bolsheviks. When the SRs were prosecuted in the show trial of 1922, however, Gorky sent Lenin an ultimatum, threatening to cut off relations, if the executions were carried out. They were not, but Lenin and Trotsky launched a campaign against Gorky, who was branded a political illiterate.[167]

Gorky's diatribe against the Russian peasantry,[168] in turn, aroused the indignation of both the Kremlin and part of the anti-communist emigration as well.[169] Indeed, the somber picture, which Gorky presented, was one of indescribable sadism, vandalism and stupidity. There is no denying, however, that the examples he described were common knowledge at that time and, to a great extent, do seem to have been true.[170]

Until the beginning of the Stalinist 1930s, Gorky's relations with Soviet Russia were characterized by a certain distance. Although living in Italy, Gorky was constantly under surveillance by GPU agents. From 1928 he began to entertain the idea of a return to Russia, which he had visited every now and then. It was the drastic measures undertaken by the regime to transform the country and the people which seem to have incited his enthusiasm. One example of such measures, which was particularly dear to him, was the "correction" of the personality of juvenile delinquents in GPU colonies, one of which was named after him.[171]

The plight of the petty bourgeois. The party program

The programs of the Communist Party of the Soviet Union are documents of the utmost importance, as the party pretended to be not just another political organization, but one that was pursuing strictly scientific principles and representing the incarnation of the most important forces of the historical progress of humanity. The authority of the program of the Bolshevik party was no less than that of the dogmas of the Catholic Church. The program contained an analysis both of the relevant world-historic epoch and its main dynamic, as well as, of the future, which would inevitably be consciously created by the world proletariat and its vanguard. The Bolsheviks' first program, adopted in 1903, saw its task as social revolution, which would be realized by a dictatorship of the proletariat. It foresaw an absolute worsening of the situation of the world proletariat and predicted that the revolution would be international, although the immediate tasks would vary in different countries. In Russia they included electing a Constituent Assembly by the whole people.[172]

The next, or second, program of the party, now officially The All-Russian Communist party (Bolsheviks), was approved in the VIII party congress in 18-23 March 1919.

Now it was time to make sense of the "proletarian" revolution, which had brought the Bolsheviks to power and, at the same time, had already brought about many unforeseen developments, from a standing army to "bourgeois specialists," from bureaucracy to harassing poverty. Now, there was an authoritative document, which determined what socialism was about.

According to the official interpretation, the dictatorship of the proletariat was put into effect on 25 October 1917. Thereafter, the proletariat "with the support of the poorest peasantry or semi-proletariat, began to create the foundations of the communist society." The tasks of the party included raising the cultural level of the masses to ensure the full functioning of the higher form of democracy, which had been established. This meant that the issues of the position of the intelligentsia and petty bourgeoisie were quite important.

The Soviets were necessary for the annihilation of the old administrative apparatus, it was proclaimed. Because of the low cultural level and lack of administrative skills of the broad masses, it was necessary to take some former bourgeois specialists into the administration. It was already recognized that bureaucracy had been reborn in the Soviet system of administration. It would, however, be fought with determination. Every member of the Soviets would be drawn into administrative work and as the tasks would be rotated, by and by, the entire "toiling population" would be drawn into administering the state.

Simplifying the functions of administration and raising the cultural level of the masses would result in the elimination of state power. In popular education, the schools, which were instruments of class-domination for the bourgeoisie, would be transformed into instruments for the total annihilation of social classes. Higher learning would be open to all, who wanted to study, in the first instance to workers. In like manner, treasures of art would also be made the property of the "toilers."

In production, the old regime's specialists should be widely used. The party proclaimed that ultimately it wanted equal pay for all and any kind of work and full communism, but that, as a temporary measure, higher salaries were necessary for specialists. These specialists should be

> drawn into the process of comradely work, hand in hand with rank-and-file workers and be supervised by conscious communists and in this way contribute to the mutual understanding and rapprochement of physical and mental workers, whom capitalism had separated from each other."[173]

As regards working conditions, working time would be shortened in order to provide time for studying. In the future, the working day would be no longer than 6 hours, which would be achieved without lowering wages. Moreover, there would be two hours of obligatory study in the theory of production technology, of administration, and military skills.[174]

It is clear that the central anti-intelligent tenets of the *State and Revolution* had not been forsaken. Socialism (at this time, the word "communism" was used to denote the same thing) still meant maximum equality, for example, in wages and salaries. It also meant the abolition of the state and of money. Exceptions to these principles, it was explained, were temporary and would soon be liquidated. The country was supposed to be constantly advancing towards an egalitarian, moneyless society, where the broad masses would take care of administration and where bureaucrats no longer existed.

True, there were some amendments to *State and Revolution*. The broad masses were understood to be unprepared for administrating the state and even for working for the common good in a disciplined way. Not only did they lack necessary and important skills (which Lenin had supposed everybody already possessed), but they needed no thing less than total re-education in order to become conscientious workers for their own state and to unlearn the detrimental effects of bourgeois society. The liquidation of democracy in the army was concealed behind the slightest of fig-leaves. In fact, the specialists had dominated the Red army ever since its creation. So, instead of an egalitarian rule, hierarchical structures remained in place. Those with special skills (the intelligentsia) had higher incomes and more power.

The term "petty bourgeois" was not used in the party program at all. Instead, some of the peasants were dubbed "proletarian" and still others were called "semi-proletarian." While the kulaks were immediately classified as "bourgeois," the status of important group of the so called "middle peasants" (*seredniaki*) was left mysteriously vague. It was said that the party was constantly engaged in trying to win them over to its side, but whatever the tactics of the party, there was no changing the fact that in a strictly Marxist sense, the *seredniaki* were actually petty bourgeois.

All in all, politically, the program of the Communist Party openly discriminated against "petty bourgeois" elements and, on the other hand, promised for them favors both in the towns and in the countryside: the specialists would get higher salaries and the serednyaks would be given some unspecified favors. Anyway, the worth and importance of one peasant, in terms of political influence, was assessed at no more than a quarter of that of a worker. All this was to be provisory, it was promised, as full equality was the goal, which, clearly, was not far off. But promises are promises. There was no denying that petty bourgeois elements were not considered equal citizens of the Soviet Union.

Lenin besieged. The proletarian petty bourgeois emerges on the left

In the spring of 1920 Lenin wrote a new booklet: *The Infantile Disease of Leftism in Communism*. This was a new note for the international audience as Lenin observed that Bolshevism had developed in a long battle against "petty-bourgeois revolutionism, which smacked of anarchism, or borrowed something from it". This odious tradition "deviates in all essentials from the conditions and demands of the consistent class-struggle of the proletariat."[175] This "leftist" tendency had its class-base in the petty bourgeoisie, said Lenin. After the revolution the mass of petty producers still survived and reproduced itself every day, Lenin explained. Anything that undermined the iron discipline of the proletarian party was, in effect, playing into the hands of the bourgeoisie. For instance, the trade unions were an inferior form of proletarian organization compared to the revolutionary party. If the former were in conflict with the latter, their role was unavoidably reactionary.[176] In effect, Lenin had already developed here the idea of the "general line" of the party, which would later become so notorious. The general line was always right and it alone was right; deviations from it, either to the left, or to the right were "petty bourgeois" in character. Moreover, Lenin, not content with just a declaration of the "objective" harmfulness of the left deviation, even maintained that the "White guards" were posing as communists and making their ultra-leftist initiatives in order to undermine the proletarian revolution.[177]

Accordingly, the petty bourgeois danger was threatening from all directions. An infallible method of recognizing this danger was the party line test: either you unflinchingly supported it, or you were a petty bourgeois (if not a White guard. By 1921 there was no essential difference). In retrospect, one is inclined to think that Lenin forsook almost all the formerly central "proletarian" values by subordinating them to party-faithfulness. The pragmatic task of keeping the party in power was not compatible with traditional proletarian ideas. A proletarian, who insisted on pursuing traditional "proletarian" values, but in so doing, resisted the party, was transformed into a petty bourgeois. Actually, Lenin hardly realized the inherent implications of his thinking.

What "proletarian" values did Lenin and the party still recognize? One of the central and most sacred goals of Bolshevism was egalitarianism. It is necessary to emphasize this fact, because this principle has been ridiculed so much, not least by the Bolsheviks themselves, that it is hard to remember that when the Bolsheviks, and those who supported them, spoke about a socialist society in 1917-18, they had in mind society of complete equality. Redistributing property was the "self-evident" goal of expropriating the expropriators. The same principle was to be used in paying wages. In "State and Revolution," Lenin wrote that Marx's idea of lowering the salaries of all civil servants to the level of a workman's wages deserved "special attention." This, along with the recruitment and dismissal of civil servants, was no less and no more than the "bridge, which leads from capitalism to socialism."[178] The Bolsheviks" second party program in 1919 stated that "even while it keeps aiming at equal pay for all work and at full communism, Soviet power cannot set as its goal the immediate realization of this equality at this moment... Therefore, it will be necessary, for a given time to maintain a higher payment for specialists, so that they could work not worse, but better than before." For the same purpose there would also be premiums for successful specialists, especially for organizational work.[179]

At the beginning of NEP Lenin reflected on the history of the Bolsheviks' retreat from their principles (as a result of unforeseen circumstances, as he put it). He said that it had not been foreseen that specialists would have exceptionally "bourgeois" salaries and that this was in conflict with several decrees, issued at the end of 1917. But, at the beginning of 1918 the party had already given orders to that effect and on 29 April 1918 the All-Russian Executive Central Committee (VTsIK) had taken a corresponding general decision.

All in all, if we look at the ideological premises of the Bolsheviks, the urge towards egalitarianism loomed very large in early party policy. Leveling of income and property was the moving force which the party exploited against the well-to-do. In this phase, Lenin never hinted at the possibility that there would be something petty bourgeois in it. Quite the contrary, it was the petty bourgeois, who dared not use this "bridge from capitalism to communism." Although there were, according to Lenin, even "White guards," who used the idea of egalitarianism against communism, it was totally clear that egalitarianism as such was a value in itself for communists and that a retreat from it was a retreat, albeit temporary, from the goals of communism in general.[180] A general retreat was proclaimed when NEP was adopted in 1921. This happened when violent attempts at the immediate introduction of a "socialist," equal and moneyless, economy had resulted in catastrophe.[181]

Jan Machajski and the anti-intelligent current

Among revolutionary theorists in pre- First World War Europe, there was one, whose central thesis was that the main enemies of the working class were the intellectuals. A socialist revolution, which only confiscated the property of the capitalists, was not enough, for this would merely substitute the intellectuals for the capitalists. This theoretician was Jan Machajski, a Pole, who took part in the Russian revolution and published one volume of a journal, entitled *The Workers' Revolution (Rabochaia revolutsiia)* in 1918, under the alias A. Volskii. The financial and other concessions to the specialists, which Lenin had granted, were, for Machajski, a confirmation of his theory about the non-working-class nature of a Bolshevik style socialist revolution.[182] Machajski concluded that a new bureaucracy of *intelligenty* and "semi-intelligents" was now holding power. A new revolution, the real workers" revolution, was still needed. Like some other representatives of the Russian revolutionary movement, Machajski sketched out the future of the intellectuals in dismal colors. The intelligentsia, he warned, would perish "under the knife of the ragged tramp. The people in rags will beat, burn, and cut up the well-dressed teachers of the socialist ideal."[183]

From the Bolshevik point of view, of course, "Makhaevism," as it was called, was a heresy. Instead of class, it took the nature of work as its starting point. Machajski himself did not gather a sizable following, but Lenin pointed out that factions in the party, such as the Workers" Opposition in 1920-21, as well as the anarchists, which had been a quite remarkable group in the spring of 1918, were using Machajski's argumentation.[184]

In fact Machajski hit the Bolsheviks on a sore spot: if the intelligentsia was to be defined as a socio-economic category and if it was a part of the petty bourgeoisie, then, necessarily, Bolshevik *intelligenty* were also petty bourgeois. Makhaevism was the *reductio ad absurdum* of the socio-economic definition of the intelligentsia, as the eminent *intelligent* Ivanov-Razumnik had said before the revolution. He argued that the only solution was to consider the intelligentsia as an ethical category.[185] Along with other early oppositional groups, Makhaevism fell into oblivion during the NEP years. The term was, however, brought back into daily use in the aftermath of the great terror, in 1938, when Pravda recalled the erroneous theories of Makhaevism and stressed the inviolability of the Soviet intelligentsia.[186]

After the dispersal of the Workers' Opposition, a conspiratorial group called *Workers' Truth (Rabochaia Pravda)* lingered on. In 1922 it was still agitating for the creation of a Russian Workers' party. This group maintained that the "so-called responsible employees, directors of factories, leaders of trusts, chairmen of executive committees" and so on, constituted a new bourgeoisie. It said that the technical and organizational intelligentsia was being increasingly promoted and that the methods of work and the ideology of this intelligentsia were thoroughly bourgeois. The Party itself had become the party of this organizational intelligentsia which should now be dethroned. The intelligentsia had been able to cheat a sizable number of workers, the argument went on. It could be defeated in the field of culture, for example, by fighting philistine (*meshchanskie*) and authoritarian tendencies within the working class and by promoting, in various ways, proletarian organizations of culture.   Workers from the factory bench should be used for cultural, educational, political and professional work.[187]

Workers' *Truth* did not share the ideas of *Workers' Opposition*, which, it claimed, was trying to roll back the wheel of history to War Communism. Its ideology seems to have come from A.A. Bogdanov, whom we have met before.[188]

Among the anarchists, there were others, who were no less angry about the *intelligenty* than Machajski. The well-known Gordin brothers, whose ideology purported to change radically man's, and especially woman's, position in the universe, were hostile to bourgeois science in general, and considered even Newton a counterrevolutionary.[189] Another representative of the extreme radicals, E. Enchmen maintained that after the dethroning of the exploiting classes, a mass process of withering away of "reason" and "knowledge" would ensue. There should be a "real, genuine, final destruction, total annihilation of the bourgeois and of the bourgeois *intelligent*."[190]

Guilt by presumption. The plight of the intelligentsia

The Bolshevik revolution proved to be more long-lasting than the majority of the intelligents had expected and hoped. From the autumn of 1918 it began to occur to many of them that if the Bolsheviks were violently suppressed, the ensuing reaction could extinguish all that was potentially progressive and democratic in Russia. Many people thought that even the Bolsheviks could serve the progressive cause better than the White terror that would follow a victory of White generals. Many believed that he moment of truth for the self-defeating policies of the Bolsheviks would come soon, anyway. Then, the real representatives of the people would be given power.

For various reasons, people who were not Bolsheviks began to cooperate with the regime. The symbiosis, however, had a one-sided nature. The material and intellectual conditions of the revolutionary period came as a shock to all categories of the intelligentsia. This was also true for the petty bourgeoisie, and, indeed, practically everybody, for the new elite had ruined the life of everybody for the time being. It also waged an outright war on the peasantry[191] and crushed the workers by violence, when they dared to resist.

The intelligentsia emigrated by the hundreds of thousands. The rest was decimated. Only a few scattered groups of intelligents supported the Bolsheviks. In 1917 the majority of soldiers had clearly supported the Bolsheviks' slogan about ending the war, which for them, simply meant that they could, and did, go home. Furthermore, they were not prepared to let the Bolsheviks order them about any more than anybody else. The "sick organ," the Imperial Army was demobilized. The Red Army, which came to replace it, was created by conscription and relied mostly on the peasantry for recruits. It is difficult to argue that the army was popular.[192] The fact that it finally won the Civil War, does not prove anything in this respect.

Did nobody support the Bolsheviks, then, apart from a few thousand sailors and a couple of Latvian regiments? Obviously, they did have more support than that, but at the end of 1917 and the beginning of 1918 much was not needed.[193] Serious armed resistance only developed later, and with time the party gained more and more ground, especially when it became obvious that they were firmly in the saddle. However, being the master of the country did not necessarily mean being popular. As Zinoviev had said in 1918; at first the petty bourgeois intelligentsia had been hostile and resorted to sabotage, but soon it had realized that "we were not fooling around and that there was no other master nor could there be."[194]

As was concluded at the time, and as modern research confirms, the ruthless use of violence attracted support.[195] The other parties, constantly harassed by the Bolsheviks, lost more and more ground; and in the thick of the struggle of the Civil War, some of their members even supported the Bolsheviks against the Whites, especially after the democratic Komuch had miscarried in 1918.[196] Success breeds success, but by 1921 the only success of the Bolsheviks was that they were still in power and all their rivals had been uprooted or terrorized. It was also true that serving the Bolshevik state was practically the only refuge for intellectuals, if they wanted to survive. Of course, this did not presuppose being a member of the party. As Lenin had stressed in 1918, the idea of converting and re-educating the bourgeoisie was ridiculous; instead, it was realistic to employ them as they were.[197]

Politics, under the Bolshevik dictatorship, was confined to the limits of the one and only "party." If the *intelligenty* wanted to influence politics, they could do so only through the party. And many did. It has been said that the party "seduced" a part of the intelligentsia.[198] This might be an apt formulation. But the leap involved may not always have been too big, given the quasi totalitarian quality in the tradition of the Russian intelligentsia, as described by Tibor Szamuely.[199] Many intellectuals who occupied leading positions in the Bolshevik party in the 1920s were former SRs or Mensheviks who had joined the party after the Bolshevik revolution. In the rank and file membership of the party, there were also masses of former members of those "petty bourgeois" parties. In the1930s they would be a special target of the Great Terror. Among the intellectuals, who were still in Soviet Russia by the end of the Civil War, were some former avant-garde artists and writers who genuinely supported the revolution. Amongst the technical intelligentsia and in academic circles, the Bolsheviks had few friends.[200]

The different segments of the educated classes, although they were often lumped together under the term "intelligentsia," had never been close to each other. Now they were probably even more estranged from each other: the elements which were most hostile to the Bolsheviks had emigrated or had been exterminated, whilst others worked as specialists in the Bolshevik administration and production and some were members of the party.

The void between the radical and the conservative part of the intelligentsia is well illustrated in a couple of citations from the diary of professor I. V. Got'e, who survived in Soviet Russia ("Sovdepia," as it was then called), but who was forced to do seasonal manual work in the countryside in order to survive; something unprecedented for his generation. Got'e described an occasional acquaintance in the following way: "… a typical socialistic youth from among the Russian intelligentsia: a superficial, stupid, ignorant neophyte of the new religion of socialism."[201] Analyzing the reasons why he himself had never been infected by revolutionarism, this representative of upper reaches of the scholarly intelligentsia concluded:

Recently I have been thinking often about why I did not become a revolutionary, when in the days of my youth, just as now, all Russia was divided into two camps –those in authority, and those, who questioned authority. I never remained indifferent to this 'fateful struggle' and never identified myself with the former, because I was unprivileged, not a nobleman, not a member of the ruling class, and always too independent to seek my fortune in that sector; but I always hated with all my power the blind moles who gnawed the roots of their own country. I could never feel close to the Russian revolutionaries because I was always sickened by their unprincipled lack of discipline, their barbarity, rudeness, and purely Pugachevian cruelty, combined with their impenetrable stupidity and thick-headedness."[202]

Got'e may have been more or less accurate about the social origins of the opposition-minded intelligentsia, but no doubt he expressed the sentiments of a sizable segment of the higher echelons of the scholarly world.

But what about the motley crowd of radical intelligents, who had been revolutionary? Mary McAuley has summed up the fate of the group of public-spirited radicals who called themselves "the intelligentsia:" "The intelligentsia had lost its material privileges, its social status and its self-image as the voice of the people. The poor had laughed at such a claim, and the new state, although repressive, was championing the cause of education and culture for all."[203] This sounds plausible, if we do not consider the Bolshevik party to be, first of all, an organization led by a group of intellectuals. The masses, however, were unable to substitute for the old elite, and McAuley maintains that although it had been badly damaged in many ways, the cultural intelligentsia "retained its dominance in the sphere of culture and education."[204]

As V. Buldakov has aptly summed up the story of the intelligentsia (having in mind the revolutionary majority of it, which believed itself entitled to this title of honor): There is no doubt that the intelligentsia suicidally and on purpose provoked the revolution. On the other hand, the damage, which the explosion of a bomb makes, cannot be ascribed to the one, who sets it off.[205]

Paradoxically, those, who had sought the liberation of the popular masses, and had fought both the ferocious autocracy and the philistine society, which had supported it, were now subordinated by a regime, which claimed to represent those very masses and which dismissed the intelligents themselves as philistines, who had a flawed consciousness.

The intelligentsia as a social estate had traditionally shared a feeling of guilt. Now it was also being declared guilty on every side.

4
After the Revolution

The setting

The Revolutionary period in Russian history has been defined in various ways. It has been suggested that the period of revolution and civil war came to an end, when the Soviet government introduced NEP in the spring of 1921, which signified a drastic change of course in politics and in the economy. Alternatively, the end of 1922, when the last pockets of White resistance were eliminated and the Union of Soviet Socialist Republics was formed might also be regarded as a turning point. It is also possible to see the autumn of 1923, when the last hopes of an imminent world revolution vanished with the inglorious crash of the "German October rising" is another dividing line.

As regards the policies of the Bolshevik party towards the intelligentsia, none of the above dates and events is a major turning point. The control and surveillance of the intelligentsia did not slacken with the introduction of NEP, for instance, on the contrary.

NEP meant a political retreat for the Bolsheviks, whose policies had ruined the Russian economy to an enormous extent. Now they had to disavow the very politics, which had generally been considered the nucleus of their credo. In a normal state, this kind of political bankruptcy would automatically have resulted in a loss of power. The Bolsheviks had a different philosophy. Their central tenet was that they would never in any circumstances relinquish power. Political bankruptcy was, for them, just a reason for stricter discipline.

As Lenin put it, the communists were in retreat and as with an army; discipline was now "a hundred times more necessary."[1] The "petty bourgeois counterrevolution," which had now been activated, so Lenin concluded, was "doubtlessly more dangerous than Denikin, Yudenich and Kolchak taken together."[2] It must also be recalled that Lenin classified all leftist political currents outside the Bolsheviks as "petty bourgeois."

Some have argued that Lenin allegedly was a democrat deep in his heart, had meant the restrictions on freedom to be temporary. This, however, was hardly the case. There are no signs that Lenin was thinking about the reintroduction of civic liberties. It seems that Lenin had also forsaken for good his sketchy ideas set out in *State and Revolution*, which had displayed a naïve faith in a built-in harmony of political will of "the toiling masses."[3] In the real world, violence and surveillance were always necessary, just as they were in capitalist societies, as Lenin was always ready to assert with an *intelligent*'s arrogance. Despite all the restrictions on freedom, the workers' state was "a million times" more democratic than any capitalist state. The best proof of the democratic nature of the regime was that it had confiscated all the best buildings.[4] "Petty bourgeois" views were now the danger par excellence for Lenin. He kept inveighing against petty bourgeois, philistine ideas and the "narcissistic Hamlets," who were spreading them. Orthodox Marxists like Karl Kautsky in particular aroused Lenin's anger. Lenin called Kautsky a "*Iudushka*" (allusion to Saltykov-Shchedrin's novel) and mocked him: "He would prefer that sweet little petty bourgeois *intelligenty* and philistines (*sladenkie intelligentiki-meshchane i filistery*) in night-caps would first, before the movement of the masses... write for them reasonable and accurate rules for the development of revolution...."[5]

As was discussed earlier, there were several oppositional groupings within the Communist party, which had so far been tolerated, but in 1922 the idea of "democratic centralism" was ultimately interpreted (by the party, not by the opposition with the same name) to mean that no faction whatever was tolerated in the party. This meant that oppositional groupings "Democratic Centralists," the Workers' Opposition and others were to be politically and organizationally eliminated. From the point of view of the intelligentsia, this was not a bad thing at all, for both of the opposition groups were rabidly anti-intelligentsia, wanting to push aside "bourgeoisified false communists."[6]

For non-Bolshevik intelligents, the beginning of NEP was a difficult time. Not unnaturally, some of them had been active in anti-Bolshevik scheming; for instance, in the organization led by Professor Tagantsev, which was discovered in 1921.[7] As a result, several *intelligenty* including the famous poet Nikolai Gumilev, Anna Akhmatova's former husband were executed.

Non-Bolshevik leftist *intelligenty*, which included the SRs, Mensheviks, and others, had been sympathetic to the Bolshevik regime for some time during 1918 and 1919, when it seemed to be in danger of being crushed by a reactionary counterrevolution. For their services, they received small favors, including the possibility of publishing their own newspapers for some time.[8] However, as the Soviet government began to feel safe, it took a stand against its former allies and attacked the Mensheviks and SRs in the course of 1922. For the politically active *intelligenty*, the "conscience of the revolution," the NEP period also began with show-processes and violence.

As regards the creative intelligentsia, the "masters of culture," a sizable part of it was also being harassed by the representatives of "proletarian" culture, especially by the so called Proletkults, who wanted to force all culture into their own mould.[9] Like the futurists, the Proletkults were also scornful about the culture of the bourgeois past. There were, indeed, some, like the poet Kirillov, who proclaimed, "In the name of our tomorrow, we today burn Rafael, we destroy the museums and stamp under our feet the blooms of art."[10]

This was not exactly the practice of the Proletkults, but it reflected the way in which zealots looked at the products of bourgeois *intelligenty*. After the revolution, it seemed, at first, to these enthusiasts simply a matter of course that the party would take over political power; the trade unions economic power; and the Proletkults, cultural power.[11] This, however, did not happen.

Lenin did not like the political aspirations of the Proletkult any more than Gorky and Lunacharsky and even considered its "proletarian" arrogance ridiculous.[12] The Proletkult, however, also had a problem. Quite a lot of its leaders were *intelligenty*, even though fighting the influence of the intelligentsia was an essential part of their program. There were a lot of radical egalitarians in this movement and some maintained that the new society would not need an intelligentsia at all. Others held that there should be no methods (like scholarships, contests etc.), to elevate some workers in the cultural field any higher than anyone else.[13]

In December 1920 a Central Committee decree "On the Proletkults" put an end to the pretensions of this organization. A letter of the Party Central Committee, published in Pravda charged that the Proletkult had become a "haven for petty-bourgeois and socially alien elements." The organization was allegedly dominated by dissatisfied intellectuals, who tried to pass off their decadent artistic tastes and reactionary politics under the label of proletarian culture.[14] This dialectical identification of leftism with petty-bourgeoisie was not the first time this had happened in Soviet history and it would not be the last.

The importance of the Proletkult waned in the first half of the 1920s, but its place as the spearhead of zealots attacking the old intelligentsia was taken by other organizations like the associations of proletarian writers (VAPP/RAPP), and other kindred organizations of proletarian artists, composers, architects, and so on. The non-party intelligentsia, which still had their organizations (in literature such groups as the Serapion Brothers,

Pereval, LEF, and the Literary Centre of Constructivists) was harassed by leftist zealots. In 1925 the Party Central Committee finally ordered a truce and issued a decree "On the Policy of the Party in the Field of Literature." The resolution seems to have been influenced by Bukharin and, maybe, even by Gorky, who had made his opinion known to the party leadership from his place of exile in Italy.[15]

Thereafter, a period of more or less "peaceful" coexistence commenced and lasted until 1928. With Lunacharsky as the People's Commissar of Enlightenment and A.K. Vorovsky as the editor of the journal *Krasnaia Nov'*, non-party writers now had a refuge amid otherwise hostile surroundings. Similarly, non-party *intelligenty* were tolerated in Soviet society in general until the unleashing of the "cultural revolution," which began simultaneously with the first five-year plan and collectivization and signaled a new start for extremist policies.

As has been observed, "culture" in the 1920s was synonymous with high culture, literature, scholarship, and the arts, and the Russian intelligentsia was seen as its guardian and the incarnation of higher cultural values.[16] Emancipated labor was now free to become a *kulturtraeger* itself. A higher man was coming into being, whose culture would be refined, modeled on the classics, and not on the authentic brutish existence of the "toiling masses." Nikolai Bukharin formulated the idea in 1928, "We are creating and will create a civilization in comparison with which capitalist civilization will seem like a vulgar street-dance in comparison with the heroic symphonies of Beethoven."[17] Lev Trotsky proclaimed in 1923 that the coming superman would "rise to the heights of an Aristotle, a Goethe or a Marx. And above this ridge new peaks will rise".[18] This clearly also meant that the street dances, which were enjoyed by the workers, were on a lower level than bourgeois culture. There was supposed to be an objective hierarchy in culture, and there was no denying that the masses were still on a lower level than the former exploiters.

Not unnaturally, the Bolsheviks often argued that the intelligentsia represented bourgeois culture, the past, remnants of which were lingering in the present "toilers' society" but did not really belong to it. After all, the majority of the *intelligenty* did not support the Bolsheviks, and the revolution in politics had not meant a revolution in culture. The task of creating a proletarian culture had yet to be accomplished and what was called culture had been inherited from "bourgeois" society. The idea of being called "bourgeois" naturally infuriated the socially conscious part of the old intelligentsia, who had understood their fate to be engaged in a struggle against "petty bourgeois," philistine" values as Ivanov-Razumnik had conceived it.

To a certain extent, however, "culture" was considered a class-neutral concept, which simply denoted the degree of education, enlightenment, intellectual skills and refinement. Its opposite was lack of culture, which was also class-neutral and could well be found among representatives of the bourgeoisie, as was shown in the case of Gorky's merchants, "petty-bourgeois" kulaks and so on.

It was in this sense, enlightenment, education, and skills, that Lenin in his last writings understood "culture." For him, culture had a dominantly instrumental value and was the *sine qua non* of a socialist society. The "three Rs", which in 1918 Lenin had thought to be sufficient for the building of a new society, proved to be too little, and even they were not in sufficient supply. But Lenin also respected the masters of old high culture. Artistic mastery as such was also something class-neutral and could not be replaced by mere class-instinct. This attitude was shared by Stalin and Gorky. Gorky's influence on Soviet culture in the 1930s was second only to Stalin's. Gorky had an almost religious respect for the "artistic" in literature.[19] Opinions on this issue, however, were not definitely fixed until the late 1930s. The egalitarian zealots had their say for a long time and were even sometimes the dominant voices.

Sheila Fitzpatrick has examined the relationship of the intelligentsia and the Bolsheviks in terms of a struggle for mastery. She juxtaposes "power," with the Bolsheviks representing "power," and "culture" represented by the intelligentsia.[20] Using her terms, in the 1920s "power" fought "culture" for power in culture.[21] This, of course, does not mean that "power" would have been just the opposite of culture. In practice, there were several factions on both sides: on the side of "power" were the militant "young Turks" like the RAPPists as well as moderates like A.V. Lunacharsky, the former "God-builder," who had much in common with the traditions of the non-bolshevik intelligentsia. Whilst on the side of "culture" were separate, and often mutually hostile, groups of avant-gardes, traditionalists, realists, Marxists and more or less willing fellow-travelers, non-political groups, and irrevocably hostile elements.

As Fitzpatrick points out, a contingent of the "Young Turks" from the intelligentsia, the avant-gardes, who were trying to seize control of the agenda, were marginalized during the 1920s as they were attacked not only by the Bolsheviks but by also the non-avant-garde mainstream as well. As a result it was to be "eternal," preservationist, humanist, apolitical, more or less pluralistic cultural values, which came to be accepted as the intelligentsia's values.[22] Fitzpatrick believes that the mutually hostile contingents of the intelligentsia had a lot in common: the party's early leaders came from the intelligentsia and understood culture as something which an enlightened minority should bring to the masses from above. All shared a developed sense of historical mission and moral superiority. Last but not least, both the Bolshevik and the non-Bolshevik intelligentsia were elite groups, yet both denied this. Fitzpatrick believes that "the relationship of the Bolshevik party and the Russian intelligentsia in the 1920s is best understood as two competing elites, resentfully interdependent, jealously jockeying for position and withal constituting the only possible claimants for leadership in a fragmented and unsettled post-revolutionary society."[23] This formulation may make too much of the non-party intelligentsia's chances of leadership. Out of necessity, it had to be passive politically. All that it could do was to try to preserve as much as possible of the culture it represented.

In the NEP period the Soviet government was forced to make concessions to groups or sectors of society. The "petty bourgeois" peasants were allowed, with intermittent campaigns of persuasion and bullying, to utilize a part of the surpluses which they themselves had created. The intelligentsia, another "petty bourgeois" group was also tolerated as an unavoidable evil, but was constantly harassed by militants and kept under surveillance by the security organs.

The *intelligenty* were also necessary for a time in order to push through the "cultural revolution," which Lenin, in his last writings, considered to be the main precondition of a socialist society. The Cultural Revolution as a process of raising the educational level of the masses had to be done largely with the hands of rank-and-file intelligents: professors and teachers and specialists in all branches. Reconstruction after the terrible devastation caused by the revolution and civil war presupposed the contribution of the old "bourgeois" engineers and other specialists, whose usefulness Lenin had already recognized in1918.

As regards the old "masters of culture," the artists and writers, their usefulness for the new society was easier to contest, but the top leaders in the Bolshevik hierarchy did not launch an attack on them until the First Five-Year Plan.

The famous "Philosophers' ship" (actually several ships) which left Russia in 1922 has already been mentioned. The idea was Lenin's who also nominated many of the passengers. This operation was called the "first warning" by the party's central organ Pravda.[24] Prominent Bolshevik functionaries had come to understand the danger posed by a certain section of the *intelligenty*, who were considered a weightier element than their number would have indicated, since they were potential opinion leaders. The Leningrad secret police, GPU, in 1924 considered that negative attitudes towards Soviet power and its representatives, had their origin in the intelligentsia.[25] Felix Dzerzhinsky went so far as to order that there should be a file on each intelligent and that all literature should be monitored by the security organs.[26]

The problem for the Bolsheviks was that the other revolutionary parties, the SRs, the Mensheviks, and the anarchists and so on, were no longer allies but the most dangerous enemies of the Bolsheviks. According to Bolshevik logic, they were worse than the bourgeoisie and no sharing of power with them was possible. But sympathy for the Bolsheviks could also be found. Many "romantic antibourgeois" artists and writers admired the drastic transformation of society. The futurists, for example, were, to a great extent, true to their idea of destroying the old world, and this Bolsheviks were doing. In 1912 the futurists' manifesto had exhorted throwing "Pushkin, Dostoevsky, Tolstoy and so on and so forth overboard and off the steamer of the new age."[27]

After the Bolshevik revolution, many futurists cherished the hope of becoming the adopted bards of the revolution. Overzealous futurists sometimes proclaimed their movement to be the "art of the government" and pretended to represent "truly proletarian art." This role was rebuffed by the representatives of the state, but the futurists were not depressed. Mayakovsky's role in the service of the Bolshevik agitation front is a well-known example of this activism. There was also a group called Komfut (futurist communists), which saw the struggle against old art as one of the main tasks of the whole communist revolution and a *sine qua non* for its continuation. For this group the policies of the Bolsheviks seemed all-too conservative.[28]

But the Bolsheviks thought that the futurists were more leftist than they were themselves and, hence, too leftist. As P.M. Kerzhentsev concluded, the futurists" corresponding group in politics were the anarchists. Both were symptoms of the dissolution of bourgeois society and reflected individualist (petty)bourgeois psychology. It was no accident that the Italian futurist Filippo Marinetti had become an apologist of war and imperialism.[29]

Gradually, almost all the writers who wanted to continue their existence as writers had to adapt themselves to the new conditions. Some, like Vladimir Mayakovsky or Alexander Blok, had been with the Bolsheviks ever since their coup; but others, like Sergei Esenin, were carried away by the revolutionary rhetoric, at least initially.[30] Valery Bryusov, Nikolai Klyuev, Boris Pilnyak, Isaac Babel, and many others, more or less willingly, began to cooperate with the Bolsheviks.[31] In 1922 the journal Krasnaia nov was given the task of taking care of "bourgeois" writers, by trying to assimilate and re-educate them for the benefit of Soviet society. In 1923 this element was dubbed "the fellow-travelers, by Trotsky and this was the label by which they were known.[32] In retrospect, this solution may seem the natural outcome of a situation where the Bolsheviks needed the services of the educated classes and where the latter also little choice but to agree, if they wanted to survive. In fact, however, this was a tumultuous liaison, where the party tried to save face in front of the intellectual world at home and abroad, but had in turn to regret the politically incorrect influence of non-party intellectuals. In the case of Esenin, ideologically incorrect consequences seemed to endanger a whole generation with its "petty bourgeois" contamination.[33]

The *intelligenty* as the ersatz-bourgeoisie

During a period which could more or less aptly be called "the heroic era" of the Bolshevik revolution, it had not been at all clear that the Bolsheviks would adopt a policy of cooperation with the non-Bolshevik intelligentsia. They had put all their trust in the workers. Despite the relative numerical weakness of the Bolsheviks, Lenin had pointed out that that the gentry in its day had been even weaker but had nevertheless been able to rule the country.[34] However, after the revolution the prospects were gloomy. Not only had the number of industrial workers rapidly fallen during the civil-war period, but the ruin of the means of production had been almost total. Suffice it to say that the production of pig iron, which in 1913 had been 4.2 million tons, was now a mere 0.1 million tons. The respective figures for steel were 4.3 and 0.2 In 1913 Russia had imported foreign goods worth 1374 millions "1913" rubles, now the figure was 208 million. In exports, the respective figures of 1520 million and 20 million were still more drastic.[35] The level of destruction is hard to overemphasize. Cannibalism and epidemics were common in 1921-22. The calamitous situation corrupted also the GPU. In the Ukraine, female agents of the GPU were forced to resort to prostitution in order to escape dying of hunger. Male chekists ("tens, if not hundreds of them") were robbing people in order to survive.[36]

The breakdown of industry unavoidably entailed a serious fall in the numbers of industrial workers. Compared to 1913, there were less than half of them left in 1921.[37] The real proletarians, of course, were a sacrosanct element for the Bolshevik government, which pretended to represent the vanguard of this vanishing flock. Masses of former industrial laborers left for the countryside to survive and it was commonly feared that they would revert back to being peasants, as many of them had been until quite recently. The situation in the countryside was also not promising from a Marxist point of view. A massive process of leveling out of rural holdings had taken place during the revolution and civil war period. The well-to-do peasants" holdings, as well as the nobles" and the church's, had been taken over, as the Bolsheviks had exhorted. At the same time, the land communes, which had been partly liquidated as a result of Stolypin's reforms, were now re-established everywhere. The countryside had experienced a revolution which had little to do with Marxist predictions.

Instead of developing in a capitalist way, the countryside was archaized, as Moshe Lewin has put it. [38] From the ideological point of view, the situation was precarious, to say the least. The Bolshevik party had, in effect, become, or was rapidly becoming, "the vanguard of a non-existent class" a contemporary critic quipped.[39]

By the beginning of NEP in the spring of 1921, a truly new society had been born. To a great extent, it could be called classless. There were no longer classes of proprietors or capitalists. In effect, all the "exploiters" had been liquidated (in terms of their position in the economy) and so had many of the exploited. What remained was a mass of people, struggling on the verge of subsistence in an equality of poverty, who were materially in a very similar condition.

In this situation, it was impossible to find genuine members of "classes" in the Marxist sense (with the possible exception of the lumpenproletariat and the peasantry). Instead, people could be divided into different groups by virtue of their loyalty towards the new regime or their former position in the class based society of pre-Revolutionary Russia.

However, loyalty to the new regime could not be taken for granted. When War Communism was liquidated and NEP introduced, not only were former capitalists and proprietors hostile towards the new regime, so were many peasants, workers, and soldiers.

The Kronstadt mutiny of 1921, which finally prompted the party's decision to change its policies a full 180 degrees, was a symbolic shock for the Bolshevik party. The very element, which had played the most prominent role in the October revolution, the sailors, now rose in armed resistance against the regime.

It was unavoidable that the background to the mutiny had to be explained in Marxist terms. Not unnaturally, it was declared that the Kronstadt sailors of 1921 no longer consisted of workers, as had been the case with the majority of the sailors in 1918. Instead, a "petty-bourgeois element" had become dominant.[40] But it was not only Kronstadt that had been contaminated with alien elements. At the XI Party congress it was realized that the enemy was everywhere. According to Lenin, even in the factories could be found not only real proletarians, but "all kinds of accidental elements."[41] Bukharin went so far as to draw the theoretical conclusion that, in a time of breakdown, the proletariat would transform itself into a petty bourgeoisie and begin to defend its interests.[42]

In a sense, from a Marxist point of view, the situation had an air of unreality. It did not make sense to determine one's class position in terms of production, for there was next to no production. Therefore, it was natural that people would be allocated a social category, not according to their actual position in Soviet society, but on the basis of their former position

in pre-Revolutionary Tsarist Russia. It was the heritage of pre-Revolutionary Russia, which, a priori, decided the class-nature of the citizens of Soviet society. According to the Marxism, class struggle was the engine of
all social progress. A classless, non-socialist society, with the exception of
primitive communism, was unthinkable. Therefore, the class-enemy had
to be found, exposed, and fought.

Not unnaturally, the intelligentsia was highlighted as a class-enemy.
The Cheka classified it as part of the petty bourgeoisie.[43] Understood as
a hostile element, it became, a priori, a "surrogate bourgeoisie" as Sheila
Fitzpatrick has dubbed it, and attracted the attention of the baffled party
elite. The party faced the prospect of being left alone before a malevolent
"petty bourgeois" peasantry and an undependable working-class, which
was under the influence of various petty-bourgeois anarchist elements."[44]

The intelligentsia, here understood as representatives of the educated
classes in the service of the Soviet economy, was now collectively dubbed
"bourgeois specialists," which implied that their hostility towards the regime and class-alien character were presupposed, even though they were
given the honor of being employed by the new regime. In principle, the
policy of cooperating with an alien element did not mean giving concessions to it, let alone ideological concessions.

During NEP, and also afterwards, as it turned out, the "petty bourgeois" peasants and *intelligenty* remained, in principle, a source of evil,
from where all kinds of vices emanated, including the instinct of proprietorship as well as demands for anarchism. Even the party was not considered immune to the influence of the petty bourgeoisie.[45] A *smychka*, the
truce, or alliance, between the town and the countryside (the peasantry
and the workers) was, however, inevitable in order to put an end to starvation, which had already claimed millions of victims. Analogously, tol-
eration towards the intelligentsia was inevitable in order to ensure the
accomplishment of the Cultural Revolution.[46]

Needless to say, NEP was not meant to last forever, nor was the tolera-
tion shown towards the "bourgeois" intelligentsia. Neither would survive
in a socialist society. This was a truism even if the date for the dawn of
socialism was left open. In 1920, Lenin had spoken about a period of 10-20
years, but after 1921 the perspectives had changed.[47]

The epithet "bourgeois specialist" was somewhat problematic. Not
every member of the educated classes (the intelligentsia in a general sense)
could be classified as such. The majority of the Bolshevik party leadership
also consisted of *intelligenty*. Lenin himself was of bourgeois origins, defined
himself as a journalist (literator), had received higher learning, and also
happened to have had the status of a noble in pre-Revolutionary Tsarist
society. Obviously, the category of bourgeois specialists did not include

professional revolutionaries, but who else of the educated contingent could claim that they were themselves free of the stigma of "bourgeois"? Tentatively, we may assume that the intelligentsia was bourgeois a priori, including those who cooperated with the Bolshevik regime. To rid oneself of one's past seems to have been possible by joining the Bolshevik party. The Manichean logic of Bolshevism always held that "one who is not with us is against us." By the same token, it could be concluded that "everybody, who is not against us, is with us." For the Bolsheviks, who took the scientific nature of their doctrine very seriously, this was not, however, self-evident. After all, if somebody was a representative of a hostile class, which had objectively determined his or her consciousness, what conditions were needed in order to change this? Was it really possible to overcome objective factors through a subjective change of mind?

Many people, including representatives of the intelligentsia, joined the party before the "dawn of socialism" (which officially took place in 1936), but they also remained a dubious element, which would suffer severely in the great purges. But one must be careful not to come to conclusions about the beginning of the 1920s on the basis of later developments. At the beginning of NEP, many questions were still open including the party's attitude towards the educated classes. Another question remained: if the specialists were "bourgeois" in character, did this mean that they were petty bourgeois? As regards the peasantry, this was evidently the case, for they only served their own petty household. But the intelligents might well have been the immediate promoters of big capital's interests, not just masters of small private plots as was the case with the peasants. While leaving this question open, we may glance at the struggle waged over the "bourgeois specialists'" position at the beginning of NEP.

NEP was commenced abruptly and without warning at the X Party congress in March 1921. Quite naturally, not all the new issues that were raised, if only by implication, by this sudden change of events could be thoroughly discussed at this dramatic congress, which was busy saving Bolshevik power and even sent a contingent of its members to attack Kronstadt, the citadel of the uprising, with weapons in hand. It was at the XI Party Congress in 1922 that the ideological implications of the new situation were discussed and the scores between factions settled. The typical, and well-founded, complaint of all sides concerned the vanishing of the proletariat and the ever-growing petty bourgeois danger. The representatives of the former oppositional factions which had been outlawed at the X Party Congress, were all against the "excessive" ideological retreat of the party, including the over-lenient attitude towards bourgeois specialists.

A policy of class-struggle against the educated classes or the intelligentsia in general meant, according to the party mainstream, indulging in the heresy of makhaevism,[48] which was unscientific, because it treated the intelligentsia as a class, which exploited the workers. Members of the officially non-existent Workers' Opposition were condemned by the congress for "specialist-baiting." Yet it seems evident that the general mood of the rank and file was very much in line with the opposition. After all, it had been Lenin himself, who had invented the use of "petty leveling" as a "bridge to socialism." Now there were complaints that there was no equality any more: the specialists were giving orders, they were paid better and they were making demands, and so on. There may have been little more to expropriate from this ravaged group, but the privileged status of the "alien element" as compared with the official ruling class not unnaturally aroused anger. The specialists were once more "oppressing the workers just as they used to do."[49]

In 1918 Lenin had written that oppressing the well-to-do was readily understandable for any worker. If that was so, it is also logical to assume that the new policy of endorsing the specialist was going to be equally difficult to understand.[50]

The resolution of the XIII Party Conference "On Petty Bourgeois Distortions in the Party" was approved with only three votes against the decision, but this not unanimously, as would always be the case later. It stated that the opposition "objectively reflects the pressure of the petty bourgeoisie against the party of the proletariat and its policies...."[51]

In fact, the opposition was mostly supported by young radicals; for instance, by members of the Moscow Komsomol. The specialists, who were supposedly behind the opposition and giving it, its petty bourgeois character, did not, in fact, support the opposition, although many saw its existence as an encouraging sign of increasing "democratism."[52]

The Bolshevik party, the vanguard of the proletariat, was led by intellectuals. At the end of the civil war, about 40 per cent of the members of the party were workers, the rest were peasants and intellectuals in equal number. But the leadership consisted predominantly of intelligents. In 1921 no less than 42 per cent of the Central Committee were workers (at least former workers), but of the members of the politburo only one had been a worker, the other seven were all intellectuals.[53] No wonder then that the party staunchly rejected initiatives from the grassroots to purge the party of intellectuals. Still, the lack of a proletarian element in the vanguard party of that very class was recognized as a problem and it was purportedly solved in 1924 by the "Lenin levy," when masses of real workers from the bench were recruited by the party.[54]

What has been called the "soft line in culture,"[55] denoting the tactics of "peaceful coexistence" with the specialists in particular and the educated classes in general, was adopted much against the will of the rank and file of the party and had to be energetically defended from attacks by the radicals at the beginning of the 1920s. As regards the intelligents proper, whose group only partly overlapped that of the specialists, the party chose a tactic of stick and carrot. All the major intellectuals were regularly monitored by the GPU, as Lenin had personally ordered in 1922[56].

On the other hand, certain specialists such as some university professors and academicians retained ample opportunities to continue their scholarly work without party intervention. The general level of subsistence, however, remained low and this led to professors' strikes in Moscow, Petrograd, and Kazan in 1921-22.[57] In some cases, as in the study of history, the work of non-Bolshevik specialists did, indeed, have a "bourgeois" character, for the old specialists made no effort to adopt Marxist jargon or methods in their work. In order to disseminate the Marxist "super science" and raise new Marxist cadres, the party founded several new institutions, such as the Institute of Red Professors. It also had its bridgehead in the old academic institutions; but, up to 1928, Marxist scholarship in these old institutions existed in isolation and was treated with contempt by members of the old intelligentsia.[58]

For their part, leading intellectuals such as the academicians largely understood that a frontal attack against the Bolshevik regime would have ended in their own demise. Accordingly, the academicians, with few exceptions like the physiologist Ivan Pavlov, who never cared to conceal his enmity, adopted a cautious attitude towards the new regime, voicing their opposition only on secondary issues. They wanted to preserve the Academy of Sciences as an institution and to serve the interests of science. Many also had patriotic interests, which they considered possible to serve even under Bolshevik rule. It has been maintained that the majority of the old academicians did not sympathize with the White movement. However, they did not identify with the Bolsheviks and, with the notable exception of Peter Struve, who had emigrated, felt no responsibility for the revolution, which had resulted in Bolshevik rule.[59]

Professional organizations were allowed to hold meetings only with the consent of the GPU. A politburo decision to that effect was made in 1922 after the all-Russian conference of physicians in 1922 had shown signs of political activity.[60] Universities also housed many "bourgeois" intelligents. As often happens the offspring of the educated classes represented a higher proportion of those in education, than their numerical share of the population warranted. The Bolsheviks tried to fight this by various means; for example, by discriminating against intelligents and promoting the study of young and older people of proletarian origin. This was resented by the students, who often made their opinions known quite openly.[61] The academic world as a whole, with a few exceptions, like the historian M.N. Pokrovsky and the linguist N.I. Marr, was a dubious element for the GPU. But so were all the other categories of intelligentsia: writers, creative artists, and even artists of operetta and variety shows.[62]

The Smena vekh—Changed Signposts

After the revolution, many people both in Russia and abroad did not consider the split of the Russian intelligentsia into emigrants and residents of Soviet Russia to be final. In speaking of the "Russian intelligentsia," many had in mind both those who were in Russia and those who were abroad. Most representatives of the sizable Russian emigration were, naturally, hostile to the Bolshevik revolution. By and by, however, currents sympathetic towards the Bolsheviks' historical role emerged. They first became evident during the Polish war in 1920, when some former tsarist generals volunteered to defend Russia from its old arch-enemy. These currents were nationalistic. One of them was Eurasianism, whose proponents welcomed the Bolshevik revolution as Russia's turn away from the West, which was regarded as its eternal enemy.[63]

Another current was the Smena vekh, which, like Eurasianism, was nationalistic in essence and saw the Bolsheviks as the continuers of the Russian idea. It was sponsored by the Bolsheviks and it has been considered as yet another ruse of the GPU. On the other hand, it can also be considered the beginning of National Bolshevism, which developed later, under Stalin.[64] The importance of Smena vekh was much advertised at the time, and its very name contained a refutation of the views of the Vekhi group, who with reason could say that their prophecy had been fulfilled. The intelligentsia's traditional mission of serving the people should now be seen in a new light, Smena vekh proclaimed.

At the beginning of the 1920s, many representatives of the old intelligentsia did not even pretend to be sympathetic towards the Bolsheviks. The end of Bolshevik power seemed to be just around the corner.[65] However, in 1922, according to information gathered by interviewing 230 engineers about their attitude to the Soviet power, the mood was preponderantly cooperative. The figures were as follows[66]:

12 inimical
46 lukewarm
28 sympathetic

110 smenovekhist
37 did not answer

The Smena vekh movement was claimed to have been an astounding success in Russia. It is also possible that the respondents' attitudes were interpreted as "smenovekhist" without their authorization. Other forms of manipulation cannot be ruled out either.

In any case, the movement, which got its name from an almanac published in Berlin in 1921, became quite well-known among the intelligentsia, both in Russia and abroad. In fact, it symbolically proclaimed that the wait and see approach of those intellectuals who had looked forward to the crushing of Bolshevism had come to an end.

1921 had raised many hopes among liberals who were delighted to see the retreat from War Communism. The Bolsheviks seemed to recognize their own political bankruptcy, and the adoption of NEP really drove many a leftist enthusiast to despair and suicide.[67] Smena vekh recognized the Bolsheviks as the heirs of the Russian state idea. This had been reinforced by the restitution (albeit incomplete) of the territorial integrity of the former Russian empire. Smena vekh addressed the Russian intelligentsia, both at home and abroad. It was more or less supported by the Bolshevik authorities, and its newspaper *Nakanune* (*On the Eve*) was also for sale in Soviet Russia.[68]

In the almanac the role of the Russian intelligentsia was still presented with high hopes. S.S. Chakhonin speculated that a peasant party would doubtless be unavoidable in Russia, and maybe also a party of the intelligentsia.[69] Chakhonin had come to believe that, in fact, the Bolsheviks shared the same ideals as the Russian intelligentsia and that only their violent methods had been alien and odious to the intelligentsia.[70] The intelligentsia, for its part, had nothing to regret as regards its role in the revolution for it could not have behaved in another way. Now its patriotic duty was to give all its energies to the reconstruction of the ruined fatherland.[71] For some of the authors, it was the blood that had been spilt that made cooperation with the Bolsheviks necessary.[72] Others argued, in the traditional way, that Europe belonged to yesterday, while tomorrow belonged to Russia.[73] Iu. Kluchnikov, who soon entered the service of the People's Commissariat of Foreign Affairs, asserted that the Russian intelligentsia's state of mind (*umonastroenie*) had, for the most part, always been Bolshevik.[74] In his opinion, it was possible and, indeed, imperative that the Russian intelligentsia become a leading force in the Bolshevik state in order to serve the eternal values of good and beauty and to fight philistinism (*meshchanstvo*).[75]

Nakanune, the newspaper of the movement, which was also distributed in Moscow ("in order to fight counterrevolutionary tendencies among the upper echelons of the intelligentsia") preached a truly intelligentsia attitude towards the Bolshevik state: the intelligentsia should become "workmanlike" (*trudovaia*) and work for the common good, motivated by a truly *intelligent* will to benefit the common good, while the well-paid *spets* (specialist) was motivated by his own selfish interests.[76]

Among the émigrés, Smena vekh was not a great success. Some did return to Russia, among them Aleksei Tolstoy, but the "philosophers' ship" was enough to remind others, what return entailed.

The intelligentsia and the philistines

Krasnaia nov' represented a conciliatory line towards the intelligentsia and also tolerated fellow travelers on its pages. This did not mean that it was toothless in matters political or towards the intelligents and the petty bourgeoisie in general. The journal started in 1921 and in its first year dedicated many of its pages to polemics about Smena vekh and the intelligentsia in general. Smena vekh was reviewed in 1923 by N. Meshcheryakov, who was very critical.[77] He stated that the entire Russian intelligentsia had struggled against the revolution, but that after its defeat it had fallen into mutually conflicting pieces. The smenovekhists were mystics, nationalists, and slavophiles like those who had composed Vekhi. For *Krasnaia nov'*, the Russian intelligentsia, including those who had actually remained in Russia and those, who were abroad, still represented one whole. The editor, Voronsky, pointed out that the Russian intelligentsia had forsaken its former rationalism and was becoming more and more "stupid" (*glupyi*) while it veered to the right. Now it was beginning to believe in all kinds of charlatans including anti-Semites and so on. Scientists were practicing spiritism, jurists were ready to stage any number of Beilis-trials, and the democrats of yesterday considered the people to be a "barbarian" (*kham*) or the monster of the Apocalypse[78] In general, the intelligents' life abroad was not worth envying, another author reasoned. Russian literature had always heroically fought philistinism (*meshchanstvo*). To live in a rotting and philistine Western Europe was evidently a torture, which would make many intelligents return.[79]

But in the NEP period, wrote Voronsky, the petty bourgeois was also let loose in Soviet Russia. He was trading in the famous Moscow Sukharevka market, and not only there. Among the intelligentsia, which hated and despised the people or had become openly apolitical like Andrei Bely, and even among the communists who were devoured by everyday routines, the philistine was insisting on having his own literature.[80] In the new situation it was clear that the intelligentsia's former role and position had been lost and one could expect that further drastic changes were still to come. A certain M. Levidov prophesied in Krasnaia nov in 1923 that the revolution was supposed to be fatal for some "especially hothouse-grown" species in culture, including the intelligentsia. The existence of an intelligentsia implied "psychological inequality," which had to be liquidated. In fact, the author maintained, the "accursed" word "*intelligent*" was no longer used by the younger generation. The very word was "boneless, soft, melancholic and wretched." Instead, a brisk, comely and sounding word "*spets*" was used. The *intelligenty* had outlived their usefulness and were doomed to extinction. In 20-30 years the tribe of the *intelligenty* would have disappeared from the face of Russia.[81] Vyacheslav Polonsky prophesied in the same journal that the intelligentsia would be dissolved in the triumphant class.[82] Professor M.A. Reisner also foresaw the liquidation of the intelligentsia, but considered that this would happen in a future classless society.[83]

Voronsky argued that the future intelligentsia would be mostly technical and practical, without Chekhovian traits, freed from endlessly eschewing the "eternal" and "accursed" problems.[84] The general tone, in this most liberal of Soviet intelligentsia's journals was that the intelligentsia's role in society was inevitably changing. It was a good guess in a state which would not tolerate a "conscience" or a "brain of the people" independent of itself. What it wanted was specialists and "masters of culture," who would be its docile servants.

The debate about the role of the intelligentsia in the new society also took place in other forums. In 1925 the Moscow committee of the VKP(b) published a booklet, in which P.I.Sakulin, N.I.Bukharin, and Iu.V. Klyuchnikov discussed the role of intelligentsia with Lunacharsky.[85] The general tone of the discussion was rather depressing for the intelligentsia. It was predicted that the intelligentsia would disappear as a special social layer of people, although it was not considered possible to go straight to an epoch without an intelligentsia (*bezintelligentskaia epokha*) as somebody from the audience had optimistically proposed. It was true that philistinism (*meshchanstvo*) had to be fought, but it was not right to maintain that an intelligent, a creative being was the natural opposite of the philistine, the passive being, Lunacharsky stated, thus, refuting the old "idealist" and pessimist SR stance of Ivanov-Razumnik. There were no grounds for adopting the "obscurantist" view, according to which there would always be a certain number of vulgar (*poshlye*) people.[86]

Soviet everyday life and the petty bourgeois

The true Soviet man, like the pre-Revolutionary intelligent, was supposed to despise things which belonged to everyday life: the material condition of his family and himself, good housing, comfortable clothing, the schooling of his children, and so on. It is, to some extent, obvious that the Bolsheviks made a virtue of necessity: material goods were simply not available for everyone; what one person took was taken from another. The material situation, especially in the early NEP period and during the First Five-Year Plan was appalling and probably appeared quite hopeless. A good Bolshevik or a good citizen in general, was not supposed to lose heart or envy those who had more than he did. The ideal Bolshevik was someone, who was not interested in matters material, strange as that may seem for the proponents of a supposedly materialist creed. The "trade-unionist" psychology, which was considered notoriously petty bourgeois,[87] although in a way it was "natural" for the working class, had no room in socialist society. True, the Bolsheviks knew that the masses were not able to rise above trade-unionist consciousness without the help of the party, and the party was there precisely to guarantee this most important move to a new order of values.[88] Soviet society did not exploit working people, and, therefore, they in principle should not have had anything against working harder and being paid less. In reality the consciousness of many people was lagging behind the objective state of production relations. The classics of Soviet literature describing the NEP period are full of passages where conscious activists struggle against the inert masses to raise them from their petty bourgeois lethargy.[89]

In reality, things were no better, to say the least. The Bolsheviks very soon realised that even workers from the biggest, "most proletarian" factories proved unruly.[90] The GPU's opinion surveillance files regularly informed about the attitudes of the workers and provided statistics about strikes.[91]

In theory, the ideal Soviet citizen, both Bolshevik and non-party, was supposed to bear the hardships which life under the revolutionary government had to offer without complaint. The natural vanguard in this respect was the factory workers, who "had been boiled in the kettle of the workshop." Obviously, the genuine proletariat of the modern giant plants had to be the most conscious part of the masses, whereas people, who had roots in the petty bourgeois countryside, were likely to look to their own petty interests. Reality defied theory. Workers" protests and complaints were concentrated in places where there should not have been any fertile soil for any petty bourgeois ideas or interests: Leningrad, Moscow and Ivanovo, factories like "Krasnyi Putilovets" and "Krasnyi Treugolnik" were constantly reporting workers' protests.[92] It was the working class, not the peasantry or intelligentsia that was the biggest headache for the government, which pretended to be the collective brain of that same class which reputedly was also now realizing its dictatorship.

5
The Precarious Truce

The new life and new culture. The ideological front of the NEP period

In Lenin's last writings the problems of culture and philistinism (*melkobur-zhuaznost'*) had become more and more important. In his brochure "The Infantile Disease of Leftism in Communism," which was published in the spring of 1920, Lenin sketched out the nature of the danger: "The dictatorship of the proletariat is the most ruthless and most merciless (*samaia bez-zavetnaia i samaia besposhchadnaia*) war of the new class against a mightier enemy." The might of the enemy was entrenched not only in the capitalist countries, but also in the "power of custom, the power of petty production. For petty production still exists on the earth, unfortunately there is very, very much of it and petty production gives rise to capitalism and the bourgeoisie constantly, every day, every hour, spontaneously and on a mass scale."[1] It is not uninteresting to note that this conclusion was made three and a half years after the utopian reflections of *State and Revolution* about the supposedly astonishing ease of adopting new socialist practices. There was less than a year until the adoption of NEP.

In a sequel to the "Infantile Disease" brochure Lenin concluded that many petty bourgeois intelligents had entered the party, the Soviets, the courts and administration, and that it was impossible to solve the petty bourgeois problem by destroying this element, the only way was to re-educate it, which would be a long struggle. Part of the problem was that workers themselves were not free of petty bourgeois prejudices and could not be emancipated from them at a single blow, but only through an extensive struggle against petty bourgeois influences.

One example of the petty bourgeois phenomenon was the new institution of Soviet "defenders of rights" (*pravozastupniki*), who had emerged after the institution of bourgeois advocates had been liquidated –the same institution had now returned in a new guise.[2] In Lenin's analysis the importance of the struggle against philistinism (*melkoburzhuaznost'*) was crucial especially because NEP was about to be introduced. At the X Party Congress, Lenin considered that the party had to educate (*vospitat'*) and organize the trade unions of the proletariat, and the latter had the same task regarding the "half-philistine and positively petty bourgeois masses of toilers." This role was endangered by the aspirations for "production democracy," pursued by the left communists, and this was one more reason for the suppression of their program.[3]

In his last writings, Lenin reflected on the fundamental problems of the Russian revolution and concluded that the low cultural level of the masses had had a fateful effect on the revolution, and that the raising of their cultural level was now the main task in Russia.

> In fact, we have 'only' one task left: to make our population civilized enough that it would understand the virtues of everybody's taking part in cooperation and would organize this partaking. 'Only' that. We need no other super-wisdom now in order to go to socialism. But in order to accomplish this 'only,' a whole revolution is needed...."[4]

The stress was now on cultural work, *kul'turnichestvo*. The Bolsheviks even had to learn how to trade in a civilized way.[5]

In hindsight, Lenin's last writings seem more or less like a proclamation of political bankruptcy. Now he acknowledged the facts, which the "philistines" had been pointing to for a long time, and for which they had only received angry scorn from Lenin. Had not the *Vekhi* group warned of a revolution, which would only bring about anarchy and disaster if the people itself were not culturally and morally developed? Maxim Gorky himself, who had, at the time of the *Vekhi* dispute, been scornful of the philistinism of the conservatives and had hailed the coming revolution, had already understood in 1917 that without culture, which also meant discipline and respect for fellow-citizens, there would be disaster: "Only by arming ourselves with knowledge will we become invincible in the struggle for life, only by resorting to broad cultural work at once, can we re-educate ourselves and save our country from disaster," Gorky had written in 1917.[6] Now, Lenin was saying the same thing. True, he maintained that the Bolshevik revolution had been justified even in a culturally underdeveloped country, for it had created the necessary conditions for cultural work, which could now be done.[7] A socialist society, which at the end of 1917 had seemed so near at hand, had not been realized by the revolution. The conscious elements of society (the party and those who agreed with it) were a small minority. There were no more capitalists, but there was the petty bourgeoisie, and this was an enemy, which trespassed everywhere.

As Lenin had written, the proletariat was now a small minority fighting an overpowering enemy. The methods used in this fight were educational, for the time being. This analysis was taken in earnest, and consequently a vast literature on the questions of cultural work appeared in the mid-twenties, during this "epoch of *kul'turnichestvo*," as Trotsky called it.[8]

The central topics of the discussions of this period (1921-28) were those of culture and the way of life (*byt*). There was little talk about "the new life" in the countryside, however, as these discussions were largely confined to the workers, especially the young in the Komsomol. A way of life and culture also implied questions of morals, both sexual and in the more general sense. It goes without saying that the morality in question was conceived as class-bound. This was also what Lenin had stressed in his address to the Komsomol congress at the end of 1920.[9] Not unnaturally, the vicious dimension in the class-bound system of morality was understood as "petty bourgeois." This was a danger that was penetrating society and had to be fought everywhere, in the towns and countryside, in the party and the factory.

In his analysis of the workers' culture of the 1920s, Stefan Plaggenborg concludes that during this epoch, the Bolsheviks saw the "revolutionizing of heads" as their main task.[10] This sounds drastic, but more often than not, it just meant that the "new people" would love communism and would be ready to fight for it, they would have the will to transform things and the power to do it, they would be disciplined at work, willing to learn and would have knowledge, they would be technically talented and have a predisposition to communal life and collectivism.[11] This was a nice ideal as such, but did not sound very utopian. It was a far cry from the radicalism of China of the 1960s, for instance. To a large extent the task was one of teaching the "petty bourgeois" (although non-urban) peasantry the social skills of industrial society. A "culture of work" had to be developed, for better labor productivity of was a precondition for socialism. Taylorism was one of the solutions, which was offered in a Sovietized form (NOT –Scientific organization of work). A.K. Gastev's and P.M. Kerzhentsev's League of Time even wanted to propose a thoroughgoing "mechanization of life."[12]

To some extent, raising the cultural level of the people was seen as a way to achieve increased production and improved distribution and, ultimately, an improvement in people's everyday life. This also was what Lenin had in mind when he spoke about Cultural Revolution as the precondition for socialism.

There were voices which pointed to the high cultural level of western countries as a model to be emulated. The well-known journalist Lev Sosnovsky was one of them. In Paris, for instance, he pointed out, milk and bread were being left at the door of houses in the morning and nobody stole them. In Denmark, the peasants left their milk by the highway and nobody stole it. One could compare this to Moscow where even the spittoons, which nobody used, had to be tied down with chains.[13] In the west, shop assistants served a greater clientele than in the Soviet Union, the factories were cleaner and the cows gave three times more milk. Diseases like cholera, typhus, or plague were non-existent –and all this was due to a higher level of culture.[14]

Sosnovsky's challenge did not go unheeded. The issue became a major one on the pages of Komsomolskaia pravda and passions became heated in the ensuing discussion, which lasted a long time. Both well-known figures like Taras Kostrov,[15] Anatoli Lunacharsky, and grass-roots activists became involved. For many activists taking care of personal hygiene and dress was equated with philistinism and taking the capitalist West as a model for the Soviet Union sounded blasphemous.[16] It was also clear that for many people questions of civilized manners were not real political questions, but belonged to some lower order of issues. Komsomolskaia pravda allowed different opinions to be expressed, but its own stand was easy to see in its cartoons, which ridiculed shabby clothing and lack of hygiene.[17] The paper also published a leader, where the importance of cultural work as political work was stressed.[18] On the other hand, philistinism was really considered a major danger, even among the youth: it was made clear that not only modern dances and chic clothes were philistine, but also religion, drink, and hooliganism.[19]

As regards the new man's physical constitution, developing it was also a matter of culture. The term "physical culture" (fizkul'tura) came into use in the 1920s and the People's Commissar for Health, Nikolai Semashko promoted it for the masses and praised exemplary western models.[20] Health, discipline, and endurance also interested the chief of military training (vsevobukh), Nikolai Podvoisky.[21] These were values, which did not have much in common with the élan of the rebellious masses of 1917-18. Instead of rebelling and defending his personal rights, which in a workers' state was clearly petty bourgeois, the new citizen had to learn to serve his superiors as loyally as possible. A model citizen, fit for socialism, and devoid of philistinism was a cultured, public-spirited, loyal, and healthy person. In fact, these were values which in bourgeois societies were typical of the petty bourgeoisie, but which in the Soviet Union had a different class nature.

But what about the worker, whom one could see every day and who had few of those qualities? Such workers were no rarity. They stole other people's property without their consent, did not respect other people's work, threw litter on the floor, walked around and lay in bed with filthy boots, did not wash themselves, used foul language and spat on the floor. They abused those who did not behave as badly as they did and called them *"intelligenty,"* which was pronounced in the same tone as a "gendarme" or a "snooper." A girl, who resisted sexual harassment from this type of worker was called a "philistine."[22]

This kind of person was clearly inferior and it was clear that socialism could not be built by such people: he was too lazy, unenlightened, ineffective, and probably unhealthy. But was he wasn't a worker at all, but a petty bourgeois?

Whatever the definition, the problem persisted. The average toiler did not see very much sense in becoming like the ideal citizen of the *kul'turniki*. Equal pay, which was more or less a reality in the 1920s, did not provide much incentive for developing oneself. Free from the "petty bourgeois" drive to obtain material comforts, the unenlightened proletarian was happy enough as long as he could avoid becoming overtired and was able to indulge in vodka, makhorka-tobacco, and cards. This was denounced by the government, which tried to restrict these favored proletarian pastimes.[23] Incentives for developing oneself were provided by the trade unions, which issued tickets to sanatoriums where the toilers could become acquainted with cultured surroundings. This policy, however, applied mostly to those workers, who were more or less exemplary. The more problem-ridden were taken care of by the militia.

Then there were of course the criminals. Professional "thieves" (*vory*) had a developed subculture in Russia and a mere drunkard or petty offender did not qualify just because he had been thrown into jail. As Maxim Gorky explained in the 1930s, criminals were the product of the past era of capitalism, more specifically they were the "offspring and heirs of philistinism" (*potomki i nasledniki meshchanstva*). They were re-educated in the jails and camps of the NKVD. Astonishingly, this scum of society had also some virtues also: they had the "zoological anarchism of a beast of prey," but to re-educate them could be simpler than re-educating an intelligent, who came from the petty bourgeoisie. The criminals didn't at all have the "instinct for ambition," which dominated the petty bourgeois. Robbing and stealing was, for criminals, just a means of living, a craft (*remeslo*).[24]

This line of thinking was true to the idea of communist morality, which Lenin had unveiled at the Congress of the Komsomol in 1920. After all, if criminals offended against the life and property of the propertied classes, they were not really petty bourgeois (or bourgeois) themselves but something else. It was quite another matter with those, who attacked the property and prerogatives of the proletarian state. However, the thieves could not be defined in terms of the socialist state, because they were not, and could not have been, produced by this state. Analogously, it was supposed that there could not be prostitutes in the full sense of the word in the Soviet Union. Accordingly, it was sometimes maintained that even the very word did not exist any more.[25] The one and only existing antisocial element in the workers" state, which had an existence in its own right was the petty bourgeoisie. All the other delinquents received their vices from the petty bourgeoisie, in the same way as the moon gets its light from the sun. In the 1920s, attacks by criminals against well-to do "nepmen" were, in fact more or less looked upon with *Schadenfreude* by Soviet officials and the Soviet press." Class approach" was recommended for cases of hooliganism, which was not promising from the point of view of petty bourgeois intelligents. The majority of hooligans were of worker origin and the dormitories of workers were especially ridden with hooliganism and debauchery. [26] Hooligans remained a nuisance in spite of the virtues of the new toilers' society. They mugged their superiors in the workplace ("Bykovshchina"[27]), which although was impermissible, but could still be understood in class terms. More serious and ideologically baffling was that they also began also to harass party and Komsomol activists. In 1926, in connection with a notorious case of gang rape in Leningrad,[28] hooliganism began to be interpreted as banditry, and the death sentence began to be used in dealing with it. Later, in the 1930s, hooliganism was in many cases interpreted as political crime. Harassment of "peredoviks,"[29] abusing the "stakhanovites," swearing at portraits of Lenin was all no longer regarded as hooliganism, but as counterrevolutionary agitation and terrorism.[30] The intelligent was not necessarily a better human being than a professional criminal, from an ideological point of view. Rather the opposite. No wonder that rogues and thugs used the word "intelligent" as a term of abuse. The official ideology offered them moral support.

Fighting the philistine everyday practices

During the NEP period the Bolsheviks clearly did not enjoy the support of the majority of the population. As Lenin had said, they were fighting a superior enemy. There is no denying, however, that the Bolsheviks had some mass support. In a society where all the instruments of power and coercion were in their hands, an active minority could do a great deal. The strategically important group, from the Bolshevik point of view, was the youth, who had not grown up in a capitalist society. It was naturally the vanguard of the new society and, according to Lenin, it would see the Promised Land; in 10-20 years it would be living in a communist society.[31] Not unnaturally the party, was able to find enthusiastic support for its radical ideas among the youth. True, in some cases the representatives of the youth were disappointed with the realpolitik, insufficient radicalism, intellectual dishonesty, or blatant injustice of the party. Therefore, from the point of view of those in power the youth also remained a suspect group, which might give its support to Trotskyites and other opposition-ists and might even set up its own, clandestine, "organizations."[32] It was a fact that the majority of hooligans consisted of "toiling" youth, peasants in the countryside, workers in towns.[33] On the other hand, the Komsomol also recruited masses of youths who were very serious about the new or-ganization and proper norms of everyday life, which meant, above all, living in a proletarian way and avoiding philistinism.

Several surveys were conducted about the youth and about their val-ues and their actual way of life. Very often the concerns of the youth were about sexual relations and living conditions. According to Klara Zetkin, Lenin himself had asserted that the "proletariat, the rising class... does not need intoxication, which would soothe or excite it. It does not need intoxication either from sexual license or intoxication from alcohol."[34] This was in theory, but it meant, a priori, that such aberrations were petty bourgeois. Vodka, which had been banned in 1914, reappeared in shops in 1924. Although the petty bourgeois vice of drinking was supposed to wither away, this did not happen. On the contrary, alcoholism once more became a problem and drinking increased rapidly towards the end of the 1920s.[35] Swearing was also common even among workers and the com-munists, as surveys of workers revealed. Coarseness of manners was un-derstood by many to be "revolutionary." Trotsky himself asserted that tact and politeness were not petty bourgeois in essence, but "the necessary grease of everyday relations."[36] According to Trotsky, rudeness had partly peasant, partly gentry (*barskii*) origins. As regards rude words, used by writers and intellectuals as an "artistic" measure, Trotsky asserted that the foremost part of the workers were organically hostile to it and saw in it the stamp of the old slavery.[37]

As regards sex, the petty bourgeois peril was exemplified in the "wrong" attitude to a woman that is, considering her, not as a comrade, but as a sex object. A proper sexual life was a difficult equation, for, on the one hand, there should not be too much license but, on the other hand, neither should there be asceticism. The class-aspect was always present even in things sexual. According to the famous formulation of Aron Zal-kind, a renowned specialist of his time, sexual attraction to a class enemy was as unnatural as that to a crocodile or to an orangutang.[38]

The male sexual drive as such, which evidently was more or less iden-tical with an "uncomradely relation" to a woman, was, every now and then, branded a product of the old society. The ideal in sexuality was dif-ficult to attain, because it could never be clearly defined in terms of class.

It seems to be that sexual pleasure as such was understood to have a petty bourgeois essence.[39] The case was analogous with religion: everything that distracted a person from his true mission was a sin. Accordingly, sexual pleasure, when it became an end in itself, was philistine.

It was assumed that the situation could be ameliorated by intense cultural work among men.[40] In practice the struggle with philistinism was not easy, although the Komsomols frequently claimed that they did not need the cheap intoxication of alcohol, but would rather arrange cultural evenings with tea.[41]

A direct road to philistinism seemed to be the acquisition of material goods. In the 1920s it was still assumed that somebody, who had no personal property at all, but who shared all his belongings with the other members of a commune, was behaving in a non-philistine way. In the 1930s ideas like this would be authoritatively and devastatingly refuted. But in the 1920s, when NEP began to make material goods available, some of them became symbols of philistinism as such. As a matter of fact, having too much of any kind of property was considered to be petty bourgeois. Members of the party could not, in principle, earn more than a skilled worker. At a Komsomol conference in Leningrad in 1929 the rooms of "an activist" and "a philistine" were exhibited for comparison. In the former, there was a simple iron bed with only one pillow. On the table was a newspaper and on the wall a portrait of Lenin, and nothing else. The window had no curtains. There was also a cupboard and a gramophone. The petty bourgeois for his part, had flowers on the window sill, family portraits on the wall, and even an icon. There were several upholstered chairs, and two large pillows on the bed. A gramophone occupied a conspicuous place.[42] Similar instructive comparisons were quite popular. The moral always remained the same: the person, who was worthy enough to enter the future communist society suppressed his personal needs and submitted everything to the cause of his class; that is, to the construction of the new society.

Unfortunately, the radicalism of the youth was not always directed where the party wanted. Soviet students were as unruly and bohemian as their pre-revolutionary colleagues had been. Some would go into auditoriums in caps and smoke there. Aversion to washing was widespread. Nikolai Bukharin, in the middle of the 1920s, tried to persuade the youth that this was philistine: this kind of "protest" in a workers" society was madness. Instead, the builders of the new society should be orderly and disciplined.[43]

Early Soviet society was not able to set, or fulfill, high norms of welfare. Instead, it was able to set a ceiling on opulent consumption. A full equality never succeeded, even though the Bolsheviks were, according to their program, bound to accomplish it in the future. There were still differences in income and even large-scale unemployment. In principle a communist could not earn more than a qualified worker, but in practice this was a dead letter. The communists, who held the commanding posts, were able to acquire for themselves and their relatives ample privileges in terms of housing and services.[44] For the average citizen, however, there was not much room for philistinism, for the norm for living space was first 14, then 10 and from 1930 a mere 9 sq. meters per person.[45] This did not at all mean that everybody was guaranteed that amount of living space, but that anybody with more than this amount could expect it to be taken away.

The state effectively confiscated what was considered to be "surperfluous" for an individual private person. Pianos and private libraries were taken away from representatives of the old intelligentsia, and distributed to workers' clubs and libraries. Now the state was interested only in houses, books and comparable items of lasting value –this was a new situation, for even clothing had been confiscated during the period of War Communism.[46]

Most people still had to wear old and outworn clothes in the beginning of the 1920s. It was calculated that in 1923 a white-collar worker used daily 0, 9 hours daily for repairing his clothes and a worker 0,7 hours, on week-days.[47] But even so, for some, it was possible to clothe oneself in a petty bourgeois way. A well-known party man A.A. Solts explained, in 1925, to students of the Sverdlov communist university that a member of the party should not wear clothing which suggested that he was removed from working life.

According to Natalia Lebina, a genuine war against "bourgeois" fashion was waged by the party and the Komsomol in the 1920s.[48] Silk shirts and other luxurious items were branded as "bourgeois dissolution."[49] Hats, other than peaked caps, also aroused the ire of the proletarians, for they were considered a sign of the intelligentsia, even though hats were still worn at the end of the 1920s. Other petty bourgeois signs were ties and starched collars. Spectacles, which betrayed a person who was used to reading and writing, were also a symbol of the intelligentsia. Wearing spectacles was so compromising for the image of a proletarian leader that the prominent Bolshevik Sergei Kirov never used them in public in spite of his grave myopia. Even worse than spectacles was the *pince-nez*, which was an exclusively intelligentsia device.[50]

Somebody's petty bourgeois character could also be revealed by their social life and leisure. Sensuous music, such as gypsy romances and the foxtrot was petty bourgeois. "Proletarian" musicians even considered it a kind of narcotic, which was positively detrimental to the reconstruction of the new society.[51] Unfortunately, the masses liked them. Even on an occasion like the October revolution anniversary demonstration in 1930, 44 per cent of the songs sung by the marchers were "petty bourgeois" in the opinion of a "proletarian" critic.[52] In music halls most songs were petty bourgeois in nature and were directed at a "petty bourgeois intelligent" audience and, according to the censors, were totally alien to the ideology of the proletariat.[53]

Modern dances were also seen as frivolous and, therefore, petty bourgeois. The fox trot, shimmy, one-step, and so on, were all clearly designed to excite the lowliest instincts of man; the fox trot was nothing other than a "salon" imitation of the sexual act. In the worker atmosphere of the Soviet republics, which were transforming life and throwing away the "filth of philistine dissolution" (gnil' meshschanskogo upadnichestva) dance should, it was agreed, be different: brisk, happy, and bright (svetlyi). It was forbidden to present petty bourgeois dances as special items in a program.[54]

Cheap novels, Western films, and frivolous plays abounded in Soviet Russia in the 1920s. The report of the OGPU committee for the political control of plays concluded in 1923 that the repertoire of theatres had a strong tendency to ridicule "not only petty bourgeois (obyvatelskie) shortcomings... but also the prevailing system, NEP, responsible workers and the communist party. There is also no lack of pornographic and cheap (poshlyi) contents."[55]

Plays like as Charley's Aunt, The Black Force (Chernaia sila) and others were presented in clubs. The security organs concluded that they idealized criminality and promoted anti-Semitism, pornography, and "sentimentality with its petty-bourgeois ideology."[56] The purity of the vanguard class, and the innocence of immature elements, was guarded by differentiating between different audiences. Until the beginning of 1924, when plays and shows were given the censor's imprimatur, it was also indicated which kind of audience they could be presented to.[57]

Some theatres, like that of Vsevolod Meyerhold, repeatedly showed petty bourgeois plays, the organs reported. The banquet for the 100 year jubilee of the Maliy Theatre was organized in a completely West-European manner: with dresses, dances (foxtrot, shimmy), chansons, wine, and champagne. All this reflected the psychology of other academic theatres as well, the competent security organs concluded.[58] As for cinema, in 1925 the OGPU estimated that 75 per cent of the films in local theatres were of foreign origin. This repertoire was for the most part unsuitable for worker and peasant audiences, but served the local petty bourgeoisie (obyvatel'shchina).[59] The OGPU maintained, probably incorrectly, that workers and peasants were not interested in detective films, whereas nepmen and petty bourgeois intelligent (nepmanskaia i meshchansko-intellgentskaia publika) audiences loved them.[60]

The elegance of high society was only accessible for the few; mostly nepmen and the party elite and some other small groups such as creative artists. Luxury did return to Soviet Russia in the 1920s. In 1923 the CC suppressed the public use of diamonds and other jewels,[61] but it goes without saying that this practice flourished on less public occasions. In a climate of general scarcity and poverty even the most modest instances of elegance and refinement were stigmatized as "petty bourgeois." There was also real luxury in NEP society, but it is clear that the general mood of the masses was resentful of any signs of opulence. The petty bourgeois, the main enemy in the midst of the people, was unpopular. To escape stigmatization, it was better to avoid signs and manners, which before the revolution, had been typical for the intelligentsia. A voluminous literature tried to convince people that being cultured did not mean being petty bourgeois, but the assiduous repeating of this truism just showed how difficult, if not impossible, it was for ordinary people to make this distinction.

Reconnaissance of the enemy. The secret surveillance of Soviet popular opinion

A vast apparatus was used for secret opinion surveillance in the Soviet Union. From 1922 the moods of the population were systematically monitored. By 1924 this work had attained a mature and organized character. Chronicles recording the mood of different sections of the population were produced on a daily basis and general surveys covering the whole of the Soviet Union were compiled monthly. The idea of these surveys was to provide the central governing elite with feedback about the reactions of the Soviet public to the current policies of the party. The focus of these surveys was on the grassroots level, and what interested the leadership, were anti-Soviet occurrences, evidence of discontent, or other developments that were potentially dangerous to the regime. The information also contained cases of activity on the part of forbidden parties, such as anarchists, SRs, Mensheviks, and Kadets. The bulk of the information, however, was about the workers and peasants. Only occasionally were there surveys about the mood of the intelligentsia or about the "petty bourgeoisie" in town and countryside.

The very fact of the lack of interest by the security organs in the intelligentsia reveals the feeble position of the intelligentsia, here meaning the educated classes, as a group: it was too small to pose a serious political threat to the regime and its work had little impact on production. The intelligentsia was, in general, too well-behaved to do anything that might cause a public scandal or engage in acts of hooliganism against the regime. Those sections of the intelligentsia whose work was vital for production, the *spetsy*, were attracted into serving the system with ample remuneration. "Non-productive" groups, such as physicians, teachers, and many white-collar groups, had only marginal importance for the regime which saw its main tasks as ensuring the support of the workers and the worst-off peasants. True, the opinions of the top echelons of the creative intelligentsia, writers, the film makers, artists, and so on, were important for the regime, for their productive work directly affected the public opinion. This group, however, was quite small and its opinions and especially its work were the subject of special surveillance and attention, even on an individual basis. As regards the mass opinion surveys, the intelligentsia and other "petty bourgeois" groups (except the peasants) were a second-class priority.

The opinion surveillance materials of 1922-30, which I have had at my disposal,[62] provide a wealth of detailed information which makes it possible to draw a general picture of the climate of opinion, and to understand, how the communists saw the intelligentsia. To get an idea about the place of the intelligentsia in the opinion survey reports, it is necessary to say something about the general substance of the reports.

As for the vast majority of the population, the peasants, it was not treated as a more or less homogenous, "petty bourgeois" mass. The official division of the peasantry into "kulaks" and the well-to-do (*zazhitochnye*) peasants, the middle peasants (*seredniaki*), the poor peasants (*bedniaki*), and the landless "batraks" was used in the analysis of the data. In principle, the village poor, bednyaki, and batraki were imagined to be natural allies of the Bolsheviks, and the middle-peasants (*seredniaki*) were thought to be potential allies. The split in the countryside, with the kulaks and well-to-do on the one side and the rest of the peasants on the other was always the goal of Bolshevik policy. Since the adoption of NEP, however, the *smychka* between town and countryside was reduced the need for class struggle in the countryside or so it was thought.

Rural life, as depicted in the reports, was hard. It is not easy to tell what exactly was normal." The reports reveal a sea of hardship, pauperism, unjust administration, cruelty, violence, and discontent. There were hundreds and thousands of cases of grave misdeeds, offences, abuse, and defiance. However, one has to remember that there were millions of peasant households in the Soviet Union. It seems clear that there was a great deal of variation at the local level as regards such things as the mutual relations of different sections of rural society, the economic situation of the peasantry and the officials, the prevalence of hooliganism and banditry, and so on.

It seems fair to say that the general mood of the Russian countryside was at all times unsympathetic towards Soviet power. One clear indication of this is the popularity of the idea of a peasant union (*Krestianskii soiuz*). In 1924 the files reported 25 cases where this idea had surfaced. In 1925 the popularity of the idea grew rapidly and there were dozens of cases every month. In December there were 71 cases. In 1926 the idea had become the slogan of the day. Almost every month more than a hundred cases where a peasants" union was demanded were reported. In December there were 207 such cases. To understand this rapid growth we must remember that the notorious "scissors crisis" between the town and the countryside was developing: the town produced insufficient amount consumer goods and the price of grain was so low that the peasants had little incentive to sell it. In 1926 a new tax system, requiring payment in cash and a progressive taxation was introduced. It was immensely unpopular and led to all kinds of protests. The demand for a peasants' union was just one of this general protest, but it was important, because it implied that the peasants regarded the system as unjust and did not recognize the Bolsheviks as the legitimate masters of the country. Bolshevik rule was regarded as incompetent, unjust, and ineffective. A united peasant front, where all the different layers of the rural society were united against the towns, seemed to be developing in 1924, with the kulaks and the well-to-do taking the local Soviet apparatus into their hands, which, of course, alarmed the party.

The peasantry resented the prevailing lawlessness: hooligans and bandits terrorized large areas of rural Russia. Bandits abounded especially in frontier and mountain areas, but hooligans ruled openly in many districts and engaged in robbery, arson and murder with impunity. There were constant complaints that Soviet power did not punish hooligans harshly enough.[63] In those rare cases, when severe punishment was used, it won the unanimous support of the peasants. By the autumn of 1926 hooliganism (which often developed into banditry, as the official formulation put it) had become a real nuisance. An unending array of cases was revealed by the informers, they had probably been specially told to concentrate their attention on them.[64]

The violence was partly political. In cases where officials, party members, or poor villagers were the victims, the files spoke about "terror." This was not very widespread. In 1924, 338 cases were reported; but in 1925 there were 159 cases in January alone and about one hundred in each of the following months. "Terror" did not always mean homicide; mostly it meant assault, arson or injury. This "normal" situation changed in 1929, the "year of the great break." Officially the idea of collectivization was gaining mass support. The message of the reports was very different. Mass disorders became the order of the day. Already during the first half of 1929, there were 520 mass demonstrations (*vystuplenia*) against Soviet power in the countryside. The term "demonstration" often referred to the appearance of a mob, sometimes 1000-2000 strong, which beat the agents of the state, liberated people, who had been arrested, took back the grain, which the officials had confiscated, and so on. The meetings were often summoned by the ringing of church bells. Usually, the most active demonstrators were women, who were more leniently treated than the men who often deliberately sent their wives to demonstrate, almost always the uprising (*bunt*) succeeded in expelling the officials. A handful of GPU men, even with a *tachanka* (a horse-driven cart with a machine gun,) could only flee when faced with hundreds of enraged women.

During the first half of 1929, 1480 cases of "terror" were also recorded. In this case terror" meant violence against the Bolsheviks and Soviet power.[65] Terror in the countryside was, however, not just "kulak terror," nor was "hooliganism" just acts of violence by country youths against the Komsomols and other activists, who, for example, arranged demonstrations for the 1st of May, or engaged in atheist propaganda. There was also "red banditry." This was murder or arson carried out by the Bolsheviks. The former red partisans of Siberia were especially active in this field. The victims could be, for instance, kulaks, who had reclaimed their possessions which had been expropriated during the Civil War. Cases of "Red terror" were rather conspicuous in the files in 1925 although this does not seem to have been a mass phenomenon.

Apart from the peasants, who constituted the majority of the population, the workers, supposedly the masters of Soviet society were another element which gave the Bolsheviks much to fear. Soviet power was unable to provide full employment, pay wages in time, or provide good housing or work conditions. In many cases, the state also harshly cut the number of workers in order to raise productivity, wages were lowered, and working norms increased. All this affected the attitude of the workers to the Bolshevik party. Other causes of resentment were the "too good wages" of some specialists and communists and the deficit of goods. In 1929, in particular, there was a massive shortage of the most basic necessities of everyday life: bread, oil (for lighting), clothes, and so on. Queues of hundreds, even thousands, of people appeared everywhere. As for the quality of products, "Soviet" quality had became notorious, which meant that they were not like goods in the old days, which lasted, that were the "real" thing, and were well-made.

The files also contain a wealth of information about the mood of the intelligentsia and other "petty bourgeois" elements, although it seems that interest in this was on the wane after 1924. The reason for this may be that, in 1926, the structural problem of city – countryside relations was growing so acute that small pockets of intelligentsia dissent or discontent were seen as less important by comparison. In 1924 the GPU made some generalizations based on its material pointing out that the petty bourgeois element (*melkoburzhuaznaia stikhiia*) was on the march and that this explained the various negative phenomena in society. The enmity of the urban intelligentsia was growing and its views were veering to the right. The causes of discontent included unemployment (for instance, amongst former tsarist officers, who had served in the Civil War, and had been fired) and the "utterly low remuneration" for professors and teachers. By 1924 the mood had changed from what it had been earlier: there was now no talk about "going to Canossa" as there had been in the days of the Smena vekh. Now the intelligentsia was looking forward to a "political NEP" and was trying to organize its own professional organizations. As regards rural teachers, this was an element, which had "undoubtedly" begun to be sovietized. This was also seen at a general Congress of Teachers and on some other occasions. The students in universities were becoming more active and some even had terrorist aspirations.[66]

In 1925 there were many references to an anti-specialist mood, with badly paid workers resenting the high salaries of some specialists. There were also cases of peasants demanding that the salaries of officials be lowered and their labor-day lengthened.[67] On the other hand, white-collar workers were, in some cases, quite miserably paid. There was one case, when of official killing himself after getting his low salary.

The concept of "petty bourgeois" was very seldom used in the files. Sometimes there was talk about the "petty bourgeois nature" (*melkoburzhuaznaia stikhiia*) on a general level. About "philistine" conduct, there was hardly any mention at all. The "scientific" nature of the reports restricted their interest to the "hard" facts of class-origin and the like. Interpretation was left to the high-standing receivers of the files. The word *meshchanin* was used to denote small dealers, peddlers, artisans (*kustary*), and so on. The word *obyvatel'* was used interchangeably with *meshchanin*. Sometimes the use of words gives rise to even more complications. For instance, in 1929 it was reported that there was a rise in the "anti-Soviet activity of the non-working (*netrudovoe*) town population, the merchants, and the petty bourgeois (*obyvateli*)." In Samara the petty bourgeois (*obyvateli*) had arranged a meeting of 5000 people on the market square. On the KVZhD (Chinese Eastern Railway in Manchuria) an anti-soviet petty bourgeoisie (*obyvatel'shchina*) operated, which consisted of: "*lishentsy* (former "exploiters", who had now been deprived of civil rights), merchants, servants of the church, and so on, and also some specialists and the officials." In Astrakhan there had been an action (*vystuplenie*) of about 1000 people from the "non-working" (*netrudovoe*) population: merchants, petty bourgeois (*obyvateli*) and dockers (*gruzchiki*) (!).

It would appear that the words denoting representatives of the petty bourgeoisie were not used entirely consistently. Quite often references to officials were kept separate from references to the intelligentsia and even the *spetsy* in these report. Clearly, this was because the officials were often members of the party, whereas the term intelligentsia denoted a petty bourgeois group. As regards the *spetsy*, they might in some cases be considered not just petty bourgeois, but real bourgeois like the "nepmen." The word *obyvatel'* seems to have had virtually the same meaning as "petty bourgeois" (*meshchanin*). It clearly had a slighting, even mocking tone, which connoted a lack of culture and idealism.

On the basis of the admittedly incomplete material available to me, it is difficult to arrive at very broad conclusions about the intelligentsia and the petty bourgeoisie of the 1920s or the mutual relations of the intelligentsia and other social groups. It seems clear, however, that the lot of the intelligents was for the most part unenviable. There were cases when specialists were paid well, but more typical was poverty, even misery. The Soviet state had very little spare money to remunerate those layers of society which did not directly produce material goods. In 1926 this principle was formulated in a VKP(b) resolution as follows: "...to realize in the whole country a harsh regime of saving and economizing and a merciless struggle against all unnecessary non-productive expenditures."[68] No wonder that teachers who remembered Lenin's words about the exceptionally high material status of the future Soviet teachers, felt that they had been deceived.[69]

All in all, the secret opinion surveillance had very little positive to say about the attitudes of the intelligentsia towards Soviet power. Only a certain section of rural teachers were found to have developed a "Soviet" attitude, but many kept saying that they should work "according to the salary."[70]

The problems of the specialists

As has been mentioned above, during the NEP period the Soviet leadership adopted what has been called "the soft line on culture."[71] The "softness" of this line must not be exaggerated since the term merely indicates that a "harder" line also existed, but was mostly kept in check until the unleashing of the "cultural revolution" in 1928. The civil war years had been a hard time for all sections of the old (pre-revolutionary) intelligentsia. In the mid-1920s the situation improved. The new regime believed in the primacy of material production and this had always had an impact on policies. Accordingly, the "technical intelligentsia" could be rather well-paid, while professors in "non-productive" fields were worse off. At first they had to survive at almost the same salary as schoolteachers. The latter had been notoriously underpaid even in tsarist times and for them the situation was not improving.[72] By the middle of the 1920s academics were already better off than average workers, but as members of a group, which, in principle was supposed to be under the dictatorship of the proletariat, they still faced several handicaps. Perhaps most depressing of all was that their offspring were discriminated against in admissions to higher education. It was also not easy to do scientific work in a communal apartment. This kind of hardships may well have hindered the academics' zeal in carrying out their work and in the mid 1920s they were also given some special privileges regarding housing. It seems, however, that the "privileges" of this group were not secured in practice. The rank and file of the Soviet bureaucracy did not respect very much the rights of the old intelligentsia.[73]

Schoolteachers were, of course, much worse off than academics. Surviving on starvation rations, they were also looked askance by many Bolshevik grassroots activists for being "petty bourgeois." The teachers' standard of living or the class-nature of their employer did not exactly provide bourgeois status, but it does seem to have been true that during the civil war the majority of teachers had been more or less actively opposed to the Bolsheviks. A delegate at the XIII party congress maintained that "50 per cent" of teachers were offspring of the clergy.[74] The party leadership in the middle of the 1920s made some gestures in favor of the rural teachers, but the grassroots Bolshevik officials seem to have gone on treating the teachers as a kind of class-enemy. Dismissals, transfers and other kinds of repressive measures were taken against the teachers. For rural "pioneers" and komsomols, teachers often represented the only available target, bourgeois *intelligenshchina*, which they could attack.[75]

For a representative of the old intelligentsia, the urban scene of Moscow at the end of NEP looked coarse and mediocre. The grandiose boasting about a new superculture which would make Beethoven look like a vulgar second-rate musician was a matter for resigned irony. Ivan Ivanovich Shitts,[76] a historian in his fifties mentioned in his diary in 1928 a huge poster, with a slogan about surpassing Beethoven and continued gloomily:

And there is this philistinism (*meshchanstvo*), philistinism, which is trampling us from all sides. At 4 o'clock this grey mass of people, who are in dirty clothes and physically not well-washed fills the streets...they have unwashed galoshes and worn-out peaked caps, their tobacco is wretched and their conversations spiritless (*poshlye*)—about living space, party cells, protection, lottery loans and cheap cinemas (*kinoshki*). Those are the amusements: on Sundays people leave their "living spaces" and just loiter around, slackly, gloomily, jostling and trampling each others' feet, and if they are a little bit tipsy, they let loose their reservoirs of shameful words and yell with full voice.[77]

True, everything was not perfectly uniform, as he continued:

And along with all this there are those, who want to stand out of the crowd in the usual way: some groups of soldiers, the pilots for instance, try to have their shoes cleaned and keep a good bearing, even to be "chivalrous" with women. But all this resembles more the old lower ranks of police officers than the old guards.[78]

Shitts may probably be regarded as a typical representative of the old intelligentsia. For him the class struggle, which the Bolsheviks were organizing, was nothing more than a lowering of the canons of culture to the level of the mob. No new words for describing those phenomena were needed: *meshchanstvo* and *poshlost'* were perfectly adequate for his venomous pen.

As regards the "creative intelligentsia," the "bourgeois" non-party contingent was constantly under fire. After the Proletkult had been liquidated, not least because of its ideological susceptibility, the "proletarian" writers" organization VAPP (since 1928 RAPP) continued to attack "bourgeois" writers. The "proletarian" journal *Na postu* and the VAPP's leader Leopold Averbakh attacked, not only non-party intelligents, but also overtly lenient Soviet institutions such as the Narkompros (and its leader Lunacharsky) and the "thick" journal *Krasnaia nov'* which protected "fellow-travellers," The VAPP"s world-view, as manifested in its programmatic documents, was terribly simplistic and the principle of struggling against all other literary currents, using any methods, was made an article of faith.[79] The VAPPists used "smear tactics" and had some success even at the level of the Narkompros, but they did not attain the organizational power they wanted in order to destroy bourgeois literature altogether and establish their "proletarian" rule.[80] The State Publishing House and the Narkompros were in the hands of representatives of the "soft" line until 1928. Theatrical affairs were also under the control of the "soft" Lunacharsky. Therefore, it remained possible for the non-party intelligentsia to continue its activities despite attacks by hardliners, which did not only come from the VAPP.[81]

NEP debates on the intelligentsia. Lunacharsky and the idea of containment

The journal *Revoliutsiia i kul'tura* published a couple of authoritative articles about the intelligentsia in 1927, one of which was Anatoli Lunacharsky's "The intelligentsia and its place in the socialist construction."[82] By intelligentsia, Lunacharsky meant all the specialists who did mental work. Common clerks did not belong to this group. The intelligentsia had to be divided into the "new" and the "old," taking into account that the "new" also included the old communists, who were doing mental work. It should be remembered that not only there was the peak of the intelligentsia, which comprised the academicians, top scientists, engineers, and so on, but there was also a middle layer between the top echelons and the clerks. Now, the proletariat had to create its own intelligentsia, and it had to do so with care in order to avoid creating a new petty bourgeoisie.

The old intelligentsia, wrote Lunacharsky, was not Marxist, it was mostly apolitical in a dull, philistine way, it was under a strong influence of philistine ethics with its egoism, vanity, and, "apartness" from others in work. Cooperation and tact towards the old intelligentsia was necessary. In a class society the intelligentsia would be its brain and conscience. This, Lunacharsky stated, was what some of its representatives were willing to be even now, but they did not take into account the new class nature of the new society, and spoke about Man, Mankind, Duty, Science and Art with capital letters, in an abstract way. Sometimes, this type of intelligent was a representative of soft-minded humanism and did not understand the ways of the Bolsheviks. However, this type of intelligent could understand the objectives of the Bolsheviks and cooperate with them, while criticizing their practices, Lunacharsky stated.

Here the author touched upon the main divisive issue of pre-Revolutionary debates, whilst trying to minimize the source of disagreement. The hard core radicals, Bolsheviks, Populists, and Nietzscheans had considered that all means for the great end were permissible, while, the softliners had disagreed resolutely. But now one might think that the revolution was already a *fait accompli* and that the laudable "ends" had been realized to some extent at least. There was also another matter of principle, Lunacharsky admitted. The old intelligentsia consisted mostly of westernizers but the Bolshevik revolution had not brought Europeanization. In this respect, the Bolsheviks could do nothing, for they had to keep to their principles.

As regards the material situation of the intelligentsia, it should be improved, for that would win sympathy for the Bolsheviks. Another item concerned paying proper respect to the intelligentsia. The teachers, for instance, were unduly bullied and abused. Of course, the intelligentsia should be kept under surveillance, for it could wreck things in many ways, by, for example, a docile implementation of stupid ideas forwarded by Soviet officials, who were not enlightened enough to understand the implications of their actions.

A new intelligentsia was emerging but that did not automatically mean that problems were being solved: the offspring of the old intelligentsia was still disproportionately represented in the universities, and even people of proletarian origin could be contaminated by the attitudes, which prevailed in the universities. The task was not easy, but it was very important for the party to take care of the *serednyak* intelligent[83] and to win him over to the Bolshevik side, so Lunacharsky finished his article.

Nikolai Bukharin and the power of education

Another party luminary, who published an article about the intelligentsia in *Revoliutsia i kul'tura* in 1927[84], was Nikolai Bukharin. At this time Bukharin was at the peak of his career, one of a troika with Stalin, and Rykov and yet to be accused of rightist heresy (that came the following year). This old left-communist had had some new thoughts regarding the traditions of the intelligentsia and about philistinism.

In a truly Leninist way Bukharin explained that in politics everything had its time and that it was impossible to transfer old slogans mechanically from one period to the next. What might have been progressive for one period might be reactionary in another and so on. Without referring to Vekhi, Bukharin explained that in the bourgeois period, the Bolsheviks had concentrated their efforts on destroying the old society, and had, therefore, not been interested in learning sciences or in other practical issues. However, in 1918 Lenin himself had already stressed the necessity of learning practical things: "take care of bookkeeping accurately and conscientiously, be economic, don't idle, don't steal, take care of the strictest labour discipline...." In a bourgeois society this attitude would have been mere philistinism, but now it was a necessary condition for the construction of socialism. Now, it was time for proletarian discipline and order.

But, the power of tradition was such that even people who wanted to join together with the proletariat were professing ideas, which purported to be directed against the petty bourgeoisie, but which, in the current situation, were producing philistinism. In poetry, the bohemian Esenin was in fact a representative of the petty bourgeoisie, Bukharin maintained, and even Mayakovsky had been contaminated. Although the latter had written a good many revolutionary poems, now he sometimes returned to such tones, which smelt of anarchism and debauchery, which might have been progressive in bourgeois society, for this society had to be destroyed, but not in a socialist one. In the new society, the old ideal type of the "good chap," who drank, swore, and brawled, had to give way to a civilized "soldier of labor."

For some sophisticated little intelligent, Bukharin told, this perhaps sounded like praising the virtues of philistinism. Maybe he would even cite Nietzsche's irony: "we have a small satisfaction for the day and a little satisfaction for the night. But we take care of health." But this irony did not work any more, Bukharin insisted. Now, it was the everyday work of the "best people" of socialist society that was most revolutionary. Only this work was upturning the old society. Masses of exemplary "soldiers of labor" could be produced, but, for this end, a systematic and aggressive preaching of the values of culture, work, and order, had to be organized. This was now needed, instead of dissolution, slovenliness, or "aristocrat-ic," "barefooter," or "philistine" individualism.

Old traditions also had to be fought among the intelligentsia. Philis-tinism had to be hit, over and over again. As Lenin had said, the petty bourgeois surrounded the proletariat on all sides and caused "lack of will, disunity, individualism, and depression" in the ranks of the proletariat. "The power of custom of millions and tens of millions –this is the most formidable power," Lenin had said. This power of custom had to be "torn into pieces" in the interests of the great future, for which the proletariat was fighting.

In part, Bukharin's views echoed the disillusionment, which the Bol-sheviks had faced at the very beginning of their rule. On the other hand, there was also an element of the idea of the "changed essence" of the new society, where signs of social values had been changed to their opposites.

Mikhail Reisner and the struggle against the non-intelligent philistine

Professor Mikhail Reisner's[85] article "*Meshchanstvo*" in the first issue of *Krasnaia nov'* in 1927[86] had pretensions to scientific rigor and also referred to the authority of Marx and Engels. His subject was the meshchantvo's psychology. The roots of this psychology, he contended, lay in the class position of a group, which constantly wanted to climb the social ladder and feared slipping down that same ladder. In essence, the petty bourgeoisie was a class without hope: its rise into the upper class was not possible and its constant attempts to attain the impossible were both tragic and comical. Together with the better-off peasants and city-*lumpenproletarians* (*bosiaki*), the petty bourgeoisie had often been the henchmen of the oppressors.

Under fascism, the petty bourgeoisie were given a free hand to destroy, kill, and loot, and a patriotic ideology gave it a semblance of unity, a false escape from its isolation. The psychology of the group had a dual character: on the one hand, it was utterly cowardly, on the other utterly cruel, the sadist of history. It was terribly greedy but could also indulge in hair-raising vandalism, Reisner explained. His readers could hardly help thinking about recent Russian history. The petty bourgeoisie was individualistic, the author told, and was divided into mutually hostile units. The reader didn't need to be reminded of the virtues of the supposedly monolithic unity of the Bolshevik party.

Paradoxically, the petty bourgeoisie was ascetic, but also craved unnecessary decorations and would do anything to obtain them, the old Bolshevik mocked, almost anticipating the return of decorations and uniforms, which happened a few years later. The petty bourgeoisie was also a slave to tradition and routine and inimical to any innovations. He was as much attracted to the "strictest tyranny" as he was to anarchy. The petty bourgeois family was a "real nest of false sentimentality and hypocrisy." In art, the petty bourgeois also vacillated between banality and sentimentalism, prudery and adultery.

The stronghold of philistinism, in the land of Soviets, was the country-side, where the "idiocy of rural life" still reigned, and the *bolshaki* (peasant heads of household) perpetuated the tyrannical traditions of their forefathers. The retrograde nature of this element was clear to everybody. But, the intelligentsia, which worked in white-collar jobs was also part of the petty bourgeoisie, Reisner reminded. It was naïve to suppose that a worker, who had become an official, would be safe from philistinism. The philistine nature of the milieu would engulf and swallow a proletarian. A *déclassé* worker turned bureaucrat was an especially repulsive type, resembling the prodigal son of a merchant. Worst of all, even the workers were in danger of being contaminated by philistinism. This was partly due to the heritage of the past, when many factories had had a close connection with the countryside. Another cause for concern was the state factories, where the government had bribed part of the workers with privileges. Such places were nests of dissolute life, drunkenness, card-playing, and Orthodox religiosity. In such places, the people did not regard Soviet power their power. People were drawn to petty bourgeois ways: namely old patriarchal ways at home and petty bourgeois rebellion outside the home: vodka and hooliganism. The sad fact was that factory work as such did not guarantee the level of culture, required by the workers, especially by members of a triumphant proletariat.

As can be seen, Reisner did not resist the temptation to explain all the undesirable and repulsive elements in society as a result of petty bourgeois influences. What was strange in his analysis, however, was the infectious nature of this state of mind, which in theory should have been a class-bound phenomenon. There was, however, a remedy: cultural work. The toilers had to be given their share of culture. Every worker should become an inventor and an innovator, a "fighter for scientific truth and artistic organization."

Human personality itself had to be "organized." An individual was not yet a personality (*lichnost'*). This organizing work was the first task to be undertaken and the first real blow to philistinism and hooligan rebellion (*khuliganskii bunt*), which was organically connected with it.

Now, during NEP, the land of the Soviets was under a petty bourgeois siege and was constantly under bombardment by films and books from abroad. It was not yet possible to do something about petty proprietorship, but it was possible to attack the monotonous narrowness of life. In the land of the Soviets the proletariat was not alone in defending its interests, and its allies could be "magnificently organized against our philistinism."

On closer analysis, Reisner's article does not look very Marxist. Rather, it seems to mix the petty bourgeois with what Marx called the *lumpenproletariat*.[87] As regards the revolution, it tries to whitewash the proletariat, explaining anything that was destructive in it and any senseless violence or vandalism the work of the petty bourgeoisie. The most startling claim in the analysis was that it was not only the vast majority, the peasants, that still led an archaic petty bourgeois way of life, but that large sections of the master class of workers itself were contaminated.

In my view, the stress which Reisner laid on hooliganism deserves special attention. Hooliganism was clearly a major nuisance in that time and there is no denying that the workers played an active part in it. Before the revolution, hooliganism had been explained by intelligents like Merezhkovsky as having a philistine essence. Gorky had also seen this connection, but believed that that the hooligan was an Oedipus, who would murder his father. Now both father and son seemed to have become a problem for the new social order.

Reisner's attempts to explain hooliganism as "philistinism" and connect it to the power of the traditional family and religion were hardly very convincing. For Reisner, the concept of philistinism seems to be little more than a device, which makes it possible to separate the pure nucleus of the ideal working class from the ugly traits of contemporary reality. The obvious fact was, as the opinion surveillance files showed, that a considerable section of the workers did not give a damn for a revolution, which had nothing to offer them. It was unavoidable that they were interested in recreation as a counterpoise to their often monotonous and exhausting

work. Card-playing, vodka, sex, and hooliganism were not what Marxist intellectuals had expected from the workers. Their individualism and
hostility towards the high-brow language of official ideology were shocking for those, who had taken Gorky's *Mother* earnestly, or who, for some
other reason, had expected to see an emancipated new man in the representatives of the vanguard class, which was leading humanity to a more
elevated state of being.

Taras Kostrov. Fighting the perils of the humdrum life

Taras Kostrov[88], whose article was published in *Krasnaia nov'* at the end of
1927,[89] was a representative of the young generation and the editor of *Komsomolskaia Pravda*. He wanted to put the current discussion about culture
and philistinism into historical context. This discussion had not been initiated by journalists, he maintained, but by the masses. It had several phases. First, when NEP was introduced, the topic had been culture. For some
young activists the return of signs of a cultured life, such as a vestibule in a
club, a warm supper, or billiards had been "philistine." In fact these were
just parts of civilized life, which had no class essence as such. After some
years, the discussion had started anew. Now the *kul'turniki* were on the
offensive. They spoke in favor of civilized behavior and against rudeness
(*khamstvo*). Some, like Lev Sosnovsky, pointed to the west as a model.

Culture in the Soviet Union should not be bourgeois, Kostrov concluded, it would contain some of the ingredients of its predecessor, but the
totality would be different.

Philistinism (meshchanstvo) then, was the ideology of the petty bourgeoisie. The philistine by his nature could not be organically united in a
collective (*slitsia s kollektivom*). Ethical norms, rules of conduct, and prejudices he saw as fixed and eternal, Kostrov concluded, echoing the hard-lin-
ers of pre-Revolutionary discussions, which had hardly read at the time.

Philistinism was manifested in the relation between man and society.
It was just ridiculous to brand some things "philistine" as such, be it a tie,
a suit, or even a gramophone. But it was a different case, if somebody's attitude to a person was changed if he wore or did not wear a tie. The criteria
by which one should judge a person and whether he was a philistine or
not, were his attitudes towards a comrade, towards voluntary work (obshchestvennaia rabota), towards women, towards the family, and towards
society. There were Russian sayings, which had philistine content: "My
own shirt is closest to the body." "Work is no wolf; it will not flee into the
forest." "A hen is not a bird and a woman is not human." "Would it be
right to neglect one's family?" "Don't bring the quarrel out of the house."

In other words, Kostrov was also branding as philistine the normal traditional ways of life, and these proverbs were probably no less in use among the workers than among the peasants. Unlike many others, Kostrov did not think that the task was just a matter of raising the cultural standards of the people. Earlier, the lack of culture had been the main danger, now the main danger was the uncritical attitude towards the old bourgeois culture. The "fire" should be directed towards philistinism, which crawled into the sphere of the working youth. As examples from Komsomolskaia pravda showed, there was a demand for foreign popular culture. Moreover, in the cinemas foreign films were in a majority but even Soviet ones only sold by hinting at sexuality. Even the workers' clubs had gipsy romances in their repertoire. Sensationalism, sex, and violence was clearly also part of culture, though not of the real culture but of fake bourgeois civilization. The struggle against philistinism should be "waged on all fronts," for the development of real culture was impossible without it.

Kostrov also stressed the all-encompassing role of politics in the life of a new man. It was philistine, he maintained, to try to separate the private sphere from the public one. Attitude to the members of one's own family was not preferential on part of the non-philistine. All members of a collective were to get equal treatment. Even conflicts within the family were not private matters. At the time, this was a very radical approach, which paved the way for the creation of a totalitarian state.

As these representative examples show, the discussion about philistinism at the end of the NEP period was still rather peaceful in tone and had a somewhat academic nature. The frontal attack against the "petty bourgeois" began shortly thereafter, during the First Five-Year Plan with its collectivisation and "cultural revolution."

Gladkov's *Cement*. Fighting philistinism among the workers

The petty bourgeois philistine was, of course, also described in the literature of the 1920s. At the first congress of Soviet Writers in 1934 a couple of books were pointed out as models for socialist realism. One was F.B. Gladkov's *Cement*.[90] This novel, each edition of which was corrected by the author in order to take into account the changing trends,[91] was about restarting a cement plant somewhere in Southern Russia, whilst the class enemy was present both in the form of armed bandits in neighboring mountains and also in the form of foreign representatives from the capitalist world and émigrés arriving by ship. The hero is a demobilized red army soldier, who returns home after three years of fighting in the Civil War. The former factory makes a desolate sight. Production has stopped and the machines are ruined. The workers' village has been transformed into a stinking rural area, where goats and swine are herded. The psychology of the majority of the former workers has been transformed into some kind of amalgam of petty bourgeois greed and the idiocy of rural life. The very physiognomy of the workers has changed. They no longer think about industrial production, but just make cigarette lighters and sell them to the peasants and try to steal anything of value from the ruins of the factory. The nurses in the kindergarten are even worse, not to mention the soviet and party bureaucrats. Even the party—represented by the purge commission, makes grave mistakes. The unquestioned heroes of the book are proletarians, the former soldier Gleb Chumalov wand his wife Dasha. The *intelligent*, Sergei Zhidkii is also portrayed sympathetically despite the fact that he is the son of an *intelligent* and the brother of a white guard colonel. Gleb and There is nothing petty bourgeois about Gleb and Dasha. For certain reasons, they do not even have sex together, even though Gleb wants to very much. Their home is not a petty bourgeois one: the wife has put her daughter into the kindergarten and spends her evenings at the women's club and doing other social work. She pays a high price for this as her daughter dies, but there is no alternative for a party-minded woman like Dasha. The heroes succeed in restarting the factory, despite the resistance of bandits and bureaucrats, but a new enemy emerges. With the introduction of NEP, a petty bourgeois mentality awakens in the very ranks of the proletariat, and "market, cafés, shop windows, sweets, coziness, and alcohol" begin to distract the workers.

NEP is difficult to fathom even for the best of the proletarians. Some would like to use physical violence against the depravity that has settled in the Holy Land of socialism, which has been bought with proletarian blood.

The most zealous of them are then purged by the party commission, which seems to work mechanically and destroys the best representatives of the working class, and also solid fighters for the cause such as the intelligent Sergei Zhidkii. In the end, however, Sergei receives the thanks he deserves. After all, NEP is the party's policy and is the correct political line although it has also unleashed the petty bourgeoisie and is unpalatable to working-class instincts.

Gladkov's novel certainly dealt with topical issues. It pointed out that it was not just any workers, but the most conscious people among the workers and even the intellectuals that bore the torch of the working class. Of Gladkov's heroes, Gleb was almost totally free of philistinism, except for his sexual desire for Dasha which represented his lower, animal nature. It was not individual gain that drove Gleb forward. Real life, for this proletarian spirit, was the "song of the machines." As for Dasha, her ideological purity seems totally immaculate. Nothing could hinder her from becoming a more conscious person, neither her husband's craving for physical love, which apparently could have been degrading for her, because she was not yet willing to accept it, nor the starvation and the death of her daughter. The domestic hearth, the shrine of philistinism, had been completely extinguished, and it seemed that all concerned had gained from this even though the child had died. The reader might even get the impression that Gladkov wants to say, like Paul the apostle: "It is good for them if they abide even as I. But if they cannot contain, let them marry, for it is better to marry than to burn." Clearly, the single life or even celibacy in marriage was not meant for everybody, not even all the most conscious of workers. But it was not an inferior alternative.

All in all, the restarting of the factory, a phenomenon of the material world which seems to have reached some very deep ontological dimension, is the result of the conscious work of certain individuals. The masses as such are inert and do not have the proper consciousness until the creative processes of production are awakened. Gladkov's heroes are not really the proletariat, but two individuals: a man and a woman with iron will, new people who can drag the inert masses out of the abyss of petty bourgeois idiocy and into action. In this, he more or less, follows the tradition of hardliners of the old Russian intelligentsia, from Chernyshevsky to Nechaev, from Tkachev to Lenin.

The triumph of the will. Ostrovsky's Korchagin

Nikolai Ostrovsky's book *How the Steel Was Tempered*[92] acquired real cult status among Soviet youth. Its hero was not only the officially approved model of the Komsomol, but seems to have been a genuinely successful model for Soviet youth.

Like many other examples of this genre, the book is a kind of grass-roots history of a certain period and a certain generation. Here we have all the phases of the Civil War as it was experienced in a certain town in Ukraine. Their town was taken in turn by the German army, the Ukrainian nationalists, the Poles, the Makhnovites and several groups of bandits. There is the depravity of NEP and the heroism of reconstruction. Above all, this is a book about the iron will of its hero, Pavel Korchagin. A typical representative of the Bolshevik old guard, so the book tells, he develops from being an ignorant and unruly boy into a conscious Bolshevik whose character constantly develops, even as he loses his health and becomes physically weaker and weaker. Against all the odds, Pavel writes a book even though he has become almost a total invalid. His belief that he can accomplish this feat is strengthened by Stalin's words, "There are no fortresses, which the Bolsheviks cannot take."[93]

Pavel actually was a real hero, because the author was describing his own life. He also had about him something of "the new man" who had entered Russian literature with Chernyshevsky's Rakhmetov. Pavel was certainly no philistine. He fell in love with a petty bourgeois girl, but left her, unable to stand the cheap "individualism" of her clothes.[94] Pavel was physically brave and had killed several enemies both at the front and in his home town. He was unswerving ideologically and became a commissar of the Red Army. He hated philistinism in all its incarnations: the stupid games of youth, the dissolute fox-trot, bureaucracy, and the like. He unfailingly denounced all depravity in the party, using both the party machinery and his fists. Chekists were his best friends. But even he was not totally flawless: he had to confess that once, when shooting at bandits, he had killed one, but let two of them get away, because he had not been calm enough.[95]

Pavel Korchagin's personal life was exemplary. Together with some comrades, he founded a commune. He quit smoking and stopped swearing. His manners were simple, like those of his comrades. Marriages were confirmed with a minimum of formality, sometimes none at all. Pavel's own marriage had a higher goal: to make his wife a conscious communist. Their union would be "holy" until this goal had been achieved, thereafter his wife would be free of all liabilities.[96] Petty bourgeois spontaneity is represented both by *intelligenty* and by some workers. It is most obvious among the peasantry. Pavel succeeded in pacifying the furious inhabitants of two villages, who nearly killed each other arguing over boundaries. Pavel succeeded in resolving the dispute by using his superior rationality. But petty bourgeois psychology was contagious. Pavel's own brother, a worker, was living in a village, which had clearly had a negative effect on the purity of his proletarian instincts.[97] The book ends on an optimistic note: although the hero is almost dead and can barely move his right hand, he finishes writing his book and it is accepted by a publisher. Certainly, Ostrovsky's book has something of a Wild West story about it. The hero would have felt equally at home in James Oliver Curwood's or Zane Grey's books. His book was supposedly describing actual historical events and, more precisely, the heroic life of its author. The heroes, including Pavel, were, indeed, well-read in literature. The difference, however, was that while Pavel read about the deeds of the Garibaldians, the philistines read James Fennimore Cooper and detective stories.[98] Like Gladkov, Ostrovsky also continued the traditional mission of the Russian intelligentsia of heightening their readers' consciousness. In this case, by showing how heroic individuals could contribute to the realization of the historic mission of the working class.

Critics praised Ostrovsky, who was given the Order of Lenin in 1935.[99] One critic explained that the book symbolized the tremendous energies being emancipated by the new society. Its positive hero was real he was really quite like the author of the book himself. The author was a product of Soviet society, and he was not alone, there were thousands of them, wrote another.[100] The readers were carried away by the realism and truthfulness of the book and its hero, "the new man," wrote a third.[101] A reviewer in the journal *Znamia* said that the book showed the struggle to create a new society. Only here this kind of book could be realistic. Mirabile dictu, there was not a trace of asceticism or sentimentalism in it, the critic asserted. Here, romantics had turned into a force of tremendous real action.[102]

Paradoxically, Ostrovsky's hero (and indeed, Ostrovsky) was able to be happy even though he was, apparently, in a physically hopeless state, whereas, in Pushkin's time, even the physically healthy and materially well-to-do geniuses were sometimes desperate. The novelty was due to the new kind of community that now existed between people, observed the novelist Andrei Platonov in the somber days of late 1937.[103]

Sex, marriage, and the family as citadels of philistinism

Quite a lot has been written about the Bolsheviks' attitude towards sex. The findings have been conflicting. The traditional view, one shared by contemporaries of the time, was that the Bolsheviks liberated sex. Soviet Russia, in its early years, became a kind of Mecca for all kinds of cranks: there was even a movement for overcoming the petty-bourgeoisie's shame of nudity, whose members travelled in Moscow's trams without any clothes.[104] Free abortion, of course, was a radical novelty. The institution of a simple registration procedure instead of a more formal marriage ceremony symbolically made sexual relationships more rational and a matter of private agreement. This was a far cry from the old institution of marriage, which had been sacralized and which was a cardinal element of the bourgeois society.

It has been pointed out that the famous "theory of a glass of water," which has been attributed to Alexandra Kollontai, and which claimed that having sex is no more complicated an affair than drinking a glass of water, in fact hardly existed at all. Bolsheviks were sexual radicals in theory, but their practices were hardly as radical as some of their theories.[105]

Studying the sexual discourse of the Bolsheviks, Eric Naiman discovered that in fact the dominant ideal was not sexual license, but abstinence.[106] This may seem contradictory, but is understandable if we take into account that sex, like anything else of a personal nature, was to be subordinated to the common cause. This naturally implied that sex would be deprived of its mystical qualities. It was not a sin as such, because there was no sin, but it could become a sin if it separated the individual from his collective, class, or their party. Sex was a matter of pleasure, but the pursuit of pleasure for its own sake was petty-bourgeois poshlost. Romantic love, traditionally depicted as the greatest force in the world, was philistinism par excellence. For the Bolshevik, pleasure was always a matter of rational choice, not passion. Passions were saved for the political sphere. Gypsy romances and the foxtrot were of no interest to a true proletarian. A representative of the opposite sex was, to a communist, a comrade, who was entitled to a comradely attitude.[107]

This general ethos for demystifying sex was not without its share of problems. Alexandra Kollontai, with her idea of the "winged Eros" came dangerously close to making sex an end in itself. Kollontai praised the commune and cursed the family, which kept both parents and the children in petty-bourgeois captivity. For her, full-fledged sex was what any human being deserved.[108] Her ideas were sound, from the Bolshevik point of view, except that too great a stress on the importance of sex and love would obviously make the whole thing petty-bourgeois.

The once notorious idea that the Bolsheviks had "socialized" women seems to have arisen from provocative false accusations, which the Bolsheviks had themselves made about the anarchists in 1918. According to a booklet, which the Bolsheviks had distributed, the anarchists had on various occasions proclaimed that "private property in women" had been liquidated. According to this falsification, women would have been obliged to register in "houses of free love," where every man of a certain age would have had the right to choose a partner. The fruits of this rationally arranged love would be reared by society in children's homes.[109] This rather funny piece of disinformation was sexy enough to become one of the best-known pieces of news, from Russia, in the West. Not unnaturally, the story was somewhat modified and, in the Western press, the Bolsheviks assumed the role of the anarchists, who had "socialized women."[110]

In any event, Bolshevism was also a radical creed also in matters sexual. Its goals included the disappearance of the family, which was believed to be an element of bourgeois society and a product of capitalist relations of production. This idea had already been presented in the "Communist manifesto" of Marx and Engels in 1848. Later it was developed by Engels and it was generally believed to be one of the central tenets of the Bolshevik creed as it related to the future, under full communism.[111] According to Marxist (or "Engelsist") theory, private families were part of the bourgeois social system, units of small production and distribution, and almost as idiotic as the peasant household.

The opposite of the bourgeois family, then, was the commune. Communal living in the proper sense of the word became not very common in the early years of Bolshevik power. True, more and more people were forced to live in *kommunalki*, which provided little privacy for their inhabitants. A *kommunalka*, then, was not a commune at all. It did not have a system for the centralized production of meals or for rearing children. The only things that people shared in common were the kitchen and the toilet. In practice, this did not help bring about mutual care and brotherly love, quite the opposite, everybody assiduously tried to defend their own rights and keep their property away from the others.[112]

There were also genuine communes, some in the countryside and some in the towns. These were mostly founded by intellectuals and laughed at by the neighboring peasants. It seems to be clear that people in communes believed they were living according to the ideals of the society. The communes did not pay according to the amount of work, but according to the number of "eaters" *(edoki)* or "according to the needs" of the members. The beginning of NEP was a severe blow to the communes, and the number of communes fell from 3040 in 1921 to no more than 1448 in 1922 . The communards were mostly young and it seems that adults, especially women with children, found it difficult to adapt to communal life.[113]

In the imagination of the peasants, the commune meant a "common blanket," perhaps of huge proportions, in order to house all the members of the commune.[114] For most peasants, however, the commune was a frightening prospect for quite realistic reasons.

Leading Bolsheviks were deadly serious about the liquidation of the family under socialism. P.M. Kerzhentsev, writing in 1921, was happy to foresee the liquidation of the bourgeois home, which was impregnated with individualist and proprietary tendencies. As he saw it, the family was now vanishing and this was a necessity caused by economic forces. Some progress had already been made: open clubs replaced the former closed drawing-rooms and children were reared in the healthy atmosphere of the school, not at home. A feeling of comradeship *(chuvstvo tovarishchestva)* was replacing reverence for parents, and egoism and individualism were giving way to collectivism.[115]

In hindsight it seems that what Kerzhentsev praised, was hardly a specifically socialist novelty, but a common trend for any industrial society. Trotsky was also optimistic. In 1923 he wrote that the old family was already vanishing and that there would be a new one, where the functions of the family would be given to social institutions: a communal laundry would wash the linen and a good communal restaurant would prepare the food. The children would be taught by good pedagogues. All this would create a true equality of the spouses: they would be drawn together only by mutual attraction (*vzaimnym vlecheniem*). And, therefore, the marriage would also be stable.

What was needed for this future ideal state was, first, the cultural education of the working class and, second, its material enrichment. In the present situation, however, the process of liquidating the old family should be begun. There was a way out of the dead end of the family: exemplary dormitories (communes) should be founded, as the Commissar of Health, Nikolai Semashko had also proposed, and the needs of the new type of marriage should be kept in mind when new houses were planned. In Trotsky's opinion, the socialist way of life could only be realized on a small scale for now, because of the material and mental underdevelopment of society. As a rule, for now, the communal kitchens would be worse than private ones and the linen in the communal laundries would be stolen.[116]

Thus, the Bolsheviks were entirely serious about the necessity of liquidating such crucial elements of bourgeois society as the petty bourgeois family and philistine sex. In the NEP years, however, even the most radical Bolshevik had to recognize that, for the time being, communes were possible only for a restricted number of enthusiasts. Nevertheless, the building of a real socialist society was the raison d'être of the whole Soviet system. Petty bourgeois elements were, for the moment, a necessary evil. How long, nobody could say. Nor could anyone say what would actually happen to petty bourgeois institutions and the petty bourgeoisie when socialism arrived. Marx and Engels were of little help and Lenin had ended his analysis with a simplistic slogan about raising the cultural level of the people.

6
The Cultural Revolution

The class war

By the winter of 1927-28 the policies of NEP were in crisis. The peasants were refusing to sell their grain to the government at the prices offered by the state. The party hardliners, headed by Stalin, resorted to violence. "The Urals-Siberian method", which Stalin praised, meant confiscating the peasants' grain at gunpoint. At the same time the first five-year plan was being drawn up. It was launched in October 1928.

Stalin's concept of class war was extremely radical and hazardous. It was inevitable that he would also have to fight considerable opposition from within the party. Stalin, who always spoke in the name of the "general line" of the party, launched a massive campaign against the "right deviation," whose representatives included Bukharin and Rykov and, on the cultural front, Lunacharsky.

This "Great Turn" (*velikii perelom*), which meant a return to the methods of the Civil war, was quite obviously risky. A number of explanations have been suggested as to why Stalin adopted this new campaign. This economic *cul de sac* could have been avoided of course by simply returning to normal market mechanisms such as offering the peasants a higher price for their grain. However, as a dogmatic Bolshevik, Stalin could not use this option.[1] It has been said that for most of us it is possible to choose between a cheese sandwich and a ham sandwich. For an orthodox rabbi, however, there is no choice. Similarly, Stalin thought there was no choice. Sheila Fitzpatrick has pointed out that there was discontent, amongst proletarian activists, with the realities of NEP. In other words, there was grassroots support for radical policies, which Stalin decided to exploit by resorting once again to a policy which promoted class-struggle. Vladimir Brovkin, referring to the results of secret opinion surveillance, comes to the conclusion that there was no support "from below," and that if anything, activist opinion was against the Bolsheviks. Bolshevik power, and especially the control of the centre over the periphery, was being challenged. In this situation Stalin decided to attack. In Brovkin's words "It was an admission of failure to generate voluntary social support. It was a new war on society to preserve dictatorship. It was a matter of constructing a centralized state, to be represented as "constructing socialism."[2]

The turn to the left of the Bolshevik party coincided with the beginning of the great depression in the west. Not unnaturally, Stalin connected these international events with domestic developments. An extremely radical policy of "class against class" was unleashed not just in the Soviet Union, but in the rest of the world. The Komintern, supported by Stalin, concentrated its fire on the "right deviation" in national parties, and particularly against the social democrats, who were denounced as   fascists and called, "social fascists" accordingly.[3] The pacifism of the "petty bourgeois" social democrats was, for Stalin, an organic part of the preparations for a new war. As for international politics, 1928 seemed to be a year of mutual goodwill and détente, symbolized by the Kellogg-Briand pact, which outlawed war as a means of international politics. Stalin, on the other hand, was already sure that war was not far off. It appears that Stalin thought that war would break out between England and the USA.[4]

Bukharin, who like many others, was appalled by Stalin's ruthless domestic policy, could nevertheless support Stalin's slogan about the social democrats being the main enemy on the international stage. In 1929 Stalin attempted to show that even this was not sufficient. Rather it was essential to understand that it was not the social democrats as such, but specifically the social democrats of the left that were the most dangerous enemy. He was at pains to show that Bukharin did not understand this. It is possible that this piece of scholastics was necessary simply in order to separate the representatives of the "general line" from the rightist heresy.[5]

The launching of a class-war against the old intelligentsia should be understood within the framework of this general policy. The first five-year plan and the collectivization of agriculture turned the Soviet Union into a society akin to a huge anthill with masses of people on the move, a "quicksand society."[6] The peasants were being driven into exile and into the swelling towns and rising new plants and factories. The violent nature of this social engineering should not be forgotten or understated. Not only did millions of people die of hunger in the Ukraine and Kazakhstan, but millions of kulaks with their families were deported to remote mines and camps. The violent nature of the state's intervention also made the peoples' daily life drab and austere: the churches were closed, priests were deported and the church bells were confiscated. The peasants' grain was seized and the belongings of kulak families were looted. Anybody trying to resist would be arrested or even shot on the spot. People were starving not just in the countryside, but in the towns as well, where the distribution network, which had been created during NEP now collapsed, as the "exploiting classes" — including the petty dealers and *lavochniki* — were liquidated in the towns and the countryside. Soviet everyday life during 1928-32 was a spectacle of incredible scarcity with immense queues together with bureaucratic violence, and violations of the individual's basic rights, the immunity of his home and his religious convictions.[7]

It was also a time of immeasurable social upheaval. Sheila Fitzpatrick has pointed out that an essential feature of this period was the upward social mobility of a remarkable cohort of mostly young people, the *vydvizhentsy*, who were taken from the workbench and moved into higher education and administrative jobs, which had multiplied after the state had taken over the administration of both distribution and small-scale production, which had largely been in private hands during NEP.[8]

The academic world, along with the countryside, had survived as a non-communist sector in the Soviet Union. On the eve of the XIII party Congress of the VKP, there had been no more than 3 percent of communists among the scientific workers (*nauchnye sotrudniki*) of the Soviet Union.[9] It was also true that many of the specialists had obtained their educational qualifications before the revolution. In 1929 there were 90, 000 specialists with higher education of which 32, 000 had graduated before the revolution.[10] The intelligentsia still clearly consisted of "class-alien" elements.

During collectivization the "petty bourgeois" groups in the towns were also attacked. The Shakhty affair began in the spring of 1928. It was announced that a group of engineers had established an organization for sabotage in the coal mining industry, led and financed by western organizations and by the former proprietors of the mines who were now living abroad. During the show trial the accused confessed to having pursued this subversive activity, namely the destruction of machines and infrastructure, for five years. This activity was portrayed as "economic intervention" against the Soviet state.[11]

Stalin drew several conclusions from the case. Firstly, that the Bolsheviks had chosen their economic cadres badly (Lenin had said that the choice of cadres was one of the fundamental issues in building socialism). It was no longer necessary to choose bourgeois specialists, as there were already communist cadres available. And it was possible to school new cadres. Stalin maintained that it was not true that communists from the workbench could not learn to understand chemical formulas and technical skills; indeed he argued that there were no fortresses, which communists could not take. Secondly, specialists should be schooled in close contact with practice. Thirdly, the workers *en masse* should be drawn into the administration of industry.[12]

Not unnaturally, Stalin was looking for allies among the young generation. The radicalism of his policies appalled mature minds but sparked enthusiasm in many young people. Another source of support was found among the workers, with tens of thousands being sent into the countryside to implement the party's policies.[13]

At the VIII congress of the Leninist Komsomol in May 1928 Stalin referred to the Shakhty affair and demanded that young communists should be more socially active: to fight bureaucracy "mercilessly" and to criticize shortcomings in Soviet practices "from below". The young should also conquer science.

Stalin argued that "Young Bolshevik specialists must be developed in all branches of knowledge; you must study, study and study most efficiently… What we need now, comrades, is a mass assault by the revolutionary youth to conquer science" and he was received with "tumultuous applause, shouts of 'hurrah!' and 'bravo!'" The whole audience stood up.[14]

This attack signaled the beginning of major policies of social engineering. During the following years over 100, 000 workers from the factories and the party apparat were sent to higher schools, especially higher technical schools. Moreover, students with a proletarian background were favored in the admissions process even more than before. As Sheila Fitzpatrick has observed this was an anti-intelligentsia and pro-worker policy.[15] The class-struggle ethos was reflected in society in many ways. Fitzpatrick states that as many as 666, 000 workers left the factories for white-collar employment or full-time study in 1930-33.[16] This was in effect a revolution in the social composition of higher education. In 1931 over 120, 000 university students were classified as workers whereas in 1928 the figure had been a mere 40, 000.[17]

This however provides only a partial insight as to the scale of the social changes taking place. The proletarian ethos was now honored everywhere. One of the major campaigns was the purging of the Soviet apparatus. The victims were officially labeled as "bureaucrats and social aliens," which to a large extent meant members of the old intelligentsia (educated classes). The purges were partly conducted in response to instructions from above, and partly spontaneous as a result of a general anti-bourgeois, or rather anti-intelligent zeal, which had penetrated every part of society. Secondary schools were purged as well as the professions, where extremely radical and often "hare-brained" ideas marched triumphantly forwards.[18]

It was maintained that the five-year plan and collectivization were necessary for the building of a new social system—socialism. It was more than natural if the activists were zealously preparing for the future socialist reality. Egalitarianism had always been one of the central tenets of socialism and it was unavoidable that the activists strove for its realization in everyday life. The commune, where all members were equal, materially and "morally" was the classic ideal of socialism and this was now beginning to be realized on a large scale in Soviet industrial centers. Communes became a mass phenomenon in the countryside, but this did not happen because of the enthusiasm of the peasants, but because of the radicalism of their oppressors. Collectivization was beginning to be synonymous with "going to the commune," and the party leadership encouraged the founding of communes.[19] In the professions those schools of thought, which foresaw a "withering away" of bourgeois institutions, were now in favor. The Pashukanis' school in jurisprudence advocated a "withering away" of law and Shulgin's disciples awaited the withering away of schools. In architecture, the antiurbanists had a grateful audience for their ideas of liquidating the great cities whilst economists, architects and other visionaries saw the family withering away in the near future as a result of new kinds of houses (socialist towns) and a rational division of labor between man, woman and society.[20]

With all its "proletarian" pathos the Cultural Revolution did not glorify the workers as they actually were in reality. A campaign was launched to transform the proletarians as they were in reality into their idealized counterparts. One of the worst vices was alcohol. Prohibition was not introduced, but it was envisaged that the use of alcohol would fall sharply in the near future and soon be forgotten, as the new socialist society was being built.[21] For the present, however, much remained to be done.[22]

The labour unions began issuing a new journal *Kul'turnaia revoliutsiia*, where the current proletarian way of life was severely criticized: the cultural improvement of the masses was possible only if vodka, the church, playing cards and so forth were replaced by cultural pastimes and organized leisure. In particular more art, sport and radio were needed.[23]

The program of another new journal, *Revoliutsiia i kul'tura* was devoted to bringing the proletarian revolution to all fields of life. It declared, without embarrassment, that a new people had to be created.[24] According to A. Deborin the working masses had created a new society, but they themselves were still standing in the filth of the old society.[25] Nikolai Bukharin put it bluntly that the task was to overcome one's own nature and that this would require constant attention. A petty bourgeois nature was constantly at work even amongst the proletariat.[26] P. Kerzhentsev stressed that forging a new culture of work was now the first task. This meant maximum efficiency, working accurately without slovenliness and without falling asleep! Rational and civilized forms of rest and recreation were organically connected with this new culture of work.[27]

Conditions for the achievement of these ideals were however not very promising during the first five-year plan. One of the problems was the sacrosanct communist ethos of equality.

The "cultural revolution" of 1928-31 has been defined by Sheila Fitzpatrick as a political confrontation between "proletarian" communists on the one hand and a "bourgeois" intelligentsia on the other.[28]

In this too the main method was the mobilization of the masses against the ubiquitous enemy, whose main bases were abroad, but which had its agents (both in the direct and indirect, "objective" sense) in the land of the Soviets as well. As regards the promotion (*vydvizhenie*) of the "proletarians," this was a policy, which Lenin had already sketched out in his article "Can the Bolsheviks Hold Political Power" and it had subsequently been tried out on a large scale during the civil war. Stalin was now in effect returning to Lenin's idea. Social engineering was a form of looting and presupposed the taking of spoils, which could then be handed over to the militants. In the case of the struggle against the old specialists and other intelligents, there were the literally warm and comfortable places in the apparat and management, which could be taken over by the activists. In the countryside the property of the kulaks, could be distributed to the poorest peasants. As early as 1928 whilst seizing the peasants' grain with the "Urals-Siberian method," Stalin made sure that the have-nots would have a stake in supporting the state's policies. It was decreed that 25% of the confiscated grain was to be given, on advantageous terms, to the poorest peasants in every village.[29]

The "proletarian" spirit extended to all walks of life. It was also felt in industry, including the mines. In former times, the foremen had had great authority among and over the workers. The latter had approached them in a subservient manner, cap in hand. Now, everything had changed. As the foreman did not have power over the workers, they just ignored him. Even worse, nobody wanted to become a foreman, as all the workers regarded him as "the spittoon." Not surprisingly discipline in the mines did not improve as a result of such attitudes.[30] The representatives of the "master class" also showed their superiority towards the physicians, who rarely dared to refuse signing a request for sick-leave.[31]

To what extent was the class war in culture spontaneous? Although the struggle was initiated by the party elite, it is evident that this was more a case of unleashing instigating rather than of administrative fiat. The party-state used its bureaucratic apparatus for the implementation of the proclaimed goals of the Cultural Revolution (including the struggle against the bureaucracy), but this was just part of the process. Ever since the beginning of NEP, and indeed earlier, there had been "proletarian" and anti-intellectual (or anti-intelligent) elements at every level of society. When the state chose to exploit these elements, it couldn't really control what these zealous people, who were often totally devoid of common sense, accomplished in practice.

The coming together of several factors, including: the gigantic social and geographic mobility; the accelerated "class-struggle;" the fearful atmosphere of a possible war (which was assiduously fanned in the press); the proclamation of a quasi-military emergency; the exaggerated promises of economic miracles; the near chaos which crippled distribution and production, and the starvation and violence all combined to create a unique atmosphere of extremism, where almost any kind of radicalism was favored and anything that had its roots in the "old", pre-revolutionary world, was suspect.[32]

The Shakhty trial was followed by the Promparty trial in 1930 and by the "Plot of the Second International" and the "Peasants' Party of Labor" affair soon thereafter. All these show trials carried the same message: the capitalist world was concentrating all its efforts in order to prevent the building of the socialist society at almost any price. For the present, this intervention was of an economic nature, but it was argued that a military intervention prepared by France and assisted by Poland and other western neighbors, was imminent.[33] The struggle for collectivization and the fulfilling of the first five-year plan was accordingly, declared to be a military duty and any attempt to sabotage it constituted high treason. The gravest of punishments were demanded for the traitors by the common people –and doubtless also by those fellow- intellectuals, who wanted to distance themselves from the infamous caste of the old intelligentsia.[34]

An abrupt retreat

It is commonly held that the Cultural Revolution came to an end in 1931.[35] This was heralded in several of Stalin's speeches, where he rehabilitated the old intelligentsia and condemned some of the central tenets of the current policies, including egalitarianism and the lack of power of managers.[36] For many people, this amounted to a condemnation of important elements of the socialist credo in general and it is hard to disagree with them on this. The party's program, issued in 1919, which proclaimed an egalitarian society, the annihilation of hierarchies, a moneyless economy and workers' power at every level of society[37], was a far cry from Stalin's theses of 1931, which summed up the experience of the party during these three years of radical policies.

As early as March 1930 Stalin in his famous letter "Dizziness from Success" had condemned those agricultural communes (the creation of which he himself had ordered), which had levelled the income of its members and abolished private property altogether. Instead, Stalin explained, the artel, which left the peasant a sizable private economy with a plot of land, a cow and some poultry, was the right solution.[38] Stalin criticized the founding of communes on the grounds that a commune represented a more developed form of the kolkhoz, which would be built only after the problems of grain procurement had been solved. Leaping too far ahead he argued was dangerous, and moreover this kind of policy could be "congenial and useful only for our sworn enemies."[39]

One may recall Lenin's analogous reaction to excessive revolutionary zeal. Later on, this idea of the equivalence of left and right opportunism was formally proclaimed in official Soviet ideological texts. The notorious *Short Course* of 1938 declared that the policy of establishing communes had in fact been initiated by the kulaks and their henchmen.[40]

In his speech "About the Tasks of Managers," which Stalin delivered on February 4th 1931 at the First All-Union Conference of Managers of Industry, he was full of optimism as regards the five-year plan and declared that it would be fulfilled in three years.

The slowing of the tempo was death, he proclaimed in the famous passage, where he prophesied a war within ten years.[41] At another managers' meeting on June 23 the same year Stalin was far more critical. There were whole areas of production, he said, where growth had slowed down, including the vital ferrous metallurgical and coal mining sectors. There were six conditions for improving the situation. First, the recruitment of the work force had to be conducted in a systematic manner, by making agreements with the kolkhozes. Second, the constant ebb and flow of the work force had to be stopped by putting an end to leveling and by arranging salaries correctly. On this point Stalin was very explicit and harsh: anyone, giving equal pay to both the qualified and the unqualified worker, was in effect forsaking Marxism and Leninism. Of course the worker had to be given the prospect of advancement and promotion. If this was not done, it was an offence which went contrary to the interests of socialist industry. Third, the irresponsibility of individuals, which was flourishing, had to be liquidated. Fourth, like all dominating classes in history, the working class also had to create it own intelligentsia, a "productive-technical intelligentsia," which would be able to defend the interests of the working class in production as the interests of the dominating class." The process of creating this intelligentsia was already in full swing, and the representatives of the new intelligentsia who were already available should be promoted into responsible positions more vigorously than was now the case. Fifth, there were signs of a change as regards the attitudes of the old technical intelligentsia. A couple of years ago, Stalin argued, referring to the Shakhty affair, the leading part of the old technical intelligentsia had been "contaminated with the pest of subversion." Soviet power had now repressed the active wreckers and attracted the loyal ones into cooperation. The situation had now changed.

The economic catastrophe and foreign intervention, which the specialists had expected, had not materialized, instead, the policies and accomplishments of Soviet power were indisputable. As a result, a significant contingent of the old specialists, who had been sympathetic to the wreckers, had now changed their attitude. A small number of active wreckers remained, but they were isolated and had been forced deep underground. Consequently Soviet power now had to change its attitude towards the old specialists, the engineers and technicians, and give them as much attention as possible and draw them into work more boldly than before. Sixth, the principle of profitability had to be established and agglomeration within industry should be increased.[42]

With this, a new note was struck. Over the next few years Stalin several times emphasized his enmity towards egalitarianism. In his interview with the German writer Emil Ludwig, Stalin dismissed leveling as the ideal of a primitive peasant "communism."[43] The final anathema to leveling was given at the XVII party congress in January 1934.[44]

Returning to the question of the agricultural commune, which he had condemned –with some reservations- as early as 1930, Stalin described the situation in a commune, where everything, including the individual kitchen garden and poultry, had been socialized. He argued that this meant that in a commune its members' "vital personal interests had not been given due attention and thus they had not been united with the interests of society, rather, they had been suffocated in the name of petty-bourgeois leveling."[45]

This did not mean that the commune was no longer the "highest level of the kolkhoz movement" only that it was a matter for the future and would then arise on a basis of affluence. When would this happen? "Of course, not soon" said Stalin answering his own question, adding that it would be "criminal" to try to artificially accelerate the process of transforming the artel into a commune.

All this was clear indeed almost elementary, Stalin argued, but he acknowledged that a certain group of party members (but not the gensek himself) had abandoned some of the tenets of socialism. The gensek chose to make an authoritative statement on this point. For Marxism, Stalin argued, equality did not mean the leveling of personal needs and living conditions, but rather the liquidation of classes. The tastes and needs of different people could never be equal, and this would not happen either in socialism or in communism. If anyone thought that socialism presupposed a levelling of the tastes, needs and personal conditions of life, or that according to Marxism everybody would have to wear uniform costumes and eat the same food in equal portions, this would be "stupidity and a blasphemy of Marxism." It was time to understand, said Stalin, that "Marxism is an enemy of equalization." There was no denying, that there had, quite lately, been another approach: there had been the drive to found communes and some people had even tried to found communes in industry, where both qualified and unqualified workers had to give up their salary to the common pool, where it was then divided into equal shares.[46]

After all, said Stalin for every Leninist, it was clear that "equalization in the sphere of requirements and personal, everyday life is reactionary, petty bourgeois absurdity."[47]

The importance of this revolution of values is hard to overstate. "Going to the commune" had been equal to supporting the Bolsheviks ever since the October revolution. Now it meant resistance to and sabotage of the party.

On balance, then, leveling had now become petty bourgeois, whereas keeping your own cow and looking after one's own individual interests had evidently ceased to be so. Now, as was the case with Lenin earlier, being petty bourgeois was synonymous with not agreeing with the party line.

Did Stalin really mean that the peasants' individualistic proprietary instincts had ceased to be petty bourgeois, provided they were kept within strictly limited material parameters as was the case in the kolkhozes?

Quite clearly he did not. The peasants were not granted equal status with the workers. Their relation to the means of production remained different as long as they still had their private plots and their share of the kolkhoz as a productive unit. This fundamental inferiority of the peasants as a class survived the introduction of the socialist society in Soviet society in 1936 and the history of the Soviet Union until perestroika may in part be seen as the story of trying to overcome the kolkhozniks' ideological inferiority and to abolish the differences between them and the urban working class.

The élan of the "cultural revolution" ebbed after 1931. Not only were the old specialists brought back into favor, but egalitarian trends were also reversed. Soon after the first five-year plan, ideological changes affected all forms of culture, from high art to the status of the country teacher, from workers' lifestyles to the contents of history textbooks. As regards the intellectuals, it was notable that Stalin himself adopted the term "intelligentsia," which had been pejorative, possibly even more pejorative than the term "bourgeois specialists." On the contrary, he said, now even the working class had its own intelligentsia, as had been the case for all ruling classes in history.[48]

In the professions, many of the pre-cultural revolution institutions were reinstated. The militant RAPP and other "proletarian" organizations were liquidated in 1932 and the old non-party "masters," who had been widely attacked, were once more given the status of authority in arts and literature. The "bourgeois" academics were given back their jobs and radical currents in several disciplines, for example history, fell from grace. Analyzing the net effect of the Cultural Revolution for the parties concerned, Sheila Fitzpatrick considers that it was the very same communist intellectuals, who had been the driving force of the class-struggle, who now were the main victims. In the aftermath of the cultural revolution they were largely branded as left (or right) deviationists, or left to work amongst the hostile but now rehabilitated old specialists and *vydvizhentsy*, who had a totally different life experience and outlook. The old intelligentsia fared better. Mostly they were rehabilitated and even received some kind of compensation. From now on, Fitzpatrick claims, they were no longer attacked within the professions or harassed on the grounds of social origin. This was an improvement in comparison not only with the Cultural Revolution period, but even with NEP.[49]

The *tertium gaudens* were the *vydvizhentsy*, which can also be regarded as the "Brezhnev generation." They have sometimes been described as a very different contingent as compared with the communist intelligentsia, which had been formed under NEP.

They were practical-minded and highly motivated, with a no-nonsense mentality[50] and they also had a developing taste for the niceties of life, as the end of the 1930s would prove. The new bosses, *nachalstvo*, who were part of this new intelligentsia received quasi-police powers in the work place and it has been claimed that rudeness towards their inferiors became one of their main outstanding virtues![51] The principle that their salary could not exceed that of a qualified worker (*partmaksimum*) was quietly abandoned in 1932, which opened new vistas for those with an enterprising spirit.[52]

The "Masters of Culture." The fates of the creative intelligentsia

During the tumultuous years of the "cultural revolution" the non-party intelligents lost their former patrons in the organs of the state and the party. Bukharin lost his position and his political line was proclaimed to be the main target for attack. Lunacharsky had to give up his chair in the People's Commissariat of Enlightenment to the barely literate apparachik Bubnov and even Voronsky, the editor of the fellow-travelers haven, the *Krasnaia nov'*, fell from grace.

All this alarmed Maxim Gorky, whose attitude to Stalin's revolution had by now become quite positive on other issues and who was about to return permanently to the Soviet Union. The zealots could not afford to neglect Gorky, who enjoyed the special protection of Stalin. Gorky tried to reconcile these enemies, but an end to the mutual struggle was not accomplished until 1932, when RAPP was liquidated by a resolution of the CC.[53] In 1928-32 the situation remained dire: the leftist zealots attacked the fellow-travelers as best they could. The latter were now deprived of their institutional protection and were at the mercy of the party leaders, who every now and then intervened to help some of the harassed "masters of culture", whom they considered worth helping.

Under pressure from the zealots, who were striving for a total unification under their command, many associations were forced to capitulate. The Serapion Brothers was dissipated in 1929.[54] The Pereval discontinued its existence, whilst the FOSP and many other groups were conquered.[55] The RAPP's slogan was: ally or enemy. The idea of fellow-traveling was never recognized by these zealots, who concentrated their fire on the remnants of the petty bourgeoisie still living in the land of the Soviets.[56]

The situation in other fields of culture, fine arts and science was similar during the "Cultural revolution".

The ethos of the Cultural Revolution also let loose the RAPPists against the fellow-travelers and also the "masters", who pushed for leadership independently of and outside the all-important proletarian class-factor. The fate of Vladimir Mayakovsky may serve as an illustration of the mood of the times. In the new climate this former futurist and member of the LEF/REF became a target for the "class-liners". Not only the zealots of the RAPP attacked Mayakovsky, but now even *Krasnaia nov'* became critical. Mayakovsky recanted and in February 1930 he too became a member of the RAPP and exhorted other members of the REF to join the association. He said that he had never had any differences of opinion with the general line of the party, which the RAPP professed to be guarding. The RAPP, however, was not satisfied. Mayakovsky was accused of being "a clandestine fellow-traveler". He was left isolated in his new surroundings. Paradoxically Mayakovsky, who had always fought philistinism as his chief enemy, was now accused of being –a philistine (*meshchanin*).[57]

The "anti-bourgeois" pressure concentrated against this champion of anti-bourgeois art was more than Mayakovsky could bear.

As has been said above, the pathos of culture was now "proletarian." Any kind of rapprochement between the spheres of art and material production was popular. The primacy of the material world and the proletarian creators of new material values were stressed in every way. Writers were sometimes called "workers of the printed word," who should get rid of the old methods of "cottage industry" (*kustarnichestvo*) and have their own production plans. Whilst earlier it had been the custom for writers to go to the proletarians in order to bring them the treasures of culture, as had been the case with the pre-Revolutionary intelligentsia, now the tables were turned. It was the factories, which were being asked to exercise patronage (*shefstvo*) over the writers.[58]

It followed quite logically from this that the proletarian heroes of the era, the shock-workers (*udarniki*) should become writers themselves and show the petty bourgeois intelligents the right way to work. After all, the creation of this new society was the historic mission of the proletariat. The "harbingers of a new literature, which would propel the country into ever greater production yields"[59] were soon multiplied into an army. Unfortunately, quantity was no substitute for quality. RAPP's membership rose from 1500 to 10, 000, 80 per cent of which were shock-workers. Evidently the hope was that the sheer weight of the new proletarian element would revolutionize the whole literary stage—in fact it merely drained the resources, available for paying professional writers. The crisis, which arose, was described, using the newly popularized production terminology, as a "breakdown" in the State Publishing House, caused by too many faulty literary products (*brak*), which could not find consumers. As a result of the shock-worker campaign, five million rubles had been paid to writers, whose manuscripts were unpublishable. As a large quantity of paper had been diverted to such ends there was not enough for the regular mass publications and the price of books had to rise by 40 per cent.[60]

Stalin never seems to have been a wholehearted supporter of "proletarian" literature. When the pressure against the fellow-travelers was at its most intense, he made a gesture, which though unofficial, was conspicuous enough to have a huge effect on his popularity amongst the intellectuals.

Mikhail Bulgakov, whose working conditions had become untenable, asked for permission to move abroad. His letter reached Stalin, who rang him up on the telephone. This unheard of gesture on the part of the vozhd may have had something to do with the fact that Gorky also liked Bulgakov's work. Gorky might have influenced Stalin's opinion about him.[61] Instead of granting Bulgakov permission to emigrate, Stalin insisted that he was needed in the Soviet Union and promised to help him in practical matters.[62] Stalin also visited the MKhAT several times to see Bulgakov's plays.

Gorky and the Stalinist revolution

Maxim Gorky's return to Russia, now transformed into the Soviet Union, coincided with the turmoil and horrors of collectivization. Stalin personally spared no energy in persuading Gorky to return to his homeland. He corresponded with the master and sent Soviet writers and a doctor to Italy to prepare for his home-coming.[63]

Gorky seemed to be flattered by the attention paid by the old comrade. Apparently he genuinely valued the collectivization of the peasantry. As he wrote to Stalin:

> since the party so energetically has begun to put the countryside onto the rails of collectivism, the social revolution has acquired a truly socialist character. This is almost a geological revolution and it is more, incomparably more, and more profound than anything that has hitherto been done by the party..."[64]

Gorky was also carried away by the show trials of the Prompartia, the Peasants' Party of Labor and the Plot of the II International and even began to write a play on this theme.[65]

Gorky gave his voice to serve Stalin's revolution with gusto and the party answered in kind: the 40-year jubilee of Gorky's literary career was fully honored in the Soviet Union. By a decision of the politburo it was ordered that a special appendix of Pravda should be dedicated to the jubilee.[66]

In fact, Gorky was honored and flattered in a quite unabashed way: A literary institute, the central park of culture and Moscow's main street, as well as the Moscow Art Theatre were named after him. He seems to have raised no objections to these genuine expressions of the new Soviet civilization.[67]

The atrocities committed during the collectivization campaign were not unknown to the western public and they became the subject of particular scrutiny, when in the autumn of 1930 a campaign against the Soviet Union's dumping of various products was launched in the western press. A central point in this campaign –at least in England- was the fact that the cheap timber, which the Soviets were dumping on the British market, was being produced in North-Western Russia by "slave labor," the inmates of the camps.

In the midst of these scandalous revelations, it was not unnatural that western intellectuals asked Gorky to offer an explanation for his pro-Soviet stance. For those, who remembered Gorky's role during the October revolution and did not understand his zoological hatred of the "petty bourgeois" peasantry, the old intellectual's support for Stalin's terrorist policies certainly seemed incomprehensible.

In January 1931, Gorky answered, on the pages of Pravda, a certain foreign correspondent's question, which though published in a very abbreviated and muddled way, nevertheless obviously suggested that the writer was cynically relishing in the despair of the masses and betraying the intellectual's traditional duty of defending the people.[68]

Gorky answered with a lengthy exposition of the cynicism of petty bourgeois European intellectuals, who did not care about the fate of the laborers in their own countries, but were eager to criticize Russia, about which they knew appallingly little, as some examples showed. To speak about an "all-human truth of love" (vsechelovecheskaia pravda liubvi) was shameless at a time when international conflict was growing as a result of the policies of Versailles; when the great powers were preparing for a new war and when workers were being killed in the West just because they wanted to eat.[69]

Gorky was defending the Soviet Union at a time, when the campaign against Soviet dumping and slave labor was at its highest in the West and when the Soviet press for its part was energetically publicizing the testimony of the show trials against the promparty and the Plot of the II International, which purported to show that the West was, at that very moment, preparing an armed intervention against the USSR. Some Western intellectuals took this information at face value. Gorky's old friend, Romain Rolland, for instance, announced that even though he was not a communist, he would, nevertheless, defend the Soviet Union against any attack.[70] There could be no other stance for an honest intellectual, Pravda commented. "Any other position would be on the side of the imperialists, who together with the social-fascists of the Second International" were preparing a "criminal war against the only proletarian state in the world, the fatherland of the world proletariat."[71] Consequently, it was stressed that the "petty bourgeois" reformists, now dubbed as "social-fascists" were making common cause with the imperialists. This was truly a tertium non datur situation and Gorky, whose return to the Soviet Union was being prepared at the time, was a model case of an intellectual, who understood the realities of the day.

In early 1931, Gorky's Soviet colleagues answered the foreign critics of the old master, using what was to become the standard format of Stalinist argumentation.

The answer came in a short article in Pravda, entitled "Hands Off Maxim Gorky,"[72] which contained the names of 56 Soviet writers (including B. Pasternak, Yu. Olesha and V. Kataev).

The undersigned referred to the London Times and other western newspapers that were attacking the master and argued that Gorky needed no defense. However, the argument surrounding Gorky was a matter for the whole of the Soviet literary establishment and a challenge to him was a challenge to it as a whole. The reaction to this challenge had been that all the groups and currents within Soviet literature were now grouped around Gorky. Gorky was the best example of all that this literature had been doing and would continue to do. He was the symbol of a true writer's service to socialism.

In May 1931 Gorky published an article in Pravda called "Answer to an *intelligent*,"[73] where he quite aggressively defended the current policy of the Soviet government against the criticisms of western intellectuals.

At first, Gorky rather arrogantly declared that the creative force of western culture had already been exhausted and that these self same western intellectuals were now living "at the expense" of Russian culture. It was not true that primitivism (dikarstvo) was to be found in the East, where women were enslaved. In fact, the enslaved female body was to be seen in western music-halls and this practice doubtless also accelerated the growth of homosexuality and lesbianism –which had their origins in housing problems. Now the "civilized" intellectuals of the West were protesting, because half a hundred crooks (sadists, who had organized the starvation of people) had been executed and because agriculture had been collectivized. It had to be understood that the policy of the Soviet government was to liberate the peasants from their zoological conservatism and anarchism. No capitalist government could have done this. The land of the Soviets did not violate the freedom of the peasants, Gorky maintained, on the contrary, zoological individualism, which was typical of all peasants around the world, was the result of exterior pressure against them in a class society. It was the personality's desperate response, in self-defense. Moreover, the individualism of the intellectuals differed from that of the peasants only in degree, not fundamentally. Philosophical pessimism, practical skepticism and other deformations of the spirit had the same source. And it was worth remembering that the homeland of pessimism was India.

Were the workers and the peasants happy with the policies of the Soviet government? In principle, yes, Gorky maintained. True, there were the well-to-do peasants, who had hoped to become still richer and to keep the poor peasants under their control. Such people might be dissatisfied, but their role was already played out.

Gorky was especially vitriolic about the western intellectuals' protests about the execution of 48 wreckers. After all, he stated, these in effect had been no less sadistic as the infamous serial murderer Kuerten, which had been caught in Germany lately.

In some sense, it may be that Gorky had found a becoming place for himself in the service of revolutionary Bolshevik policies: the party was attacking the petty bourgeois in the countryside, and Gorky was not only defending this line against his foreign petty bourgeois writer colleagues, but was even moving on to the offensive.

In 1932 Gorky published his famous article "Who are you with, Masters of Culture?"[74] In this article, Gorky once again most emphatically repeated his old credo. For him, the peasantry was the scum of the earth, whose style of life was the seed-bed for all kinds of beasts of prey and parasites. The peasant was by nature a "cultural idiot." Now, western correspondents were accusing the Soviet Union of using violence against the peasants, but they had simply missed the point. Not all compulsion was violence, Gorky explained: was it violence, if you taught children to read? In the same way, the Soviet working class was bringing social and political literacy to the peasants. All this was in the interests of the peasantry itself. In fact Gorky maintained the peasantry did not want to live in dirty villages at all but in "agrocities" (v agrogorodakh).[75]

It was also the case that Russian culture was developing and progressing whilst culture in the west was rapidly declining. Were there any talented people at all in the west these days? This cultural decline was due to the fact that the Western petty bourgeoisie was inimical to science and culture. Now it was busy closing universities.[76]

As regards cultural values, they were not and never had been universal, Gorky declared. Mutual hatred was the necessary relation within the bourgeoisie, in other words amongst themselves, and between the exploiter and the exploited. Some western correspondents were criticizing Gorky for "preaching hate" and wanted him to preach love. This was, however, immoral: "No, to preach love of the poor towards the rich, of the worker towards the master –that's not my job. I am not able to console. I know too well that the whole world is living in an atmosphere of hate. I can see that it is becoming deeper, more active, and more beneficial" (stanovitsia vsio gushche, aktivnei, blagotvornei).[77] The "humanists" should understand that there were two kinds of hate: one was born among the beasts of prey and arose from mutual competition and also from fear of the future, which was threatening the bourgeois with unavoidable destruction. The other variety of hate was the hate of the proletariat. It arose from its disgust with reality and its understanding about its right to power. Nothing, except the violent conflict of both sides, could reconcile these parties, Gorky concluded in an orthodox Bolshevist manner.[78]

The intellectuals should now decide, whose side they were on, Gorky demanded. The fate of the Russian (émigré) intelligentsia provided a lesson here. It had not sided with the Russian working people and now the old intelligents had drifted into emigration, where they were rotting and would die with the stigma of traitors.[79]

The passage about the virtues of hate became famous, but there was nothing novel or new in it in regard to Gorky's own works. When the newspaper "Pravda" had its 15th anniversary (1927), Gorky had told its staff about class hate, using as an example a friend of his, who had a special talent for this: he "understood and felt the truth of hate so well."[80] This friend, commenting on a novel he was analyzing, had asked: "do you know, what's good about it? It's the hate of the author, the truth of hate. It must be so: calmly, with resolution, without polishing. When people speak about a holy, great or other kind of truth, I understand it only as the truth of hate. There is no other truth. Any other truth is a lie! This is the way Lenin understands it."[81]

Gorky was, indeed, preaching hate and explaining away the atrocities, which had taken place in the Soviet countryside and about which he could not but help know. At this stage, as always, the point of Gorky's vehemence was directed against the peasantry, the "petty bourgeois" mass, for which he obviously held a genuine hatred. But was Gorky's personal hate really of that lofty proletarian variety, which he praised?

In fact, Gorky's thinking—and his own life story—did not provide evidence of a true proletarian nature. Before his canonization as the master of socialist realism many people had diagnosed Gorky as a "writer of the revolutionary petty bourgeoisie" or as a "*déclassé* writer from the petty bourgeoisie of the town of Okurov, who had fallen into the working class."[82] Accordingly, Gorky's hatred of the old world was not so much the hatred of the proletarian towards the bourgeois-capitalist system, but, rather, a hatred of the petty bourgeoisie of the ultra-philistine town of Okurov, that is to say, the attitude of somebody, who had dropped out of that petty bourgeoisie and, had therefore become its irreconcilable enemy.[83] The idea that Gorky was a petty bourgeois by class origin, became a widely held view.[84]

In the class-conscious, militant atmosphere of the Cultural Revolution, all the old "masters" of culture were exposed and attacked by the militants. Like Mayakovsky, Gorky might have been a predictable victim. However, when in 1929 a Siberian journal dubbed Gorky the "mouthpiece and shield of the whole reactionary part of Soviet literature" and maintained that Gorky was defending all the Soviet "Pilniakovism" (pilniakovshchina), the party reacted. A decision of the party politburo no less, condemned such "hooliganism" (bearing in mind that hooliganism was a petty bourgeois phenomenon) and ordered the removal of the editor of the journal.[85]

It was Gorky's ideas about the nature of philistinism, not those of the proletarian zealots that would prevail in Soviet culture. Even in the midst of a general struggle against all kinds of "masters," Gorky was too precious for the Soviet leadership to be left at the mercy of second-rate proletarian scribes.

Literary heroes. Veresaev's *Sisters*

Vikenti Vikentevich Veresaev[86], a rather well-known and outstanding man of letters, described the class-war of the cultural revolution realistically in literary form. His novel *Sisters* (Sestry)[87] was written during that period and published in 1933. It experienced some trouble with the censor before its publication.[88]

Veresaev's novel had the ingredients of socialist realism *avant le mot*. Like Gladkov and Ostrovsky, he described the political maturing of his heroes in the struggle against philistinism.

The heroes were two sisters, Lelka and Ninka, who come from an intelligentsia family and are carried away by the revolutionary upsurge during the period of the first five-year plan. The more radical of the two, Lelka, leaves her university studies and goes to work in a factory. The novel goes on to describe Lelka's—an *intelligent*'s—acculturation in the workers' milieu; her political development; emancipated sex-life, and Komsomol activities of the time such as "light cavalry" operations[89] and the organizing of socialist competition. The final part of the book contains a description of worker activists during collectivization and ends with the publication of Stalin's famous article "Dizziness from Successes", which leaves the zealots confused and casts doubt on their political correctness. On the final pages, the less radical of the sisters, Ninka seems to fare better, in ideological terms, than the zealot Lelka. The problem, however, is that the reader is given almost no information about Ninka's political development, whereas Lelka's political growth and struggle is described in considerable detail and in a clearly admiring tone. The moral seems to be that in the final analysis the party is the repository of a higher wisdom. While the Komsomol zealots are heroic and show a healthy class-instinct, the highest truth is not accessible to them by virtue of their class-position, but must be conveyed from above, from the vanguard of the vanguard, namely the party.

In any event, the description of the young komsomols' activities is always sympathetic and even admiring. The righteous ones are always morally impeccable and the enemy gets what it deserves. The enemy par excellence is philistinism: it tempts not only those, who are from an alien class origin, but even the workers. Incidentally, the workers are not a homogenous mass, but contain different cohorts. Those, who come from the countryside, are almost enemies: they are petty bourgeois, who are not interested in the fate either of the five-year plan or even their own factory. Instead of working in the factory, which has trouble in fulfilling the plan, the country people stay for days in their village in order to help out in private agriculture.[90] Moreover, not all workers, however proletarian, become activists, in fact, only a small minority does[91]. Despite their class, the mass of the workers are still bearers of the old psychology, they work just like they did under the capitalists: they resent the lowering of their wages and the rising of the norms, they loathe the denunciations but still like drinking, smoking and swearing.

The philistinism of everyday life and the struggle against it is described in detail in the book. The young workers hate the intellectual types, who are easily recognized by their spectacles, and jostle them on the street and in the tramway.[92] This is the primitive stage of class-hate, but this hate as such is a magnificent proletarian quality. Lelka's most loved partner, Vedernikov is a class-hater par excellence and therewith, earns Lelka's admiration: " she loved him for his grim gaze and his proud lips, admiring his unquenchable, vehement class-hate, which knew no compromise."[93] At first Vedernikov's hate is even directed against Lelka, who is a representative of an alien social sphere –the intelligentsia.[94] Lelka's sincere proletarian activism make things better, until their love becomes flawless, at which point they begin to work together in the countryside, promoting collectivization.

The uncompromising class-line is being implemented in the party and in the Komsomol. A young man of bourgeois origin, who has come to the factory in order to get the opportunity to study at the university is turned down. The class-line means that he must be prevented from entering not only the Komsomol but the university as well, for class is inherited and cannot be earned by working in the factory. This sounds rather illogical, because in Lelka's case, the inherited class is being transgressed.

The activities of the "light cavalry" are also ruthless and violate the old codes of worker solidarity. They do not honor the philistine codes of personal friendship, but make even their friends' vices public. The problem is that the old psychology of the workers has not developed to the required level.[95]

The petty-bourgeois qualities of the young workers become apparent in many ways: a boy wants to have a cosmetic operation, whilst another young comrade changes his name from Vasili Tsarapkin to Valentin Yelsky. The same person opposes a reduction in his salary, although it is large enough for him to buy such petty-bourgeois things as a nickel bed, which had brass balls on its columns. The blanket was of blue satin. The front of the wardrobe had a mirror and the man also used perfumes. At the same time, he happened to be not just a member of the Komsomol, but an activist. When his petty bourgeois nature was revealed, the activists understood that he had to be fought like any other class-enemy.[96]

The heroes understand that humanitarian considerations are typical for the *intelligenty*. Vedernikov throws himself body and soul into the collectivization campaign with Lelka's enthusiastic support.[97] Although quite a number of their actions are inhuman there is no sign that the writer is critical of most of them. Finally, at one point, the heroes of the campaign make a mistake: they found a commune and, in doing so, ignore the opinion of the peasants and ruin the whole venture. In fact the real culprit turns out to be a certain individual, comrade Oska Golovastov from the same factory. Oska was not in fact a true proletarian, but a garrulous careerist, who received sadistic satisfaction from being able to decide other peoples' destinies.[98]

When Stalin's famous letter turns the tables, the proletarian heroes are upset. In fact they had not realized what they had been doing. The novel ends in a somewhat oracular way, but there is no hint that the writer does not share the ideas, about the intelligents and the philistines, which his heroes profess.

Veresaev's book may be considered a rather accurate description of contemporary moods and practices. *Literaturnyi kritik* published a review of the book, where the main criticism was that the heroines were not really representatives of the new generation of the intelligentsia, but figures from the beginning of the century, who had been mechanically transplanted into the new era. Several cases of political incorrectness were also pointed out, but even this critic stated that Veresaev could never be accused of insincerity. [99] The critic argued that being an intelligent was no longer seen as a stigma during the first five year plan and that Veresaev was presenting attitudes such as "Makhaevism" and *komchvanstvo*, which had been condemned by the party.

This amounts to saying that Veresaev should not have described undesirable phenomena, which, however, existed.

Veresaev had several quarrels with the censors, who maintained that the exhausting and unwholesome work, which was described in the novel work (which entailed breathing vapors of petrol) was no longer being carried out. However, it turned out that the author had in fact spent a long time in the factory he described, when planning his book. The censors also cut passages, which described how the workers stole some of the rubber that they were producing.

Subsequently Veresaev was to claim that the picture, he had drawn was accurate. The characters in the book were easily recognized by their real-life counterparts, which caused some consternation on their part. Whilst agreeing that the picture was not false, they questioned the need for it to be described in literary form. The passages about sex in particular led to protests and it was asked, what workers abroad might think about them. In his defense Veresaev argued that the English critics had been astonished to recognize that sexual manners in Russia, about which so much had been written during the last decade or so, were very similar to those in Great Britain.[100]

The *intelligent* as caricature. Vasisuali Lokhankin

The "bourgeois" intelligent was repeatedly depicted in the Soviet press and in literature. A genuine "bourgeois *intelligent*" was someone, who had received his education during the pre-Revolutionary period and had not been converted to communism. In the new society he was a remnant of the past in a more direct sense than a common philistine, who might be simply a passive member of the working class lacking in class-consciousness.

A stereotypical image of the *intelligent* was presented by the satirical duo Ilya Ilf and Evgeny Petrov (Ilya Petrov) in their novel *The Golden Calf*.[101] In the 1920's this literary duo had published the hugely popular *12 chairs*, which was a satire of the NEP period. Now they described their heroes in the new surroundings of the first five-year plan.

The book is built around the picaresque journey around Russia of a group of swindlers and contains scores of caricatures of different categories of Soviet people, whom the heroes meet during their mission. One of these is the *intelligent*, Vasisuali Lokhankin who, though his character and style of life are briefly described in the book, does not seem to have a real role in the novel, or indeed in Soviet society either. Nevertheless, one of the chapters of the book is called "Vasisuali Lokhankin and His Contribution to the Russian Revolution" where it becomes clear that though this contribution is indeed non-existent, the hero considers it to be of great importance. This self-avowed greatness is due to Vasisuali's supposedly high moral standards. Actually, Vasisuali is doing nothing useful at all in this world. He is incomprehensibly lazy (reminiscent in this respect of some of Gorky's heroes), and, at the same time, dissolute. He does not work but is maintained by his wife. He is not even educated; just a secondary school dropout. All this notwithstanding, Vasisuali understands that an occupation worthy of himself may be found in the contemplation of such topics as "Vasisuali Lokhankin and his importance"; "Lokhankin and his importance in the Russian Revolution"; and "Lokhankin and the Tragedy of Russian Liberalism." He has quite a special literary taste, and his favorite book is called *Man and Woman*, which is well printed and apparently contains much interesting visual material.

Unable to live without his wife, for several reasons, Vasisuali follows her like a dog, when she leaves him for another man. The authors make fun of the intelligentsia's fighting traditions by making Vasisuali go on hunger strike to force his wife to return. When Lokhankin receives a thrashing from his neighbours for systematically refusing to turn the light off when leaving the toilet of the *kommunalka* where he lives, he sees this as a kind of martyrdom, which maybe serves some higher purpose. In any event, he suffered for the sake of truth like Galilei (he had been contemplating the importance of the Russian intelligentsia). Perhaps his personal drama hid a "greater truth." But it was not only Vasisuali, the self-proclaimed *intelligent*, but all the other swindlers on the journey who were understood to be petty bourgeois elements. The book supposedly showed how hopeless life in the Soviet Union was for these remnants of the past, who were dreaming about making a million.[102]

The point of this satirical picture may have been directed against the pre-revolutionary non-Bolshevik intelligentsia, who kept paying homage to their old, non-Bolshevik moral norms, in an attempt to "defend their philistine practices by means of the old '*intelligent*' glossary."[103] The caricature, of course, was overtly hyperbolic, but might have contributed to the general anti-*intelligent* climate.

Whereas Ilf and Petrov created a shameless caricature of the philistinism of an *intelligent*, the general spirit of more "proletarian" writers such as Gladkov, Ostrovsky and Veresaev was less harsh from the *intelligent*'s point of view. There were, they maintained, *intelligenty*, who were also good communists. However, the really ideal communists were not from such *intelligent* origins. Rather, they resembled Korchagin and other similar proletarian heroes, who had attained their precious class-instinct (class hate) thanks to their social origin and later became a new kind of *intelligenty*, conquering the peaks of knowledge. *Intelligenty* can become good communists, but the inevitable class-instinct, which guides their activity, comes from genuine proletarian surroundings. Real proletarians are also able to conquer the peaks of culture, as indeed Korchagin does. The ideal communist is a class-conscious practical man with an outstanding ability for action. He is uninhibited by *intelligent* soul-searching, but at the same time he too can master culture if necessary. The negative type of intelligent, on the other hand is one, who is sentimental, impractical, lazy and dissolute.

Mayakovsky's last battle: The *Bedbug* and the *Bathhouse*

Vladimir Mayakovsky also took part in the discussion about the philistine, by writing two plays on the topic. They were not, as soon became clear, in tune with the spirit of the times. Mayakovsky dedicated his two last plays, *The Bedbug* (*Klop*) and *The Bathhouse* (*Bania*) to the struggle against philistinism.

Mayakovsky described *The Bedbug* as "a fairy-tale play", which he considered to be "a theatrical variety of the fundamental theme, on which I have written poems and epics, drawn posters and leaflets. This theme is the struggle with philistinism"[104].

The hero, or rather anti-hero of the play, Prisypkin, was in fact a synthesis of the petty bourgeois phenomena, which had been harassed in the press, especially in *Komsomolskaia Pravda*, in recent years. The former worker Prisypkin changed his name to Pierre Skripkin. A similar phenomenon had been described in both *Komsomolskaia Pravda* and in Veresaev's *Sisters*.[105]

The new philistine pretended to be revolutionary and liked things red, such as "red ham, bottles with red corks and other red items." Prisypkin, was a self-seeker, who abandoned the workingman's difficult life, only to die in a fire. However, after 50 years he was resurrected by scientists and caused an epidemic. It was discovered that the cause of the epidemic was not an ordinary bedbug *"klopus normalis,"* but a species of parasite, personified by Prisypkin himself: *"obyvatelius vulgaris,"* which lives with the whole of humanity. Nobody could cure the vodka-consuming Prisypkin, who is not actually human at all. In the end he is isolated in a cage.[106]

The Bathhouse was about an inventor, who had invented a time-machine. Bureaucrats of course tried to resist the novelty, but in the end wanted to use the machine in order to go straight to communism. The length of the journey made it also possible to demand daily allowance for 100 years.[107]

Both *The Bedbug* and *The Bathhouse* were presented in Meyerhold's theater in 1929. The avantgarde mise-en-scène, as well as the text, were severely criticised, especially by representatives of the militant youth. During the reading of *The Bathhouse* in the Polytechnic Museum somebody, typical of the period, asked the author, for whom was he writing since the workers did not read Mayakovsky and the intelligentsia was abusing him. Mayakovsky answered in a calm tone, remarking that the word "intelligentsia" itself was a term of abuse and that the workers could hardly claim that they could not understand his plays if they hadn't read them. Mayakovsky tried to defend himself by pointing out that there was, after all, a workers' intelligentsia.[108]

For all his party-mindedness, Mayakovsky found himself up a blind alley. Philistinism and bureaucratism, as one of its forms, were in effect outlawed by the party and the "light cavalry" of the Komsomol kept attacking them on all levels. Mayakovsky, an old master and authority, was, in any case, too flagrant a stumbling stone for the egalitarians, whilst in his private life, his tastes were too "petty-bourgeois" to go unpunished by the zealots. The young activists continued their attacks on Mayakovsky, and in the tumultuous and violent year of 1930, he shot himself.

In the context of the general mood of the times, it would appear that Mayakovsky's sin was twofold; not only did he lack the required commitment to egalitarianism but he was also just too pessimistic. Enthusiasts foresaw communism as being just around the corner, whilst for many people a new way of life and the creation of "the new man" seemed to be a present-day reality. Mayakovsky, on the other hand, was cynical enough to prophesy the return of the petty bourgeoisie, which was in the process of being liquidated.

The international scene. The pilgrims

The story of the Western pilgrims to Russia is famous enough. It is well known how a contingent of western intellectuals was carried away by the romanticism of the Stalinist five-year plans, and how quite a few believed in the authenticity of the show trials of the Great Terror (and perhaps, wanted, even more, to hush up this ugly episode in the history of the adored New Society). It is also generally accepted that western intellectuals' enthusiasm for the Soviet Union fell away dramatically after Stalin's death, when the regime adopted less murderous methods. However, the Soviet Union retained its attraction for western intellectuals right up to its end. Even thereafter, some have been trying to whitewash its record of coercion and violence. In fact, the first (minor) wave of disappointment came during the great purges. The second can perhaps be discerned at the time of the Nazi-Soviet cooperation. Some Western intellectuals, who had been enthusiastic about the Soviet Union, were eventually to be disappointed with it, by the late forties.[109] A large number, however, remained loyal to the idea that some kind of higher, socialist society had been built in Russia.[110]

It has traditionally been maintained that the Russian intelligentsia and its western counterparts had always been very different. The Russians in the pre-1917 period had seen the social role of the intelligentsia in Russia as the main factor, which set them apart from the intellectuals in the West. Western intellectuals were often dismissed as socially passive and even cynical, whereas the Russians were seen as selfless and moralistic champions of the popular good—even though this manifested itself mainly on a symbolic or illegal level, as the Russian *intelligenty* did not take part in practical social or political work, if it meant cooperating with the state. Western intellectuals were considered to be more practical and down-to-earth.

This may be true, but it must also be recognized that the Russian intelligentsia and its western counterparts had a very different history as regards their relationship to the structures of power: both to absolutism and to the totalitarian Moloch.

The Russian intelligentsia was tackled by the totalitarian regime. Its politically active part—insofar as it was not enthusiastic about the new regime—was forced into silence, emigration, or annihilated. The creative intelligentsia was bribed or intimidated and kept under surveillance.

Undoubtedly, it was also the case that the Russian intelligentsia, or at least a part of it, was carried away by the grandiose scale of Stalin's social construction. Western intellectuals, on their pilgrimages to the Soviet Union, met Soviet colleagues, who were enthusiastic about the prospects of socialist construction. However, the Soviet intelligents inevitably had a different kind of contact with the realities of the socialist life than their western guests could ever experience. What, for the westerners, was theory with beautiful words and handsome syntax, full of promises and broad perspectives, was, for the Russians, the harsh reality of their daily lives, with its stubborn irrationalism and lack of freedom.

The Soviet leadership staged worldwide actions by which means the intellectuals of the world could express their solidarity with the USSR.[111] These took place both in the 1930s and after the Second World War and the tradition continued, in the shape of campaigns against western missiles, right through to the early 1980s. These Soviet initiatives always had an enthusiastic audience in the west, but the situation among the Soviet intelligentsia was different. Certainly, there was not much public protest against these official Soviet "peace actions." In any event, by the 1960's the vanguard of the Russian intelligentsia had either ceased to serve the totalitarian regime, or at least considered it to be morally dubious.[112] Ironically, whilst western intellectuals were reluctant to believe that the Soviet regime could be more oppressive and dictatorial than their own societies, there were few Soviet intellectuals, worthy of the name, who thought like this, even though their knowledge of the western world was severely handicapped by the ubiquitous censorship. The lack of information worked both ways.

Paul Hollander, in his study of western intellectuals' "pilgrimages" to the Soviet Union and other totalitarian countries, provides a general picture of the politically active intellectuals.[113] He concludes that, the intellectuals are generally defined on the basis of shared attitudes, interests and predispositions, rather than on the basis of either occupational specialization, or the substantive content of the ideas they adhere to. The emphasis is on a 'mindset' more than anything else."

As regards moral-ethical aspects, they are regarded as "idealistic, critical, irreverent, iconoclastic, imbued with altruistic ameliorative impulses, deep moral concerns and commitments". As for their social roles, they are usually regarded as "outsiders, yet the conscience of society".[114] Intellectuals are also considered to be alienated from their societies, indeed, alienation from corruptive power was considered to be a virtue, even an obligation. In some cases, as Hollander observes, the intellectuals have paid lip-service to the idea that they should "never get involved" in the sordid business of the 'establishment," which is reminiscent of the Vekhist critique of the old Russian intelligentsia.[115]

In reality, it was typically the case that while intellectuals believed that they should under no circumstances get mixed up with "bad political systems," they also thought that nothing should restrain them from a total commitment to a "good" political cause or system. As in pre-Revolutionary Russia, western intellectuals are also supposed to serve the "masses." The concept of the "masses" is elusive, but as Hollander remarks, for some intellectuals at least, it amounted to an "abstraction apparently made up of equal imaginary parts of authenticity, innocence, strength and simplicity, qualities intellectuals either rarely experience or do not have in sufficient supply."[116]

In fact, this description, which is mainly concerned with western intellectuals after the First World War and indeed later, would fit the Russian intelligentsia of XIX Century and pre-1917 period almost perfectly. Before the Russian revolution, the Russians considered their intelligentsia to be unique, largely because of its benign and progressive social character as a group, its alienation from corrupt power, and its moral commitment. It may well be that the Russian intelligentsia really was unique for its time. This does not mean, however, that it would be unique for all times. In fact, western societies after the First World War also developed the same kind of fighting order –or corps. Such groups emerged in several countries in the 1930s if not earlier. By that time, a sizable contingent of western intellectuals had become alienated from their respective societies, which were experiencing serious difficulties at the time, and, thus estranged, they were attracted by the utopia, being built on earth, namely, the Soviet Union. On their pilgrimages in the 1930s western colleagues could, sometimes, met the remnants of the pre-revolutionary generation of *intelligenty*, or at least those of them who were involved in building the new society and who, for the most part, were to be liquidated in the great purges. In a symbolic way, the old Russian intelligentsia left the baton to their western colleagues. At the same time, a new kind of intelligentsia was emerging in the Soviet Union. A new spirit was gaining ground in a state, where the intelligentsia's position had been totally changed. The changes were, the result of the party's conscious efforts on the one hand, and a reaction to totalitarian rule, which the intellectuals were forced to experience at close quarters and in whose grip they were obliged to live out their lives, on the other.

It is generally known that there were some western pilgrims to Russia even in the early days of the Revolution when Lenin was in control; namely, John Reed and a handful of others. However, the Bolshevik revolution, not to mention its immediate aftermath, had very little constructive to offer, which could impress a western observer. The NEP was an even unhappier period, as far as western pilgrimages to the USSR are concerned, for, in essence, it was nothing other than an inglorious retreat from communist principles. It was only the Soviet Union of the five-year plans (starting from October 1928) that could boast really magnificent views of, reconstruction, of a new world, and a new man.[117]

The timing of the socialist offensive was perfect when compared with conditions in the capitalist world. The whole western world was in the grip of an unprecedented economic crisis, which started at almost exactly the same time as the launch of the first five-year plan. The crisis severely shook the foundations of western self-conceit. The leading capitalist countries were forced to accept the reality of mass-unemployment, the ruin of small and large entrepreneurs, hunger, and despair. In this atmosphere, the phenomenon, which Hollander has called "the first wave of estrangement," was born.[118]

The appeal of Soviet society for western intellectuals was manifold. Everybody seemed to find, in the Soviet Union, just what he was looking for. For many, bolshevism seemed "a new, more gloriously intransigent bohemianism" devoid of the bourgeois hypocrisy of the west. Strange and bizarre though it may appear, for many it also seemed to be a "paradise for rebels". Many were convinced that social justice and equality had been realized in the USSR and that it offered everybody a sense of purpose and cohesive values. In the Soviet people the visitors saw the sum of all imaginable virtues, beginning with good health and ending in wisdom and simple authenticity. As Paul Hollander sums up, it was "an image that combined time-honored elements of the Noble Savage, the Earthy Peasant, the Happy Poor, the Powerful Proletarian and a glimmer of the Renaissance man of Utopia."[119]

The gullibility of the western pilgrims is famous. The visitors wondered at model prisons and concentration camps, praising the potential of the OGPU, which was achieving "triumph in human regeneration". Many critical intellectuals were also totally convinced of the authenticity of the show trials of the great terror.[120]

All this was achieved by using a variety of techniques, including a selective exposition of reality, lavish hospitality and so on. It is clear too that, their estrangement from their own societies made western intellectuals more susceptible to their hosts' influence. We must also remember that their hosts treated them very skillfully, massaging their egos. In the Soviet Union many a Western intellectual though a nonentity in his own country, was treated like a king or at least like a very important person. This naturally convinced them of the high intellectual level of the USSR and made them yearn for the same kind of rationalism in their own countries.[121]

The psychological profile of these western intellectuals seems to be quite similar to that of their pre-1917 Russian counterparts: there was the denouncement of one's own society and the enthusiastic approval of an ideal one. In the case of western intellectuals the estrangement from their own society may not, however, have been as total as that of their pre-1917 Russian colleagues and the "ideal society" had existed for the pre-revolutionary Russians only as an ideal, without an incarnated form. Also, for the western guests, the ideal society existed, largely in their own minds. What they saw, just served as an illustration of the theory, which was stronger than any facts. Both groups, included champions of a non-bourgeois, emancipated way of life and both groups adored the "people." Another similarity should be noticed: a craving for abrupt changes effected by a heroic action had been typical of the old Russian intelligentsia. Many of them had dreamed about a new Peter the Great, who would remold Russian society. Their western guests were scandalized by the fact that capitalist society seemed to be unable to do anything at all to solve the appalling problems of society during the great depression. In the Soviet Union, by way of contrast, not only was "something" being done, a vast amount was apparently being achieved, and the regime was not restricting itself to petty-bourgeois half-measures, but was apparently ruthless enough to use all possible means to attain its goals. Western governments seemed cowardly and wavering as compared with the imposing Soviet giant, which was reporting incredible growth rates, and where unemployment was being liquidated at the very same time that it was rising in the west to unheard of levels.

A large section of the intelligentsia had always believed that all social problems could be resolved if only the government would be radical and ruthless enough. This now seemed to be happening in the Soviet Union.

The violence, which would be needed to make "a perfect" society in Russia seemed to be no problem for such remarkable intellectuals as G.B. Shaw, who made fun of it with gusto.[122]

There were, however, moments, in the development of Soviet ideology, which in principle should have been uncongenial to western radicals. For instance, egalitarianism, after 1931, was no longer on the march. All kinds of radical doctrines in society and culture were gradually being extinguished during the second five-year plan including new methods in schooling, trends towards the withering away of law, lenient views in criminology, sexual radicalism, artistic avant-gardism and so on. The Soviet Union of the 1930s rapidly became less and less "radical;" least of all was it the paradise for rebels, which many had supposed it to be. Instead, it increasingly began to resemble a petty bourgeois society, something that both the old Russian intelligentsia and the western guests abhorred. Of course it might, reasonably, be admitted that the kind of "petty bourgeoisie," which emerged in the Soviet Union at the end of the 1930 s was not of quite the same variety, as that experienced by the western guests in their own countries. The great terror and other, specifically Soviet, phenomena certainly added their own ingredients to the general picture of the land of the Soviets. In any event, the real situation in Soviet Union by the end of the 1930s represented a development that was a far cry from the ideas of the first five-year plan, when the building of the utopia had started.

Some of the Western guests, in fact, thought that the industrialization of Russia, which the five-year plan heralded, meant the "Americanization" of Russia.[123]

Indeed, one of the slogans of the first five-year plan, "technology decides everything" (tekhnika reshaet vse), could easily give the impression that the most important development in the Soviet Union was in fact merely an attempt to introduce modern machines plus Taylorism and Fordism. Many Western capitalists, including Ford himself, believed that Russia would have to follow the same path as other modernizing countries and that there was now a good opportunity to influence Russia by means of technical and economic cooperation.[124]

On the other hand, Americanization was precisely what many representatives of the old Russian intelligentsia most detested. At least, this was the case if Americanization was understood to be "mere striving for the colossal, devoid of spirituality, empty collective worship of technology." This was the way in which a contemporary conservative critic of the modern world, Julius Evola and many others saw it.[125]

During the first five-year plan more and more reliable first hand information about the reality of Soviet socialism became available. Tens of thousands of Western specialists went to the USSR to take part in construction work and more than a few books were published.[126] In fact, there was no shortage of accurate information about the USSR at the time of the first five-year plan. Even a tragedy like the famine of 1932-33 was rather well known, not only on a popular level in neighboring countries, but also in the literature of the time.[127] It was the attitude of the reader, which, most of all, determined the quality of the picture of the Soviet Union. In 1928-32 the other important factor, which influenced the image of the USSR was the great depression, which, for many, seemed to signify the beginning of the final act in the decline of the West, a development, which had been prophesied since time immemorial, especially in Russia.[128] Nazism, as another remarkable factor influencing the image of the USSR, only became really important after 1933.

During the "cultural revolution" of 1928-31, when the radical Soviet intelligentsia and western pilgrims could still meet on even ground as it were, a utopia was in the making and radical ideals were still being taken seriously by the Soviet leadership. They were also driven through with a ferocity which had never been possible in a bourgeois or absolutist regime. At least this was not petty bourgeois. There really were young Soviet intellectuals like Lev Kopelev, who participated, with enthusiasm, in ruining the lives of countless numbers of peasants and representatives of the hallowed "people" or "masses," in order to make them resemble increasingly some notion of their "ideal self," which would be emancipated in the near future, in the egalitarian and affluent socialist society.[129]

In 1932 a collection of writings by prominent western intellectuals was published, in which more than a hundred people presented their opinions of the Soviet Union. Amongst the contributors were Heinrich and Thomas Mann, Erwin Kisch, Ernst Toller, Anatole France, Henri Barbusse, Romain Rolland, André Maurois, G.B. Shaw, H.G. Wells, Theodore Dreiser, Stuart Chase, Anna Louise Strong, Albert Rhys Williams, John Dos Passos, Upton Sinclair, Martin Andersen Nexö and George Lukacs.[130] Needless to say, everybody's opinion was positive as regards the objective of the USSR, and although the views expressed were not always orthodox or conventional, this hardly diminished its value for the Soviets. Not surprisingly, the book was published in Russian, to give the Russian audience an objective, outsiders' view, as it were, of their country.

The "anti-Soviet dumping" campaign and the White Sea Canal

The global economic crisis, known as the Great Depression in the USA, swept through all the western countries. The shock it caused was at its most severe at precisely the same time that Stalin's revolution began in the

Soviet Union. The Soviet Union had been largely autarchic in the 1920s, but forced industrialization implied capital goods, which could only be obtained from the West. The capitalist countries did not like the Soviet system and the fear that the Soviets would export their revolution was not without some foundation. However, when the markets collapsed, exports to the Soviet Union were tempting for western countries. These exports, of course, had to be paid for somehow, but all the Soviet Union had to offer, except gold, was its agricultural products and raw-materials, like timber. Soviet exports boomed: by 1928 they had returned to the levels of 1913, and by 1932 they were 2,7 times more –and by 1940 still 1,5 times more.[131] Unfortunately, the depression had already forced prices down to very low levels. The sudden flow of Soviet goods did not help the situation at all.

The fact that the inmates of Soviet labor camps, where numbers had grown as a result of collectivisation and the "liquidation of the exploiting classes", were used for producing timber for export, became known in the west almost immediately.

Several inmates escaped from the camps –mostly to Finland- and readily described what life was like in the "workers' paradise". As early as January 1930, Mr. Bellairs, a British M.P., questioned the Foreign Minister, Arthur Henderson, about the import of timber, being produced by "slave labor." This happened to be against the Foreign Prisonmade Goods Act of 1897.[132]

The Labour government was not easily persuaded of the horrors of the Soviet labor camps, although masses of information filled the pages of the press. At the end of the year, however, Soviet dumping became an international issue. France led the way, by raising tariffs and import quotas on Soviet goods (e.g. wheat and other agricultural products, whose low prices were ruining small French farmers). The French government tried to organize a wider international action, but was not very successful.[133]

Nevertheless, the anti-Soviet campaign gathered momentum, even in England. In 1931 both the conservatives and the liberals returned to the issue of Soviet forced labor and the dumping of goods on western markets, several times, both in the House of Commons and the House of Lords.[134] An "Anti Soviet Persecution & Slave Labour League" was founded and at the beginning of 1932 it boasted of having organized as many as 80 meetings and of issuing a quarter of a million leaflets.[135] The Antislavery and Aborigine Protection Society also presented a report on Soviet timber production.[136]

The campaign in England became particularly venomous in July 1931 with the Morning Post leading the way. It interviewed dealers and importers of goods throughout the British Isles and was happy to report that almost no one was willing to buy or sell Soviet goods. It was not only Soviet timber that was regarded as odious, Soviet butter, for instance, was found to be "disease-laden filth," which was highly dangerous to eat.[137]

Unfortunately for the supporters of the anti-Soviet campaign, the Labour government did not join the boycott, but, on the contrary, even consented to long-term export credits to the Soviet Union.[138]

All this notwithstanding, the Soviet Union's exports to England did not recover. In 1931 they had represented 32.8 per cent of her exports, whereas by 1932 they had fallen to just 24.1 per cent of its total exports. British exports to the Soviet Union experienced a short boom so that in 1932 they constituted 13.0 per cent of the Soviet Union's total imports, whereas in 1931 they had only been 6.6 per cent.[139]

The campaign against Soviet dumping was not restricted to England or France, but encompassed several countries, including Austria, Finland and the Netherlands. In fact, the campaign was not too serious for the Soviet Union, which in the dire situation caused by the economic crisis, was a rather attractive trading partner for many western companies and countries. However, this campaign did damage the public image of the Soviet Union. The Soviets resorted to a policy with manifold tactics. On the one hand they declared that the whole campaign was yet further proof of the hostility of the capitalist countries and of the imminent danger of an intervention, which was to be begun by France. The campaign, as well as the "call for a crusade" by the Pope, was portrayed as part of the psychological preparations for a military attack on the USSR. Other parts of the same plan were the "plots" of the wrecking organizations, which, it was claimed, were directed by France and its foreign minister Briand.[140]

The Soviet Union responded to the foreign "slander" on an authoritative level. At the VI congress of Soviets the President of the Council of People's Commissars, Molotov, in his report, discussed the topic of "slave labor" at length.[141] The main thrust of Molotov's argument was based on Marx, who had shown that the workers under capitalism were factually, if not formally, in no better a situation than slaves. In the Soviet Union he asserted the picture was totally different. Whereas the working-day was becoming longer and longer in the capitalist world it was in the process of being reduced to 7 hours in the Soviet Union whilst wages were rising. Furthermore, there was a growing enthusiasm for work amongst Soviet workers.

However, Molotov said, the Soviet Government never purported to conceal the fact that it, was indeed also using the labor of healthy, able-bodies prisoners for some publicly useful projects such as the building of highways and railways. Of special importance was the building of the Baltic-White Sea Canal. About 60, 000 people were engaged in these public works. They had an 8-hour working-day and were receiving a salary of

20-30 rubles a month. The workers were not under guard and cultural and educational work was well organized. The conditions of work, in general, were so good, that thousands and thousands of unemployed workers in capitalist countries were envious of them. This was the "bitter truth," the orator quipped.

As regards the cutting of timber, the prisoners were not used for this work. Molotov also rejected the idea of a foreign "investigation" commission, which had been proposed, arguing that no sovereign country could accept such terms. Instead, he declared that an exchange of workers' delegations would be welcome and that the Soviet Union would promote the publication of the reports of the delegations.[142]

In 1931-34 a canal connecting the Baltic Sea with the White Sea was, indeed, built. The building of this waterway was made possible due to the existence of hundreds of thousands of *zeks* (prisoners of the forced labor camps) who were easily available thanks to the "collectivization" and "liquidation of the exploiting classes" campaigns. The engineers that were needed were supplied by the NKVD, which fabricated so-called "plots of wreckers," who supposedly had been preparing the ground for foreign intervention. Living conditions and working conditions were appallingly primitive and the convicts died *en masse*.[143] It has been estimated that hundreds of thousands of people perished whilst doing this work. The reasons for building the Canal seem to have been mainly strategic in character –the canal was supposed to enable the passage of Soviet submarines to the Barents Sea when and as required. Why the canal had to be built at such a breathtaking pace has defied rational explanation. Solzhenitsyn has suggested that the idea was to kill people.[144]

This more or less rational reason for the enterprise was not mentioned at the time, rather it was emphasized that the natural riches of the Karelian Autonomous Republic (which were scarce enough, consisting mainly of wood) could now be transported all over the world.[145]

For the Soviet Union, however, the building of the canal was just another project, which was realized because there was a large number of prisoners and a badly educated population, which could be used for primitive manual labor, which elsewhere would have been done by horses and machines. On the map, this grandiose project was large enough to make such feats of engineering as the Suez, Panama, and Kiel canals seem quite modest.[146] The Soviet propaganda machine never missed such opportunities for advertising its unique achievements.

Another unique achievement of Soviet propaganda was the image of a new kind of socialist, collective work. According to this propaganda, socialist work in the camps could turn morally depraved elements, such as swindlers, thieves, prostitutes, enemies of Soviet power, and wreckers into new people in just a couple of years. A merely symbolic staff of 37 chekists was needed for guarding this massive work force, which consisted of tens of thousands of people at a time. In fact, guarding was not even the right word, since the chekists did not act as prison warders but rather guided and conducted, in a comradely way, whilst all the time respecting the human dignity of the so-called "canal-army people" (kanaloarmeitsy).[147] All this, of course, as the author stressed, compared very favorably with places of detention in capitalist countries like the USA, Nazi Germany, or "fascist" Finland.[148] The Communist party and the OGPU ordered Soviet writers to produce a worthy description of the building of the canal and a brigade of 35 writers, headed by Maxim Gorky, was organized to accomplish the task.

The result was a masterpiece of socialist realism, collectively written and replete with minute details, lively interviews, characteristic anecdotes and convincing portraits. It turned out that the lifespan of this book was to be short, for in 1937 all copies were confiscated from libraries and destroyed. The reason was obvious: the book had presented a whole gallery of heroes, who in 1937 were exposed as traitors and enemies, including the main hero, Genrikh Yagoda, head of the OGPU/NKVD. Many of the authors were to perish later in the great purges of 1937-38.[149]

When it was published the book was an anthem to a new kind of relationship towards labour. For Gorky himself, as he described it, the project was a triumph over philistinism.

Gorky claimed that the building of the White Sea canal was yet another project to join a succession of famous and honorable feats, which were already common in the land of the Soviets. Moreover, it was a splendid success in the task of transforming former enemies of the proletarian dictatorship into qualified members of the working class and even enthusiasts of work, which was necessary for the government.

The rapid triumph over the fiendishly hostile natural environment was impressive, but even more impressive was the triumph over the former nature of the people, who until recently had been under the anarchic, beastly power of a tyrannical philistinism (anarkhizirovannye nedavnei, zverinoi vlastiu samoderzhavnogo meshchanstva).[150]

Once more the policy of the OGPU of education through labor had succeeded. The proletariat in power had once more won the right to proclaim: "I don't struggle in order to kill, as the bourgeoisie does, but in order to wake up laboring mankind to a new life. I kill only when it is impossible to erase from a person his entrenched habit of nourishing himself with the flesh and blood of other people".[151]

In the philistine (meshchanskoe) society, Gorky pondered, romanticism was born out of the injuries and violations of the individual by society. But philistinism was not able to foster self-esteem in man, for in a class-society everybody necessarily remained somebody else's lackey. Philistinism did not teach people to think but to believe in the unthinkable. This is how the romantic came to separate himself from society.

A less elevated and more common reaction was easier. People just came to think that it was more worthwhile to be crooks (*vory*) than lackeys. Still others became "enemies of society" because the philistine life was dull, and hopelessly grey (*nishcheski sera*). For many people the natural romanticism of their youth turned into an evil and anarchistic romanticism of despair and beastliness: if my life is worth a kopeck, why should yours be worth two? Gorky concluded, echoing the pathos of his early works.[152]

The "truth of collective labor" had now been able to create human beings even out of such half-human kulak types and worshipers of private property, who had hidden their grain and had preferred to let people die rather than reveal where they had hidden their treasure.[153] Another peasant had been accustomed to stuffing himself with milk and porridge, which had caused ulcers but on the canal he had begun to eat like the poor and his stomach had been healed as a result.[154]

Twenty months of labor had transformed thousands of former enemies into qualified constructors, who had been through a school of strict discipline, Gorky asserted. They had been cured of the poisoning, which had been inflicted by rotten philistinism. This was a disease, which still ailed millions of people and which could only be cured by a "feat of fame and honor" and by "feats of prowess and heroism" that is, by honest and proud work, needed for the reconstruction of the first socialist society in the world.[155]

True, Gorky observed, there had been some reports that in some cases the "real" workers had adopted a "cheap American-style philistine attitude" (*sluchai amerikansko-meschanskogo poshlenkogo otnosheniia*) towards the former "socially dangerous" elements. If this was true, Gorky argued then it was shameful of the workers of the Soviet Union and could only be explained by an "idiotic philistine conceit" (*idioticheski meshchanskim chvanstvom*). This was an evil disease and required a serious cure. It would suffice to take a group of the canal-army shock workers to a factory and make them show yesterday's peasants how one can work with enthusiasm and discipline.[156]

Here, as everywhere, Gorky was true to his idea that philistinism was the ultimate evil in capitalist society and that the peasantry was its true stronghold. Now, however, the final solution of this problem in Russia was at hand.

As regards the cure for this disease, Gorky's account was just not plausible. Was not the dictatorship of the proletariat in the Soviet Union based on the assumption that class was hereditary in the sense that it was not determined by one's current occupation but by one's "origin," i.e. by the position of one's parents? How could it be claimed that some 20 months of the dictatorship of the proletariat—even allowing for the fact that it was spent under the iron discipline of the Guard of the Proletariat, the GPU—could remake somebody's consciousness?

Obviously, the competent organs of the state did not share Gorky's ideas. The notion of class-origin in the passports of the Canal-army veterans was not changed in spite of their service. This kind of information remained in every Soviet citizen's passport, and the Soviet state, the party, and its repressive organs continued to determine the social trustworthiness of Soviet citizens by the same criteria and in the same way as those workers, whom Gorky had accused of "cheap American style philistinism."

The building of the White Sea Canal was a strange event in Soviet history. Certainly, it was a phenomenon of the "heroic" age of the first five-year plan. The initiators of this enterprise had tried to arouse the enthusiasm of the workers. In some sense, it can be argued that they had tried, by force, to realize in practice some theoretical tenets about the alleged beneficial effects of physical work for a new society and its ability to create enthusiasm. On the other hand, it is all-too evident that the masses of people, who suffered and perished in the camps, had no less a sarcastic attitude to the official liturgy than had Solzhenitsyn in his description of it. The vast amount of "White Sea Canal-text," which was published, had an obvious function: it was needed as an ideological counterattack against the anti-Soviet campaigns in the west. For a political thinker like Gorky, both collectivization and the "reforging" of the peasants in the labor camps were part of the same, fundamentally important project; that of liquidating the petty bourgeois community and the psychology of its inhabitants.

Constructing a new self. The Comintern cadres fight philistinism

The OGPU achieved sensational successes in fighting philistinism in former kulaks and amongst all kinds of rogues. Undoubtedly, therefore, the conditions in camps like that of the Belomorkanal must have been well nigh perfect for this metamorphosis: there was physical labor, a great and comprehensible goal, and the impact of the collective. Work in such a camp could be considered, no doubt, as full-time education in socialism.

Not everybody was as happy as that. At the beginning of the 1930s there emerged, for instance, a new group of foreign workers. Foreign specialists were invited to take part in the construction of socialism and tens of thousands of them arrived. In 1932 their number reached 42,000 which was probably its peak.[157] The newcomers were, in some cases, highly qualified like the Germans, who helped to start the production of electric light bulbs.[158] A similar elite element was the group of approximately 6000 Finns, who arrived in Soviet Karelia from North America.[159] On the other hand, there were about 15,000, largely unqualified, Finns who crossed the border illegally in the 1930s to seek their fortunes in the land of the Soviets, which had advertised its progressive society and just social practices.[160]

The foreigners were a problematic and, a priori, dubious element. Those trespassers, who arrived illegally from Finland, were invariably sent first to a filtering camp for some time. Thereafter, they might expect to receive their freedom with or without restrictions regarding their place of residence. Their fate was in most cases very tragic.[161]

However, many foreigners were extremely serious about the task of constructing socialism. Very often well-to-do people sacrificed their fortunes and careers in order to contribute to the great cause. In the Promised Land they often lost their loved ones, their freedom, and their life.

Amongst these foreign workers was a rather special group, who were to be schooled in the Komintern schools. It goes without saying that this group consisted of people, who were politically active –although not always well educated. From the Soviet point of view they suffered from a quite special and detrimental handicap: they had grown up in a capitalist society.

Like the inmates of the Belomorkanal camps, the foreigners needed re-education. This was given to them by the party collective, where each, in turn, had to practice criticism and self-criticism. This system was quite similar to normal Soviet practices, but certainly the foreigners had specific problems of their own.

In their book, which is based on a huge amount of material consisting of party biographies and protocols, Brigitte Studer and Berthold Unfried describe how the young cadres understood that they were fighting philistinism, which isolated them from a true proletarian mentality like original sin. The struggle had to be waged in many ways: one had to become conscious of one's philistine self, which worked like a fifth column in one's psyche.[162] The goal was to change one's consciousness, transforming it into that of a proper proletarian.[163]

Philistinism makes itself felt in countless ways, but apparently the most serious damage was the result of the egoism and individualism, which it entailed.[164] There were also other forms of philistinism such as sentimentality for instance.[165] Yet another was the inclination to self-justification, whereas a communist would have to confess his mistakes and vices.[166]

Many, perhaps most, young foreign cadres in the Komintern schools took the struggle against philistinism very seriously, but ultimate success was extremely hard to achieve. In every "unfinished" cadre there was a petty bourgeois that thought "bad thoughts," uttered incorrect verdicts and indulged in philistine conduct. As one comrade said: "when somebody says to me: 'there are no petty bourgeois remnants in me,' I'll say: 'You are wrong.' In all of us there are some."[167] For those people, who took the idea of socialism very seriously, this was a logical conclusion. As regards such matters as sexual license, which would be understood by some Western bohemians as anti-philistine conduct, this was condemned in the party rituals as "moral dissolution." For a person, who indulged in promiscuity could also deceive the party.[168]

At the end of the 1930s the foreign element as a whole was considered unreliable and it suffered enormous losses in the purges. Inside the Komintern many parties were bled white; the Polish party for instance was completely destroyed. The fate of these people seems to have had astonishingly little influence on the political pilgrims, discussed above, who visited the Soviet Union under scrupulous guidance.[169]

7
The New Covenant

The intelligentsia rehabilitated

The cultural revolution of 1928-1931, a period of class war, had been a terrible time for the entire petty bourgeoisie, including the peasants, *nepmen*, specialists, masters and superiors of all kinds, intellectual fellow-travellers and party functionaries, who were not sufficiently proletarian-minded to fulfil the zealots' criteria. This period was characterized by an attempt to annihilate the petty bourgeoisie *en masse*. It had been a vital part of the grand project of constructing the edifice of a classless socialist society.

But Stalin apparently thought in terms of material production rather than abstract classes and their supposed psychology. In general, he was especially concerned with the economic outcome of his policies. What for the zealots seemed to be the very essence of the struggle and its essential goal; that is, an attack against the proprietary instincts of the peasants, driving them into the commune, the destruction of the petty bourgeois family and so on, soon appeared to have a detrimental effect on the economy of the country. The leadership was not slow to react.

As has already been pointed out, the cultural revolution, which in essence was an attack on "petty bourgeois" values, had already been on the ebb since 1931—even since the spring of 1930 when Stalin suddenly adopted a policy of a return to authority and hierarchy, where the workers would certainly not be the topmost layer.[1]

Here we can trace the first instances of the rehabilitation of "petty bourgeois" values. This was the beginning of a process, which lasted for several years and ended in an ideology, which was totally different from and hostile to the "revolutionary" anti-philistine and egalitarian values, which the Bolsheviks had preached during the revolution. Vera Dunham, who has studied Stalinist literature, speaks about a "Big Deal," whereby the Stalinist state bought the support of the new Soviet middle class by satisfying its material and—restricted—moral interests.[2]

The first five-year plan was successfully fulfilled in four years, in 1932, or so it was claimed. Undoubtedly, this was largely achieved thanks to a retreat from the egalitarian and levelling tendencies, which had begun in 1930-31. A further step saw the strengthening of discipline and the widespread introduction of draconian methods. These new methods were introduced in 1932. Draconic measures against the pilfering of socialist property, the restoration of the authority of the leadership on all levels, the fastening of the peasants to the land, the introduction of the work-book system, and so on, may well have been necessary to ensure the functioning of the system. In any event, the Bolsheviks were by no means ashamed of the fact that the system used coercion. On the contrary, they prided themselves on the fact that they could use coercion with such impressive effect. According to Marxist theory, the state, and that meant any state, was an instrument of violence, and the Bolsheviks had always been free from any petty-bourgeois prejudice concerning the nature and methods of political battle: this was total war, which knew no mercy and no compromise.[3]

Stalin's extremely useful idea of the "general line" of the party was developed in the battles against both the "right" and "left" opposition. In practice, this meant that when he attacked his adversaries, he accused them of deviation either to the "right" or to the "left" of the "general line," which he himself always represented and which had been established by Lenin. This line, which was the incarnation of the collective wisdom of the vanguard of the proletariat, obviously could not be wrong. On the other hand, any other line or policy was, necessarily, always wrong. This was as unavoidable as the meeting of nonparallel lines on the Euclidian plain.

Deviations, both the rightist one and the leftist one, would produce the same result, namely, the restoration of capitalism. Consequently they both had the same kind of character, namely, a petty bourgeois one.[4]

Had the party been imprudent enough to begin the building of socialism before the preconditions for this existed, the project would have failed. Ultimately, the process would have resulted in the restoration of capitalism. Similarly, had the party tried to introduce petty bourgeois communes in the countryside (as class-enemies, doubtlessly camouflaged, were doing), this process too would have ended in the restoration of capitalism. Had the rightists abandoned the programme of collectivisation and begun to endorse the petty bourgeois peasant economy –this would also have resulted in the restoration of capitalism.[5]

The Short Course's conclusion that Stalin's general line prevented a catastrophe is hardly convincing as it caused the greatest peacetime famine in European history. On the other hand, it is not implausible to think that a "petty bourgeois" political line, too eager in its desire for social levelling, too anti-authoritarian, or too lenient in its use of violence against enemies of the regime, would have resulted in a society very different from the "socialist" Soviet Union that was built in the 1930s.

According to Stalin's logic, if the proprietary instincts of the people could be made to serve the socialist society, then they were socialist by nature, not petty bourgeois, for nothing in the world could have a fixed class nature as such—it always depended on what ends it served.

For some reason Marxist theory had presupposed that the proletarians (who had only their chains to lose) would, by the logic of things, be collectively rational in pursuing their material interests, and would not want to stop with personal gain, but would want to annihilate the old system as a whole. The petty bourgeoisie and the *lumpenproletariat*, on the other hand, naturally pursued their individual interests.

In real life, however, both Lenin and Stalin took care to take into account the individual material interests of the workers. In a very real sense they built their social engineering on what someone, who hadn't recognized its socialist nature, might quite aptly have called petty bourgeois greed. In 1918 and (in principle) in 1930 the rioting of the masses had been organized by the party. The state took care of the machinery of violence, but the rank and file of the progressive classes (the workers and poor peasants) were always driven forward and persuaded by appealing to their personal material interest—which obviously for all materialists was very respectable and real.

As regards the petty bourgeois peril among the toiling classes, it was, of course, present even amongst this social group. It was present wherever there was material remuneration (or sexual, or moral, for that matter, as literature had shown), which distracted the individual from the service of the cause. I hope that the reader has already been convinced by my conclusion that, for the Bolsheviks, commodities themselves could not spoil a human being. This could result from his surroundings, both past and present (which was more or less equal to his class position). A pure, proletarian soul would not need to live in a commune at starvation level in order to preserve his class-consciousness. The essence of his class-consciousness was his relation to the collective (which was the party, in the last instance).

In fact, it was the petty bourgeois instinct, which was having its orgies in communes, where everybody was made to "eat the same porridge in identical portions." This was nothing but a distortion of Marxism, a blasphemy, so Stalin declared at the XVII party congress.[6] Its petty bourgeois nature was not evident to everybody, as Stalin implied in his angry remark. Perhaps Stalin had this in mind: the excessive interest in equality was proof of envy—a motive that had been amply exploited by Lenin during the revolution, but which, understandably, could no longer have a progressive role in a society, which was becoming socialist. Quite the contrary: as the tables had been turned and the socialist state had begun to remunerate its best sons and daughters according to their merits, it was anti-social and, thus, bourgeois (in this case petty bourgeois, for it had no roots in the prevailing social order) to envy them.

Indeed, on whom was the Soviet state lavishing remunerations, moral and pecuniary? It was the best workers and the most precious functionaries of the socialist state, not to parasites, who had inherited their wealth and lived at the expense of the exploitation of the workers. It was unthinkable that a Soviet labourer could feel hate towards his superiors. Could this be class-hate? a feeling which, as Gorky had said, had a benign and progressive character. Obviously not. Such a subversive attitude was necessarily anti-Soviet and benefited the enemies of socialism.

The group, which was officially called the "intelligentsia" comprised not only the creative intelligentsia and the specialists. The lower apparachiks, the higher administration and even the ruling oligarchy also began to be called the "intelligentsia" after the cultural revolution. Its numbers grew very rapidly in the 1930s. It has been concluded that the "overwhelming majority of it consisted of officials with little education and a low level of professional skill."[7] However, this was a group, whose lifestyle was becoming increasingly different from that of the actual proletarians. It was not self-evident that this should be so in a socialist state. The situation was rationalized by stressing the "proletarian" character of this "new" class.

In the past the *intelligenty* had not belonged to the "people." In 1934 the writer A. Avdeenko related how his father had hated and despised the *intelligenty*, the engineers, the French and Belgians, who constituted the leadership and proprietors of the local factories. These people were neatly dressed, smelt good and behaved in a strangely careless and free manner. Avdeenko's father explained that these people were *intelligenty*, and pronounced the word like a curse. Now, Avdeenko himself had been invited to a meeting of the "Soviet intelligentsia" of the town. He laughed and wondered and began to think about the great transformation.[8]

Yes, he was an *intelligent* himself, he wrote books, he rejoiced, he loved a woman in a new way, he was living in a powerful, famous and vast country, not worried about the future. He attended the theatre, and elected those in power –for all this he thanked Soviet power. Avdeenko also used to wake up early, wash himself with cold water, do calisthenics and run about the flat, laughing at the abundance of his energy. He was going to live under socialism where everyone would be like brethren. He would also see socialism come to Europe and America. There were no obstacles to his creative energy and he would be happy into old age.

He would write a book about his gratefulness towards Soviet power and make his hero pay a visit to his father's grave. There the hero would tell his father, the new kind of meaning the concept of an *intelligent* now had. And the father would answer: "You are happy, my son. Live and rejoice for thyself and for your children and grandchildren!"

Now, being an *intelligent* had begun to mean having a cultured, happy, healthy and worthy life. Did the offspring of the exploited toilers of pre-revolutionary times not deserve it?If there was an institution, which had the right to decide what was petty bourgeois and what was not –for there had to be such an institution if scientific socialism was worthy of its name- then it was certainly the vanguard of the proletariat of the socialist state: the All-Union Communist Party (Bolsheviks).

Material goods, cultured manners and all the niceties of life did not –automatically- spoil those who had earnt them, whereas absolute equality and poverty almost certainly spoilt the unworthy, philistine soul. In capitalist society someone, who earnt a lot, had cultivated manners and a cosy home was likely to be a slave of this property – a philistine, or so we learn from Gorky's works. In the socialist Soviet Union, someone in a similar position was likely to be a leading representative of the proletariat and presumably would have the psychology of a collectivist, not a philistine.

In my opinion, it is important to note that this kind of revolution in concepts was bound to happen, when society was in the process of reaching the stage of "socialism." Indeed, this officially happened as the result of the second five-year plan, after 1936 (that is: in 1937). As a result of the changed nature of society, the nationalities policy was revolutionized. In pre-socialist society, national prejudices were unavoidable. In order to overcome these prejudices, Soviet power had adopted a policy called *korenizatsiia* or indigenisation. This meant in practice (ideally at least) that the representatives of the minority nationalities were, in every way, given precedence over Russians in their national republics and autonomous units. This had been necessary in order to fight petty-bourgeois national prejudices, which were, in turn, the product of bourgeois society.

As soon as socialism was realized in the Soviet Union, however, this kind of policy became obsolete and was now reversed. By this logic, it was unavoidable that the national elites, which had been promoted to leading posts in the national territories by Soviet power, were found to be perpetuating the wrong policy for a socialist society. Petty-bourgeois nationalism, which had not only been excusable, but even unavoidable and objectively useful for the progress of the communist cause before the triumph of socialism, was now seen as having a detrimental anti-Soviet character.[9] For instance, it had been correct to give precedence to non-Russians in their national republics before the triumph of socialism, as this was instrumental in winning the trust of those nationalities. The triumph of socialism by the end of the second five-year plan also meant that national prejudices had been overcome. In this new situation, favoring the minority nationalities at the expense of the Russians was tantamount to being guilty of segregation, which was a cardinal sin against the ethos of socialism.

The triumph of socialism meant, in principle,that the whole country had been purged not only of bourgeois elements, but also of the petty bourgeoisie, represented by the nepmen and the peasantry.

This was the discourse Stalin used and he went on to prove that it was meant to be taken extremely seriously. The only bourgeois influences in the socialist Soviet Union (after 1936) could now come only from outside, for in the Land of the Soviets, there was "no social base" for such influences. Consequently, all bourgeois phenomena (e.g. bourgeois nationalism) were foreign in nature (and by connection) and, accordingly, a merciless attitude was needed in dealing with them.[10]

The new society

It was intended that a socialist society would be built by the end of the second five-year plan. This would secure its material basis. With the stimulating knowledge of the approach of socialism, people were filled with enthusiasm (at least officially) and looked forward to an imminent future, which would totally transform their lives. This alone could explain the wonderful transformation of the kulaks in the Belomorkanal camps. The kolkhozniks, for their part, learned from Stalin himself that they would all be "prosperous" and their life would become "fully cultured."[11] Everyone could look forward to the abolition of material scarcity. Some progress had already been made in this direction, as bread rationing was abolished in 1934. Accordingly, the following year, Stalin could say with reason that "Life has become better, life has become merrier."[12]

There was no denying, however, that not everybody was happy with the policies of the party. Anti-Soviet agitation was also in evidence. The Peoples Commissariat for Justice realized, however, that such agitation was not happening simply along class-lines. It was not true that the workers were always loyal and petty bourgeois elements always anti-Soviet. For instance, among those, who were convicted of anti-Soviet agitation during the third quarter of 1935, 24.5 percent were workers, 13,9 percent *kolkhozniki*, 32,5 percent kulaks or *edinolichniki*, 24,3 percent officials (*sluzhashchie*), and 3,9 percent others.[13] True, officials, who might be suspected of having petty bourgeois, non worker sentiments, were over-represented, but, on the other hand, the kolkhozhniki, who were— or just a couple of years before had been- petty bourgeois, were grossly underrepresented. The percentage of workers was alarming. As regards the extent of this kind of behavior, narkom Krylenko reported to Stalin that it was sharply rising.[14] All this was happening just at the very moment, when society was reaching a qualitatively new, and higher stage.

A real harbinger of the new society was the Stakhanovite movement, which began in 1935. It showed, in effect, that the Soviet worker had conquered technology. He was a new kind of man, not just a worker but an intelligent too.

The following year, a large movement to raise the cultural level of the people both at home and at the workshop was begun. Its protagonists, the obshchestvennitsy or the wives of the technical leadership, were to bring the blessings of cultured life to the masses.[15]

Classical culture was also to return. Whilst the RAPP radicals wanted to throw away the whole body of the old literary heritage as unnecessary ballast and had attacked the "masters," they no longer had the support of the authorities for their activities. On the contrary, their own organizations were liquidated in 1932. When the new Union of Soviet Writers was established in 1934, it professed an ethos of literary mastery and a respect for the classics of world literature.

Similar changes affected the other unions of the creative intelligentsia. "Proletarian" organizations were liquidated and replaced by "Soviet" organizations, which respected classic forms.[16]

As for the avantgardists, who had been among the few friends the Bolsheviks had had during and after the revolution, even they were silenced drastically and effectively. In 1936 Pravda launched a campaign against "formalism" in all fields of art, which was a complete success.[17]

In sum, if we try sympathetically to sketch the ideal new citizen of this socialist society as he was depicted in the propaganda around 1936, we get the following: the Soviet citizen was now becoming cultured, well-to-do and happy. Being cultured meant adopting both the skills and traditions of urban life and a knowledge of both classical culture and current Soviet politics. The tastes of the cultured citizen were conventional and so was his way of life. As the results of the 1936 all-union discussion about the new family laws purportedly showed, the family was found to be the fundamental cell of the new socialist society.[18] Whilst being an impeccable family man, rearing his children to become good and loyal Soviet citizens, the new Soviet man was also a hero: his heroism was expressed in his dedication to his work and the party and in his readiness to defend the fatherland.

The Soviet man was no longer being exploited by anybody and no longer had to waste his energy in struggling with the elemental vices of a pre-socialist society, where lack of planning and petty bourgeois instinctiveness defied rational approach. Now, society was becoming entirely rational. The structures of society, the "objective conditions," could be blamed for only ten per cent of any deficiencies, Stalin argued in 1934 —all the rest lay on the shoulders of the individual, and could be cured by improved control, and cadre work.[19] This was a proud and responsible position for Man, who was no longer the wretched product of wretched social conditions.

Moreover this was also true for the new Soviet woman, who in principle also had to excel both in work and in defence. In addition, the new Soviet woman was also the main keeper of the family hearth, and had to have an eye for the niceties of life.[20] This was not to be confused with philistinism, which had afflicted the women in the pre-socialist society (and even later, after the revolution, or so Gladkov's novel, among others, argued), for in the new socialist society everybody received his or her due, no less and no more.

All this seemed quite idyllic, almost pastoral. No wonder that people began to ask when the state would finally die away as the program of the communist party predicted and as even Lenin had already presaged in the tumultuous years of the revolution.

Here general line of the party had corrected the old tenets of socialist theory. In 1935 Stalin revealed that the state in the Soviet Union would not wither away as long as there was bourgeois encirclement. The bourgeois world was sending its agents into the first socialist country and its enmity towards the Soviet Union would grow in proportion to the latter's successes on its own forward leading path.[21]

In fact, this meant that the class struggle even inside the Soviet Union would not relax, but would, on the contrary, grow more and more fierce. This might have seemed contradictory, in that class struggle was now going to happen in a classless society. But, contradiction was one of the basic concepts of bolshevism, and the highest institution, which could decide on such an issue would, of course, be the vanguard of the leading class.

The coming of the new social system unavoidably presupposed a new constitution for the Soviet state. This document, which was clearly regarded as having tremendous significance for the whole of humanity, was prepared with great labor in 1936. An all-union popular discussion about the new constitution was launched, but ultimately Stalin's opinion was the most authoritative and was given great publicity, even being published alongside the law-text itself.

In his comments,[22] Stalin concluded that the class-structure of the Soviet Union had changed in a fundamental way. All the exploiting classes had been liquidated. There remained only the working class, the class of peasants, and the intelligentsia. But even these groups had changed in character. The working class, for instance, could no longer be called a proletariat, for it was not exploited and owned, together with the rest of the population, the means of production. Such a working class had never existed in history before. The peasantry was also free from exploitation. Its subsistence was not based on individual work on private plots using primitive technology. It was based not on private property but on collective property, which grew on the basis of collective work.

As for "the intelligentsia, the engineering and technical functionaries, functionaries of the cultural front, the white collar workers in general and so on", this group had also radically changed. It was no longer "that inveterate intelligentsia, which tried to set itself over the classes, while it in fact in most cases served the landlords and the capitalists." "Our Soviet intelligentsia" said Stalin "is a wholly new intelligentsia, which is tied by its roots tied to the workers and peasants." The offspring of the gentry and bourgeoisie now formed a tiny part of the intelligentsia, whilst 80 to 90 percent came from the working layers of society. The very character of the intelligentsia had changed and it now served the working classes which was building a classless society.

Moreover, the differences between these groups within socialist society were disappearing: both the economic contradictions and, therefore, the political contradictions between these groups were disappearing.

In any case, even though Stalin declared that a new Soviet man had been born and that Soviet socialist society had a new nature, this did not mean that everything in the great transformation process had already happened.

There were no antagonistic contradictions between social groups, the two classes and the layer of the intelligentsia, but clearly there were still non-antagonistic contradictions, of both an economic and a political nature: there was, for instance, the different kind of relation to the means of production of the workers and peasants. The latter owned their share of the kolkhozes and, accordingly, were a particular kind of petty proprietor. There was also the difference between mental and physical work, which had yet to be overcome.

The essence and structure of the intelligentsia had been transformed throughout the Soviet Union. This had happened not only in the urban centers, and not only in Russia proper. In 1936, a country teacher, Sofron Ivanov described in Pravda, what had happened in his native village, Tiurlem, in Chuvassia. The text was originally a speech that had been delivered at a village meeting.[23]

Between the reforms of the 1860s and the revolution—that is, over the course of half a century—the speaker stated, Tiurlem had given the country about twenty *intelligenty*, among them nine priests. Among the rest there were three, second lieutenants, one *fel'dsher* (medical assistant) and three telegraphists. After the revolution about two hundred *intelligenty* had come from the village, among them 11 engineers, 30 commanders of the Red army, 22 teachers, 29 bookkeepers, 50 electricians, 15 electric mechanics, 29 technicians, 30 specialists of telegraphy, two station masters and seven deputy station masters, and so on. Life in the village was more cultured: there were schools, clubs and a library. There were a "Radiocabine*t*," a "Party cabinet," a "House of Defence" and a "Park of culture and rest." The kolkhozniks were now interested in Pushkin and there were 93 complete editions of Pushkin's works in the *rayon*. There had been well-attended literary conferences about Sholokhov's *Virgin Soil Upturned*, Furmanov's *Chapaev* and Gorky's *Mother*. Culture was now held in honor, whereas before the revolution the uncivilized local merchant did not even shake hands with the teacher.

Indeed, as comrade Stalin had said, the new Soviet intelligentsia was a totally new intelligentsia, which had its roots in the working class and the peasantry. Indeed, the progress described, sounded imposing, even if we accept that the report contained an unavoidable amount of so-called *lipa* (sham). As for Stalin's proclamation about the new nature of the intelligentsia, it was obviously true: now the term was being used of any employees doing mental work, all foremen and directors or having education. It is doubtful that priests and deacons before the revolution would have considered themselves members of "intelligentsia," at all. It is also true that the general educational level of the new intelligentsia was often very low.[24]

To be sure, despite Stalin's rather simplistic presentation of the mutual relations of the communists, their non-party supporters and the bourgeoisie, which left little room for any domestic non-socialist elements, there were apparently some "petty bourgeois" phenomena, which could not be explained by the presence of some immediate foreign contact. Some "remnants of the past" unavoidably survived in the psychology of the older generation, which had received its education under capitalism. Now, everybody had, in principle, been liberated from the burden of his past and had become a Soviet citizen, with an equal right to vote and to work. But the remnants lingered on. Viacheslav Molotov, speaking on the 20th anniversary jubilee of the October revolution, explained that socialism had won on the political level in 1917.However, on the economic level the triumph of socialism had happened along with collectivization, that is, at the beginning of the 1930s. But on the cultural level, it was still too early to speak about the triumph of socialism.[25]

Now, the social position of a person was in principle (but not in practice!) determined by his profession and not by his former class position in the previous capitalist and pre-socialist Soviet society.

The only classes now were the workers (who were no longer "proletarians") and the peasants. It was not openly acknowledged in the constitution, but clearly the peasants were still regarded as somewhat "petty bourgeois" and consequently the workers were recognized as their superiors.[26] The intellectuals were now regarded as a social "layer," which represented the ideas of these two "classes" and had no independent existence. On the other hand, given the nature of the work of intellectuals, they were clearly the group, which could most readily serve the exploiting classes that still existed, namely, those abroad.

The birth of Socialist Realism

The radical "proletarian" culture, which had fought against more traditional forms in art, had had its zealots among the post-revolutionary Proletkults. The heyday of proletarian culture had been during the tumultuous years of the First Five-Year Plan, which Western scholars later dubbed the "Cultural Revolution," echoing the parallel of the Chinese experience of the 1960s.

The First Five-Year Plan had been a period of wild optimism, of harebrained schemes, fierce class struggle and callous atrocities including the starvation of millions of people. The whole country was in flux and sizable contingents of young activists—including many intellectuals of the new generation—attacked the "fortresses" of the "exploiters" and petty bourgeoisie everywhere. In the countryside, the kulak was "liquidated," torn off his homestead and deported; in the administration, the old specialists and "bureaucrats" were attacked; in the workshop, the young, proletarian *praktik* (man from the workshop) replaced the old engineer; in the arts, old "masters" were toppled from their pedestals; at school, the authority of the teacher was contested and so on. The "petty bourgeois" intellectual was also going to be replaced by a "proletarian" intellectual in the field of culture.

The "Great Retreat" from radicalism since 1931 was felt in all walks of life. The authority of the directors in workshops was restored and the drive towards egalitarianism was reversed. The school study program returned to being conventional, the heroes of Russia's national past were resurrected and the idea of the importance of great men in history was reinstated.

The liquidation of the Union of Proletarian Writers (RAPP) and its numerous local sister unions in 1932 was a logical and necessary step in this process, which was a sort of conservative restoration, which lasted from the end of the First Five-Year Plan (1931) to the beginning of WW II. Similarly, all unions of "proletarian" artists—and there were scores of them—were liquidated by the second half of the 1930s, many being replaced with a corresponding "Soviet" organization, which gave the work of the creative artists involved a more disciplined, unified and conservative character.

The doctrine of socialist realism, and, indeed, the term itself, were invented in the years 1932-34. This happened with the active participation of Stalin and other party luminaries. The term "socialist realism" was chosen by Stalin himself, but the epithet of the writers as "engineers of the human soul" was invented by a writer, and former RAPPist, Kirshon.[27]

RAPP was also liquidated and its members were not even allowed to found their own section in the new organization that replaced it. This was decided at a meeting, held in October 1932, at which Stalin, Molotov, Kaganovich and Voroshilov, as well as about 45 writers were present. This meeting also decided that Gorky should be considered as the founder of socialist realism.[28]

The slogan of the new literary method was also developed in the years 1932-34. The main aim was to tell the "truth," or to reflect correctly Soviet reality. Socialist realism was the antidote to RAPP, which had pretended to use a dialectical-materialist method. The new method could not deny the fact that reality had a dialectical nature, but it maintained that the dialectical method did not exist.[29] Stalin himself was sceptical and ironic about verse that would be created by a master of dialectics.[30] It was explained that one did not need to know dialectical materialism to write well, but that it would help one to write better than ever.[31]

By 1934 the slogan of socialist realism had come to be formulated as follows: "Socialist realism, which is the main method of Soviet literature and literary criticism, presupposes from the writer faithfulness to reality, and the historically concrete presentation of reality in its revolutionary development. Faithfulness to reality and historical accuracy must be united with the tasks of the ideological reforging and education of the toiling people in the spirit of socialism."[32]

New practices were more important than formal definitions of the tasks of literature. They included, for instance, the rehabilitation of the fellow-travelers. This was not a final peace treaty, but rather an armistice, which lasted until the spring of 1936, when the campaign against the formalists was launched.[33]

It may sound paradoxical that the arts in the new socialist society would be more or less freed from the dialectical method. The explanation may be that the writers and artists were now liberated from the task of solving the cardinal tasks of understanding ontological, or any other philosophical questions, for themselves. These were to be solved by the top leadership and it was enough, that the artist contributed to the flourishing of the party line, instead of inventing problems and solutions for himself.

The general slogans of the party were good inspiration for the creative intelligentsia. When Stalin proclaimed in 1935 that life had become better and merrier, no *intelligent* denied the veracity of that assessment. The intelligentsia had better accept this and try to depict life as it was supposed to be. Indeed, it was not even possible to publish anything melancholic, as this was prevented by the censor.[34]

This did not mean that they were simply supposed to write clumsy panegyrics of current Soviet reality. They also had to show up the problems and contradictions. "Varnishing" reality was detrimental to the cause of socialism, because it lacked credibility. Instead, the author had to "minimize the void between everyday life and the optimistic tendencies of the collective history."[35]

Socialist realism was not intended only to apply to literature. Its principles were also valid in the fields of painting, sculpture, architecture and even music. Everywhere, there was a return to conservative forms. "Middle-class values" rose to a place of honor and individual heroes began to emerge.[36] The hero was no longer just a representative of the class—a collective entity. The hero was an individual. In historiography, great men were rediscovered and returned to history lessons after 1934. In art, great men were even found to exist among the leaders of the party as well as among other remarkable representatives of the working classes (and no other classes existed in the state of the Soviets). At the top stood Stalin, who came to be regarded as the "father" of the Soviet family, whilst the lesser heroes were his "sons."[37]

According to the self-understanding of socialist society, the future belonged to this progressive social system. This by no means presupposed that the heritage of the past was worthless; on the contrary, all that was best in the past was part of the painful preparation for the dawn of socialism, which would finally put an end to the prehistory of man and usher in his real, true history as the conscious creator of his fate.

Accordingly, the best (progressive) part of the cultural heritage of humanity was proclaimed to have an innate worth, which was why every cultured person had to know it. It may be recalled that, Lenin had already stressed the importance of knowing the classical heritage, when he had spoken about the future communist society ("after 10-20 years") to the komsomols in 1922.[38]

There was nothing anomalous in making the classics serve the revolutionary class after the revolution. The Bolsheviks had expropriated the property of the former governing classes and put it at their disposal. Why not make Rubens, Rembrandt and Repin serve the working class?[39]

This implied that the intelligentsia was not deprived of the opportunity of studying classical literature and art, and these subjects were also taught to the youth. This was even useful, to a certain extent, for the purposes of the party-state: it gave prestige to the new society and its artists, and it offered an outlet and an escape to those, who found socialist everyday life suffocating. And, after all, it was true that the value of avant-garde art could be plausibly contested — the mainstream in most countries did precisely that, but everyone acknowledged the value of classical art. Consequently, the formerly bohemian and rebellious cultural scene of the socialist Soviet Union now quickly became a haven for the classical purist. Soviet intellectuals became, with time, famous for their knowledge of classical culture. Part of the Russian intelligentsia had looked for spiritual guidance to Tolstoy, Dostoevsky and Pushkin before the revolution and continued to do so after it. For many intellectuals, the classics became a real passion.[40]

It has been said that socialist realism was to be a *Gesamtkunstwerk*. In fact its principles encompassed the representation of Soviet life in its entirety. In a socialist society everything was supposed to be perfect: happy, effective, heroic, popular and party-minded. The Socialist society had not been entirely constructed in 1934, but everybody knew that it would be by 1937. I think that it makes sense to see the development of the cultural front during the Second Five-Year Plan as a planned preparation for the impending socialist society. When using the word "planning" I don't mean that the future development of culture could have been foreseen. The Bolsheviks believed both in the importance of planning and also in the revolutionary, qualitative jump, which would occur with the introduction of the socialist system. Who could tell? Perhaps there would be new forms in art and culture, but this was not important. The essence was, in any case, absolutely new and forms as such did not have value in themselves. Socialist art could not just repeat old forms even if it used them, because its new essence also gave them new meaning.[41]

A masterpiece is found. Furmanov's *Chapaev*

By 1934 it was understood that the masterpiece par excellence of socialist realism was Gorky's *Mother*, which has been described above. Some other books, which had been written several years previously, were also selected to be models of the new literary school. Gladkov's *Cement* and Dmitry Furmanov's *Chapaev* belonged to this group.

It was, of course, not an accident that the late Furmanov's novel became another model for socialist realism. Its protagonist was a famous red warlord of peasant origin, who was a born military genius although he was also a narrow-minded and unenlightened person, who was barely literate. He had naïve ideas about society and politics, was childishly capricious in his behavior, — and was very much in need of guidance.

The other hero is the political commissar, Fedor Klychkov, whom the reader easily recognizes as, in fact, the narrator himself.

The narrative and message of the book is very clear-cut. Chapaev, who is representative of the simple muzhik, is suspicious about his superiors, the officers, the intelligents, the "headquarters," and "the center" in general. He only trusts simple folk and despises the intelligents' "idle talk." Chapaev is like a wild horse of the steppes; left alone he could even be dangerous and detrimental to the great cause, but harnessed to its service he becomes a most precious ally. Therefore, the commissar undertakes to "light the way for this man and put him on the right track."[42] Chapaev was very much like his soldiers, who were simple peasants. His whole unit was quite different from the neighboring one, which consisted of workers; the weavers of Ivanovo-Voznesensk. Their antipathy was mutual.[43]

In fact, Chapaev was not very talented, and not even especially brave. He became a symbolic hero because he was so much like his men.[44] For the reader it is clear that without the guidance of the party, which represents the collective wisdom of the proletariat as interpreted by the commissar, this semi-anarchistic mass could only be destructive. It mercilessly destroyed, the life and resources of the Cossacks, which was, indeed, vitally important, but left alone this primitive natural force might have turned against the hated and despised "center" itself, against those who were superior in consciousness and education.

Furmanov does not use the word "petty bourgeois" about his subject and in the given context it would, indeed, sound very funny. According to Marxist analysis, however, Chapaev and his men were "petty bourgeois" by class. The party guided them through the efforts of a man, who was also, clearly, a petty bourgeois — an intellectual by class. Everything, however, turned out for the best, after all. The workers of the neighboring unit, the workers from Ivanovo-Voznesensk, did their duty impeccably, which must have been almost a truism, but Chapaev's men also served the cause with honor, although even their leader did not really understand what socialism was about.

The message of the book is quite clear; it is only the superior knowledge of the party that is able to direct the blind passions of the dark masses to serve the cause of progress. The commoner's instinctive hatred of superiors and of more developed comrades is just peasant/petty bourgeois backwardness and has nothing to do with the real objectives of class struggle. Whatever its credibility, this position happened to fit extremely well the needs of the "real socialism," at least that form of real socialism that was in the process of being born in the 1930s. Like Gorky's *Mother*, Furmanov's *Chapaev* had the considerable merit of having been written in the past and, accordingly, it was a time-honored proof of the permanent validity of the principles it illustrated. It served as evidence that the idea of the superior knowledge of the party over the masses was not a novel invention of the present government.

In 1936, 10 years after Furmanov's death, his *chef-d'oeuvre*—and a new film about it—were still widely discussed. Its rather simplistic political message was always at the center of attention.[45]

Here, one can perhaps point out that later in the 1960s, Chapaev, undoubtedly thanks to Furmanov's book and the film made about it- became the hero of countless anecdotes, which made fun of Marxist-Leninist jargon and the orthodox explanations (rationalizations) of the rather grim realities of Soviet socialist society. In these jokes Chapaev plays the role of a homemade intelligent (who hits the bull's eye better than the party Pharisees) as his friend Petka asks him about vital issues, of interest to the masses.

The First Congress of Soviet Writers attacks the enemy on both sides

The new organization, which was to replace RAPP, the Union of Soviet Writers, was founded in August 1934. That moment in Soviet history is reputed to have been full of official optimism. The First Five-Year Plan had been declared a tremendous success, and the XVII Party congress in January of 1934 was depicted as "The Party congress of the Victors," referring to the claim that the plan of building a socialist society had achieved a decisive victory. Undoubtedly there were real achievements in heavy industry, but there was also terrible misery in the countryside (especially the famine in the Ukraine and Kazakhstan in 1932-33) and a widespread and very serious deterioration in living conditions.[46] In 1934 bread rationing, which had been introduced during the First Five-Year Plan, was abolished, which, for many people, did not bring about a noticeable improvement, but could offer some hope of a better future.

All the hardship notwithstanding, the mood of the ruling elite and many of the intellectuals was probably rather optimistic. As a result of the successful Second Five-Year Plan, a new socialist society was to be built, and this did not mean just an increase in the standard of living, but also an intellectual or mental revolution. The "Cultural revolution," in the official contemporary sense, or the campaign for civilizing the masses and changing their psychology, was still on the march and would produce tremendous results in the near future.

The task of the Writers' congress and their new union, itself a creation of the congress, was to organize the writers to best serve the world-historic transformation, which was taking place. Their calling was to become engineers of the human soul, to use the term Stalin had coined somewhat earlier (with the help of the writers).

At the congress, there were 377 writers with the right to a deciding vote and 220 with a consultative vote. Forty foreign writers were also present. No less than 96,3 percent of the delegates were men, 49,1 percent were communists (60,4 percent if candidates and komsomols are taken into account), 27,3 percent were workers, 42,6 percent were peasants, 2,4 percent came from the petty bourgeoisie (*meshchane*), 12,9 percent represented the 'working intelligentsia,' 5,5 percent were civil servants, 2,4 percent were of gentry origin, 1,4 percent were merchants, 1,4 percent were servants of cult (clergy) by origin and 3,8 percent were kustars (craftmen). This meant that no less than 30,1 percent of the writers present at the congress (or literati, for critics and journalists were also represented) were of petty bourgeois or noble origin. If we consider that the peasants were petty bourgeois, as the party did, it is clear that only 27,3 percent of the delegates were of proletarian origin (probably less, for there must have been non-proletarian representatives of the labor aristocracy among the writers of worker origin).

It was officially calculated that there were no more than 201 Russians present, but as many as 322 actually wrote in Russian. The second largest group was the Jews, who numbered 113, although only 24 of them wrote in their national language (Yiddish). The majority of the delegates had begun their literary careers after the revolution. Only 139 had practiced the literary craft before 1917, while 257 had begun in 1918-1926. No less than 151 had joined the republic of letters during the tumultuous years of 1927-1931.[47]

To summarize, the congregation assembled in the hall was almost totally male, preponderantly young, pro-communist and wrote in Russian.

On the other hand, there were substantial contingents of non-party and non-Russian elements and people with a personal knowledge of prerevolutionary Russia. It was also true that a formidable number of them came from a petty bourgeois background. This was a typical instance of the party's general tactics. The party would always remain the active vanguard. The role of the party as an organization unifying the most active individuals in each institution inevitably created an atmosphere of tension between the activists and the others, as the reader will remember from the example of Veresaev's factory. The plight of the party was to be engaged in an eternal struggle for progress and at the same time a permanent purge of its rank and file. In the ideal case, those who were not members of the party would recognize its authority and join the common struggle under its guidance. Those who were against the party would be destroyed, but even those who were for the party would not and could not comply with its standards to an equal degree. Some were stronger and some were weaker in their faith in the party and the struggle. There would be a constant struggle for higher standards with the party showing the way.

The congress was opened on the 17th August by Maxim Gorky. Before the congress Gorky had sent Stalin a letter, enclosing his speech for inspection and expressing his thoughts about suitable candidates for the leading posts in the Writers' Union. Personally Gorky wished to decline the role of chairman of the Union, referring to his age, the amount of work and his inability to act as a chairman. Gorky also used this opportunity to express his concern that many people still considered that the peasants had just pretended to have become collectivists, and that if there was a war, a counterrevolution could restore capitalism. Moreover, it was not only the petty bourgeoisie and the philistines (*meshchanin, obyvatel'*) who were saying this, even some party people were expressing such views and this was what was disturbing. Gorky also referred to some phenomena in Ukraine, which allegedly witnessed of "wrecking" at school and "contaminating children with philistinism" (probably he hinted to "local nationalism"). All these phenomena convinced Gorky of the necessity of paying serious attention to literature. Literature had to be the medium, which "brought ideas to life," and not just ideas, but the proper mood too.[48]

Gorky acted as the chairman of the congress. In his speech, which had also been given to Stalin for inspection, he pointed out that this was the first time that the literature of the USSR, which had hitherto been scattered in numerous fragments, had appeared in front of the world proletariat as a unified whole. "We are," Gorky proclaimed on behalf of his audience, "people, who profess real humanism, the humanism of the revolutionary proletariat, of a force, which is destined by history to liberate the toilers of the whole earth from envy and bribery, from all those diseases that have centuries have been deforming working people for centuries." "We are," Gorky went on, "enemies of property -that terrible and vile goddess of the bourgeois world, enemies of the beastly individualism, which this goddess has made its religion."[49] The "anti-philistine" ethos, which was at the core of Gorky's thinking, was very emphatically expressed here at the very beginning of socialist realism, which purported to offer a new way forward for the Soviet people and the world. The authoritative ideological contribution of the politburo was delivered by a secretary of the Central Committee, A.A. Zhdanov.

In his speech Zhdanov pointed to the pretentious tenet of the party that the socialist system (*uklad*) had triumphed in the Soviet Union "irrevocably and definitively." He mentioned Stalin's words at the party congress in January, where the leader had explained that the difficulties now being encountered in the work of building socialism were just due to a lack of organization. The party was now organizing the masses for the final liquidation of capitalist elements and for the destruction of the remnants of capitalism in economics and in the consciousness of people. The destruction of the remnants of capitalism in the consciousness of the people meant struggling with the remnants of all kinds of bourgeois influences on the proletariat: unsteadiness, laziness, petty bourgeois (*melkoburzhuaznyi*) indecency and individualism, greed and a non-conscientious attitude to social property.

Soviet literature had now developed into a new kind of literature, Zhdanov argued. It was an organic part of the new society of workers and peasants. It received its inspiration from the construction of the new society and enjoyed the "tactful, daily guidance" of the central committee and of Stalin himself.

As regards bourgeois literature and culture in general, they were already incapable of creating great works. The inclination to mysticism and pornography was characteristic of the depreciation and rottenness of contemporary bourgeois culture. The "famous people" of bourgeois literature were now thieves, detectives, prostitutes and hooligans, whereas Soviet literature described workers and peasants, party people, engineers, komsomols and pioneers. Soviet literature was optimistic, full of enthusiasm and heroism. It was also openly tendentious. Every Soviet writer could say to any dull-witted bourgeois, any philistine (*filister*) that this literature was tendentious and that he was proud of it, for this tendency was directed towards liberating the whole of humanity from the capitalist yoke.

Soviet writers, the engineers of the human soul, as Stalin had called them, had to be able to portray heroes and the future for the people. This was not utopian, for tomorrow was already being systematically built today.

The proletariat was also the lawful heir of the best that had been created in world literature, Zhdanov stressed and hoped that writers would create works of high craftsmanship (*masterstvo*), and be the most active organizers of the change of consciousness in the spirit of socialism, and be in the forefront of the construction of a classless, socialist society.[50]

From Zhdanov's words, it was evident that classical literature would have its place of honor in Soviet culture, but that the depravity and pessimism, which ailed bourgeois literature would not be tolerated. As engineers of the human souls, writers had a great practical task to undertake in the cause of the "party and the class." Literature fulfilled its mission in showing the splendid phenomena of the socialist present and future. The message here for the individual writer was that life in the land of the Soviets was splendid in essence and could not be depicted in any other light in practice.

As regards philistinism, the party was fighting to erase it from the consciousness of the whole Soviet people and here too writers would be at the forefront. Writers as such were not depicted as special people even though Soviet literature was unique and worthy of many superlatives. Its grandeur was due to the fact that it was an organic and ineradicable part of socialist construction ("flesh of its flesh and bone of its bone").[51]

After Zhdanov's speech (rech'), Gorky presented a report (doklad) about Soviet literature. As was becoming for an event of world-historic significance, Gorky began with philosophic musings about the emergence of man on the earth and the significance of work and society for his progress towards humanity. Gorky also gave a brief review of all literature that had been written hitherto and then concentrated on the present century, with some excursions into the past. The critique of his paper was directed at the bourgeoisie and especially against the petty bourgeoisie.

The bourgeoisie's attitude to culture had always been nonchalant, he said. "There is good reason to hope" (sic!), he said, "that when the history of culture is written by Marxists, we will come to know that the role of the bourgeoisie in the history of cultural creation has been greatly inflated, especially in literature..."[52] The bourgeoisie never thought that the cultural level of humanity should be raised. In fact, it denied the right of the workers and peasants to an education. Instead, it tried to give them ideas that served its own interests, which ultimately were nothing other than the idiotic greed of a petty vendor (lavochnik).[53]

The petty bourgeoisie (meshchanstvo) was situated between the hammer of capital and the anvil of the working people. It was skeptical, ignorant and low-minded (poshlyi). The European philistines (meshchane) had an ardent love for crime novels, along with detectives, gentlemen-thieves had become its favorite characters. Drama and comedy had deteriorated and "great people" had disappeared. Most characteristic of contemporary European literature was the "superfluous man."[54]

As regards Russian literature, there had been two lines of development (as there was in the West): critical realism (Fonvizin, Griboedov, Gogol, Chekhov, Bunin) and "purely petty bourgeois" literature (Bulgarin, Masal'sky, Zotov, Golitsynsky, Vonliarliarsky, Vsevolod Krestovsky, Vsevolod Solovyev, Leikin, Averchenko etc.).

Bourgeois romanticism of the individual was barren and not connected with reality. There was the egocentric type, the social degenerate, as sketched by Dostoevsky, who had influenced Nietzsche, the spiritual father of contemporary fascism. There was the decadence of Boris Savinkov, who had said that there was no moral, only beauty and the unrestrained development of the personality. There were the *Vekhi*, Merezhkovsky, and many others, who had expressed reactionary ideas during the period 1907-1917, which deserved to be called the "most shameful and unabashed decade in the history of the Russian intelligentsia."[55]

The principal hero of Soviet literature should be work itself, Gorky said. Work understood as creation. In the Soviet Union there could be no "superfluous men" as there were in bourgeois literature. Here, the writer had full freedom to develop his talents and only one claim was made of him; that he be honest. It might be deduced from this that the writer also bore responsibility for any instances of petty-bourgeois low-mindedness (*meshchanskaia poshlost'*), meanness (*podlost'*), duplicity (*dvoedushie*) and unprincipledness.[56]

Somewhat unexpectedly, given the ovations, which the leaders of the Land of the Soviets had received at the congress, Gorky referred to a bourgeois disease of the time called *vozhdizm* (the idolatry of leaders). In Gorky's mind, this phenomenon was the result of the lowered vitality of the petty philistine (*melkoe meshchanstvo*). It was true that, as an inheritance from the petty bourgeoisie, there were still some people in the Soviet Union who did not understand the difference between *vozhdizm* and guidance (*rukovodstvo*). The point was that guidance would find the best way to achieve the best results, whilst philistinism (*meshchanstvo*) was merely the individualistic struggle to rise over the heads of ones comrades.

Indeed, philistinism still had a serious presence amongst the writers, which was expressed in envy, greed, low-minded gossip and mutual slander. It should be remembered that the petty bourgeoisie (*meshchanstvo*) was a large class of parasites, who were producing nothing, but would like to swallow as much as possible. Low-mindedness (*poshlost'*) was typical of the philistine, who was occupied solely with the facts of everyday life, not the questions of work. It produced only lethal poison.

In the Soviet Union the philistine had been expelled from his nests, from the hundreds of provincial towns, but had crept back, even into Lenin's party, from where he was ousted in every party purge. All this notwithstanding, he existed like a microbe causing shameful diseases.

Philistinism should, of course, be eradicated from Soviet literature, which should be organized into a collective unity (*kollektivnoe tseloe*). Socialist individualism could develop only in conditions of collective work.[57]

It was also Gorky, who made the final speech to the congress. He noticed that non-party writers had also recognized that bolshevism was the only leading idea in creative work. Writers were the engineers of souls and should help to liberate the minds of the people from the remnants of the past, from class-history, which had converted working people into slaves and the intellectuals (*intelligenty*) into duplicitous or indifferent anarchists or renegades, sceptics or critics, or reconcilers of the irreconcilable.

Gorky made also some practical initiatives, including one about erecting a monument in honor of the "hero-pioneer" Pavel (Pavlik) Morozov.

As the new protocol required, the final speech ended with a greeting to the leader (*vozhd*) of the party, Iosif Stalin, followed by tempestuous (*burnye*), long-lasting applause, which became an ovation. Finally everyone stood up and sang the "International."[58]

It is clear that for Gorky, there was still a lot of philistinism present amongst rank and file writers. Although he sometimes used the word with the meaning of a social group ("class") and declared that it had been destroyed in Russia, it was also equally clear that by virtue of some hidden logic its properties still lingered on.

The pathos of Gorky's speeches may have been sincere, and it is well-known that high-class intelligents of the caliber of Pasternak were moved to tears by the rhetoric of the congress. In hindsight, Gorky's boldness consisted of having the nerve to flatly deny what was obvious to everyone: *vozhdizm* was ridiculed and denigrated, yet the mere mention of the name of the vozhd of the Soviet Union caused an obligatory ovation. The freedom of creation was proclaimed to be boundless, whilst collectivism and strict guidance by the party were extolled.

As soon became clear, the work of the writer, as an organic part of the reconstruction of socialism, would inescapably be organized by the party, the vanguard of the proletariat. In essence, the freedom of the man of letters was reduced to his/her voluntary acceptance of the inevitable. The party was now the supreme intellectual, which waged war on the philistine, and the writer's moral and intellectual qualities were proportionate to his faithfulness to the party-line.

But, at the 1934 congress the party-line itself was not at all clear. A good illustration of the difficulties involved is provided by Nikolai Bukharin, who made a long speech on the tasks of poetic creation in the USSR.[59]

As the OGPU observed, Bukharin's speech was the subject of a very lively discussion.[60] His "liberalism" was rather shocking, as he said that socialist realism should describe any phenomena of the epoch and should use all sorts of different forms.[61] At some points in his speech, such as when he endorsed Mayakovsky, he was met with the spontaneous applause of the audience.[62] On the other hand, Bukharin was rather stingy in giving praise to the poets in the audience and this infuriated some of those concerned. He had to take back some of his words in the discussion and again during the final session of the congress.[63] Judging by the reactions, it is clear that the independent thinking that Bukharin voiced shocked the audience. Bukharin was still considered a first-class political figure, but he was soon to lose all his influence. For some reason, however, the party cell of the presidium of the congress, led by Zhdanov, prevented attempts to attack Bukharin on political grounds.[64]

Under the surface. Remnants of the petty bourgeois past linger on

The OGPU agents, who gathered information in the corridors of the congress building and in the banquets, had a lot of precious material to report to their employer.

A mysterious letter circulated among the delegates of the Writers' Congress.[65] It was an anonymous letter, typewritten and addressed to the foreign guests who were attending the meeting. Unfortunately, it was written in Russian and it remains a mystery, whether its message ever reached its intended recipients. Strangely enough, the authors (apparently a group) claimed to represent the real opinion of the majority of Russian writers, although they explained that most of them would present totally different views in the public -and even private- discussions of the meeting Congress.

The letter was not the first of its kind. In 1927 a similar letter had been addressed to the "writers of the world" and had been published in the émigré press.[66]

It is an understatement to say that the tenor of the letter was critical. It was a murderous invective and its sarcastic passages could have been written by Solzhenitsyn and published in his "GULAG Archipelago." Evidently, the authorship of the letter remained a mystery, as did the extent to which its ideas were representative. In any event, we now know that many writers were very critical of the meeting, its pompous hollowness, Gorky's role, his pedestrian lack of enthusiasm, and the whole idea of regimenting writers and the suppression of any and all criticism.[67] It is fair to say that many of the writers -if not the majority- would have signed the letter, if they had been completely free to do so; that is, without fearing for their personal safety and their careers.

The year was 1934, not 1937 and all this happened before the murder of Kirov, which was to transform the whole atmosphere of the country at a single blow. It was also one of those "idyllic" years, when the horrors of collectivization and famine were behind and nobody foresaw the great terror.

What, then, was the message of the author who professed to speak on behalf of the silenced? In brief, the message was that everything said, shown and told at the Congress, was just a great lie. Russian writers, it read, were like prostitutes, who could not escape from the brothel that was the Soviet Union. They were forced to lie, not only for their own safety, but for the safety of their families. Their stance was, perhaps, despicable, but it was understandable given the circumstances. But what on earth could make foreign intellectuals join the chorus? Nothing prevented them from telling the truth, which was obvious enough. Or was it? Did they really not understand the nature of the trials against so-called wreckers? Did they not read what Pravda wrote about the progress the greatest writers had made in understanding the philosophy of Marx, Engels, Lenin and Stalin (this seminar dropout)? Did they understand, what that meant?

Western intellectuals were busy organizing meetings and campaigns on behalf of the victims of fascism, but they never uttered a word on behalf of the victims of the Bolsheviks, and yet, the number of completely innocent victims of Soviet fascism since the World War, were incomparably greater than those of all the other dictatorships taken together.

Western intellectuals enthusiastically applauded Litvinov's peace initiatives. Had they really lost any normal capacity for understanding plain facts? They must see that the whole USSR had been transformed into one vast military camp. The hungry, but well-armed masses could quite possibly come to the West, bringing Soviet philosophy on their bayonets.

> Do you understand all that has been said here?" the author asked rhetorically. "Do you understand which kind of game you are playing? Or, maybe you too, like us, are prostituting your feelings, your conscience and your duty. But in that case we will never forgive you. We are prostitutes by virtue of a terrible and abominable necessity. We have no other way out of the USSR than death. But what about you??? Or maybe you are not like this, after all. We really hope that you aren't. In that case, take on yourselves the task of defending us in your own countries. Give us your moral support. Otherwise, we will not have the strength to carry on living...![68]

As the GPU reports showed, the foreign guests were not as innocent simple-minded applauders of the Soviet system, which might be the impression obtained from reading the official proceedings. Almost certainly some of the covertly dissident writers told them something of their real thoughts.

There were, indeed, some, like Andre Gide, who later, in 1936, told the truth back in his own country. But the great majority seems to have been carried away by the rhetoric of the anti-fascist struggle. As the GPU reports reveal, the similarity of the fascist and communist dictatorships was well understood by some intelligents in the Soviet Union,[69] but few in the western intellectual elite took this seriously.

It is clear that a special kind of politically correct atmosphere had been created at the congress and it was too great a taboo for anyone to break. Just as the anonymous author of the letter had assumed, people outwardly maintained impeccable Soviet unanimity, even in private conversations. They went even further. Andre Gide, who was in fact critical of Soviet reality, praised it to Isaac Babel, who was also critical, but who answered in like manner. Evidently, both of them doubted the integrity of the other. In Babel's opinion Gide was as "smart as the devil". Gorky was "a mere country sexton when compared with him."[70]

In general, the foreign guests spoke in a predictable way, greeting the congress on behalf of their organizations, thanking the patrons and praising the role of the Soviet Union in the struggle with fascism.

Occasionally, there were unexpected expressions of a critical attitude. So, André Malraux in his speech praised the great work being done in the Soviet Union, including what had been done on the White Sea canal project. In the future people would refer to these years as a time when the people were trusted. But it seemed that the writers, the engineers of the human soul, were not trusted. However, the chief task of an engineer was to invent, not to implement.[71] Malraux had, perhaps, sugared the pill to such an extent, that it hardly made any effect on the general sweetness of the atmosphere.

The solemn decision of the Congress was formulated by the Central Committee of the party and accepted by the congress with minor corrections.[72] On paper, the congress seemed to be a mighty demonstration of optimism and enthusiasm, which in theory were necessary attributes of the representatives of the triumphant working class, which was now assuming hegemony in world history. In fact, the atmosphere seems to have been rather depressing. According to the GPU reports, some writer said that it was torture to listen to Gorky, who spoke mechanically, without "a gram" of enthusiasm.[73] Another said that the congress was as dead as a tsarist parade. He also thought that nobody abroad would believe in the authenticity of the parade. The Soviet press could tell stupid lies about the "colossal enthusiasm" of the delegates, but foreign correspondents were present and they would tell the truth on their return home.[74]

A Ukrainian writer said that, looking at the hollow ceremonies, he felt a maniacal impulse to throw a bit of shit or a dead fish at the presidium. Maybe that would have stirred things up a bit. In fact, he concluded, at least half of the audience, especially the representatives of the minority nationalities, wanted to speak out about the huge number of problems and injustices, to protest and to speak in a human way and not like lackeys. Now they were made to listen to totally false stories about how good everything was. Here people applauded like soldiers in service, while real artists of the word and fighters for national culture were rotting in the bogs of Karelia or in the jails of the GPU.[75]

The national literatures of the Soviet republics were given great attention at the congress. The national cultures were at that time supposed to be undergoing a stormy process of development and attaining a state of "flourishing." The process was just culminating and Stalin would soon realize that local nationalism had developed to a dangerous degree. So far, anyway, the masters of culture had been busy developing national cultures, languages were being Latinized and the treasures of literature were being translated from one language into another.

At the writers' congress it was found that quite a few of the Russian writers, who had been translating the national minorities' literature from the minority language into Russian, had opinions, which revealed certain great-power chauvinism on their part. Somebody said that it was in fact the Russian writers, who were "making poets" of the national writers and in so doing had to neglect their own work. Moreover, many of the national poets were arrogant and showed no gratitude. In fact, it was clear that whole nations were "deeply untalented" in literature.[76]

In many ways, the first congress of Soviet writers was a milestone of socialist realism. The principles of this doctrine were now firmly established and all the members of the Writers Union were obliged to respect them. But socialist realism also triumphed in another sense. The congress showed that a new politically correct way of speaking had been born. Although people might have been hurt by the obviously false liturgy, which was officially served, nobody had the nerve to say this out loud. This would, indeed, have been equal to throwing shit at the presidium. Everybody knew the truth but they also knew the rules of the game, which included using the words and concepts, which had been introduced by the elites. As Boris Groys has aptly said, Stalinism purported to be a "*Gesamtkunstwerk.*"[77] It implied a way of speaking, which painted a polished and varnished picture of the world. At the same time, this glacier was transparent and could at any moment be penetrated by a political joke, a poem, a story or a novel, which was not necessarily of an overtly political nature. The subtext was so well-known by all the intellectuals that even the subtlest hints were always noticed.

This was also understood by the party. The GPU reports made clear that many intellectuals were just pretending to be loyal soldiers of the party, while; in fact, they were often deeply inimical to even the most basic tenets of the official ideology and were psychologically ready to accept any means to destroy communist tyranny.[78] Stalin called such people "double-dealers" (*dvurushniki*). In 1937-38 he undertook some operations whose aim was to destroy this element *en masse*.

The fate of formalism

Lenin, in his time, did not like avant-gardism — or any "isms" for that matter. In a letter to Klara Zetkin he reasoned that to hail novelty just because it was new made no sense at all.[79]

It was certainly awkward for the "formalists" that most of the people simply did not understand it. Nikolai Punin tried to overcome this by explaining that it was the philistine *lumpenproletariat*, which did not understand the avant-garde, whilst the genuine proletariat would immediately identify with it.[80] But this was just wishful thinking.

Whatever the real class-nature of the avant-garde and their opponents, both coexisted in the Soviet Union up to the 1930s. Doubtless this had something to do with the fact that the Bolsheviks had so few friends among the intelligentsia that it could not afford to dispense with the anti-bourgeois avant-garde, even though the leadership, including Lenin, did not like its work.

"Formalism" had become a term of abuse in Soviet culture as early as the middle of the 1920s. At that time moderate communists like Lunacharski and Bukharin had denounced it in principle, although they thought that it should be tolerated in practice. Bukharin thought that formalism in art was comparable to the narrow specialization found in science; it didn't make revolutions possible, and its approach was obsolete, scholastic and metaphysical. Therefore it had to play a secondary role in Soviet culture.[81]

Lunacharsky stressed the class connection: before the revolution, the Russian bourgeoisie had created a group of well-to-do intelligentsia, whose style of life had gradually become similar to that of the bourgeoisie itself. For the most part, this group within the intelligentsia reflected the liberalism of the Kadet party. Had there been no October revolution, it could be said with certainty, Lunacharsky argued, that formalism would now be the dominating tendency in art and art research.

However, after the revolution a new popular intelligentsia was in the making and it was instinctively inimical towards formalist art. This new group had, however, not yet found its own forms. Before October 1917, formalism had been a "season's delicacy," but now it had become a remnant of the past. Now it was the podium around which that part of the intelligentsia, which thought in a bourgeois-European way was waging its battles. While it was unthinkable that the Kadets would now openly fight Marxism, formalism was doing precisely that. But this was not dangerous. It would just strengthen Marxism. In Lunacaharsky's opinion, formalism was "the imported fruit of the fully ripened or slightly overripe bourgeoisie."[82]

While the adoption of socialist realism had meant a certain rehabilitation of the "bourgeois" masters of the past and the fellow-travelers of the present, it was becoming more and more evident that this rehabilitation did not apply to the formalists. Lunacharsky in the 1920s had already observed that there was an aversion on the part of the new intelligentsia to "bourgeois" formalists (an epithet, which they would certainly have rejected with indignation). He might have been right. Whatever the reasons, "formalism" — and to a lesser degree "naturalism" — became, for socialist realism, words of abuse. A general campaign against formalism in 1936 destroyed what had been left of the heritage of the Soviet avant-garde in art and literature.

As is generally known, unlike the avant-garde, socialist realism was oriented towards classicism in many senses of the word. The masters of past epochs returned to grace, and painters and sculptors began to strive for "quiet grandeur" and "noble simplicity." The Greco-Roman heritage was amply exploited in the visual arts. The heroes of the Second Five-Year Plan were portrayed much in the same way as David or Phidias had depicted theirs. The new palaces of the working people (including their homes) were drawn in a classical manner with details from several periods of western art, from antiquity through the Renaissance to Empire style. The fascination with antique forms and the urge to create a species of Hellenic works of art was not restricted to the Soviet Union. Nazi Germany cultivated very similar forms and claimed to be the lawful heir of classical antiquity, dismissing "bourgeois" art as decadent. Incidentally, the Bolsheviks claimed that "corrupt" modern art was "petty bourgeois" and had a "fascist" character, whereas the Nazis claimed that it was "Bolshevist." Consistently, both parties recognized that the ideological opponent did not allow "corrupt art" to be put on its own walls, but instead, sent its agents to poison the culture of its adversary.[83] Whatever the reasons, the pavilions of the Soviet Union and Nazi Germany, which stood opposite each other at the world exhibition in Paris in 1937, certainly resembled each other with their pseudo-classical pomposity.[84]

The recycling of antique forms was not retrograde, let alone reactionary, from the point of view of socialist realism, for it was essence, not form, which was important in a work of art.[85] From the Marxist point of view the essential thing was class. Moreover, classicism as a style had not been reactionary at the time of its flourishing and, by the logic of Stalinism, could not be so now. Post WWII Soviet encyclopedia summed up that classicism had been progressive from the seventeenth century up to the beginning of the nineteenth century. In fact, it had embodied many of the most precious values, which Soviet socialism also found to be worth cultivating: rationalism instead of religion, and reason and civic duty instead of individualism were precious achievements of lasting value for any age. The struggle against religious-ascetic scholasticism was now over in the Soviet Union, but its virtues were still trumpeted by Soviet socialism to the less developed cultures of the world. In art, classicism had striven for social and heroic content and for sublime, clear-cut and rational figures.[86] Needless to say, these things were very relevant in the Soviet Union of the 1930s.

In 1935 Stalin had given the country a new slogan: "Cadres decide everything." Now it was the heroes—and individual ones at that-, who artists had to introduce to the people. True, the heroes were not "absolute," perfect beings in their own right. Rather, they were "children" of Stalin, whose exploits had become possible by virtue of the general line of the party, which the great leader embodied and—not infrequently- by virtue of the immediate intervention of Stalin himself.[87]

It has been argued that this campaign to promote "heroes" was in fact the applause the party bureaucracy ordered for its own debut as an unashamedly opulent layer with petty-bourgeois preferences. Some writers have even equated this layer as the new "popular intelligentsia."[88]

Maxim Gorky had anticipated the emergence of the heroic "higher" man in his writings at the beginning of the century and predicted that a new mass heroism would find its incarnation in the working class.[89] This brave new breed, full of creative potential and free from philistine preconceptions was now emerging in the form of the Stakhanovites, heroic pilots and polar explorers. These new men and women had an unspoiled taste and did not want to enjoy "formalist" art or be depicted in painting or sculpture as hard-to-recognize symbols, preferring instead the conventional language of forms and preserved likeness in representation. This was what "adequately reflecting reality" meant in the epoch of socialism. There was no need for an art, which would "épater le bourgeois," for there were no bourgeois in the Soviet Union any more. According to its own self-understanding, socialist realism was an absolutely new phenomenon. It was new in essence. Therefore, it could borrow any form from any other epoch, without this did changing its own essence.[90]

Whatever the reasons socialist realism preferred conservative form, and stressed the importance of "essence" before form. It has been aptly said that the creation of the totalitarian *Gesamtkunstwerk*—an idea, which, arguably, Stalin got from Hitler- meant total realism, monumentality, classicism, appealing to the people and heroism.[91] In 1936 a campaign to erase the disturbing elements of formalism from Soviet culture was launched.

This campaign was a violent attack on the traditional liberty of the creative intelligentsia. Certainly, this liberty had not been allowed to develop freely after the Bolshevik revolution, but the new offensive had a remarkably arrogant character even in the prevailing atmosphere. To understand the background of the campaign, it is useful to know that the members of the creative intelligentsia themselves had been in a quite belligerent mood towards the bosses. At a "creative conference" of Moscow artists at the end of 1935, which was also attended by writers and actors, including figures, like honored artist (zasluzhennyi deiatel' iskusstva), a certain Shterenberg directed very harsh criticism against the restrictions on creative work. It was reported that Shterenberg's "counterrevolutionary" ideas received considerable support among the audience. One artist also complained about unpaid salaries and even starvation. Even two members of the party threatened to commit suicide as the only escape from their hopeless situation. Many talented artists were starving and living in unbearable conditions.[92]

The tone in the Pravda campaign against formalism was shockingly coarse. "Formalism" had been criticized before and critics had often struck their victims with hard blows. The representatives of RAPP especially had not spared their opponents political labeling and personal denigration. The Pravda articles, however, were different. They were anonymous, but absolutely authoritative. Everybody understood that the party leadership was behind these words, which could not be criticized or answered in kind. The Politburo or Central Committee might just as well have issued a party resolution, or the VTsIK a law, denying formalism and naturalism in art.

Maxim Gorky's article about formalism[93] illustrated what was meant by formalism. On the ontological level, formalism was idealism, Gorky explained, and had been born with Plato. Formalism in art had a parallel in jurisprudence, where it meant primacy of the letter of the law over its spirit. In literature, formalism was expressed in verbal ornaments and endless details, which left facts and images (obraztsy) in the shadows. To understand the difference, one could compare what Shakespeare, Pushkin and Tolstoy had written and what Proust, Joyce, Dos Passos "and all kinds of Hemingways" had created. More often than not, formalism served to hide emptiness or a poverty of the spirit. Certain writers would have liked to speak to people, but had nothing to say and resorted to garrulity and a fatiguing stream of words, which sometimes could be neatly ordered. They were just describing what they saw, but could not, would not or dared not understand what they saw. Formalism was used out of fear of the simple, clear, and sometimes even rude, word, and out of an unwillingness to take responsibility for that word. Some even used formalism to hide their inimical attitude to reality, Gorky declared.

The journal *Literaturnyi kritik* elaborated on the meaning of *Pravda*'s articles. Its editorial[94] proclaimed that the Pravda articles echoed the voice of millions of readers, watchers and listeners. Art was now being more closely controlled by the broad masses than ever before.

Formalism was alien to the great masses and incomprehensible for them, the editorial said. Formalism put itself beyond the control of the masses and therefore it often served as a refuge for the untalented and for charlatans. Formalism could be compared with bureaucracy, it too was lifeless, artisan like (*tsekhovoe*) and antidemocratic. It was uninterested in life, its theorists had "souls of paper." Formalism was a purely bourgeois phenomenon and in the USSR it was a remnant of the past. In the ideological arsenal of the formalists one could find "vulgar sociologism," the eclectic mixing of Marxism and bourgeois sociology, and the theories of the Second International and Bogdanov and so on.[95]

The other deviation was naturalism, which fixed its gaze on details and could not see the whole.

The *Pravda* articles had now given impetus to genuine self-criticism in literature, the article explained. In the new epoch, which had given birth to Stakhanovism and a mighty wave of amateur art (*samodeiatel'nost'*), the existence of remnants of a bourgeois past, which had no roots in Soviet reality, was intolerable.

In other words, the new society needed a new kind of art, but it was not clear that all old art had now become obsolete. Gorky in *Pravda* had mentioned Shakespeare, Tolstoy and Pushkin as positive examples, yet *Literaturnyi kritik* did not mention the old classics at all.

Former members of RAPP had by no means been beyond reproach when it came to the sin of formalism. However, some were willing to show the authenticity of their conversion and made their own contribution to the anti-formalism campaign, such as

V. Kirpotin's article in *Pravda* called "Popularity and Simplicity" (*Narodnost' i prostota*), on the 3rd April 1936.

Kirpotin concentrated on the present, stressing that the new society required a new literature, not just new in essence but new in form. The people was fighting a revolutionary struggle and taking one fortress after another. The goal of this struggle was, in a sense, the people itself; that is, their happy communist life. The people did not want the heroes of its art to be alien people, or wavering thoughtful intelligents. They wanted an art, which would help burn out (*vykorchevyvat'*) the remnants of private proprietorship from its conscience, "as Stalin had said." The people want-ed a literature that would help form new habits and relations in the new communist world and would provide models for emulation. But what was suitable for emulation? Only what was natural, easy (*neprinuzhden-nyi*), clear, benign, heroic and simple could be inspiring.

Formalism was antipopular (*antinaroden*), anti-democratic and inimi-cal to the truth. But neither did naturalism have the virtue of expressing the truth and richness of life, fixed as it was on detail and thus not seeing the whole.

The people, wrote Kirpotin, demanded a new socialist art which did not mean repeating the past, but fulfilling new grandiose tasks.

Kirpotin wrote in Pravda, he spoke in the name of the people and used a very militant tone. And yet this did not save him from becoming a victim of the purges a year later. True, he was spared his life, which was somewhat unusual.

The struggle against formalism, which in fact was already a purge, continued in 1937. Now, "mistakes" didn't just result in a "civic execu-tion," as in the days of Chernyshevsky, but often a real one. Meyerhold and his theatre were among the victims. P. Kerzhentsev, who had already played the role of anti-formalist hangman in 1936 wrote a murderous arti-cle in Pravda called "An Alien Theatre," where he "unveiled" Meyerhold's political sins, which included the "fact" that in Erdman's play *The Suicide* (*Samoubiitsa*) he had defended the right of the philistine (*meshchanin*) to an existence and voiced the protest of the liquidated class against the dicta-torship of the proletariat.[96] Meyerhold's tragic fate is well-known.

The campaign against formalism was not just a struggle against a par-ticular current in the arts. First of all it was a campaign of the party lead-ership to subdue the creative intelligentsia, a motley crowd, which was often bohemian, independent and incalculable.

The new standards for socialist realism, which were emerging, fully deserved the epithet *poshlost'*, which the intelligentsia had always attached to philistinism.[97]

The official iconography pointed the way: the leaders were depicted in a quasi-hagiographical way and with a naïve imagery of flawless per-fection, often in the quasi-antique, classic, or baroque forms which were preferred in works of art.

The heritage of *intelligentnost'* survived, but this happened more or less clandestinely. Its haven was classic literature, which the regime did not destroy and which attained a more and more important function for those who did not betray the traditional ideals of *intelligentnost'*, even if the regime did all it could to hammer home its will.

Behind the curtains. A victory without enthusiasm

"Formalism", thus became a word of abuse in socialist realism. In fact, it was used for any unconventional form of presentation in painting, architecture, literature, and even in music.[98]

The campaign against "formalism", which was launched in *Pravda*, in several articles during the spring of 1936, was noticed by every member of the creative intelligentsia. It was also evident that every writer had to take the new formulation of the party line into account in his work. The writers in Moscow organized no less than three meetings where they discussed the questions of formalism.[99]

The NKVD reports revealed that the atmosphere at the beginning of the campaign was far from enthusiastic. The whole thing was badly prepared and the writers were unwilling to voice their opinions. Almost overnight, however, everything suddenly changed, thanks to Boris Pasternak. The poet said what the majority clearly thought and was met with much applause, laughter and approval. Soon, however, the audience became more careful, when it turned out that Pasternak's presentation had "a purely anti-Soviet character," as a NKDV informer explained. In Pasternak's opinion formalism was nothing more than a antiquated relic of yesterday's youth, which was now in its fifties. Moreover, why should literary criticism now begin to use such concepts as "formalism" or "naturalism," when it was much more important if a literary piece was "bad," "weak" or "unsuccessful."

Pasternak had broken the spell of political correctness. He did not mention the Pravda article, but everybody understood that he was speaking about it. But what had given Pasternak such, almost suicidal, prowess? The NKVD informer supposed that a meeting with Andre Malraux, who was inimical towards the anti-formalist campaign, had added to the "aggressiveness" of Pasternak. Anyway, at the next meeting Pasternak gave another speech, where he, in effect, took back the most offending parts of his first presentation.

One writer was reported to have said that Pasternak in effect presented the opinion of the majority of people who were simply afraid to speak out[100]. Anyway, there were also voices of disapproval, claiming that the poet was a "counterrevolutionary." A model of politically correct behavior was Marietta Shaginian, who admitted to having been "beaten" up by the party, but who also said that during this process and because of this beating, she had felt the power of the collective.

Boris Pilniak was disgusted by Shaginian's speech and said that she had been like a wet hen and that he had felt ashamed for her.

Pasternak was the only one who expressed his opinion openly. But others let it be understood, what they thought about the new party invention. When Kirpotin and Korabelnikov presented their views, they were asked to stop, as people were not listening, and, indeed, were leaving the hall.

Yury Olesha, for his part, played by the rules of the party game; he used the official terminology and tried to explain away the "formalist danger." However, people did not believe in the honesty of his presentation, the NKDV informer reported.

The whole thing had something surrealistic about it. But the great terror had not yet begun. Konstantin Paustovsky could still tell a joke: "Hi there, what is new?" "Nothing special. I just noticed how a militiaman took two formalists to the station".

Quite a few members of the creative intelligentsia were, of course, arrested and killed over the next two years. It seems fair to conclude that the majority of writers really would have liked to dismiss the whole campaign against formalism as irrelevant and anti-intellectual. As regards the similar campaign against formalism in music, it may have enjoyed greater popularity, and there were even some genuine voices of support at the grassroots level and also among some composers.[101] However, the NKVD concluded that in this case, the reaction among the writers was, in general, positive. In any event, cases of "negative and anti-Soviet" reactions were reported and the agent described no less than ten of "the most typical" instances, which included comparisons with the Nazis and the burning of books.[102]

Among the intellectuals there was always a group, which never approved of the Soviet dictatorship and was deeply inimical to it. In order to survive everybody had to take the rules of the game into account. Only by doing so was it possible to live and, possibly, publish. To go point blank against the totalitarian state was tantamount to committing suicide.

However, obsequious subservience was openly despised. When two writers, Kirpotin and Korabelnikov, proposed, during anti-formalist discussions, "a unified type of Soviet writer," they were heckled and ignored.[103] Olesha, who also used the official terminology, but was, in fact, against the regimentation of writers, received enthusiastic support. On the other hand, it seems that a certain number of writers really absorbed official Soviet values and had no intention of transgressing the official codex.[104]

As regards the issue of philistinism, socialist realism was—as understood by one of its chief founders, Gorky- the general line in culture, which was struggling against philistinism on the "right" (or "up"), which was formalism, which was more or less equal to bourgeois elitism. It also fought philistinism on the "left" (or "down"), which could embody itself as pornography or cheapness (*poshlost'*).

Gypsy romances as well as atonalism, constructivism, traditionalism, the stream-of-consciousness, as well as detective novels were all philistine for Gorky. The key to Gorky's thinking in these matters may be found in one of his letters to Stalin in 1934 where he said: literature should make the ideas of socialism "into flesh;" the great task of socialism was the liberation of mankind from philistinism.[105]

Newspeak is born. Censorship on guard for political correctness

The idea of politically correct language is hardly compatible with a non-totalitarian society, where single norms for correctness don't exist. In the totalitarian Soviet Union, on the other hand, the imperative of politically correct language, which Orwell had aptly dubbed "newspeak" in the 1940s, was unavoidably developed.[106]

The first stage of newspeak came into being almost immediately after the Bolshevik revolution: the very words, which were used by and about the new leaders and functionaries of the state, were new in kind. The new words had a formal structure, which implied a denotation, pretending to be diametrically opposite to their actual import. There was no government, let alone a cabinet, in Soviet Russia: there was only the Soviet (or council) of people's commissars. There was no police, but a popular militia instead. There were no soldiers, but so-called red-army men (*krasnoarmeitsy*). There were not even banknotes, but "state marks" (*gosznak*) etc. Someone who wanted to exhibit his anti-Soviet, petty bourgeois cast of mind, could still do so relatively safely in the 1920s, by using the "bourgeois" word "soldiers" (*soldaty*), instead of the new soviet term *krasnoarmeitsy*, for instance.

One of the characteristic traits of newspeak was that it absolutely lacked a sense of humor. This is understandable, as humor, which plays with hidden meanings and unleashes suppressed associations, is the worst enemy of newspeak. Any totalitarian regime is challenged by jokes and, for its part, will persecute their authors. For some reason, this tradition has now appeared in many Western countries, which have adopted the idea of "political correctness," but insist that they have, nevertheless, preserved democracy (a claim also made by the Soviet Union under Stalin).

In the Soviet Union, newspeak was by no means just "propaganda" or a set of euphemisms. It reflected a new way of thinking, it was consistent, and it was meant to be taken deadly seriously. Sinyavsky was probably right, when he said that in this language "words replace knowledge: it's enough to know a specific set of words to feel on top of the situation."[107] Quite soon a pseudoscientific way of speaking was also developed. It absolutely loved substantives (maybe due to the idea that the thing behind the phenomena is also in itself known to be a material substance). So, for instance, there was a profusion of "isms." As Sinyavsky quips, for instance, the expression "I don't give a damn" produced "I-don't-give-a-damnism," that is, indifference toward the State's ideals words and deeds; an indifference that everyone was supposed to fight."[108] Where Dal's famous nineteenth century dictionary had only 79 "isms," Ushakov's dictionary from 1935-40 referred to no less than 415.[109] Many of the "isms" had a pejorative meaning. In fact, there was only one correct "ism," namely, Marxism-Leninism; all its rivals were heretic usurpers. So, for instance, "liberalism" during high Stalinism was defined as "criminal permissiveness, laxity, rotten liberalism…"[110]

The Soviet State was by no means indifferent towards indifference. Ever since its founding, the Soviet state was understood to be *sui generis*. According to the official state ideology, as proclaimed in the constitution of 1924, the dictator class was keeping the *plenitudo potestatis* of state power and would not share it with anybody. Any system that ensured a division of powers or checks and balances was rejected a priori.[111]

Introducing newspeak was part of the process of creating the new man. It was not enough to teach the upcoming generation to speak and think in a new way; it was also extremely important to create a new politically correct milieu, where people would not be contaminated by the old bourgeois, philistine and cheap (*poshlyi*) ways of thinking and speaking.

Freedom of speech, once one of the most sacrosanct values of the Russian intelligentsia, was suppressed soon after the Bolshevik takeover. The Bolshevik excuses for this were as logical as they were outrageous to the intelligents: the published word was a mighty weapon, and at a moment of heightened class-struggle it was as impossible to give their enemies freedom of the press as it was to give them artillery and machine guns. The Bolsheviks could avoid theoretical problems as long as they consistently identified themselves with the working class, which they, of course, incarnated, and at the same time portrayed all their rivals and enemies as the enemies of the working class.

A dictatorship was not content with simply suppressing the press of its adversaries. There was a lot more to do. A new kind of censorship was created and it would not just suppress unwanted texts, but would also decide what could be written and how that should be written.[112]

Political and philosophical literature was—from the point of view of the dictatorship—a natural target for attack. It goes without saying that the works of contemporary thinkers who were considered counterrevolutionary or petty bourgeois (which soon came to mean the same thing) were suppressed. True, there were still some question marks left about the classics, which were of no immediate relevance to the current political situation.

Keeping an eye on what was being published in the Soviet Union was not that difficult, for the state controlled the printing press and the supply of paper. It had promised that these would be used for the "toiling masses,"[113] which meant that they were not available for the bourgeoisie or anybody else the party suspected of serving the class enemy. But apart from the contemporary press, there was also the heritage of the past and the threat of "ideological diversion" in the form of imported material from the bourgeois world outside the USSR. It was not just political and philosophical literature that had an ideological content, but also the belles-lettres, plays, films, and songs and dances, which had been produced by the "old" people for the "old" society.

Clearly, the dictatorship of the proletariat had to fight this ideological danger and in order to do that more or less consistent rules had to be formulated. Glavlit, the bureau for censorship, which was founded in 1922,[114] was responsible for the administration of censorship, and its agents, which were soon to be found in all newspapers, publishing houses and post offices, ensured that unsuitable information, language, and ideas were not published. Libraries were also purged of odious literature and the public presentation of plays and songs was monitored.

As for the most problematic aspect of the censors' work; namely, that concerned with the censoring of belles-lettres, most of that responsibility was left in the hands of the editors of the publishing houses. The work of the best writers and other members of the creative intelligentsia were deemed so important that the top Bolshevik leadership, including Stalin, devoted quite a lot of time to it.[115] Here, we will look at the ideology that lay behind the daily activities and practices of the censorship and try to establish the nature of its ideas about the "petty bourgeois" danger and the ways in which it tried to save the emerging new Soviet man from its polluting effect.

Glavlit was only one of many organs, which took interest in the publishing of printed material and had a role in deciding its content. There was also self-censorship, which, in all probability, played the greatest role in the process of adapting texts to make them fit into the mould of political correctness. Glavlit was the final instance before printing in the normal procedure. It hardly could cope with complicated questions of ideology, but it was the ultimate gatekeeper and it also took care that blasphemous misprints did not go unpunished.

Statistics from the 1920s show that even Glavlit's role was far from negligible. In the peaceful year of 1925, for instance, it suppressed 110 manuscripts. The motivation was "political" in 23 cases, which meant that there was some deviation from the political course of the party, such as disfiguring the revolution, etc. In one case, the reason was the "counter-revolutionary" nature of the manuscript; "ideological" motives (mysticism, idealism, religiosity, bourgeois morals) were the reason for suppression in 12 cases. Pornography and foul language were responsible for 4 cases; "antiscientific or unsuitable" material for instruction was the reason in 13 cases. In 18 cases there were "formal" reasons and in 10 cases the issue was the presence of information, the dissemination of which was prohibited because it was included in a list of forbidden subjects; the so-called "military and economic list."[116]

How many of the suppressed manuscripts were "petty bourgeois"? It is difficult to provide a direct answer to this question from the sources that were available to me, but clearly most of the "ideological" cases, some of the "political" ones and perhaps the "pornographic" ones could be so classified.

In 1927 for instance, books by Gabriele D'Annunzio, Nikolai Leskov and Arthur Conan Doyle were suppressed for "ideological" reasons, while Kornei Chukovsky's "Barmalei" was thought unfit from a pedagogical point of view.[117] In 1925, 683 manuscripts, that is, about 10% of the total, had been "corrected" or shortened. Many books, including the classics, were only published with Marxist forewords, in order to help the reader see them in the proper light.

All this concerned belles-lettres. A huge amount of work was done in other fields, such as journals, newspapers, radio, etc. We must also remember that Glavlit was only the last link in a chain of censorship, which could consist of, say, five stages.[118] It is very unlikely that any Soviet manuscript arrived at Glavlit without having been altered in some way.

As regards the attitude of the censors, it may be possible to draw conclusions about their ideals from the thoughts of one of the directors (1935-37) of Glavlit, Sergei Ingulov. In the late 1920s, Ingulov wrote about Soviet criticism, saying: "In the Soviet press, criticism is not ridiculous or malicious, philistine (obyvatelskoe) giggling, but the rough heavy hand of the (working) class, which, falling on the back of the enemy, smashes his spine and shoulders. "Finish with him!" — this is the exhortation, which is heard in all the speeches of the leaders of the Soviet state...."[119] Although this was undoubtedly a piece of RAPPist oratory from 1928, there was something prophetical in it, for in 1938 Ingulov was liquidated as a wrecker. Even if it is reasonable to assume that rank and file censors did not always share the savagery of Ingulov, the pathos no doubt holds for the ideal censor: no petty bourgeois compromises or intelligents' scruples, but a clear class line and destructive blows directed at the culprits.

The 1920s were a hard time for the classics. The zealots' school of criticism, which was later called "vulgar sociologism," thought that even the classics were first and foremost representatives of their "class" and its ideology. In the middle of the 1930s this changed and a leader in *Pravda* in 1936 urged that schoolchildren should be taught to love classical literature.[120] The historian of Soviet censorship, A.V. Blium, maintains that there was not a single collection of the works of any Russian classical author, which did not suffer from Soviet censorship.[121] Works by Tolstoi, Pushkin, Chekhov and even Saltykov-Shchedrin were mutilated. The last named was accused of pornography.[122] As for Chekhov, his affinity with the petty bourgeois intelligentsia was all too evident.[123] The case of Dostoevsky seems natural enough, if we remember the ethos of his *The Devils*, for instance. Despite all the difficulties, the classics were published. Even *The Devils* and some other highly explosive material, from the Bolshevik point of view, were published. But in each case the circumstances were carefully considered. Of course, said the chief censor, Lebedev-Poliansky, in 1931, it was impossible to publish *The Devils* in a cheap edition of 500,000, but an academic edition of 5,000-6,000 was another matter.[124] After all, *The Devils* was about a current in the revolutionary movement, which the Bolsheviks condemned.

One of the problems with the items of the "old culture" (which the censors divided into "classic" and "philistine") was that they used scarce resources, which were in short supply even for the politically correct new cultural products. In 1926, the Glavrepertkom, the committee, which took care of the censorship of theatrical programs, announced that "philistine" elements should not be tolerated in theatres. "Monarchist" and "feudal" operas like *Lohengrin*, *Faust*, *Queen of Spades*, *The Decembrists*, *The Stony Guest* and so on, were among the bad examples.[125]

Then there was the literature that had been published abroad. As regards Russian emigré literature, it became odious in 1927, when fellow traveling smenavekhist items were also prohibited.[126] However, quite a lot of contemporary foreign literature was published. The works of "progressive" writers like Romain Rolland, Louis Aragon, Bertolt Brecht and Pablo Neruda were published and works by Ernest Hemingway, John Steinbeck, John Dos Passos and Thomas Mann were available. Even Marcel Proust's *In Search of Lost Time* and James Joyce's *Ulysses* were published, although they were not widely available and could not be found at just any bookstall.[127] Even Hitler's *Mein Kampf* was translated and made available to a very restricted audience.[128]

Children's literature was quite an important part of the education of the new man. No wonder that at the first congress of Soviet writers in

1934, the other main report (besides Gorky's) was delivered by a children's writer, S. Ia. Marshak.[129] Children's literature was a "mighty weapon of communist education," said N. K. Krupskaia.[130]

But the importance of children's literature also meant that it was under careful control. Even leading figures in the field like Kornei Chukovsky and S. Ia. Marshak, and Mayakovsky's and Olesha's children's books, had trouble with the censors. Later classics like *Barmalei* and *Mukha tchokotukha* were initially suppressed by the censorship. The authors also found themselves in serious trouble at the end of the 1930s.[131]

The mental surroundings of adult people were also guarded by the state. At various times, "old literature," which was considered to be harmful for the creation of the new man, was purged from libraries, antiquarian bookshops and other places. This process began soon after the revolution, but in the 1930s became so serious that A.V. Blium has called it "total bibliocide." In the hysteria of the great terror, people on all levels competed to demonstrate their vigilance and as a result masses of books that were believed to contain even the slightest sign of having been influenced by newly unveiled diversionists were destroyed. Some of these books were preserved, but kept in a "special holding" (*spetskhran*). Even Tolstoy's *War and Peace* could end up in a *spetskhran* and not given to readers by a vigilant librarian.[132] The toll was high. During 1938-39 as many as 16,453 titles and 24 million copies were destroyed.[133]

Naturally, the state jealously guarded its self-image in the press. The censors had at their disposal a weighty book, called *The Talmud*, which contained a list of forbidden topics. For instance, at the time of dekulakization, it was forbidden to report on or disclose information about mass demonstrations against Soviet power or about the "terror" perpetrated by the kulaks (if there was no mention of the immediate punishment of the culprits) or about the fate of the kulaks and their families either during dekulakization or in exile.[134]

After 1935, when Stalin had said that life had become merrier, it was forbidden to show sad faces and depressing images in the press. Everything was happy and flourishing in the socialist virtual world.[135]

At the time of the great terror the heightened vigilance of party functionaries began to see anti-Soviet phenomena everywhere. Scores of cases involving the malevolent production of enemy symbolism (swastikas) were reported. The top leadership of the Soviet state seems to have spent a lot of its time examining these cases. It is perhaps difficult for us now to understand why such symbols were seen as so dangerous by the Stalinist regime.

Another anti-Soviet activity, which was apparently widespread, was wrecking with the help of "so-called" misprints. This widespread phenomenon involved the substitution of certain words by others, which might sound the same, but which meant something very different to that intended. So, for example the word "socialism" would replace the word "capitalism," or the adjective "financial"(*kassovyi*) would replace the adjective "class" (*klassovyi*). The word "terrible" (*strashnyi*) would replace "fearless" (*besstrashnyi*), "viciousness" (*porochnost'*) would become "stability" (*prochnost'*). Worst of all, "chairman" (*predsedatel'*) often became "traitor" (*predatel'*).[136] There were, it has to be said rather "funny" misprints; for example, Kliment Voroshilov's first name was changed to "*Aliment.*" There were crossword puzzles, which asked "the name of a Red Army commander" and on the next line "voice of an animal." The party and its agent, Glavlit had absolutely no sense of humor in dealing with these cases. Frequently they were given over to the GPU/NKVD for investigation and "measures." Censors who were not vigilant enough would soon find themselves on the bench of the accused.[137]

Glavlit was also interested in music. The public presentation of songs had to have Glavlit's permission and in many cases it would not be given. During the tumultuous years of the Cultural Revolution, Glavlit forbade a stunning number of songs. In 1929 900 "songs and romances" were on a list of forbidden songs. By 1932 the number had risen to more than 3,000. Many well-known popular songs, such as "*Variag,*" "*Chaika*" or "*Vechernii zvon*" were forbidden, as was a record containing the song to Lermontov's words "*Vykhozhu odin ia na dorogu,*" which was deemed to be "mystical." Another song, "*Para gnedykh,*" described a woman as an object of pleasure. Indeed, in 1925 it was decreed that any record that contained "monarchist, patriotic and imperialist" ideas, that was pornographic, that denigrated women or that reflected a *barin's* (gentleman's) attitude to the *muzhik*, (peasant) was to be confiscated by the GPU.[138]

As regards plays and films, in the 1920s they were divided into several categories. Some were only to be permitted in the so called central region and some were permitted on condition that they would not be shown to audiences of workers and peasants.[139] Later this differentiation was removed, although the peasants were not, according to the 1936 constitution, supposed to be completely equal with the workers.

The virtual world of Soviet socialism guarded its integrity with impeccable consistency. Anything that officially did not exist could not be shown. Officially there was no censorship at all. No wonder, therefore, that when the director of Glavlit published a booklet during the war called *The Tasks of Censorship During the War*, it was quickly confiscated, because it concerned something that, officially at least, did not exist and, therefore, had to be lying.[140]

In short, the Soviet system of surveillance had had a very firm hold over the press ever since the October 1917 coup. As early as the 1920s, the publication and public presentation of pre-Revolutionary and foreign items of culture were very closely controlled. As regards the product of the creative intelligentsia, the stranglehold of the state was gradually stiffened and after the terror of 1936-38 hardly anyone even tried to defy the system. Someone like Zoshchenko, who had an "underdeveloped instinct of self-preservation," could try, but could not succeed.[141] In fact, Zoshchenko had born the stigma of a being a "philistine" and a *poshliak* ever since the 1920s. In his view, this was due to the fact that the authorities thought that the characters in his books represented his own opinions.[142] For some reason, however, he survived the great terror and became one of the scapegoats of a new cultural purge after the war.

In the west, many radicals saw the Soviet Union as a country where culture was really free, where philistines and prudes did not restrict the bohemian liberty of writers and other intellectuals.[143] Quite clearly, western intellectuals who saw in Soviet Russia the incarnation of a new, revolutionary, non-philistine culture did not understand what a labyrinth of restrictions bedevilled not only the work of the Soviet creative intelligentsia but even the everyday life of the ordinary man in the street. According to the official Soviet view, this kind of restriction was not petty bourgeois, but its very antithesis. Not socialist norms, but the "leaden weight" of the past was supposed to be the factor, which kept the ideal human being in captivity. It was also pointed out that the petty bourgeoisie and its petty bourgeois values had given birth to fascism, whereas Bolshevism was totally opposed to fascism.[144]

The story would, however, be incomplete if we forgot that the dawn of socialism did not just involve purges, censorship and terror for the creative intelligentsia. True, its freedom was increasingly restricted as regards style and communication with foreigners. On the other hand, the state also offered incentives and inducements; there was a carrot too. In professional matters some representatives of the cultural elite obtained immense powers. After the 1930s the best artists and especially those writers fortunate enough to sell millions of copies could lead a very opulent and materially carefree existence. The state gave more and more dachas, cars and sanatorium tickets to successful intelligents, although being successful did not necessarily mean that these particular writers or intelligents were the figures most esteemed by their colleagues.[145] The editions of books grew to enormous sizes. While 130 million books had been published in 1914 and 265 million in 1928, the figure was no less than 693 million in 1938.[146] Even if we accept that Soviet figures are probably inflated, there was certainly real growth. Some books were very effectively distributed: there were already eight million copies of Gorky's *Mother* in print by 1934. A single edition of Sholokhov's voluminous *And Quiet Flows the Don* amounted to no less than 3.5 million copies.[147]

8
The Terror

Trotskyism and the men of letters

Somebody has said that Stalin had good literary taste and that just a couple of great writers were destroyed in the purges, while intellectuals in other groups were harder hit. This was not exactly the case. Quite a lot of even the best writers suffered. But one can say that many talented writers, who were clearly inimical to Stalin's regime and whose attitudes were known to the secret police, for some reason survived.[1] The terror of 1936-38 hit hard many groups of the old intelligentsia, for instance, the academics,[2] the old Bolsheviks and former SRs, the Mensheviks and other revolutionaries. It is not clear, whether the intelligents suffered more or less in comparison to some other segments of the society, but it is evident that the purges hit, in an essential way, the very core of the intelligents' domain. The purges proved in a very concrete way that the intelligents would only survive on one condition: they had to agree that it was the party that had the right to explain reality.

As is well-known, the arch-enemy of Soviet socialism, on whom all wrecking, diversion, espionage, and other anti-Soviet activities could be blamed, in the years of the great terror, was, officially, the "Judas Trotsky." Just why Trotsky was given the honor of representing everything anti-Soviet, from imperialism to petty-bourgeoisie, may, in part, be explained by Stalin's personal life-history and his psychological makeup. The grand story, which the secret police fabricated during the great terror and which "proved" that all the enemies of socialism, both from the right and the left, had formed a grand alliance with the imperialists to destroy Soviet socialism and restore capitalism, implied that a real world-wide anti-Soviet plot existed. Having its centers and class-base in the capitalist world, which was encircling Soviet socialism; imperialism also had hired agents inside the Soviet Union. Mostly these were former oppositionists who had only one thing in common; their refusal to accept the idea that a socialist society existed in the Soviet Union. Usually, it was announced that they were "paid agents." In most cases, the secret police tried to squeeze a confession from their victims, which included an admission of this vital link with the capitalist world: the "dark powers" did not exist in the Soviet Union, accordingly, they could extend their influence in the country of socialism only through such occasional depraved elements, which still existed there as remnants of the past.

According to the official truth, the essence of Trotskyism was anti-sovietism. It was manifested in the fact that the Trotskyites bluntly denied that a socialist society had been built in the Soviet Union. Trotsky himself ridiculed the Soviet system and spoke about "The Stalin School of falsification." The Trotskyites, as well as the fascists, the imperialists, and other enemies claimed that the new Soviet society was only held together by terror and violence. Tentatively, at least, we may infer that anyone who denied the socialist essence of the Soviet Union could be accused of being a Trotskyite. This denial proved that he was an alien element. The task of detecting the mechanism, through which this abnormal phenomenon of anti-sovietism had come into being within the Soviet state belonged to the domain of the competent repressive organs.

To understand the mood of the newly-born socialist society of 1937, where almost everybody voted in free elections and where almost everyone voted for the Stalinist coalition of communists and non-party candidates, we must remember that this was already a time, when everybody had a friend or relative, who had disappeared during the night. This was a time, when people were frequently summoned to meetings to demand the death sentence for someone, who just a couple years previously had been, more or less, genuinely honored, and who had, in any event, been respected and high-standing members of the party elite. This was a time, when Stalin was creating the elements for the *weltanschauung* of the new intelligentsia.

The magnum opus of the epoch, written by Stalin, together with some outstanding ideologues, was published in 1938 under the name of *Short Course of the History of the VKP* (bolsheviks). The article on Marxism-Leninism in this book was of Stalin's own doing. In fact, the famous term "Marxism-Leninism" was first introduced in this book.

The title of the "Short course" was modest enough, but that was all that was modest about it. The book aspired to teach the essentials of both Marxism-Leninism and its correct application in practice in the history of the Soviet (All-Union) Communist party. This party had a world-historic role and significance and studying its history helped people "to understand Bolshevism and heightens our political vigilance," the book proclaimed. This history "armed us with the knowledge of the laws of social development and the moving forces of revolution." Finally, the study of this history "strengthens confidence to the final victory of the great cause of the party of Lenin and Stalin, the victory of communism in the whole world."[3]

The new intelligentsia, that is to say, those, who were in commanding positions or intellectual professions, was supposed to study this book methodically and thoroughly. Study aids were soon published. This studying was to happen under leadership and surveillance; discussion clubs were no longer tolerated. Ideological study was taken really seriously by Stalin. It was at the infamous February-March plenum of the CC of the VKP in 1937, the same occasion, when the "machinations" of Bukharin and his comrades were "exposed," that Stalin stressed very strongly the necessity of political study. The whole of party life had to be rebuilt in order to give all part leaders time for political study. For this purpose, party bosses on every level had to be given deputies.[4] The stage for a massive new wave of purge and promotion, *vydvizhenie*, had, thus, been set.

The importance of ideological work was caused by the novelty of the contemporary situation. Now, said Stalin, the enemies were no longer openly class-alien as had been the case in the days of the Shakhty-affair or with the "Promparty." Now the enemies were "double-dealers (*dvu-rushniki*)," who pretended to be loyal party men, but who were, in effect, just waiting for the opportunity to strike –this could happen on the eve of, or during, a war. Now new methods were needed to fight them: no more discussions, but methods of scorching and destroying (*vykorchevivaniia i razgroma*).[5] The successes of the party had been tremendous, but the shady side of this was that "political vigilance" had been lowered. Now all the leaders of the party, on all levels, had to master politics.[6]

The study material par excellence, the *Short Course*, was published no earlier than 1938 and this meant that it was mainly used, not by those, who had been bosses in 1937, but by the deputies, who had by then been appointed to them. These deputies were for the most part representatives of what later came to be called "Brezhnev generation." This was, indeed, the new Soviet intelligentsia, which had been socialized in the Soviet state and been promoted for party, and other responsible, work during the Cultural Revolution.

The *Short Course* was quickly translated into all the "national" languages of the Soviet Union and scores of other languages also. It was claimed, rather boastfully, that no less than 50 million copies had been published by 1953, which would reputedly have made the Short course the most published book in the world, even surpassing the Bible.

In order to asses the intellectual atmosphere of the Soviet Union in the years before the Second World War, and the quality of scholarship, which was considered essential for the new intelligentsia, we must briefly consider the contents of this extraordinary book.

The successes of socialism in our country delighted not only the party, the workers and the collective peasants. They delighted also our Soviet intelligentsia, all honest citizens of the Soviet Union. But ... they did not delight but enraged the followers of the crushed classes—the wretched remnants of the Bukharinians and the Trotskyites. Those gentlemen did not assess the accomplishments of the workers and the peasants from the point of view of the people, which hailed each such accomplishment, but from the point of view of the interests of their own wretched fraction, which was estranged from life and thoroughly rotten....The murder of comrade Kirov, as later was discovered, had been committed by this united Trotskyite-Bukharinist gang.... The criminals, who were caught with a smoking gun had publicly to confess at the court that they had not only arranged the murder of Kirov, but were also preparing the murder of all the other leaders of the party and the government. Investigation later showed that these scoundrels had trodden the path of wrecking and diversion. The most appalling moral and political depravity of these people, the most base meanness and perfidiousness, which they kept covering with double-dealing explanations about loyalty to the party, was exposed in the process, which was held in Moscow in 1936.

The main inspirer and organizer of this whole gang of murderers and spies was Judas Trotsky.... In 1937 new evidence against the scoundrels of the Bukharinian-Trotskyite gang were discovered ... the Bukharinians and the Troskyites, as now had been proven, had already long ago formed a common gang of enemies of the people in the form of the 'rightist-Trostkyite bloc'.... These wretched henchmen of the fascists had forgotten that the Soviet people needed just to move its finger a little and nothing would be left of them.

Soviet justice sentenced the Bukharinian-Trotskyite scoundrels to be shot.

The People's Commissariat of Domestic Affairs carried out the sentence.

The Soviet people accepted the destruction of the Bukharinian-Trotskyite gang and proceeded to deal with the things, which were in the order of the day.

In the order of the day were preparation to the election of the Supreme Soviet of the Soviet Union and accomplishing it in an organized way...."[7]

The rabidly morbid tone of the book speaks for itself. However, the story was optimistic. The communist cause had won and there were lessons to be learnt. The *Short Course* ended with six numbered paragraphs, each dedicated to a cardinal "lesson" of the history of the party. The paragraphs explained the nature of the "General line" of the party as an exclusive kind of superior wisdom, which always had to be most vigilantly defended against all kinds of deviations. The importance of the struggle against all kinds of deviations could not be exaggerated:

> opportunism in our own organizations is as intolerable as is rot in a healthy organism. The party is the leading echelon of the working class, its foremost fortress, its headquarters in battle. It cannot be tolerated that in the general staff of the working class could sit people with feeble faith, opportunists, defeatists, traitors.... To ensure victory it is first of all necessary to purge the party of the working class, the general staff of the working class, its foremost fortress, to get rid of defeatists, defectors, scabs and traitors. It cannot be considered that the Trotskyites and the Bukharinians and the representatives of the national deviations, when struggling against Lenin and the party, arrived in the same spot, where the parties of the SRs and the Mensheviks had landed: they were transformed into henchmen of fascist intelligence organizations, became spies, wreckers, murderers, diversionary agents and traitors to their country."[8]

Institutionalizing surveillance and harassment. The new literary criticism

Needless to say, these hysterical diatribes could not convince the top echelons of the old intelligentsia, still less win its sympathies. But they could scare people and make them understand that politics was not something that could be left to amateurs and philosophical discussions.

Only enemies would dare question the official truths of socialist society. The first of these official truths was that the USSR really was a socialist society. This official axiom put the intelligentsia in the same position the Catholic clergy had occupied in the Middle Ages: to seek the truth was not just an idle idea, it was blasphemous. The truth was given in the "general line" and the intelligents just had to learn it and understand, how it was reflected in reality.

It must not be forgotten that 1937 was not just the peak of the great terror: it was also the year, when socialism began and when all kinds of remnants from the past were liquidated from the new society.[9] The witch-hunt continued into the next year and the lessons of the *Short course*, which summed up the process, were given to a cowed and scared audience, which did not voice any critical comments in public.

There is no doubt that the new intelligentsia assiduously studied the new syllabus. It had no choice. The apparat also organized classes for the methodical study of the book and made sure that the message was read and understood.[10]

In his speeches at the February-March Plenum (Plenary Session of the Party CC) of 1937 Stalin had sorted out the actual tasks of party function-aries: mastering political questions, raising the level of vigilance, criticism, and self-criticism. Deputies for party bosses on all levels of organizations had been set. The stage was clear for a great purge.

Criticism and self-criticism were widely practiced everywhere at meetings in various organizations during the spring of 1937. The old lead-ership had to recognize its sins in front of the rank and file and especially the new deputies, who had recently been appointed. One of the topics that were always raised was, whether representatives of the young generation had been sufficiently helped and promoted. If it the self-criticism was not severe and genuine enough, the press reacted to this. Sometimes envoys from the center were sent to the province to "help" in the arranging of real, thoroughgoing self-criticism.[11]

All this also, naturally, concerned literature. *Pravda* on the 23rd April 1937 contained several remarkable articles. M. Serebriansky wrote about Soviet literature in the last five years, that is, since the Central Commit-tee decision about the restructuring of the literary and artistic organiza-tions.[12]

The sins of the leadership of the Writers" Union were revealed. There had been "family circles" (*gruppovshchina*) and ideological education had been substituted for commanding (*administrirovaniem*). Self-criticism had been suppressed. L Averbakh (who had already been arrested) had in-terpreted the idea of the Cultural Revolution in a Trotskyite manner, and maintained that proletarian culture was not socialist culture. "Leftist" vulgarity, ideas, which were inimical to Bolshevism, had been accepted instead of the party line in literature.

Many novels, for example those, written by Gladkov, Kataev, Ilin, Grossman, Ehrenburg, Paustovsky, Yasensky, Leonov, and others, had de-scribed the struggle and the victories, which had been achieved in social-ist construction and in creating the new man. The old problem about the relation of the intelligents to the revolution was being approached in a new way and had ceased to be a poignant problem. Mostly, Soviet writers wrote about intelligents, who had left their petty bourgeois past behind and who were free from bourgeois influences and habits of thought only thanks to Soviet power. True, one exception to the rule was Gorky's *The Life of Klim Samgin*, the story about a double-dealing, implacable enemy of the working class. The protagonist had been described by Gorky with such force that the book had to be considered as one of the best products of world literature.

The revolutionary reforging of the "human material" had been described by several authors. Avdeenko, Makarenko, Pogodin, Grekova. Mayakovsky, whom Bukharin had branded obsolete, were to be thanked for many accomplishments in Soviet poetry.

Serebriansky's article named quite a lot of exemplary writers and their works. Two books only were presented as negative example: the "cheap and untalented" (*poshlyi i bezdarnyi*) novel of G. Serebryakov *The Youth of Marx*, and Galkin's novel *Smuta* (*The Time of Troubles*), which used vulgar-sociological schemes. These books were flagrant examples of inimical attacks in literature. But, sadly enough, even Soviet writers had committed gross mistakes, for example, there were Demian Bednyi's *Bogatyri* (*The Warriors*) and Z. Davydov's *Dikii kamen'*, (*The Wild Stone*).

This proved how important it was to "struggle devotedly for the creation of good historical novels." This had to de done taking into account the remarks, which comrades Stalin, Kirov and Zhdanov had made regarding the proposals for new textbooks in history.

I.Lezhnev in his article "About Literature and Its Cadres"[13] in the same issue of *Pravda*, had other negative things to report. He also surveyed the five-year period since the Central Committee decision of 1932. In his opinion, the Writers' Union had been working badly: new talented writers had only been promoted in small numbers, and the Union had not taken care of the provinces, which, in the past, had often produced the greatest names in literature.

Ideologically, "petty-bourgeois prejudices had been overcome" and a remarkable number of writers who five years ago had been merely sympathetic to Soviet construction were now its active participants and had become non-party Bolsheviks.

However, political and educational work was being conducted badly, even in Moscow, and had been conducted wretchedly in Leningrad, where the writers' organization had been led by a certain Gorelov, "an enemy of the people." Better political work would help to "reveal those enemies of people, who still were hiding in the corners of the writers' organizations."

By the way, the double-dealing Trotskyite had still not been described in Soviet literature. This, however, would help "reveal the enemies of people, to burn out with a hot iron the Trotskyite monsters."

The general idea in liquidating RAPP and founding the united Union of Writers had been to unite the non-party writers with writers, who were members of the party and mobilize them for the tasks of socialist construction, to bring them closer to contemporary political tasks. The present leadership of the Union had not been able to do this. There was no real Bolshevist self-criticism.

The leadership had also been unable to help the writers in their literary work. Dull and immature books were being published.

All this notwithstanding, Soviet literature had become more popular (*narodnyi*) and had more and more profoundly adopted the method of socialist realism. This was proven by the existence of the best books, which had been published in the last few years, the author concluded

A truly formidable and rabidly aggressive article was written in the same issue of Pravda by the philosopher, P. Yudin.[14]

Yudin accused RAPP and its leaders of the greatest of sins, Trotskyism. The tone of the article corresponded to the gravity of the crimes, for Trotskyism was equivalent to high treason, it was the satanic and irreconcilable arch-enemy of Soviet socialism.

RAPP, Yudin wrote, had become obsolete by 1932, for the vast accomplishments in the construction of socialist society had also caused a break among the old intelligentsia: it had begun to support soviet power. Thus, no special proletarian organizations were needed any more. The political line of Averbakh, Kirshon, and others had also been wrong: they had banished all dissidents (*inakomysliashchikh*) and insufficiently submissive ones from proletarian literature. They had built a kind of personality cult and made writers waste their precious time in all kinds of idle meetings and ceremonies and, thus, cut their ties to real life. The "general line" of RAPP was founded on grounds, which were deeply inimical to Marxism-Leninism.

The main theoretician and "leader," Averbakh, was a well-known Trotskyite and ignorant double-dealer. In his brochures he had argued that the culture being built in the USSR was not socialist. This was a totally Trotskyite thesis.

The slogan of Averbakh and his comrades had been that everyone who was not a friend of RAPP was an enemy. They invented a stupid and inimical theory about a dialectically materialist method of creation, which was clearly absurd. They also produced a "harmful little theory" about the "living person," who had to have both vices and virtues. In their literary criticism, which contained Trotskyite, Bukharinist and other trash (*poshliatiny*), could be found ideas of Freud, Deborin, Fritsche and Bogdanov.

In 1932, RAPP was liquidated, but Averbakh, Kirshon, Afinogenov, and Yasensky did not stop their fractional activities and in fact began to resist the decision of the party Central Committee, Yudin concluded ominously.

The factional activities of the group continued during the preparations of the 1934 Writers" Congress. Their most flagrant deed was the concentration of resources for the well-known book about the White Sea Canal. This enterprise, which was energetically supported by Yagoda, became an appalling and repugnant marketplace for the wasting of vast amounts of state resource, the author claimed, not mentioning the conspicuous role of Gorky in the book.

Averbakh's influence in literature, which lasted for a whole epoch, caused "colossal political damage to literature," Yudin argued. The 1932 CC decision had initiated a new epoch of unity amongst writers on socialist positions. The possibilities, which had been opened, had not yet been fully exploited and the Union of Writers still had to do a lot of (*mnogo i mnogo*) work in order to become "a genuine creative organization, which would guarantee the flourishing of literature."

Maybe the most striking thing in Yudin's article was its aggressive and arrogant tone and the black and white world-view, which painted the enemy as totally black. This style or approach had been used elsewhere to describe "wreckers" and "enemies of people." After the "unveiling" of the Red Army case in the summer of 1937, this became the dominant style of the entire Soviet press.

In April of 1937, however, a more moderate tone still prevailed, as was the case, for example, with other articles in the same issue of *Pravda*.

It is not clear, which kind of assignment Yudin had had when writing this article. Anyway, he reported directly to Stalin and Kaganovich about the meeting of the party group of the presidium of the Union of Writers. In this letter, he also repeated the accusations against Kirshon, Yasensky, and Afinogenov and informed the leaders about their Trotskyite discussions and other deeds.[15]

That Yudin had named Bruno Yasensky, a Polish emigrant, among the Trotskyites, was rather startling, for Serebriansky, in the same issue of *Pravda*, had referred to his book *A Man Changes His Skin* as one of the remarkable accomplishments of Soviet literature. Yasensky was, understandably, upset by Yudin's accusation and wrote a letter to Stalin, where he explained that Yudin's animosity towards him was of a personal nature.[16] Nothing helped. Yasensky was "liquidated" and his novel *A Man Changes His Skin* was raised into notoriety as an example of "doubledealing," which was one of the central derogatory concepts of the great purges.[17]

While *Pravda* set the tone, other organs of the press followed. Literaturnaia gazeta eagerly took part in the process of condemning "enemies of the people."[18] The Kremlin and the NKVD received an endless array of reports and denunciations and were very well aware of the refurbishment of the organs of the Writers' Union.[19]

A kind of summary of the new political atmosphere and the new norm set for literary life was given in an anonymous article "For Bolshevist Vigilance in Literature," which was published in *Novyi mir*.[20]

In this article the author(s) remarked that "leading Trotskyites" like Radek and Bukharin had had a lively interest for literature. The "idiotic disease of carelessness," about which Stalin had spoken in the February-March plenum of 1937, had also been widespread in literary circles. The article repeated the "rotten theories" of the Trotskyites, which included Voronsky's and Gorbov's idea that the enemy should not be unveiled and that a "man in general" should be looked for even in a kulak. They had called this approach "humanism." In the circumstances of "capitalist encirclement" this kind of "humanism" for the enemies of socialism and of the "whole of toiling humanity" could not exist. That would be like having pity for a wolf, which would repay such a favor with new crimes and treasons. Vigilance had been lacking. Books like Bruno Yasensky's *A Man Changes His Skin* had been advertised by a fascist spy, and so on, but the best works of Soviet literature like Gorky's *The Life of Klim Samgin*, Sholokhov's *Virgin Soil Upturned*, Gladkov's *Energy*, Fadeyev's *Last of the Udeges*, Ostrovsky's *How the Steel Was Tempered*, Panferov's *Creation*, Aleksei Tolstoy's *Peter I*, Pavlenko's *In the East*, Tynianov's *Pushkin*, Sobolev's *Capital Repairs* and many others witnessed of the growth of this great literature.[21]

As regards the role of avant-garde in the history of Soviet literature and the value of "formalism" in general, these questions were answered in detail by M. Rozental in the journal *Literary Critic*.[22] The author pointed out that every kind of bourgeois intelligent, whose audience had been decadent, had believed that the revolution had been made to give them freedom to reign in art and literature. The avant-garde had not understood at all the correct order i which cultural tasks would have to be solved. They had tried to give the masses "their own, rotten ideas." Formalism was and always had been an "enemy of genuine art," and the party had always fought it and struggled for the creation of great art, worthy the people, which had accomplished the greatest deed in world history. The answer was the adoption of the classical heritage. This had to be done in a critical way, but the task was to "continue the course set by classical realism and to enrich it with the experience, which was being attained in the struggle of the workers and the peasants to construct a socialist society." The party directed Soviet literature and the whole of Soviet art towards most progressive human ideals of justice and rationality concluded Rozental.[23]

Taken together, the campaign of criticism and self-criticism, the forced raising of "vigilance," and the denunciation of past practices, which had in fact been supported by the party and state at the time, changed the atmosphere, and created new political standards of speech and writing. Things, which only recently had been matters of taste, had now become deadly serious political matters. In addition, the party was not prepared to let bygones be bygones. They did matter. Old oppositionists were "scorched" from their nests everywhere, past sins, which had been committed in a totally different situation and had perhaps even been generally accepted at the time, could now become dangerous. Moreover, the general line of the party in literature also seemed hopelessly illogical. If formalism was bad, why was Mayakovsky a great master (and why did nobody criticize his philistine suicide)? If old petty bourgeois intelligents (like Gorky's Klim Samgin) could not change, why had the struggle against fellow-travelers been wrong? If the theory about the "living person" was wrong, how could masters of socialist realism like Sholokhov create the kinds of "living" heroes, who had both vices and virtues? And so on and so forth.

It was more or less hopeless for a writer to try to decide on his own, what was right and what was not. Clearly, this had to be left to the party. True, formally, the party did not make many decisions in this field, but it could monitor the literary scene and put the right people into the right places in institutions.

The purges took their toll of the creative intelligentsia and of cultural institutions. Pilnyak, Mandelshtam, Babel, Meyerkhold and legions of lesser-known masters of culture were shot. Usually this happened after lengthy investigations, during which the NKVD extracted every piece of information possible, true and false, from its victims. Often, it was not difficult to establish that "Trotskyite" conversations, denying the socialist character of the Soviet reality, had taken place. From trifles the investigators could also piece together a connection with someone abroad and, thus, prove that their victims were agents of foreign intelligence services, as indeed, the ideological tenets of the time presupposed.[24]

In the Babel's case, there was ample evidence showing that he had understood the real nature of the great terror and spoken about it to his acquaintances.[25] Even the fact that he had declined to publish any major works for a lengthy time, despite the fact that he had been writing all the time, was proof of his Trotskyite, anti-Soviet attitudes. His silence was "dangerously eloquent."[26]

It is clear that Babel, who understood the nature of theis newly-born socialism, could not bring himself to cooperate with this barbarism. According to a witness, he had said that an author had to be sincere in what he wrote, but that sincere views could not be printed, because they were not in tune with the party line. He sensed, he said "the contradiction between my unchanged and abstractly "humanistic" viewpoint and the works about the New Man that the Soviet reading audience was waiting for, books, that in artistic form explained the present and pointed forward to the future."[27]

As regards Trotskyite connections, they were easy to find, as always. In the case of Babel they included Voronsky, the once editor of *Krasnaia nov'* and other domestic literary names, even the wife of Yezhov[28] (this case was tried in 1939) and this acquaintance was as odious for the accused in 1939 as had been that of Yagoda in 1937.

Babel's fate was very similar to that of Boris Pilnyak. Pilnyak had also been unable to praise socialist reality, and he had had foreign contacts, cooperated with Voronsky, and planned terrorist acts (this time against Yezhov!). At his trial Pilnyak, in his concluding remarks to his judges, said that he had now become a "new man" and looked at life with new eyes. He asked for the opportunity to serve the Soviet people.[29] The military tribunal condemned Pilnyak to be shot.

It is hard to escape the conclusion that both Babel and Pilnyak and, indeed, legions of others were executed because of their more or less open disbelief in the new, socialist nature of Soviet society. After all, this was nothing other than Trotskyism. As regards the endless plans to murder Stalin, Yezhov, and other luminaries, there cannot be any doubt that people, who had preserved a normal sense of good and evil, did at least in their imagination and in confidential conversations entertain the idea of tyrannicide.

The great terror destroyed intellectuals, who had not been able to become "new men." The idea of terror in general is to kill some and scare thousands. After the purges, every intellectual knew that he or she also could be shot. As the well-known theory of cognitive incongruence suggests, quite a lot of people may well have adopted the official view as their conscious image of the new Soviet reality. But, after all, who could have been safe against accusations of double-dealing, or of having contacts with the enemies of the people or their agents? In July 1938, A. A. Andreev sent to Stalin a list of names of dozens of prominent writers, about whom compromising material had been gathered by the NKVD.[30] Stalin also received special files on men of letters, like Demyan Bedny, M. S. Golodny, M. A. Svetlov, I. P. Utkin, and so on.[31]

The capitalist encirclement

Agents of the enemies of people were discovered everywhere. Any contacts with foreigners now became dangerous because of their link to capitalist encirclement, the source of all anti-Soviet activity.

Babel had also been abroad and knew André Gide and André Malraux very well. Since 1937, Gide had, of course, been considered a Trotskyite by the NKVD. And so was Malraux, a fact, he was probably unaware of, and which undoubtedly would have shocked him, had he known about it. After all, Malraux had been one of the main organizers of the pro-Soviet "cultural front" in Western Europe, and a willing supporter of Litvinov during the short flourishing of the Popular front, which had gathered together thousands of intellectuals from many countries.

Now, however, Malraux was shown to have been disloyal and to have had little faith in Soviet socialism. He had sent to Stalin a letter in behalf of no lesser a figure than Bukharin himself.[32]

Babel had had close connections with Malraux, who had been "spying," as the NKVD found out. He had, e.g. wanted to know about the fate of the peasants who had been exiled to Siberia. Babel had given him information, which "gloomily sketched the negative sides of life in the collective farms."[33]

The Poet I. P. Utkin had said, according to the denunciation, which had been given to Stalin about him, that

> Europe laughs at this constitution, which is being launched with a salute of the executioner's bullets. The intelligentsia does not accept it... Abroad, we, by and by are losing all our friends and allies... An enemy could not have harmed us as much as Stalin did with those processes of his....[34]

How was it in practice? Did Western European intelligents accept the official Stalinist version about the show trials of 1936-38? In the Soviet Union the "Trotskyites," who dismissed the trials as cynical and outrageous acts of violence, did not have in their possession Trotsky's revelations, which convincingly showed that many of the accusations, which had been "proved" in the show trials, could not have been true.

In Western Europe and America, however, ample material showing the spurious nature of the accusations was available. Predictably, therefore, many foreign intellectuals did not believe the Stalinist version of events. But, all this notwithstanding, many did. To some degree, this amounted to a certain disorder among the Western "anti-fascist" intellectuals, some of whom proved able to resist the "totalitarian temptation" and did not accept the Stalinist view, according to which there were only two alternatives: communism and fascism.

There were those, who did not actually believe the Stalinist version, but did believe that it was useful to defend the Stalinist cause. In the USA 150 intellectuals signed a declaration, where they supported the Moscow show trials and the death sentences handed down.[35]

Some people, who were actually present at the trials, like Lion Feuchtwanger, believed the Stalinis version, as did those, like Henri Barbusse, who obviously were unable to doubt the veracity of the trials. Even people, who were not communists like Walter Duranty, a reporter for the New York Times and Joseph Davies, ambassador of the United States, who were also present at the trials, believed in the authenticity of the trials.[36] Feuchtwanger published a book *Moscow 1937*, which was even published in the USSR in an edition of 200,000. Unfortunately, the following year it did not suit the new political situation and was, accordingly, was taken off the market.[37] Some friends of the Soviet Union did not believe in the authenticity of the trials, but were ready to forgive them for the sake of the great cause, which the Soviet Union represented. So, André Malraux declared that "just as the Inquisition did not affect the fundamental dignity of Christianity, so the Moscow trials have not diminished the fundamental dignity of communism."[38] Bertolt Brecht confessed privately that "freedom" did not reign in the USSR. Instead of that, he maintained, it was "in the process of coming."[39]

But there were also those, who were less optimistic. André Gide published his *Retour de l'URSS* at the end of 1936 and another volume next year, where he revealed the mechanisms of lionization and fraud, by means of which the Soviet Union was recruiting intellectuals into its sphere.[40] Gide's books were a shock to Moscow, where he had been regarded for several years as a friend of the system. Gide's "treason" was advertised in the Soviet Union, and several prominent people condemned him. Even a collective of Magnitogorsk miners sent a letter of condemnation of Gide to Romain Rolland, who, like Lion Feuchtwanger, for instance, had also condemned Gide's "double-dealing."[41] Feuchtwanger deplored the fact that Gide did not see that, for instance, what looked like the divinization of Stalin, was in fact, an expression f the gratitude that the people felt for their new found prosperity and welfare, which they associated with, and attributed to, Stalin. What looked like the "unification" of minds was the beginning of a new culture. Gide's attack against socialism had come at a time, when the fascist attack in Spain was threatening socialism in the whole world. By publishing his books at this moment, Gide had lost the right to call himself a socialist writer.[42]

In an anonymous column, *Pravda* "unveiled" Gide's class essence: he was a true son of the French petty bourgeoisie. He was a typical representative of the degenerate bourgeois intelligentsia, and an individualist, who had fallen in love with himself. Gide had rebelled against bourgeois morality, but this was just a cheap rebellion of a petty bourgeois, which might even lead to fascism. The author hinted that Gide clearly belonged to the camp of Trotskyites and fascists.[43] A literary critic, who reviewed

Gorky's *Klim Samgin* in 1937, found that Gide was just another Samgin –a conceited individualist.[44]

In fact Gide did not want to "attack" socialism, but to be a sympathetic critic of Soviet reality. Unfortunately, both the official Soviet Union and the French activists of the cultural front considered such stance impossible.[45]

There were, in France, a number of intellectuals, who were genuinely interested in finding out the truth about the Soviet Union. The well-known defector, Boris Souvarine even founded a society "The Society of the Friends of the Truth About the Soviet Union" (*Amis de la verité sur l'URSS*), which seemed necessary, because "The Society of Friends of the USSR" did not allow people with critical minds to be members. Souvarine seems to have had scant success.[46]

There were, however, people in France like Trotsky and his son Lev Sedov, who were violently anti-Stalinist, who were, in fact, able to show the spuriousness of the show trials. They were not, however, regarded as credible witnesses when it came to their "own" trials. There was a French committee for the monitoring of the Moscow show trials, but, like Romain Rolland, it came to the conclusion that the accused were guilty, although it did oppose the drastic sentences.[47]

Among the German émigré writers, who had fled Hitler, opinions were divided. Prominent figures like Rudolf Hilferding considered that the show trials had compromised the Popular front terribly.[48] Some, like Kurt Hiller, said that clearly cooperation with Stalin was only possible if one blindly submitted to his will. Any signs of individualism would lead to being branded an "individualist," "bourgeois" or "counterrevolutionary," and then he could be slandered or executed.[49]

The show trials divided the German Popular front, which existed in emigration. One of its organs, *Neue Tage-Buch* compared the trials to medieval witch-hunts. Another émigré organ, *Neue Welt-Buehne* adopted an apologetic line and printed more and more orthodox Soviet views.[50]

Against the *Neue Tage-Buch*, the NKVD resorted to what became a classic method in the "active operations" of disinformation. A letter was sent to the NTB under the name of "Marcel Strauss," in which the sender, allegedly a medical specialist, explained, how the confessions could have been obtained by using hypnosis. Soon after the publication of the letter, agents of Moscow "revealed" the spuriousness of Strauss's letter: no such person existed at the given address, they said. Unfortunately for them, they forgot to check the letter. It contained no sender's address and the nature of the trick was exposed for the reader.[51]

As regards the Russian émigré press, in the first half of the 1930s it had become more and more pro-Soviet. Even liberal organs like Miliukov"s *Poslednie novosti* (*Latest News*) had become quite pro-Soviet in the 1930s.

In 1936 Alexander Kerensky founded a new organ *Novaia Rossiia*, whose name symbolized the idea that the Soviet Union had become "Russia" once again. Interestingly enough, Stalin's collectivization had aroused admiration amongst émigré socialists and the rehabilitation of Russian nationalism and the "great retreat" in culture had appealed even to those, who were more conservative.[52]

The show trials too were received with little criticism, and even support, by the émigré press until the purges hit the leadership of the Red army.[53]

When Tukhachevsky and several other high-standing commanders of the Red Army were liquidated in the summer of 1937, the tone abruptly changed. Whereas Kerensky's paper as late as the spring of 1937 had still "understood" Stalin's struggle against the Trotskyites as part of his abandonment of political extremism, it now asked "Is Stalin Mad?"[54]

It has been noted that Stalin was impressed by the "Night of Long Knives" in 1934, when Hitler ruthlessly murdered the potential opposition, which had developed within the SA. Similarly, Stalin's ruthless policies, which certainly showed that he was no wavering philistine, impressed some fascists. The Italian Renzo Bertoni[55] wrote about the Soviet Union in 1936 in an admiring tone. Moscow often used terms like "communist," "Leninist" or "Stalinist," Bertoni wrote, to denote things, which in his opinion were essentially and distinctively "fascist." The Soviet Union, however, was still not a fully developed fascist country: it represented only the last stage of the old society, not the new (fascist) one. However, the Soviet Union was yet another case, which showed to the "old world" that capitalism was obsolete. The new way for humanity was being shown by Rome.[56]

By the end of the 1930s, the new socialist Soviet culture and society seemed as difficult to understand as ever. Even such connoisseurs of Russian culture and people as the émigrés, who had explained Stalin's return to traditional, national, and petty bourgeois values as a retreat from revolutionary extremism into "normalcy," had been disappointed. Stalinism really did seem to be a new kind of civilization, for better or worse. It was clear that this party-state had forsaken the "petty bourgeois" principles of rule of law and respect for the individual.

9
A Post-Philistine World
The New Intelligentsia and the Discourse of Soviet Socialism

The new official moralism

In "The Communist Manifesto" Karl Marx and Friedrich Engels had proclaimed that the bourgeoisie had destroyed all virtue in society. It had severed the ties of feudal society and had left only one virtue and one bond between human beings: naked greed and payment in cash. There were no longer any pious dreams or chivalrous enthusiasm, only selfish calculation. Even family ties had been turned into property relations. In fact, bourgeois society had destroyed the monogamous family by creating prostitution, which stemmed from the proletariat's misery. The wives and daughters of the proletariat were, in fact, already available for the bourgeoisie's gratification, but even so, the depraved bourgeoisie considered seducing each other's wives to be their greatest pleasure.[1]

For the bourgeoisie, including the petty bourgeoisie, all relations had a commercial character. No wonder, then, that bourgeois culture was polluted by egotism and that it gave birth to pornography, formalism in art (the fruit of individualism), and other degenerate products. All this was in line with the Stalinist cultural politics of the late 1930s. As regards the proletariat, Marx and Engels seemed convinced about its high moral standards. It was virtuous in battle and was not contaminated by individualism. It was the new rising class and the future belonged to it. Therefore, it was natural that nothing depraved or degenerate could flourish in its midst.

Indeed, the noble forms of classical antiquity proved adequate for serving the needs of the new socialist society and its progressive ruling class. This was a society, which reflected the interests of the working classes and there was no longer a bourgeoisie. But how did the new morality, which stemmed from the nature of the social system, function on the individual level? The old bourgeois society had favored the principle of *laisser-faire*. In any case it had the virtue of not being artificial. This was a potential argument for showing that it was a natural social system. The unseen hand of the market was supposedly serving the whole society even if individuals were just pursuing their own personal gain and enjoyment. Private vice was transformed into public virtue, as Bernard Mandeville had demonstrated.

If socialism, and not capitalism, was the natural social system, then it could be anticipated that the virtues, which this system promoted and which were necessary for its functioning, would also very easily stem from human nature, and there would be no need for omnipresent coercion and surveillance. Lenin in his *State and Revolution* had asserted that people would very easily get accustomed to living according to new norms (which in essence were ancient ones). But would citizens of a socialist society, whilst learning to live according to new rules, at the same time also have personal, individual freedom?

According to Marx, freedom was nothing more than the conscious approval of necessity. This was, in fact, very much in line with the thinking of the Utilitarians and even Adam Smith. For any socialist it was an axiom that the socialist social system was rational and if its citizens were also rational, they would obey its rules. In the USSR the great terror probably taught a lesson for many such people, who had been thinking that it could also be rational to disobey the rules of the new society. During the second half of the 1930s a set of socialist virtues were inculcated by the citizens of the new socialist society. In principle one had to assume that all the new socialist virtues belonged to all members of the new socialist society, if it was true that one's social being determined one's consciousness. Some of the virtues, however, were, first and foremost, supposed to be represented by the new socialist intelligentsia. *Kul'turnost'*, or culturedness was one such virtue of special social value.

Kul'turnost'

As has been repeatedly said above, the raising of cultural standards had been one of the top priorities of the Soviet leadership ever since the last writings of Lenin, where he had even maintained that it were the main task on the way to socialism.[2]

A higher cultural level, as a presupposition of socialism, clearly, first of all, a practical importance: people had to be able to run a state and understand the basics of both administration and economics. In the early 1920s the most elementary task was to teach the masses to read and write.

Education also meant liquidation of the cultural gap between the working masses and the elite, which was often simply called the intelligentsia. Schooling was also to play a major part in emancipating the toilers from the captivity of only being able to do one particular job. The unified working school was supposed to give everybody a polytechnic education, which would give them the opportunity to change jobs as and when required and was a remarkable step in the general liquidation of the division of labor, which was one of the basic novelties of the new society. The importance of this ideological task can be understood by looking at the programmatic texts of the communist party and the state. In was no accident that Krupskaia, who had been one of the main champions of polytechnic education, was overrun by Stalin at the beginning of 1930s, when the egalitarian pathos of the educational system was substituted for a performance oriented ideology. For Krupskaia, schools had been the crucial medium, through which people would be remolded. According to this view, the interests of material production were in fact secondary.[3]

From the beginning of the 1930s, the school system lost its libertarian and egalitarian character and experimental methods were substituted for traditional ones. Anton Makarenko's ideas about the pupils' collective being the central pedagogical entity, which was exploited for keeping discipline and for surveillance purposes, became the foundation of Soviet pedagogy. The courses offered and teaching methods once again became traditional. History, in the traditional form of a narrative about states and personalities, was restored to the curriculum and new textbooks were written taking into account the instructions of a high-standing jury, which included Stalin, Kirov, and Zhdanov.[4]

As regards the cultural standards of the Soviet people, the progress made since the revolution and with the dawn of socialism had been tremendous. The official figures are doubtless inflated, but much of the claimed accomplishment, the fruit of the labor of a half-starved intelligentsia, must have been real.

From the very beginning, however, the idea of raising the cultural standard of the masses had not just been utilitarian or exclusively connected to the practical tasks of production and politics. Bringing the masses to a higher cultural level had always been understood by mainstream communism to mean improving their taste and behavior, developing their spiritual talents, raising their morals, and polishing their manners.

According to the intellectual tradition, which the Bolshevik mainstream from Trotsky to Bukharin had shared in the 1920s, a cultured person combined practical skills and civic virtues with knowledge of the classical heritage: Rubens, Beethoven and Pushkin were not representatives of the proletariat, but they represented the level, which the former "dark masses" were supposed to achieve and, perhaps, surpass.

In 1937 the anniversary of Pushkin's death was not celebrated only by the intelligentsia: the whole people participated. The number of worker (especially Stakhanovite) Pushkinists was especially impressive.[5]

Cultural work directed towards educating the "dark masses," was conducted throughout the 1920s. *Kul'tura* meant a great variety of things, which were connected to the modern way of living. In the "many-formational" Soviet state, to use Lenin's phrase, there were still remnants of past epochs: back to feudalism and even more primitive phenomena. Culture meant modernization: overcoming old irrational traditions, including the Sharia in Muslim regions. It meant overcoming the "idiocy of rural life" in the Russian countryside, and the petty-bourgeois cretinism of the "Towns of Okurov," which Maxim Gorky had described.

It has occasionally been pointed out that "culturedness" (*kul'turnost'*) was, in fact, not identical with "culture" (*kul'tura*). Kul'tura can be understood as "the achievement of the intelligentsia in the sense of higher culture, a synthesis of ideas, knowledge and memories,"[6] whereas *kul'turnost'* had nothing to do with a spiritual legacy, but was a "mere program for proper conduct in public."[7] In the 1930's at least, it was not exactly so. *Kul'turnost'* meant both basic skills and proper, "gentlemanlike," conduct, which the *kul'turniki* of the 1920s had been craving for, believing that it would be a *conditio sine qua non* for the socialist society.[8] But the question was not just about behavior, it encompassed knowledge, skills, tastes, and modernization. To a large extent, the terms *kul'tura* and *kul'turnost'* were interchangeable.

Women were a special group, which the Bolsheviks wanted to civilize and liberate. In the 1920s they could be considered another "surrogate proletariat", whose potential was to be used in the service of the Bolsheviks.[9] The "right" attitude to a woman (on the part of men) was a very important criterion of culturedness. The change in the position of women in the "national *okrainy*" became a much-advertised accomplishment of Bolsheviks power in the 1930s and a symbol of their raised cultural level.

In principle, culture was something, the working class, especially the "conscious" working class already possessed to a remarkable extent. In this respect Gorky's *Mother* had referred to a commonplace. This was especially evident when the low cultural level of the primitive" national" (non-Russian) peasantry was compared with that of Russian workers.

The high cultural level of the workers was reflected, for example, in the fact that they did not have national prejudices. Logically, then, the national prejudices of the *okrainy* would be overcome by establishing industries in those regions, which would the produce for all of the "national groups," a proletariat of their own.[10]

The conscious working class had left behind the coarse and animal level of existence of the petty bourgeois peasants, as Gorky had described in *Mother*. The conscious workers represented a new and higher morality. It was also no accident that it was workers, those "best sons of the fatherland," which had been sent to the countryside to implement collectivization. It was also a sad, but predictable phenomenon that the new recruits to the working class, who arrived from the countryside, still lived in an uncultured way, and slept with their clothes and boots on. It was the "petty bourgeois" peasantry that was to blame for this. The peasantry was the main object of the civilizing mission of the Bolsheviks in the 1920s and 1930s.

The cultural level of the peasants was deplorable, by definition, up until collectivization. After collectivization and with the dawn of socialism, they were destined to become cultured. Without this, a socialist society would be unthinkable.

Stalin also promised the peasants several times to the peasants both a "well-to do" and a "wholly cultured" life. This happened in the aftermath of the collectivization and the ensuing famine.[11] It is clear that a "cultured" life presupposed a certain level of material well-being. Being cultured on the verge of a subsistence level of existence was unthinkable, for a "cultured life" also meant hygiene: good wells, unbroken windows, the destruction of vermin and cockroaches, and so on[12]. It goes without saying that using tractors instead of horses for field work, along with a knowledge of mechanics, was a step forward in culture. It was also no accident that some kolkhozes could be named "Kul'tura."

With the dawn of socialism, the development of the peasantry still lagged behind that of the workers, and this was taken into account in the 1936 constitution. Their social being (as proprietors, albeit collectively, of their means of production) and their daily work and lifestyles still preserved remnants of the petty bourgeois way of life, including the owning of a private plot. In fact, the peasants would remain second class citizens up to the end of the Soviet Union. The much-advertised liquidation of the differences between town and countryside, as well as those between mental and physical work was destined never to take place under Soviet socialism, either on a real or an imaginary, "official" level. This, however, was not foreseen at the end of the second five-year plan, which celebrated the triumph of socialism.

In 1935-37 Soviet propaganda widely advertised its cultural accomplishments, including the unprecedented kul'turnost' of the "new man." But, what were conditions really like in practice?

The campaign for culturedness began in 1935. Stalin linked kul'turnost' and a prosperous life in his speech to Stakhanovites in November 1935,[13] but the issue had become topical even before this. The Stakhanovians were supposed to be real "new people" and they were also obliged to be exemplary regarding their cultural level as well.

A cultured person took care of his hygiene, it was proclaimed. No less a person than Sergo Ordzhonikidze demanded that leading personnel in plants and factories should look tidy and shave regularly. In many places, this was soon made obligatory.[14] Mirrors were hung up in workshops, to give the personnel the opportunity to check their own appearance. The movement of the wives of the leaders (obshchestvennitsy), which held its first meeting in May 1936 and was attended by Stalin and other luminaries, began to take care of the kul'turnost' of workshops and dormitories. Often appalling hygienic conditions were improved, and an attempt was made to give workers more privacy. The quality of their food was monitored and cultural programs, including music, were organized for them. Coarse language and rudeness, not to mention wife-beating and drunkenness, were all opposed as they were regarded incompatible with kul'turnost'.[15]

An the same time, things, which in the 1920s had been considered "philistine," especially curtains, lampshades, and tablecloths, came back into favor. These things even turned into fetishes. Curtains especially "turned into a universal symbol of kul'turnost', it has been said.[16]

"Culture of speech" was another criterion, and a cultured person was expected to read both the classics and Soviet newspapers and journals. He was supposed to attend the theatre and cinema and be aware of the topical political tasks, set out by the party. In other words, a cultured Soviet citizen resembled, more or less, the old ideal of an intelligent. However, real kul'turnost' also excluded philistinism. The rehabilitation of the cosy life did not really mean a rehabilitation of philistinism: mere consumerism without the right mental attitude to it was not welcomed. Until 1937, and sometimes even after, it could be labelled "petty bourgeois.".[17]

The campaign for kulturnost' seems to have lasted from Stalin"s speech to the Stakhanovites in 1935 until the campaign of mastering Bolshevism, which was launched in September 1938 ,with the releasing of the Short Course of the History of the VKP(b).[18]

That the state tried to raise the cultural level of its people was by no means unique in European history. Something similar had been attempted in most of the other European countries. This had been called the task of civilizing the population, which most states had attempted during and after the nineteenth century. But, the Soviet campaign of the 1930s, was, of course, uncommonly abrupt and implemented in a uniquely totalitarian way.

By international comparison, it has been said that the Soviet civilizing process excelled with its "overt and unremitting emphasis on cultivation as a public and collective duty, rather than an individual and private quest" and also in its egalitarianism.[19]

Culture, kul'turnost', was declared to be available for anybody in the Soviet Union. It seems, however, that a certain minimum of kul'turnost' rapidly became a sine qua non for the top of society, which was often called the Soviet "intelligentsia," but which did not necessarily comprise all the people, who belonged to that category according to the official definition. These were people, who gave parties and conversed in a cultured way, knew how to dress for formal public occasions, how to conduct themselves at polite parties, and how to entertain guests.[20] As was stated above, the cultured life was also a well-to-do life. The future affluence of a socialist society had always been an axiom for any communist. As regards the extreme hardships of the first five-year plan, these, it was explained, were the result of having to concentrate all resources in investment. Affluence would come with the second five-year plan, which would bring socialism. Stalin had already promised this in 1933 and had referred to it as an established fact in 1935: "Life has become better, life has become merrier!"

In practice, affluence was attained only by a few, although it was not confined only to the communist leadership. Stakhanovites could earn fantastic sums, many times higher than the average salary. They had pianos and bicycles, and even cars (and chauffeurs) of their own.[21] Stakhanovites became cultured persons, they attended the theatre and their children had piano or ballet lessons. They were called the "illustrious people" (znatnye liudi), which was reminiscent of the high society (znat) of pre-Revolutionary times.

The workers, or rather Stakhanovites, as well as responsible workers in the party and the government together with the managerial and industrial elite, had access to an affluent life in the second half of the 1930s. This "virtual affluence" of the Soviet people was advertised in what has been called "consumer-goods pornography."[22] The famous Book about the Tasty and Healthy Food, which appeared on the book-market, presented an awe-inspiring array of different sorts of delicacies: dozens of different sausages, candies, and pastries. Silk stockings, suits, good drinks, and other luxury items were reported to be available in the land of the Soviets.[23] In practice, however, they were in such short supply that masses of people hardly ever even caught a glimpse of them. Scarce products were available in the so called Torgsin stores, which sold goods for hard currency or precious metals, but they were closed in 1936.[24] Thereafter, scarce goods were hardly ever seen on the shelves of ordinary shops, and those, which were, were very expensive. Since the nominal, pecuniary remuneration of people in the USSR was increasing more rapidly than the production of goods, which, Stalin proudly proclaimed, was a guarantee against depression this led to a situation, where demand widely exceeded supply, which ensured that scarce goods became the subject of black market, where prices rose to very high level. As a result, it was getting hold of goods, rather than having a lot of money, which was important in the USSR. As regards

Stakhanovites and other illustrious comrades, they had both money and access to goods. The production of luxury items like "Soviet champagne" amidst general poverty was quite sensible. It helped to create an image of "virtual" affluence and added to the credibility of the optimistic forecasts, which promised widespread prosperity within a couple of years.[25]

The scarcity of goods and the unavoidable appearance of a black market price to the scarce goods gave rise to the fact that a shop assistant had not to "sell" his product but to "give " it away to the clients. They were always ready to buy more than was available and reproached the poor clerk for the lack of goods. I was generally suspected, often with grounds, that all of the goods i shops were not mad available to the clients. This system very quickly gave rise to a "service culture," which could be called "qualitatively new". The relations between the shop assistants ad the clients resembled a state of war.

The campaign for culturedness also put a considerable stress on the need to civilize trade. The campaign coincided with the abolition of rationing, whilst the service culture had not improved under the card system. The campaign for "cultured trade" also meant a limited introduction of consumerism, and American models were advertised for the Soviet consumer, who had been waiting for the often promised affluence, which so far had arrived only for the selected few.[26]

The new culturedness of the new intelligentsia often bore the hallmark of *poshlost'*, which had been considered an attribute of the philistine (*meshchanin*). The Stakhanovites, who had become Pushkinists overnight,[27] could hardly be taken seriously by the older generation of intelligents.

But, challenging the regime had already become very risky. Although Zoshchenko made fun of the half-baked Pushkinists on the pages of the satirical journal *Krokodil*[28], even this was not necessarily safe, for the party had the power to define the boundaries of both *poshlost'* and satire, and could intervene at any moment.

The officially advertised image of the high cultural level new intelligentsia, no doubt, bore the traits of the false perfection, which was the hallmark of *poshlost'*, according to Nabokov's classic definition. No less false was the official image of the new Soviet affluence. The new intelligent was, in principle, cultured in the sense that he was supposed to have a knowledge of the classical heritage, but, according to the official image, he did not share the old intelligent weaknesses, but was true to proletarian class values, as defined by the party. He had left behind the curse of petty bourgeois philistinism forever.

Vigilance and political rectitude

"Politics" had always been a top priority for Stalin. The whole concept of "politics" in the Soviet Union came to be understood rather differently than in other countries. In practice it often meant coercion, euphemistically called "administration," which was imposed on the country by the party. The party was the heart of politics, but politics did not end with the party. One must not forget that the acronym GPU means "Main Political Administration." The kolkhozes, since 1935, had "political departments" on the Machine and Tractor Stations. The role of the party cells was to actively promote the party line in the collectives. They were the avant-garde of the ruling class. On the other hand, the security organs had a more humble mission: they took care of those, who were the least conscious, who represented remnants of the past or were even agents of imperialism, which had its bases abroad. The security organs were in fact just the rear-guard.

As regards the party, it, of course, was not a party at all, in the conventional sense of the word, for there were no other parties. Anyway, despite its monopoly in politics, the party as such did not encompass the totality but directed and monitored it. The official idea that the party was the organization of the most conscious and active part of the population, had a very real meaning. It implied that the rest of society could not be as active or as conscious.

The Komsomol was an extension of the party, as was every other organization. An organization, beyond or outside the control of the party, was unconceivable. Party cells in every organization, even in ad hoc organs, took care that the party line was being pursued. When socialism was achieved in 1936-37, practically all the remaining civic organizations, like learned and professional societies, were dispersed. The main organ of the Komsomol was unstinting in its efforts to propagate the image of the new Soviet man and the new Soviet intelligent. It was proclaimed over and over again that one's private life was not outside politics and that the Komsomol and the party had a right to intervene in one's private life when necessary.[29]

From the beginning of the 1930s, Stalin repeatedly stressed the importance of the political factor, that is, the reliability of the political apparatus. The height of the campaign for political vigilance came in 1937. In the February-March Plenum of the Central Committee, Stalin firmly and closely linked political knowledge and vigilance: the political conscience of all leading comrades was to be heightened by studying. This studying, rightly understood, clearly showed that everything that went wrong, was the result of wrecking, which had political reasons, this was, in effect, what Stalin proclaimed in the spring of 1937 and was also the message of the *Short Course of the History of the VKP(b)*, which, in 1938, became the catechism of the party and the new intelligentsia as a whole.

The new man had a new morality, which was entirely class-bound, as Lenin had envisaged. Now, in the new socialist society, there was no room for petty bourgeois scruples, for putting the individual self before the interests of the collective.

This new psychology was to be reflected not only in words, but also by actions. The "double dealers" (*dvurushniki*) became the most odious enemy, which Stalin attacked in the February-March Plenum and which he ordered to be unmasked and liquidated. The problem with the double dealers was that they did not openly reveal their inimical nature, but continued to work properly, just waiting for their opportunity, which could come at any moment. Was this just paranoid morbid hysteria, which has so often ailed omnipotent rulers since Biblical days? This may be partly so, but we must also not forget that Stalin kept getting opinion surveillance reports, where he could easily be convinced about the double-dealing of a large segment of the people. Nobody spoke out publicly, but nothing prevented people from hating their oppressors and from craving for revenge.[30]

An ideal Soviet person would spare nobody when unmasking the enemy. The family, the citadel of petty bourgeois egoism and individualism, was no exception. This was presupposed in criminal law, so that even members of a family of an "enemy of the people" were sentenced to several years in jail, if they had failed to inform the repressive organs. The "new man" exhibited his heroism, for example, in his principled relationship to his family. Pavlik Morozov was not just a boy-hero, worthy of praise by the pioneers. He was a symbolic figure for the new ideal of humanity. It was no accident that Maxim Gorky, in 1934, made the cream of the Soviet intelligentsia pay homage to Pavlik's feat (denunciation of his own father's machinations with the kulaks), and his contribution to the great struggle against the very roots of philistinism.[31]

There is no denying that the witch-hunt, which was launched to unmask double dealers, in 1937 reached a point where it lost touch with reality. There was, however, a grain of truth behind the façade. Stalin knew that a great part of the people was against him and had politically incorrect ideas about the present state of society.

The orgy of "unmaskings" reached new heights in the summer of 1937, when thousands of army officers were caught. The whole tone of the press, which had been morbid since the February-March plenum, became one of fury. Terrible crimes were revealed everywhere, but the whole process also had something positive about it: it was not only the repressive organs that fought the criminals. Rank and file citizens were also active. The masses held meetings, demanding harsh sentences for the criminals. There was seamless cooperation between ordinary citizens and the security organs. In principle, this was unavoidable, for the organs represented the people.

The hero of the day, in the summer of 1937, was Nikolai Yezhov. His virtues and exploits were presented to the whole Soviet people in a *Pravda* leader, which meant they had to be considered as, not a piece of laudatory journalism, but as scientific truth. The article was called "For a Bolshevik, Word Does Not Differ From Deed!"[32]

Nikolai Yezhov had received the order of Lenin, the article stated, for "excellent results in directing the organs of the NKVD in the implementation of tasks, given by the state." The state had the role of implementing the tasks, which were given by the party, so that Yezhov's feat was nonetheless done in the service of the party and he was praised for his party qualities and political virtues and not for his technical achievements.

Yezhov, the article said, "incarnates a Bolshevik, whose word never differs from his deed." The main virtues of Yezhov were: "the greatest revolutionary vigilance and an iron will, a sharp Bolshevist eye and organizational talent, a rare intelligence and the finest proletarian tact." These qualities were necessary for a man, whom the party had put in such a post.

Yezhov was an exemplary man, *Pravda* pointed out, but there were still windbags in the country, who used many beautiful words and did nothing. Was it not clear that these were "rotten people, who had nothing in common with Bolshevism!" For a real Bolshevik words and deeds were identical and the interests of the party were higher than anything else. The word of the party and its central committee had never differed from each other. The toiling masses knew this and, therefore, they trusted the party. True communists were conscious of their goal and their character was tough, they were able to "surpass any obstacles," as Stalin had said. This was amply demonstrated by the peredoviks, by the Stakhanovites and by all kinds of heroes, whose exploits were now filling the pages of the newspapers. The whole land of Soviet was now becoming "a land of heroes."

The strength of the Soviet Union lay in such people, and they were the source of faith in communism. People, who said one thing and did another, the party would throw away.

There were still enemies and always would be, but they would be annihilated thanks to the unique fact, unthinkable elsewhere, that the security organs were an organic part of the whole people, "flesh from their flesh and bone from their bone" *Pravda* proclaimed in the article, which surely was carefully read all over the land of the Soviets.

The masses knew, Pravda wrote, that the work of the NKVD was a most important part of the service to the working class and the cause of socialism. The masses understood that "by helping the NKVD they helped themselves," the chief organ of the party explained. The NKVD was the naked sword of the working class

> The whole people are holding this sword in its hands. Therefore, the NKVD has and will still have million of more eyes, millions of ears, millions of hands of the working people, who are led by the party of Bolsheviks and its Stalinist Central Committee. Such a force is invincible![33]

Although this very remarkable article clearly has a touch of hyperbole about it, it is sensible, nevertheless to look at it closely. In any case, it described the ideal Bolshevik and citizen at the critical moment, when the new socialist society had, in principle, became reality.

The main pathos of the article, which praised a man, who had already sent hundreds of thousands of people to their death, was that there was only one reality and that was the truth given by the party and its central committee. The new image of society was not a matter of propaganda, it was deadly serious.

This "socialist realism" was not just meant for literary people or for party people. It concerned everybody. It may be noted that the article maintained that the whole people was in the service of the NKVD. This was logical, for there were no longer antagonistic classes. Workers and peasants were not mentioned separately in the article: there were just toiling people (*trudiashchikhsia*) "members of the party and non-party Bolsheviks." On the other hand, there were also the enemies of the people but also a strange group of people, who were described as rotten, who had nothing to do with Bolshevism. Their only sin, however, seemed to be that they spoke beautiful words about the need to "do something," to "implement," or to change things" (*perestroit'*). Instead of doing their task, however, they stopped when faced with difficulties, which even often were only imaginary.[34]

Were these people not the analogy of the same lukewarm element, which had already been cursed by the author of the Apocalypse? An ideology, which had become sacral politics and had started a holocaust, could not tolerate bystanders, who were feeble in faith.

The original double dealers, against whom Stalin had declared war in February, had been accused of being agents of foreign imperialism. Now another category of people, who evidently were just inefficient, was declared to be an enemy of the people.

There is no doubt that the thrust of the attack was directed against the category of old party leaders on all levels, for whom Stalin had ordered the appointment of deputies in the spring. Now, Yezhov had set new standards for politics, and the old leadership and their new would-be replacements had to show kind of communists they were.

It was, however, not just the bosses, who were given new standards. The great transformation concerned everybody. As we know, the great purges claimed millions of victims, and by no means was even the rank and file safe. But people occupying commanding positions were the most conspicuous and the most likely to attract the attention of "vigilant" people.

The beginning of the new socialist era was promised to be hard for the classic Russian type of *intelligent*—and also for the petty bourgeois.

Lenin Had already remarked that the *intelligenty* had always excelled in making a fuss about the fate of unnecessary and odious people. It was their tradition to speak endlessly using grand words, and to stop short in front of dirty and bloody tasks. This, in fact, was the petty bourgeois trait in their character. It belonged to the past. The petty bourgeoisie, as a social group, did not exist anymore. Where did these inefficient windbags come? The unavoidable conclusion was that they were in the service of the imperialists, and that the people had to unmask and to destroy them.

In literature, the archetype of the double dealer was depicted by Maxim Gorky in his multi-volume *The Life of Klim Samgin*. As George Lukacs explained in 1936 Samgin was a "spineless individualistic bourgeois intelligent," who wanted to find a third answer to any question. In reality, however, there were only two alternatives: yes or no. Samgin started out as a narodnik but "degenerated" towards Kadet liberalism. Gorky showed how both the cruel ferocity of the kulak and the refined "culturedness" of the wrecker had their roots in the barbarous capitalism of the past. Gorky was wary of the danger of capitalism as long as the enemy had not been pulled out by its roots. Lukacs warned, as early as 1936, when the great hunt for double dealers had not even begun, that overcoming the remnants of past in the life and consciousness of the people, was a very timely task.[35]

Maxim Gorky's *The Life of Klim Samgin. Forty Years*, a voluminous and erratic description of a pre-Revolutionary intelligent, acquired new relevance, with the publication of the last volume. At the beginning of the 1930s critics had already seen the book as a devastating blow against the old "unnecessary" intelligents, whom Gorky wanted to "annihilate."[36] For this, "all Samgins from Russia and abroad, "hated Gorky –and this, a critic concluded, was a well deserved hatred."[37]

In 1937 *Klim Samgin*, which was unanimously praised as one of the great classics of the epoch and of world literature, was also understood as a deeply political and topical book, because it described the double dealer. I. Gruzdev, in Pravda, at the end of 1936, said that Samgin was "a philistine (*meshchanin*) behind the mask of an "aristocrat of spirit." The mask of "intelligentnost'" hid the agent of capitalism in the decisive and deadly struggle for the proletarian revolution. Some had regarded Samgin just a "superfluous man." This was deeply erroneous, warned Gruzdev. These double dealers and traitors were not at all "superfluous" for the fascists, who were recruiting them. In literary criticism as everywhere, the vigilance of the masses had to be raised, Gruzdev proclaimed.[38]

Gruzdev's article was directed against a certain Tamara Khmel'nitskaia, who soon published an article, where she came to the conclusion that the "superfluous" or "little" man cannot exist in socialism. Either he becomes a real and useful person or an active enemy.[39] I. Luppol, who wrote, in Pravda, about the fourth volume of Klim Samgin, did not miss the relevant political message either. At the end of the book Samgin is killed by a kick from an angry worker, who shouts: "Out of the way, you cockroach!" The critic concluded that these words not just meant for Samgin but sounded like a death sentence for all political "cockroaches," past and present.[40]

The double dealer was a type drawn from the real life. The "enemy of the people" with his connection to imperialism might have been almost totally a creature of the security organs, which had come to understand that "beating determined consciousness." If there was enough beating, there were also confessions.

There were, however, really legions of people saying one thing and doing another. The secret files gave ample evidence of this. Stalin and the highest party elite knew about the reports, but the common people had no idea of their existence. In 1937 Stalin had declared war on double dealers. According to Marxism, historical progress does not happen in a smooth and linear way, but in leaps. What Stalin was doing in 1937, when he attacked the psychology of the old leaders, was, obviously, conceived to be another major step of social engineering, which attempted a new "leap." It was not just propaganda; it was politics in its highest form as the Bolsheviks understood it.

The process of liquidating "unnecessary" intelligents, which Gorky had proclaimed, had now reached a new stage. From the point of view of Marxism-Leninism, it was, no doubt, the highest stage.

Hatred

As has been repeatedly stated above, hatred, class hatred, was a key concept for the Bolsheviks. For Lenin, it was one of the main forces that moved the proletariat. Gorky shared this enthusiasm for the creative role of this kind of hate in world history, although he was, for some time, depressed to see the fruits of this hate in practice.

After the murder of Kirov, the issue of hate became very popular in the Soviet Press. It was energetically preached by Gorky. The class enemy had killed Kirov, it tried to kill Dimitrov and it was going to kill Ernst Thaelmann, wrote Gorky in 1935, but by so doing it was just bringing its own day of doom nearer. These deeds just "organized" "more quickly and strongly the class hate of the proletariat, an energy, which already is impossible to destroy with bullets and gasses," Gorky concluded.[41]

Komsomolskaia Pravda published Gorky"s article on "Proletarian hate,"[42] where the author stressed that hate was justified not only against capitalists and *lavochniki*,[43] but no less against the "lukewarm, the idlers, the vulgar and other monsters," who still existed in the country. Now, as ever, the ultimate enemy for Gorky was the philistine, *meshchanin*, which he did not fail to mention by name.

Inspired by the words of the great proletarian writer the organ of the komsomol praised the virtues of hate as "A Great Creative Feeling."[44] Gorky's articles launched another general campaign against the philistine, who had once raised canary-birds and now excelled in sexual license and hooliganism.[45]

As the great terror developed in 1936, hate became a most relevant topic. The "enemies of the people," who had been unveiled in the show trials, were naturally depicted as class enemies, even if they had held key positions in the proletarian state. A great deal of unhappiness had alleg-edly been caused by the "enemies of the people," the wreckers, and "di-versants." They had caused explosions in mines, train collisions, shortages of food, epidemics, and so on. The "enemies of the people" were now presented as permissible targets for the hate of the tormented masses. Meetings were held, where people gave vent to their anger towards the "enemies of the people," people, who just a short time ago, had been well-paid and privileged members of the Soviet intelligentsia. As the secret files showed, it was not without a certain *schadenfreude* that the rank and file watched the fall of the greats of this world. On the other hand, the wrath of the people was also to some extent directed against the educated classes and the upper layers of society in general. It was the "scholars" (*uchenye*), not the ordinary workers, who had taken part in these abominable crimes against honest citizens.[46]

The arch-enemy of the people was, according to the official version, Lev Trotsky, who had united the right and left opposition in the service of treasonous anti-Soviet plots. Lenin had sometimes called Trotsky by the nickname "Yudushka," which referred to Saltykov-Shchedrin"s character Yudushka Golovlev. Yudushka, or Judas, became Trotsky's semi-official nickname during the great terror. Even the famous *Short Course* spoke about Judas Trotsky."[47]

Saltykov-Shchedrin had been one of Lenin's favorite writers and the 110th anniversary of his birthday coming at the end of 1936 made him the focus of attention and gave him a particular relevance. At the same time the first great show trial had highlighted the treasonous role of Trotsky. On Saltykov-Shchedrin's birthday, D. Osipov wrote about him in Pravda and reminded readers that Lenin had called Trotsky "Yudushka."[48] In the same issue an article by Maxim Gorky was published, where the master of socialist realism scrutinized the rotten intellectual types, which Shchedrin had described.[49] The main virtue of the hero of the day, as described in Pravda's articles, was his hate. "No Russian writer has spoken with his reader with such a passion, sorrow, wrath and pain as Shchedrin," wrote D. Zaslavsky.[50] The author praised Shchedrin"s phenomenal capacty for hate and concluded that he had also demanded the same capacity from his reader. This hate was directed not just against the gentry and the bureaucracy; in the school of Chernyshevsky and Dobroliubov, Shchedrin had also learned to hate liberalism and opportunism in all their forms. With "crushing force the great satirist unveiled the double dealing, mendacity, hypocrisy, and mimicry of the opportunist, his readiness to betray at any minute his ideals, his friends, and his ideological comrades of yesterday." Shchedrin had also unveiled the "mask of Judas," which the double-minded bourgeois intelligentsia was wearing. His Yudushka Golovlev was a "universal type of double dealer." Lenin had not called Trotsky by that name in vain. Shchedrin "not only described the opportunists, double dealers, and traitors of his time, he also taught the reader to hate them and his "living hate bore that of ours," Zaslavsky concluded. Shchedrin"s hate was, however, not just negative: "Shchedrin"s holy hate of the oppressors, of the hangmen and the traitors was nourished by the same source as were his ardent love for the toilers, his passionate faith in the triumph of reason and of social justice." The writer was depicted as a paragon of virtues, among which the "holy hate" was the most cardinal and most prominent. Shchedrin's only shortcoming was, that he had not found the proper solution, scientific socialism, to the ills of capitalist society, but, for his time, that was understandable and pardonable.

The new Soviet man was a great hater, for hate was the other side of love. This dialectical equation was impeccable in form. Soviet man also understood the necessity of destroying an enemy, who would not surrender. This very clearly separated him from the old petty bourgeois. The new intellectuals were also decidedly different from their petty bourgeois predecessors, who were aptly depicted in the person of Klim Samgin.[51] The new Soviet intelligents hated not only the philistine *lavochniki* as the old intelligentsia had done, they also hated the old intelligents, who, in principle, supported the party, but in practice failed to act, and who were lukewarm and feeble in their faith in communism.[52]

During the period of the Great Terror it was not only the repressive organs that chased the real, and imagined, enemies of the new totalitarian tyranny. As the Pravda leader praising Ezhov had stated, millions of ordinary people took part in the process. Whilst some were pursuing their own personal goals, many were undoubtedly carried away by the general hysteria. There is no doubt that this was not only a time of great fear, but also of great hate. In the official media at least, the old "philistine" idea that everyone had human rights and was entitled to dignity, was destroyed. The hero of this ideology now became the hangman, as Andrei Sinyavsky has said. He was the one, who did the dirty work, which was necessary for the happiness of humanity.[53]

The ideal type of the new *intelligent* lacked the very quality, which had traditionally been regarded as one of the basic ingredients of *intelligentnost'*. The ideal new *intelligent* had no general empathy towards his fellow-man. His love and hate were strictly selective and he had a quite special talent for hating and for unscrupulous action, which only the extremist faction of the old intelligentsia had had.

Heroism

Heroism was one of the basic attributes of the new Soviet man. The topic had been popular in the Soviet press ever since the days of Stakhanov's feat, but in 1937 and especially in 1938 this phenomenon rose to new heights. Almost every day the press reported outstanding feats. Now, heroism at work was a minor concern. Instead, the press concentrated on new sensational records in other fields, which became a daily phenomenon.

A large number of these achievements involved Soviet citizens using the most advanced technology of the day to beat the previous records by combining their own personal human qualities, the results of the engineers' genius, and the technical skill of the workers. For example, aviators flew from Moscow to Vladivostok, or to New York over the North Pole, and so on. Individuals reached new heights in gas balloons, parachuted from unheard-of heights, beat speed records in airplanes, drove motor cars all over the Soviet Union in record times, and so on. Others showed their heroism in more conventional ways. Someone swam from Kronstadt to Leningrad, and others sailed from Leningrad to Moscow(!) and from Murmansk to Moscow. Heroic individuals climbed the highest peaks, or covered thousands of kilometers on skis, by bicycle, or on horseback.

Some set new records in horse-jumping, and so on. As astonishing as this apparently unending array of new records and feats of incredible endurance, was the fact that very seldom were the heroes just individuals, usually it was groups of people, who, together, conquered new heights or depths, or endured strain of the seemingly impossible tasks. Another very conspicuous trait was that many of these heroic individuals were women, young communists (*komsomoltsy*), and representatives of minor and formerly not very prestigious nationalities.

A closer examination of stories carried in *Pravda* about this new social-ist heroism, it was new, because socialism a functioning social system was new, yields some interesting insights.[54]

The heroes were given a lot of space and prestige. The topic of hero-ism was present in some way in almost every issue of the "central organ." There were a lot of leading articles,[55] and quite often several pages, even in several successive issues of *Pravda*, were dedicated to particular heroic deeds.[56] The heroes were treated very much in the same way as figures of popular culture in the West: there were big idealized portraits and even some human-interest stories about the hero's character.[57]

Although the heroes were also represented as individuals, some of whom became household names like Papanin, Chkalov, Kokkinaki, Vodo-pyanov etc., the idea of a "heroic people" was repeated time and again. When A.A. Zhdanov, in a speech at the Bolshoi theatre on 21 January 1938, said: "Heroism has become part of the everyday life of our people,"[58] he was simply echoing the view of the press. The sensation was, in effect, the "new man," who was qualitatively different from the "old one."

To a great extent, these acts of heroism were in some way or anoth-er associated with military might and readiness. Even women exhibited martial abilities: a group of military female flyers flew from Moscow to the Far East,[59] and female skiers from Buryat-Mongolia skied from Ulan Ude to Moscow.[60] Women went 3,500 km by boat from Leningrad to Kherson,[61] and female chauffeurs competed in a car-rally from Moscow to Klin and back.[62] Wives of commanders of the Red Army excelled in riding sports.[63]

Border guards, who happened to be representatives of the much ac-claimed NKVD, demonstrated startling physical fitness by bicycling over 30,000 km following the borders of the fatherland.[64]

Record-breaking flights[65] and parachuting[66] had an overtly military nature. These spectacular feats were often used to advertise the socialist system and its institutions in other ways as well. When an airplane from Moscow reached Khabarovsk in 20 hours and 58 minutes, its crew did not land empty-handed: they brought with them 12,000 copies of *Pravda*, which included extracts of the just published *Short Course of the History of the CPSU*.[67] Here, the real novelty, which was breaking all the old records and remaking history, was the book, which contained the concentrated wisdom of the party and its leader.

Komsomols flew all across the Soviet Union, visiting all eleven capitals of the Soviet republics in honor of the 20-year jubilee of the Komsomol.[68]

As Katerina Clark has concluded, the new heroic Soviet citizen was not, however, heroic just on account of his own virtues. He or she always expressed their thanks to the party and, in the last instance, its leader, Stalin. The heroes were understood to be the "sons" of the "father" Stalin. Every now and then, the leader himself was depicted showing his "children" the right way forward.[69]

It goes without saying that heroism was the very opposite of philistinism. A hero was a hero because his behavior was not dictated by the imperatives of his own personal profit or comfort. The highest form of heroism was, of course, self-sacrifice. In the optimistic days of this newly-born socialism, however, this was a rare occurrence. Armed battles in Manchuria and Mongolia did provide some examples of heroic death to be described.[70] The hero was ready for battle and ready to win, for there could be no doubt about the result of the coming conflict.

Heroism was possible for youth and women, and even for once primitive peoples like the Buryats and the Nenets. The courage and endurance of the Soviet people knew no boundaries, and the engineers and workers of the land of socialism were proceeding to ever new frontiers.

But was it only physical heroism that existed? Was heroism something that could only be shown by relatively few people, in normal times at least? What about everyday life? What about mental work? What about the intellectuals?

An editorial in *Literaturnyi kritik* sought answers to these questions.[71] Heroism had become an everyday phenomenon, the author stated. Almost every day the papers wrote about the decoration of some Soviet citizens for their "heroism, and selfless efforts (*samootverzhennuiu rabotu*), for outstanding feats in defending the fatherland, and for fulfilling the assignments of the state, for attaining great results in developing art, science, sport, and so on."

But along with this, there was a mass of "unseen heroism, the everyday heroism of hundreds of thousands and millions of people, who were working in industry, agriculture, on the cultural front, in the Red Army, and in all aspects of socialist construction." Socialist heroism was a mass phenomenon.

The most heroic feat in history had been the socialist revolution. A proletarian revolution was unthinkable without heroism, for it brought about a colossal change, it destroyed the very roots of a thousand-year old exploitative society and re-educated whole peoples.

There was also bourgeois heroism, but it was principally different from socialist heroism. Bourgeois heroism belonged mostly to the "youthful period" in the development of the bourgeois society. In essence, bourgeois society was deeply inimical to heroism. It was inimical to anything that went beyond the boundaries of commercial prosaic business of the speculator's calculations and the exploiter's smartness. Even if there were individual cases of heroism in bourgeois society, they were connected with record-breaking (*rekordmenstvom*), with the wish to set oneself apart from the masses (*vydelit' sebia iz massy*), to secure one's material well-being or to beat one's competitor. The bourgeois hero did not receive the support of his society and was not fit for great deeds, which presupposed the support of the whole people.

In socialist society all this had changed. It was socialist society that had provided the airplanes for the polar flyers and given a clear goal for the record-breaking Turkmen riders. The energy and strength of character which had helped citizens to overcome all obstacles, was a social phenomenon.

According to dialectical logic, socialist heroes were both individuals, and, at the same time, collectivists. Marx had explained, how a human being's individuality was restricted in a capitalist society, the more so, the more one was an individual proprietor (*chastnyi sobstvennik*). It was bourgeois society, which had given rise to such a disgusting phenomenon as philistinism (*meshchanstvo*), which was the very opposite to a full, complete, and strong human character. In a capitalist society, it was only the workers, the proletarians, who preserved their individuality. With socialism, this became possible for all.

At the same time, the great collective was always with the individual hero. When Chkalov, Baidukov, Gromov and their comrades flew to America, they were not alone. As they themselves said, along with them flew the whole people. This was not just a beautiful metaphor, the anonymous author asserted, but an "exact description of the real situation" (sic!).

Everything Soviet heroes achieved –both the great illustrious heroes and the little rank-and-file heroes, was tied to the struggle of the whole people. The epoch of socialism could not avoid being an epoch of heroism, the author concluded.

The intellectuals were not the most likely of heroes, but heroism was in no way impossible for them. There is no doubt that someone like Nikolai Yezhov, could well have been called "a heroic intelligent," for he had shown uncommon moral qualities in serving the socialist state. As for the journalists and critics, who unveiled "enemies of people," their conduct could doubtless also be called heroic. On the other hand, sparing one's friends, family, or anybody else from the righteous sword of the

Soviet state was un-heroic, philistine. Pavlik Morozov was not perhaps an intelligent, but his moral qualities doubtless surpassed those of most representatives of the intelligentsia.

As for philistinism, it goes without saying that this quality was incompatible with heroism, and was even its opposite. Whilst philistinism meant being confined in one's own private world, heroism meant breaking out of that confinement. Soviet heroism, it was claimed, was the realization of the individual that intelligents at the turn of the century had been demanding: it supposedly reconciled the antagonism that had previously existed between the individual and society.

Joy and optimism

The conscious new man could not help but be optimistic, for the future belonged to socialism. By about 1933 newspapers had cut their coverage of burials, which had been standard stuff in the twenties.[72] In the press, censorship prevented the reporting of depressing stories[73] and presented, instead, an unending array of joyous and optimistic faces thankful to the party and its leader for their newly found happiness.

It had been after the first hard years of the second five-year plan that Stalin had observed that life had become better and more joyous. This, however, was before the second five-year plan had been completed. In 1937 life was not only better; it was supposed to be good in absolute terms.

The general optimism of the people was reflected in mass meetings and popular feasts (narodnye gulianiia), which were arranged in honor of remarkable dates events like the elections to, or the first meeting of, the Supreme Soviets of both the USSR and the republics.

The people's interest for these popular feasts was probably genuine, at least in part. It became a Soviet tradition to make scarce goods available at election time, and there were also other interesting things to look at:100, 000 people came to see the new park of culture that was opened in Leningrad to celebrate the elections.[74] 120,000 people celebrated the opening session of the Supreme Soviet in Baku.[75] In Leningrad, no less than 200,000 people even celebrated the Supreme Soviet of the USSR completing its work.[76]

The mood of the people was described in epic colors: the opening day of the work of the Supreme Soviet was a "Happy day,"[77] and someone who had seen Stalin, talked about a "Feeling of immense happiness."[78] Especially in the national republics people expressed their happiness. Headlines like "The dreams of the Ukrainian People have been realized," "Joy of the Kazakh People"[79] were common. Anyone, who did not know anything, or had only heard ephemeral rumors, about the millions of people, who had perished in these republics a couple of years ago, might really have been convinced that things had improved. Even in the remote taiga of the Northern Yenisei, trappers' meetings proclaimed that now, it was "good to live."[80]

The new joy in life was expressed both individually and collectively. Great parades and meetings of sportsmen and youth were held in all the major cities, and the press gave the impression that the mood was jubilant. Forty thousand young sportsmen marched in Moscow,[81] and 35,000 took part in similar parade in Leningrad[82]. 100,000 people celebrated the 3-year jubilee of the Stakhanovite movement, in Leningrad alone.[83] In short, there were lots of specifically Soviet jubilees, which, according to the press, were enthusiastically celebrated by the masses. Special editorials and whole pages of the "central organ of the party" were dedicated to the incomparable happiness of children in a socialist society.[84] Women, for instance, who were working as tractor-drivers in kolkhozes, were reportedly very happy.[85] The artists of the minority nationalities, whose culture was exhibited at special jubilees in Moscow and Leningrad, assured everyone that they were happy and glad.[86]

A new genre of socialist folklore of the minority nationalities was born. It praised Stalin and socialism and the happy life. One of the *beati possidentes* were the Evenki, whose poem about the new "sun," meaning the Soviets, was published in *Pravda*.[87]

This display of the inevitable happiness of the Soviet people must be seen in context. At the same time, "antisocial elements", including the *bezprizornye* (homeless children) were caught and thrown to camps. As this happiness was being reported, millions of representatives of the diaspora nationalities lost all their national cultural rights: the Ingrian Finns, the Ukrainian, and other, Germans, Poles, Estonians, Greeks, and so on. This meant that their schools, newspapers, publishing houses and libraries were destroyed. The national intelligentsias even of minority peoples, who had titular republics or other territories, were decimated or destroyed en masse.[88]

But in the virtual world of the Soviet press, all true Soviet people unanimously praised their unprecedented happiness. The mighty rise of Soviet patriotism was easy to understand in the light of this new general well-being. The press explained that in capitalist countries, workers did not have a fatherland. Instead, masses of people emigrated from their homelands and deserted from capitalist armies. This was because their life was incomparably worse than that of the new Soviet man. The Soviet socialist system had created a new kind of patriotism, which was one of the purest, most elevated and benign of human sentiments. The Soviet people also were proud of their homeland, but this did not mean that they would oppress other nationalities. The Great Russian people, it was true, was the first among equals, but this was due to its historical accomplishments. Soviet patriotism also included internationalism, and this distinguished it from bourgeois pseudo-patriotism and from petty bourgeois patriotism, which might be genuinely "patriotic," but was not able to overcome its national narrowness.[89]

The respect, which was given to the Great Russian people was, indeed, very logical. Under socialism all national prejudices had been overcome and there was no need to abstain from giving the Russians their due. Favoring the minority nationalities in the USSR would now, in effect, mean oppressing the Russians.

All this flowering of the personality of the new Soviet man, which flowed from the cornucopia of socialism, was a necessary consequence of the system. The human personality had blossomed in the Soviet Union, an author explained in the theoretical journal of the party.[90] The antagonism between the individual and the collective had been abolished in the Soviet Union, and since society was built rationally, phenomena like the overproduction of intellectuals had become impossible. Now, there were more students in the universities of Soviet Ukraine than there were in Germany, although Ukraine had a smaller population.[91]

But were there still some remnants of capitalism in Soviet society? Given the general mood of Pravda's articles, and assuming that Pravda was telling the truth, one could think that there wasn't anything left to worry about. Although there were still the "enemies of people", they were a very small minority without a mass base. The vast majority was absolutely uncorrupted, one would assume.

In the theoretical journal of the party, the picture was somewhat more nuanced, in this respect.[92] The journal explained that the class-based morality of "Soviet man" was very clear-cut: it meant love of class, the party, and the country, and, as its inevitable reverse side, the sacred hate of "enemies of the people." There were, however, people, who were immoral in their private life and this could reflect on their social, and public life. They could easily fall prey to "enemies of the people."

In fact, there was still a legion of possible sins, in which even Soviet man might indulge, from religious and national prejudice to bureaucracy, political blindness, and so on. In a speech to electors, as late as 1936, Stalin had stressed for the importance of demanding that candidates not sink to the level of political petty bourgeois (*obyvateli*), but be, like Lenin, courageous and merciless to the enemy.[93]

In principle, the petty bourgeois (*melkii burzhui*) no longer existed, but traces of his mentality (*meshchanstvo*) still lingered on. It can be noted that

Stalin used the word *obyvatel'* (man of the street), which denoted the petty bourgeois psychology, without having the direct connotation of a social category. In short, the image of the new Soviet man, during the first years of the socialist system, was described in a triumphantly congratulatory manner, and avoided speaking about "problems." Simultaneously, the propaganda machinery devoted much attention to the "wrecking" and "diversion" of the "enemies of the people." By definition, however, the "enemies of people" were not "people," but their opposite. Accordingly, they were not entitled to the optimistic and happy life of the socialist people, which was developing at the very same time, when millions of their "enemies" were being repressed.

According to the new discourse, Soviet man was a new man. He was always ready to put the values of the collective, especially those of the Soviet state, before his personal goals or those of his friends or family –it was precisely this, which separated him from the petty bourgeois. The great hate and love of the Soviet man did not reflect the personal interests and cravings of the petty individual. The question "Are you a Soviet man?" became famous. Often it was asked by the "competent" officials of repressive organs and a negative answer would have been suicidal. Even though the Great Russian nationality rose to a high place of honor during this period, the crucial question was not, and could not be, "are you a Russian Man?"

The publicity given to the role of the "petty bourgeoisie" and its spirit "philistinism" (*meshchanstvo*) was reduced almost to nothing at the moment, when the socialist state eventually and finally settled its scores with the bourgeoisie proper (its agents in the USSR). In effect, the petty bourgeois in the socialist Soviet Union became a non-person, like Trotsky. As there was Trotskyism, but no Trotsky in official Soviet history, so were there the attributes, but not the essence of the petty bourgeois creature in socialist Soviet society.

Towards the decline of the intelligentsia in a post-philistine world

As Stalin, explaining the Constitution of 1936, had stated, the intelligentsia survived in socialist society as a layer (*prosloika*). However, this was a temporary situation, for in the future classless society there would no longer be an intelligentsia, any more than there would be separate classes of workers and peasants.

General social processes in a socialist society were supposed to result in the liquidation of the differences between manual and mental work, and between town and countryside. In a communist society no special intelligentsia would be needed, because all the citizens would be *intelligenty*. As has been mentioned, the Stakhanovite movement was seen as the beginning of this process. Although the process in fact, was destined to end in the liquidation of the intelligentsia, dialectically it looked as if there was a stormy growth in its numbers. Especially since 1938, it had become a topical task to warn the proletarians about having a "wrong" attitude to the swelling numbers of the new intelligentsia.[94]

Stalin's words about the new nature of the Soviet intelligentsia were repeated over and over again, when the Marxist-Leninist education of the new intelligentsia was discussed in Pravda and other forums, during the second half of 1938.

The all-important novelty in the autumn of 1938 was, of course, the *Short Course of the History of the CPSU*, which has been discussed above. It now became obligatory reading for everybody, who wanted to be a Soviet intellectual. In leading articles of *Pravda* and in other more or less official texts, it became customary to include officials (*sluzhashchie*) in the category of the intelligents, which had not always been the case in the past. Anyway, the message was always that the Soviet intelligentsia deserved the care and esteem on of the party and that the most urgent and important task was to help the intelligentsia master Bolshevism.[95]

Conspicuously, it was announced that the party had to help the intellectuals (especially non-party ones) "master bolshevism," which certainly sounds like an intellectual feat and, thus, something, which the intellectuals were to teach others. Here, no doubt, we are dealing with the basic Bolshevik mystic of the party. To "master Bolshevism" did not mean just knowing its basic tenets. Bolshevism was incarnated in the party, which had a certain style of its own (which "whining" *intelligenty* could not share, as Lenin had repeatedly said in the days of the revolution). The party organs, which were asked to "take care" of the non-party *intelligenty*, also had many *intelligenty* in their ranks. They had to help other *intelligenty* "master Bolshevism, and work for the ideological (*ideinyi*) education and Bolshevist tempering the officials, doctors and engineers."[96]

It was the plight of the intellectuals to have special skills. Discovering ideological truth was the specialty of the party, the vanguard of the proletariat. The intellectuals undoubtedly understood that themselves having read the Short course.

Systematic political-educational work would also help fight bureaucracy, corruption in trade, and other phenomena, which were typical for people lacking in idealism (*obyvatel'skie elementy*).[97] Every Soviet intelligent had to "master Bolshevism," which had to be begun by mastering the Short Course. Thereafter, he could also read Marx's Capital and other classics.[98] Studying was to be done mainly individually, not in study groups, as had often been the case earlier.[99]

It was the Procrustean schemes of the *Short Course* and its ethos of the one and only General line, which did not recognize any rivals or deviations whatever, which became the incarnation of "the highest truth" for Soviet *intelligenty* and, indeed, everybody. This truth was given to the intelligentsia "from above," from the party and mastering it was not just a question of reason, but also of morals and faith. As the fourth point of the conclusions of the *Short Course* stated, the party would not tolerate people, who were weak in faith, since they were petty bourgeois opportunists. As the first point demonstrated, Marxism-Leninism was "not a dogma, but a guideline for action." Marxism-Leninism was constantly developing and it was opportunistic to hold to old tenets and think they would remain relevant forever.

By 1938 Soviet intellectuals had learnt, through experience that it was not up to them to argue about the right interpretation of ideological questions. This had to be left to the party. But ideological questions concerned the everyday work of the creative intelligentsia most of all. Every book or picture had an ideological content. In practice, this meant that all issues of fundamental importance, excluding purely technical and most scientific questions, had to be left to the organs of the party to decide. Inside the party, it was understood that there was very little intellectual freedom of action indeed at the grassroots. Ultimately, the supreme judge was and could only be the general secretary of the party. What the individual intelligent could do, was to "work towards the vozhd," that is, try and guess, what the leader wanted. It has been pointed out that this was also a widespread practice in Nazi Germany.[100]

Repeatedly described as equal citizens of the Soviet state, the intellectuals received several advantages. Well-to-do officials, artists, and the like were now officially protected from the envy of the rank and file. At the XVIII Party Congress, Stalin dedicated part of his report to the question of intelligentsia. He repeated the idea of the new character of the new Soviet intelligentsia and stressed the need for a positive attitude towards this social layer. There had been a "theory" about the necessity of suspecting and fighting the intelligentsia, Stalin said, but that was now obsolete. "For the new intelligentsia a new theory is needed," Stalin said, "which proves the necessity of a friendly attitude towards it, care for it, respect for it and cooperation with it in the name of the interests of the working class and the peasants."[101] Indeed, it was "astonishingly strange" that some people were still using the old theory, Stalin said.[102] In the Soviet Union at that time, it would have been impossible to make the point more strongly: the whole history of the Bolshevik party had been dedicated to the struggle against theoretical heresy, as the *Short Course* testified.

Undoubtedly, the "Big Deal" with the new intelligentsia, which was more or less the same as a new middle class, was congenial to the rank and file of this "layer of society." This group was now no more apart of the "masses," no longer guilty before the masses, it was a part of them, the "best people." Those, who had read Gorky's *Mother* and Chernyshevsky's *What Is to Be Done?* probably understood that all this had been foreseen a long time ago.

The Soviet Union was proud to proclaim that these "new masses" were astonishingly numerous: by 1939 there were 9, 5 million intelligents. Together with their families this meant 14 per cent of the population.[103]

Eighty to Ninety per cent of this social group had worker or peasant origins. It was the "salt of the earth," as an author wrote, paraphrasing Chernyshevsky, and it was armed with the highest accomplishments of Marxist-Leninist thought, thanks to the attentiveness of the party. In fact, the whole Soviet people were being transformed into "intelligent" people, who had mastered modern science and culture. As Molotov had stated, the intelligentsia had a central role in the successful fulfillment of the third five-year plan.[104]

The intellectuals could no longer assume the role of the conscience of the nation as the old *intelligenty* had done, nor could they serve as the brain of the nation. This role was strictly reserved for the higher echelons of the party. Instead, the intellectuals were supposed to adopt the traditional role of serving the people, which, in effect, meant serving the party. Mastering culture was highly esteemed and amply remunerated.

As for the old "accursed question" about their guilt before the people, this clearly survived only amongst intellectuals, who did not think that the Stalinist version of socialism was what the people deserved. It was the tactics of Stalinism to take the masses along with it so that they would share the complicity for the policies of the party. Signing condemnations and taking part in demonstrations in support of Stalinist policies was not, as a rule, obligatory. But most people took part. For those who did so against their convictions, in order to preserve their petty bourgeois individual peace and security, this complicity could become a matter of guilt.

As regards the lesser brethren in Soviet society, the people, who were less cultured, earned less money, had more disagreeable jobs, and were less esteemed in society, they were, by logical necessity, the "worst people," if the intelligentsia consisted of the best people." There could be no guilt on the part of the intelligentsia regarding their remuneration and positions, and also no envy on the part of the worse-off. Such sentiments were not just a sign of backwardness; they also revealed something more dangerous: the Makhaevist heresy, which, in essence, belonged to the lumpenproletariat, which was, in essence, petty bourgeois. Astonishingly, there were still "monstrous remnants" (*urodlivye perezhitki*) of this phenomenon in the USSR.[105]

When Stalin had proclaimed that a new intelligentsia had to be cre-ated, he certainly did not mean that there should be a new layer, which would excel by virtue of its *intelligentnost'* in the pre-revolutionary sense of the word. Rather, the idea was that there should be a layer of special-ists, which would be able to fulfill the needs of material production, which would also be "cultured," having a wide knowledge of things cultural, and which also could behave in a decent way. All that notwithstanding, it was clearly understood that there should be none of the old *"intelligentnost'"* in the habitus of the new intelligentsia. "Abstract" humanism, an inability to take ruthless action, spirituality, and, in many cases, even tact, all that was petty bourgeois ballast, and the new intelligentsia was not supposed to ex-hibit those qualities. Instead, this layer of the new socialist society, which had a proletarian class character, was to be unflinchingly loyal to the party. The new intelligentsia was also supposed to be free of philistinism. True, philistinism as such had been annihilated together with its social base, but something similar to it, persisted and the term "philistine" was occasion-ally used. For instance, Stalin told the graduates of military academies on 5 May 1941 that: "The Red Army must get used to the idea that the peaceful policy has ended, and the era of widening the front of socialism by force has begun. He who does not recognize this is a philistine and a fool."[106] We may deduce from this that "philistinism" here refers to a kind of naiveté or a stagnant psychology, which believes in eternal truths. The "Short Course" taught that yesterday's truths were not automatically the truths of today or tomorrow. To be a member of the Soviet intelligentsia, and the military elite certainly was entitled to this status, should be nei-ther naïve nor too convinced of one's own omniscience, but always open to new truths, which could be given from above.

Thus it would appear that, in the official discourse, the new intelligen-tsia paradoxically lacked what used to be called *intelligentnost'*. But this was only part of the theory. The heritage of classical literature had been saved for the intelligentsia, which was supposed to acquaint itself fully with the heritage of past progressive generations. However, the norms, values, and ideals of the great classics, with the possible exceptions of Gorky and maybe Chernyshevsky, did not coincide with those of the par-ty. Therefore, intelligents, who fulfilled the norm of attaining *kul'turnost'*, also ran the risk of imbibing *intelligentnost'*.

There are good grounds for presuming that a large part of the new in-telligentsia, and possibly even the greatest part of the "Brezhnev genera-tion" was always loyal to the Stalinist regime. It is not hard to believe that many of the "new *intelligenty*" sincerely shared those values, which the regime wanted to convey to them. Ruthlessness was one of the most im-portant qualities required from the ideal "new *intelligent*," but it was not a new idea, created by the regime. A certain cult of ruthlessness had always existed among the Russian intelligentsia, and a large part of the old intelligentsia had also, in principle, approved of it before the revolution. In fact, even then ruthlessness had been considered as a value in itself. This had been in line with the thinking of Nietzsche, Marx, Engels, and their numerous followers. The point view of the soft-minded intelligentsia had now been defeated, but it had always been of secondary importance even before the revolution.

The new intellectual climate must, in principle, have corresponded quite easily to the mindset and discourse of a sizable contingent of the intelligentsia, as indeed the proponents of *Smena vekh* had claimed in 1922. Perhaps, it is even possible to say that the dominant class, in the Gramscian sense of the word, the class, whose functions, interests, and outlook contributed most to the general character of the system, was the intelligentsia. This point has been taken up by Robert V. Daniels, who explains that the creative intelligentsia and the technical intelligentsia should be understood to form a common whole.[107] The "Ruling class," as opposed to the "dominant" one, in Stalin's Russia was the nomenklatura. To continue in Gramscian jargon, Soviet ideology can be understood as a kind of "false consciousness," but who profited most from its imposition? Daniels states that it was not the creative intelligentsia, which was a victim, but rather the nomenklatura, the technical intelligentsia, and the white-collar class.[108]

Certainly, there must have been a vast amount of self-deception and cognitive dissonance among the Soviet intelligentsia of Stalin's time. But, no doubt, there was also genuine faith in the necessity and even inevitability of Stalinism. After all, the party-state had now taken the *intelligent* under its protection and had declared that he deserved the blessings of a comfortable life, which no longer had a petty bourgeois character. One would never become a petty bourgeois provided one was loyal to the party. The party solved all problems, moral and material, for those who believed in it, and thus belief was one of the main virtues.

But there were also always those, who did not agree. These people could not speak out as open dissidents in Stalin's time. They were the "double dealers," whom Stalin had tried to destroy. But this was impossible. Every generation produced its own dissidents. This also happened with the Brezhnev-generation, despite the fact that it was a generation of true believers. At some point in their lives, people like Lev Kopelev, Alexander Solzhenitsyn, Evgenia Ginzburg, and others were turned from being true believers into dissidents. But their anti-Soviet activity belongs to a later epoch.

Conclusion

The Russians often maintain that the Russian intelligentsia is a unique phenomenon and does not have a counterpart in any other country. This may be an exaggeration, but it must be admitted that the historical fate of the Russian intelligentsia has been quite exceptional. Some knowledge of the experience of the intelligentsia as a social group is necessary for an understanding of its discourses, which often used the same concepts as Western European intellectuals, but put them in a different context.

It has been said that the Russian intelligentsia was the first remarkable dissident community of alienated intellectuals. Politically, it was a kind of subculture, which stood in irreconcilable opposition to the existing order. Revolution, as the great destiny of the intelligentsia became, even for the liberal wing of the intelligentsia, a mythical panacea, which would radically transform society and cure all ills. Any compromise or cooperation with the authorities was despised by members of the intelligentsia, who believed the tsarist autocracy to be incurably rotten.

This is, of course, not the whole story. The intelligentsia was never so monolithic. Politically, most of the Russian intelligentsia shared more or less an anti-absolutist stance, but there was always disagreement about the means of political struggle—and also about the relative worth of political struggle on the one hand and other tasks, including the self-perfection of the individual, on the other. Russian classics, of Dostoevsky, Tolstoy and Chekhov certainly also had a considerable influence among the intelligentsia. Even on the political level, there was a remarkable split in the ranks of the intelligentsia before the First World War, when a group of liberal conservatives, the *Vekhi* group rejected radical politics and warned the intelligentsia about its political course, which it argued was not only futile and suicidal for the intelligents themselves, but also detrimental for the whole of society. The main tenor of the intelligentsia, however, remained radical and revolutionary and it concentrated its efforts more on the destruction of the old structures, than on constructive development.

The fact that the Russian intelligentsia always considered itself to be outside, and in opposition to, state structures and in the service of the "people," largely determined its discourses. It has been said that the intelligentsia's attitudes were, in fact, aristocratic. And, therefore, it readily despised the petty bourgeoisie, while adoring the lower classes, who, in fact, dreamed of becoming petty bourgeois. This attitude, which seems to be specific for the Russian intelligentsia, was not typical of antibourgeois intellectuals in France, for instance.

The intelligentsia in general saw itself as the servant of the oppressed people and it also shared a feeling of guilt for its own "privileged" position in society. Famous representatives of the radical intelligentsia, like Nikolai Chernyshevsky, became martyrs, who suffered in the cause of liberating the people. Many of them were committed to this cause in a quasi-religious way. The intelligentsia also gave itself a very important role in society: it purported to be the conscience and brain of the people. By assuming for itself the grand mission of serving the people uncompromisingly, the intelligentsia sharply separated itself from the petty bourgeoisie, whom it deeply despised. Sometimes the whole mission of the intelligentsia was defined as a battle against the morally and intellectually inferior philistinism of the petty bourgeoisie. In its purest form, this idea was developed at the writings of Ivanov-Razumnik in the beginning of the twentieth century

The long-awaited revolution, when it actually came in February 1917, was basically a primitive reaction of the war-weary masses. It was supported and greeted with enthusiasm by the intelligentsia, which considered itself the "brain of society." The revolutionary intelligentsia also took it for granted that it would be given responsible posts in the new society. Very soon, it became clear that the intelligentsia was unable to cope with the anarchy that was unfolding. The anarchy was, however, exploited by that section of the intelligentsia, which formed the nucleus of the Bolshevik party. The leading role of the intelligentsia in the party of the proletariat was rationalized by Bolshevik doctrine, which was based on the assumption that the masses, left to themselves, could not rise above a trade-unionist, that is, petty bourgeois level of consciousness and that a real class consciousness had to be given to the masses by the vanguard of the proletariat. This was a vanguard which in fact consisted of intellectuals.

Bolshevik ideology bore the hallmarks of a typical *intelligent's* construction: it was based on abstract theorizing about classes and their mutual struggle and it postulated certain "unavoidable" consequences of a victory of the proletariat, including the liquidation of philistinism. The latter was, according to Lenin, the main obstacle to the creation of a new society. The supposedly thaumaturgic effects of the transformation of the "class nature" of society through a workers' revolution were never questioned.

In practice, the utopian ingredients of Bolshevik ideology were rapidly cast aside, explained away, or ignored as soon as they seemed to endanger the power of the self-proclaimed vanguard of the working-class. What remained was a system of coercion, which strived for the total control of society by a group of intellectuals. In the 1920s the ideal was still impossible to realize, but after the Stalinist revolution, which culminated in the collectivization of the peasantry and the five-year plans, the goal became more and more realistic.

The situation of the intelligentsia as the conscience of the nation, critics of the authorities, became very awkward, almost impossible in the new society. The intelligentsia in the larger sense of the educated classes, at first tried to resist the new regime by using old means: strikes and disobedience. Some individuals, like Maxim Gorky, succeeded for some time in giving voice to their protest.

The position of the intelligentsia in post-revolutionary society was aggravated by the fact that the regime considered it to be a part of the petty bourgeoisie and, hence, an element, which was to be kept in check by the dictatorship of the proletariat. Also, any dissident political voices within the party were silenced and dismissed as "petty bourgeois" by the Bolsheviks. This also applied to the workers.

It soon became clear that any notable public criticism or opposition was impossible, for the state held in its hands the keys to one's subsistence, and the tools of information and violence, and it was far more ruthless than the tsarist autocracy had been.

The Bolsheviks suppressed outright resistance with violence and expulsions. Large segments of the intelligentsia fled the country or were thrown out. As for the less politically active segments of specialists and the academic intelligentsia, the Bolsheviks adopted a policy of attracting them into cooperation, without questioning their political beliefs.

To a certain extent, this policy succeeded, although a notable contingent of the intelligentsia emigrated and was never reconciled to the new regime. The Smena vekh movement that operated among the émigrés, tried to persuade this irreconcilable intelligentsia that in the new situation, they had to continue their traditional mission of serving the people by submitting themselves to Bolshevik rule. For a couple of years, the movement gained some popularity, but, in the long run, it was not a great success.

For the intelligentsia, the price of collaboration, which in some cases was amply compensated, was its subordination to the will of the Bolsheviks. As regards the educated classes at large, this was not always a painful process. Apart from financial difficulties, the technical intelligentsia, physicians, and other specialists at first did not encounter any professional difficulties in their new role in Soviet society. They could continue their traditional role of serving the people even under Bolshevik rule. However, even the technical intelligentsia en masse became the victim of political harassment during the first five-year plan, which was launched in 1928. Its position was restored only in 1931, when Stalin himself lifted the collective indictment.

Foremost amongst the *intelligenty* who collaborated with the Bolsheviks with gusto was Maxim Gorky. Gorky believed that Stalinist policies were the final solution to the problem of philistinism. Some *intelligenty* collaborated with the regime half-heartedly and some remained hostile or indifferent, but did not actively resist the totalitarian state. The Bolshevik leadership knew about the opposition to its regime, as it regularly received secret opinion surveillance reports from the OGPU. Public criticism of the new regime was possible only in Aesopian language. Writers, who nursed critical ideas, and there were a lot of them, as secret surveillance revealed, voiced their criticism in a very cautious way, but were often punished even for that.

During the Great Terror of the 1930s, the secret and public surveillance of people's opinions became so effective, and the fear so great that critical voices completely disappeared. The Stalinist state now created a new self-image of a totally novel society, which lacked the problems and ills of capitalist society and was led by an unerring party, which enjoyed the undivided support of all the people, including the intelligentsia, which was now regarded as a layer of people, which represented the interests of the workers and peasants and had its origins in those classes.

Many intelligents, especially representatives of the old intelligentsia, obviously never believed in this propaganda, but instead, remained critical in their attitudes to the regime until the end of their life, as surveillance reports testify. Critics of society, however, had no chance of making their opinions publicly known in the Soviet Union. The only Russian criticism of the Stalinist state was now published by emigrants, but even many of them had a positive image of Stalin, whom some understood to be forsaking revolutionary utopianism, whilst others considered him to be a genuine revolutionary.

As for their colleagues in the West, Soviet *intelligenty* had few contacts with them. Only a very restricted and well-monitored number of Soviet intellectuals could visit the West. The contingent of Western intellectuals who visited Soviet Union most often, was a motley crowd of so-called political pilgrims. This group, which for the most part came to the land of utopia with its preconceived opinions, was easy prey for the Stalinist machinery. Impressed by official accounts of the wonders of socialist society, this element was as uncritical of Soviet totalitarianism as it was critical of its own society.

In a way, the heritage of the old Russian intelligentsia now became the intellectual property of Western radicals, who developed an irreconcilable opposition to their own governments and began worshipping the idea of a revolutionary panacea to cure all ills. These people were in the same way alienated from their own societies as the Russian intelligentsia had been before the revolution. At the same time, the old Russian intelligentsia now knew better.

For the old Russian intelligentsia, it was, however, impossible to convey its bitter revolutionary experience to the new Western intelligentsia. This was due to both physical and mental obstacles. The alienated totalitarian-minded Western intelligentsia filtered out any unwanted information.

A lot of books and articles, which revealed the real nature of the Bolshevik dictatorship, were published in the West by Soviet emigrants and defectors, and by critical tourists. Their limited effect was, to some extent, due to the political constellation of the day. The Soviet Union was seen as a counter balance to Nazi Germany, and many leftist intellectuals deliberately abstained from criticizing the Soviet Union.

While the old intelligentsia remained critical of Stalinist socialism, as secret surveillance showed, the attitudes of the young generation seem to have been different. It is beyond doubt that the so-called "Brezhnev generation," which grew up in Soviet society and received many favors from it, was, to a remarkable extent loyal and even fanatical in its support for the regime. The suffering and hardship for the Soviet people and even the cruelty of the regime were rationalized by faith in the great mission of the Soviet Union. The official ideology explained that the new intelligentsia now had a new class essence and was liberated from the petty bourgeois prejudices of its predecessors.

The discourses of the Russian intelligentsia must always be understood in the context of its historical experience. The subtext of this Russian discourse was often very different from that of its Western colleagues. French radicals of the late eighteenth century, whom J.L. Talmon has called the founders of "totalitarian democracy," considered that any means were justifiable in order to force people to live according to the dictates of reason. This way of thinking was adopted and thus perpetuated by nineteenth-century radicals.

At the beginning of the nineteenth century, the idea of the hero as a man of letters became popular in both Russia and Western Europe. Intertwined with it were ideas about the divinity of human nature and the mission of heroes, namely, to bring people back to their original glory by overcoming philistinism, which was regarded as a profanation of true, real human nature.

The issue of philistinism (*meshchanstvo*) has always been one of the main concerns of the Russian intelligentsia. The concept of philistinism, like that of the intelligentsia, had several meanings. Officially the meshchanstvo was a social estate in imperial Russia. It never became influential and prosperous in that country. However, in the absence of a noticeable middle-class, the poor *meshchanstvo* came to symbolize human meanness. The archetypal *meshchanin* was not a wealthy merchant, but a poor peddler or *lavochnik*, who sold junk from his stall.

Intellectually and morally the philistine was understood to be the opposite of the intelligent: he was a stupid, unprincipled, insensitive, credulous, and greedy human being, who neither strived for higher values nor recognized them. This meant, inter alia that the existence and prevalence of the philistine in society was an obstacle to a social revolution, and this, in effect, made the philistine complicit in the sufferings of the people. If his political role was not enough, the philistine was also an inferior being on his own right. He represented, as it were, a sin against the spirit.

Philistinism, understood as a lukewarm attitude towards the sufferings of the people, accompanied by consumerism and conformism, was even conceived to be the main calamity threatening the spirit of the people.

However, in this respect, the situation was not considered to be very bad in Russia. Several intelligents thought that western countries were more philistine than Russia. In this respect, America was often represented as the foremost example of philistinism, and as a possible scenario for the future of Russia.

To a certain extent, the anti-philistine mission of the Russian intelligentsia was part of a common European heritage. Romantic ideas about the sacred nature of the world and the role of the man of letters as a secular priest showing the way towards a worthy life became especially popular in Germany at the beginning of the nineteenth century. The influence of J.G. Fichte reached Russia through the Stankevich circle. In a somewhat different form it reached England through Thomas Carlyle. Throughout Europe, the gospel of anti-philistinism became very popular during the latter half of the nineteenth century. Nietzsche and Ibsen were the most famous champions of this movement.

Russian thought had always been greatly influenced by western models. However, in Russia, the intelligentsia also developed a powerful domestic anti-philistine tradition, which encompassed such different elements as the early Slavophiles, Bakunin, Herzen, the Nihilists, and the Populists. The impact of Alexander Herzen on the discourse of the Russian intelligentsia was very important. He was one of the first intelligents, who defined philistinism in Russia and maintained that Western Europe was more contaminated by philistinism than Russia. Herzen's ideas returned with new force in the discourse of Russia's Silver Age and continued to find expression in the thinking of several important thinkers.

It may be maintained that in Russia anti-philistine ideas found remarkably fertile ground. It is possible to assume that this had something to do with the general Russian mentality, which was probably influenced by ideas of the orthodox faith. For instance, there is the idea of *theosis*, or the divinization of human beings. The anti-philistinism of Dostoevsky, Tolstoy, Berdiaev, Soloviev, and other religious thinkers obviously had a religious basis. The idea of *bogochelovechestvo* or God's humanity, which lifted the meaning of life of human beings high above matters of mere subsistence, was well in line with the romantic idea of transcending the sphere of humdrum life and achieving a higher purpose for human life.

This idea was easily turned into the idea of *chelovekobozhestvo* — human divinity. The idea of human divinity was often as emotionally laden as its opposite. Fichte's pupils like Bakunin and even "unromantic" philosophical anthropologists like Chernyshevsky clearly had a religious strain to their thinking. With Maxim Gorky and the "god-builders" the quasi-religious nature of anti-philistinism came once again strongly to the fore.

In the discourse of the Silver Age, quasi-religious and genuinely religious ideas about the divine nature of man and history and the role of the man of letters as the hero, who mediates between the sacral and profane spheres, became once more quite central. The philosopher, who reinforced this discourse, was Nietzsche, although his writings must have had some kind of *dèja-vu* effect on the Russian intelligentsia. After all, Nietzsche's central themes, from God's death to human deity had been widely discussed in Russia for several decades.

The old romantic belief that humanity, which largely consisted of philistines, had to be given "consciousness" and thus saved through the action of heroes was shared not only by Nietzschean writers and philosophers and avant-garde artists, but also by different political movements, including the Bolsheviks. True, the Bolsheviks believed that they were not romantics, at all, but rather, the heirs of the rationalist heritage of the 'totalitarian democrats' of the French Revolution. Indeed, Lenin, who had a mentality as dry as dust could not stand the "God-building" of Maxim Gorky, who was borrowing enormously from both the Russian intellectual heritage and from Nietzsche. But Lenin too was a pupil of Russian radicals, notably Chernyshevsky and Tkachev. The ultimate goal of Leninism was not just general well-being or some other equally "philistine" notion, but "A New Man," no less.

On the other hand, the obsession with the political struggle and the neglect of spiritual values, which could be detected both in the philosophy of the radical section of the intelligentsia and in the actual behavior of the masses, could also be defined as "philistinism." This, indeed, was the conclusion of some non-mainstream *intelligenty* like Dmitry Merezhkovsky, who called the popular masses "barbarous." This disappointment with the popular masses was also shared by the *Vekhi* group. The *Vekhi* group considered that the radicalism and anti-philistine obsession of the intelligentsia was misguided. It argued that the intelligentsia's arrogant rejection of "philistinism" was often simply unjustified self-glorification and a cheap excuse for not doing anything useful for society.

As was argued above, the calling of the intelligentsia was to rise above the philistine consciousness of the petty bourgeoisie and show the masses the way forward to a meaningful and dignified life. This was not just a secondary issue, but rather the ultimate metaphysical and axiological one. For some intelligents like Maxim Gorky, America was the main example of a philistine society: senselessly materialist, consumerist, and conformist.

The coming of the "mass society" raised the issue of philistinism everywhere. The philistine was the bête noire of intellectuals of throughout Europe, especially since Henrik Ibsen's dramas and Nietzsche's philosophy had placed the issue on the European intellectual stage.

What seems to distinguish the Russian intelligentsia from its western, for example French, counterparts, was that in Russia the intellectuals almost always kept believing in the intrinsic worth of the masses. But the masses, left on their own, were "dark," the Russian *intelligenty* believed. It was the plight of the intellectual to bring light to the masses, not despise them. The people had to be saved from the perils of philistine consciousness, and this was the work of the intelligents.

Some intellectuals hoped for great wars and social upheavals, which would put an end to the spread of philistinism, which was threatening the people. On the other hand, there were voices, like those of Merezhkovsky, Berdiaev and the *Vekhi* group, which warned that great upheavals could, on the contrary, bring the masses to power, and they were intrinsically philistine themselves. The very concepts of "philistine" and "*intelligent*" became the subject of violent debate at the beginning of the twentieth century. The conflicting parties often defined the concepts in diametrically opposite ways. A major disagreement concerned the role of the intelligentsia as the "brain" of the masses, and the ways in which the cause of the people and the struggle against philistinism could be best served.

In reality, the Russian *meshchane* were mostly very poor. The social element which Marx had dubbed the *lumpenproletariat*, was, in Russia, considered part of the *meshchanstvo*. However, some Russian thinkers and litterateurs believed that the bosiaki, the lumpenproletarians, were amongst the most progressive of social forces, and were defying the bourgeoisie. There were also conflicting ideas about the class-character of the agrarian majority of the Russian population. The narodniki believed in the revolutionary potential of the peasants, while the Bolsheviks concluded that both the peasant majority of Russian citizens and the educated classes, that is, the intelligentsia, were all petty bourgeois.

The petty bourgeoisie including the intelligentsia, was, for the Bolsheviks, officially an enemy, which the workers were to "liquidate" as a class, when society entered the socialist stage of development. It was clearly understood to be a trivial task.

Officially, the Bolshevik revolution did not create a socialist society immediately. It was understood that petty bourgeois elements were still present even after October 1917. Accordingly, the party organized "class-struggle," in order to subjugate these elements to the service of the proletarian state. However, philistinism, the psychology of the petty bourgeoisie, proved to be not so easy to liquidate. In practice, the "petty bourgeois" element and "philistinism" soon became the culprit for all the shortcomings of the proletarian state. According to the Bolsheviks in the 1920s, philistinism became an awful, ubiquitous, and perfidious thing, whose protean physiognomy revealed itself in all kinds of places. It was not only the peasants, peddlers, merchants, and other nepmen, or so-called "former" people, and the old intelligentsia that were its bearers. During the NEP period, it was repeatedly declared that "philistinism" could also corrupt members of the Komsomol and the party, even the workers in the workshop and the leaders of the party—literally anybody.

During the first two five-year plans, philistinism was radically redefined by the Bolsheviks. The time-honored values of all anti-bourgeois radicals, such as the leveling of wages, living communally, annihilating the "petty bourgeois" institution of the family and abolishing money were forsaken by the Bolsheviks. In a breathtaking dialectical salto mortale, it was declared that those old goals of the radical community were not socialist values at all, but anti-Marxist, petty bourgeois nonsense.

Stalin redefined much of the old creed of the intelligentsia. However, he was true to the radical tradition in that he unscrupulously used any means available in order to create the new society. Stalin's social engineering was enthusiastically supported by Maxim Gorky, the former "God-builder." For Gorky, the annihilation of philistinism was the ultimate goal of politics. The new society would produce "Man with a capital M," whose coming had been predicted by the radical prophets of the nineteenth century as well as by Nietzsche and the antibourgeois radicals of the Russian Silver Age. It was Gorky, who, more than anyone else, determined the discourse of full-fledged Stalinism. As a result, Stalin's Soviet Union, far more than Lenin's, was in a way the true heir of the romantic radicals of the nineteenth century.

The end of the petty bourgeoisie as a class was declared, followed from the construction of the new socialist society. The new socialist society, which was declared to have been built in 1937 when the second five-year plan was completed, was no longer merely a "workers' state" with a petty bourgeois majority as had been the case in the Soviet Union under NEP. Now, the socialist state was supposed to have annihilated the whole social class of the petty bourgeoisie by transforming its members into workers, collective peasants or members of the working intelligentsia.

Thus, the Russian "bourgeoisie," including the independent peasants, that is, the class-base of philistinism, no longer existed. This was supposed to be a happy state of affairs, but it did not mean that a harmonious peace prevailed in Soviet society. On the contrary, Stalin declared that the class struggle was getting fiercer and fiercer all the time, for the imperialist world system, which encircled the Soviet Union was doing its utmost to damage the first ever socialist society; it wanted to annihilate it and re-store capitalism. For this purpose, it was sending its agents into the Soviet Union. Anything that was un-socialist, anything was against the tenets of socialist society was, now, no longer supposed to have merely a petty bourgeois character. Now, all deviance and resistance was declared to be "bourgeois," for it necessarily had its origins in foreign capitalist encircle-ment. It had to be "scorched out" of the land of the Soviets by fire and sword. This was the subtext of the notorious year of 1937.

The dialectics of Marxism-Leninism opened up new vistas in the struggle against philistinism. When the class-base of philistinism had been annihilated in the Soviet Union, the things, which the philistines had once cherished, could be filled with new meaning. Material well-being and cul-ture, even building one's own home and taking care of one's family were, it was now declared, no longer philistine, at all. A Stakhanovite, the model of the new Soviet man, was the opposite of the philistine. He was a kind of worker-intelligent. He earned lots of money and had many creature comforts in his home. This was socialist affluence, not philistinism. Con-ventional tastes in art, inequality in pay, knowledge of classical literature, patriotism, and so on no longer had a philistine class-essence. Formalist art, Trotskyite radicalism and Bukharinian defeatism were all annihilated. In millions of cases, the people associated with these qualities, had been physically liquidated. This was true not only of peasants, politicians, and intelligents, but also of a large group of other anti-social elements, who were considered unworthy of the new society: thieves, prostitutes and hooligans. These were also regarded as class-aliens: essentially déclassé "petty bourgeois" by essence. Bolshevism was now building its variety of human divinity. The human God was the new Soviet Man. Stalin and his associates were the heroes, who brought the people its true glory. Stalin's discourse was quasi-religious. A true Bolshevik was described as someone, who never wavered in his faith. Stalin's closest associate in 1937, Nikolai Yezhov, was depicted as a man, whose deed never differed from his word. In a sense, he too, was an heir of the romantic heroes of the beginning of the nineteenth century.

The dawn of socialism coincided with the Great Terror. This was no accident. Bolshevik ideology put its trust in violence as the highest form of class struggle. The Bolsheviks, who always took pride in the fact that they were ruthless, unlike petty-bourgeois *intelligenty*, did what they had promised to do.

The new discourse of the new socialist society was, in many respects, a true continuation of the radical classics of the eighteenth and nineteenth centuries. The "Almighty People," had a divine right to annihilate its enemy, which, in effect, was the new Satan. According to the canons of the new socialist society, the new Man was totally free in his society, and complied with the rules of the new society readily and without coercion. At the same time, the most severe forms of repression were applied to those who denied the new realities and were not, therefore, worthy of the new society.

The old, pre-Revolutionary intelligentsia had to cede its place in society, in politics as well as in culture, and within the Bolshevik party as well as outside it, to a new generational cohort in the second half of the 1930s. This new intelligentsia was really a new social element. Its origins really were preponderantly worker and peasant, and its cultural standards were low, but numerically it was large. Its consciousness had been formed during the post-revolutionary Soviet period and it had adapted to the new realities in a way, which the old intelligentsia, with its knowledge of past history, could never have done.

The Soviet regime had wanted to create a new intelligentsia, which would lack the qualities, which have been described by the word *intelligentnost'*. *Intelligentnost'* has connotations of mild manners, refinement, and gentlemanly behavior. Instead of *intelligentnost'* the new party-minded intellectuals were to be "cultured."

This "culturedness," however, also included knowledge of the Russian cultural heritage, which was largely the creation of the Russian intelligentsia. To be cultured, one also had to know the "progressive" works of classical culture. From the point of view of the Bolsheviks, this knowledge was a double-edged sword. Obviously, not all the new Soviet *intelligenty* could readily accept the idea, as they were supposed to, that the new Soviet values essentially agreed with the entire "progressive" classical heritage, and in the event of disagreement, were superior to them.

The new, "non-*intelligent*-like," but "cultured" intelligentsia had to adapt to conflicting pressures: it was supposed to master the accomplishments of the old classic culture. At the same time, it was supposed to adore and produce artifacts, which the old intelligentsia would have described as *poshlost'*, which denoted an inferior, philistine taste and an apparently naïve, but intrinsically insincere, idealization of reality.

The cream of the new intelligentsia was well remunerated. It was not, however, supposed to have any philistine consumerist instincts. In fact, consumerism was in many ways promoted among the privileged layers of the society, and critical voices were silenced and dismissed as "makhaevism," which was seen as a petty bourgeois anti-intellectual phenomenon, destined for liquidation.

This official promotion and encouragement of that upper layer of society, which was now collectively called the "intelligentsia," has been called "The Big Deal," implying that it now dominated society and shared in the spoils. However, the group, which was now officially called the intelligentsia consisted of many different groups: the top echelons of the *nomenklatura*, the technical intelligentsia, and the creative intelligentsia. In order to retain one's privileged position in Soviet society one had to comply with its norms. It has been assumed that this was not a problem for many representatives of the *nomenklatura* or even the technical intelligentsia. The creative intelligentsia, which was nearest to the heritage of the old intelligentsia, was the element which had to pay most of the moral price for the "Big Deal."

The traditional issue of the intelligentsia's guilt before the people could now be understood as the question of its guilt for the Bolshevik revolution. This issue was, of course, blasphemous in the Soviet Union and could be discussed publicly only by émigré intelligents like Berdiaev. It was also true that the intelligentsia's ideas about the viability of the Bolshevik form of socialism were divided. Many émigré intelligents even admired Stalin's achievements and abstained from criticism. The Second World War increased the prestige of the Soviet Union even further. The question of the intelligentsia's guilt for unleashing the revolution, which led to Bolshevik tyranny, became the subject of a larger discussion only during and after perestroika.

If the new Soviet socialist society had no room for the old type of philistine, it certainly generated a new species of philistine, which shared the values of the totalitarian state, or adapted to it. This was *homo sovieticus*. In its purest form it was represented by the Brezhnev-generation, which had been born before the revolution and been promoted in the course of several social upheavals in the 1920s and 1930s.

It was this generation, which was the most uncritical in its acceptance of Bolshevik ideology in its original Stalinist form. This was also a tragic generation, which suffered immense losses and underwent terrible hardship in battles for the country and the Bolshevik cause. However, this was also a generation, which had been offered a higher purpose in life than that provided by philistine values like consumption (which was, indeed, very restricted). Obviously, the immense losses and terrible suffering served only to reinforce their belief that they were. This generation reigned in the Soviet Union until the end of the Communist empire. To the eyes of a foreigner, this generation of the official Soviet intelligentsia resembled a petty-bourgeois element, which was utterly docile towards the authorities, and sought happiness in the quiet life, work, friends, love, the acquisition of scarce things, like carpets, clothes, cars, and sausages.

However, this was no longer the old philistinism of *meshchanstvo*. It was a new *meshchanstvo*, as the new intelligentsia, which stepped onto the scene in the 1950s pointed out, in the 1960s. Dudintsev's and Bek's works give good examples.

This book does not deal with post-WWII realities, but one can make some remarks about the heritage of the old Russian intelligentsia and its influence on post WWII generations. The new intelligentsia was born in totally new surroundings. It was to have a quite different mindset from that of the old mainstream Russian intelligentsia. In fact, it was obviously the product of the 'soft-minded' section of the old Russian intelligentsia, which had believed in the primacy of spiritual values, which in the 1960s became central for the new cohort of post-Stalinist Russian intelligentsia. A good example is Solzhenitsyn, who was carried away by the ideas of the *Vekhi* group. In principle, it has been argued, there was nothing subversive in the values of the "children of the 1960s." Obviously, they had been gathered from the classics, which the regime was teaching its citizens. In the 1960s the values of *intelligentnost'*, which the Soviet regime had tried to destroy and substitute with party-mindedness, were restored.

Maybe the most fundamental difference between the new intelligentsia and its radical pre-Revolutionary predecessor was that the new generation, in principle, did not feel guilty about its own social position. It could not believe in the totalitarian discourse, which praised the merits of the new Soviet Man. It had seen with its own eyes, that the Bolshevik Revolution had not created human divinity, the "Man with a capital M," as Gorky had preached, but rather the *kham* or barbarian, about whom Merezhkovsky had warned. For those who did not agree in principle with the Communist regime, conformism and silence seem to have become sources of guilt. This was the guilt of quietism, the guilt of the philistine, which the old intelligentsia had been fighting before the revolution. Later, in the 1970s some *intelligenty*, like Solzhenitsyn, declared that anybody who allowed the official lie to spread its influence through their thoughts or actions, shared the guilt for it –and that nobody was totally free of guilt.

Obviously, many representatives of the new Russian intelligentsia of the 1960s believed that they were continuing the traditions of their predecessors, but this was only partially true. Clearly, this group was also alienated from society and was critical of the state. However, at the same time, it was largely liberal, and not prone to fanaticism. In comparison with its Western counterparts, the young fanatics of the 1960s, it was humane and reasonable. All these were qualities, which the mainstream of the old intelligentsia had despised. Like their pre-Revolutionary predecessors, the new intelligentsia also despised conformist "philistines," but for them now the philistines were the stupid and cynical *apparatchiki* rather than the "dark" masses.

As regards the totalitarian psychology and traditions of the old pre-Revolutionary Russian intelligentsia, they continued their life abroad. In Western Europe and America a totalitarian-minded, alienated intelligentsia had become active in the 1930s, at the same time it was disappearing in Russia. This group also felt guilty for the "people" (at home or abroad), it also hated the petty bourgeois, non-revolutionary philistine, it too was convinced of its own intellectual and moral superiority in comparison with the respectable petty bourgeois, and it too was often ready for any sacrifice and upheaval in the name of the great revolutionary cause. The "System" was considered incurably rotten and its further development senseless. The totalitarianism of the "new left" now flourished paradoxically in the free world and its influence peaked in the turmoil of 1968. This international wave of radicalism coincided with and contributed to a cultural revolution, which, indeed, annihilated much of the "petty bourgeois" value system it attacked. It failed in trying to establish totalitarian rule, but it left a formidable intellectual and moral heritage, whose full import is, as yet, impossible to assess. This heritage is now, beginning of the 3rd millennium, a substantial part of Western civilization.

On the other hand, the tradition of the pre-revolutionary "soft-minded" Russian intelligentsia survives in Russia and the rest of the former Soviet Union. It lays stress on spirituality, and on non-material and non-egoistic values. It despises consumerism and *poshlost'*. This is the tradition, which was built on the heritage of *Vekhi* and which, during the Soviet period, was reinforced, taking its inspiration from classical literature and art. At the beginning of the 3rd millennium, this group may be one of the most remarkable intellectual and moral forces still able to criticize the ideas and practices of the new globalizing, consumerist mass society.

Notes

Chapter 1

[1] See V.V. Vinogradov, *Istoria russkikh slov* (Moscow: "Russkii iazyk," 1994), 227. The writer P. D. Boborykin has often been considered the father of the term "intelligentsia." See the entry "Intelligentsiia," in *Novyi entsiklopedicheskii slovar'* (St. Peterburg: izd. F.A. Brokgauz i I.A. Efron), (s.a., after 1910, before 1917). This has been plausibly contested. See A. Pollard, "The Russian Intelligentsia: The Mind of Russia," *Californian Slavic Studies* 3 (Berkeley: University of California Press, 1964), 1-8.

[2] See, for example, I. I. Petrunkevich, "Intelligentsia i "Vekhi"," in *Vekhi, Intelligentsia v Rossii. Sborniki statei 1909-1910*, (Moscow: Molodaia gvardiia, 1991), 210-11; Marc Raeff, *Origins of the Russian Intelligentsia. The Eighteenth Century Nobility* (New York: Harcourt, Brace & World Inc, 1966).

[3] See "intelligentsiia", *Novyi entsiklopedicheskii slovar'*; Bolshaia sovetskaia entsiklopediia tom 18., Moscow 1953. Manfred Hildermeier, The Russian Socialist Revolutionary Party Before the First World War (New York: St. Martin's Press, 2000), p. 61-69.

[4] *Slovar' russkogo yazyka,*. tom I, (Moscow: Izd. Russkii yazyk, 1981).

[5] *Rossiiskiy entsiklopedicheskiy slovar'* (Moscow: Nauchoe izdatel'stvo "BRE," 2000.

[6] The adjective seems to be younger than the word intelligentsia. It first came into use in the 1870s-80s. See Vinogradov, 227.

[7] See P.N. Miliukov, "Intelligentsiia i istoricheskaia traditsia," in *Vekhi, Intelligentsiia v Rossii, Sborniki statei 1909-1910*, 294-300.

[8] See M. Gasparov, "Intellektualy, intelligenty, intelligentnost'," in *Russkaia intelligentsiia. Istoria i sud'ba* (Moscow: Nauka,1999), 5-14.

[9] Raeff, 3.

[10] Circles of intellectuals, for instance the "Wisdom-lovers" (liubomudrye) already existed and their members were well aware of the latest currents of German philosophy. See,for example, A. Walicki, *A History of Russian Thought from the Enlightenment to Marxism* (Stanford: Stanford University Press,1979), 74-91.

[11] See,for example, A. Walicki, *The Controversy over Capitalism. Studies in the Social Philosophy of the Russian Populists* (Oxford: Clarendon Press, 1969.

[12] Walicki, *Russian Thought*, 166-70.

[13] A favorite concept of the "bourgeois" king, Louis Philippe (1830-48).

[14] Walicki, *Russian Thought*, 166-70.

[15] B.A. Uspenski, "Russkaia intelligentsiia kak spetsificheskii fenomen russkoi kultury," in *Rossiya/Russia* 2 (10) (1999) 7-16.

[16] A classic treatise about this is A. Walicki, *Controversy over Capitalism*

[17] See,for example, T. Szamuely, *The Russian Tradition* (New York: McGraw-Hill,1974), 145-47.

[18] See Walicki, *Russian Thought*, 100,170; E. Neff, *Carlyle and Mill. An Introduction to Victorian Thought* (New York: Columbia University Press, 1926) ; Frank E. Manuel, *The Prophets of Paris* (New York: Harper Torchbooks, 1965),118-19.

[19] V.R. Leikina-Svirskaia, *Intelligentsiia v Rossii vo vtoroi polovine XIX veka* (Moscow, 1971), 56.

[20] Ibid., 62, 64.

[21] V.R. Leikina-Svirskaia, *Russkaia intelligentsiia v 1900-1917gg* (Moscow, 1981), 24; Leikina-Svirskaia gives the numbers of hereditary nobles (11.8) and "personal nobles and civil servants" (36,6) for 1906 separatedly. For 19th century they are given summed together (e.g. for 1880 half and half). See Leikina-Svirskaia, *Intelligentsiia v Rossii*, 62.

[22] Leikina-Svirskaia, *Intelligentsiia v Rossii*, 317. At the same time, the author rather mysteriously says that the number of workers grew from 15,6 percent to 46,8 percent from 1884-1890 to 1901-1903.

[23] Leikina-Svirskaia, *Intelligentsiia v Rossii*, 318.

[24] Personal, i.e. non-hereditary noble status could be attained by rising to the sixth grade in the Table of ranks (table o rangakh), where all civil servants and military officers had their place.

[25] C. Read, *Culture and Power in Revolutionary Russia. The Intelligentsia and the Transition from Tsarism to Communism* (Houndmills, Basingstoke: Macmillan, 1990), 7-8.

[26] *Sovetskaia istoricheskaia entsiklopediia*, tom 6, *Sovetskaia entsiklopediia*, (Moscow), s.v. "intelligentsiia."

[27] Gasparov, 5-14. For Western European intellectuals, there is a Russian word "intellektual". It seems to be that the groups, which were called intellectuals in Germany and France (Die Intellektuellen, les intellectuels, respectively) rose into notoriety at the end of the 19th century; See Dietz Bering, *Die Intellektuellen. Geschichte eines Schimpfwortes* (Stuttgart: Klett-Cotta im Ullstein Taschenbuch, 1982.

[28] Szamuely, 151-52.

[29] In 1861 as many as 80 percent of the students of the St. Petersbug University were of noble origin. In the 1880s this number was still 54-55 percent. See Leikina-Svirskaia, *Intelligentsia v Rossii*, 61.

[30] See Ronald Hingley, *Dostoevsky. His Life and Work* (London: Paul Elek, 1978), 101-02.

[31] See P. Pomper, *Sergei Nechaev* (New Brunswick, New Jersey : Rutgers University Press, 1979); Hingley, 149-59.

[32] V.B. Kataev, "Boborykin i Chekhov," in *Russkaia intelligentsiia. Istoriia i sud'ba*, (Moscow: Nauka, 1999), 392. Chekhov considered that the contemporary Russian intelligentsia was unable to be just, or even comprehend justness.

[33] Lenin also understood the revolutionary potential of Tolstoy. He wrote: " Every sentence in Tolstoy's criticism is a slap in the face of bourgeois liberalism." See V.I. Lenin: L.N. Tolstoy, 16.(29.)11.1910; *PSS* 20: 19-24.

[34] It is increasingly felt that Chekhov's role as a writer was mostly detached, even "cold blooded". It is not possible to classify him in the same group with tendentious, let alone didactic social writers. See R. Jackson, "Perspectives on Chekhov," in *Chekhov. A Collection of Critical Essays*, ed. Robert Louis Jackson (Englewood Cliffs: Prentice Hall, 1967), 2-7.

[35] Probably the development of the archetype must be heeded here. In Checkhov's time the Bazarovs of the 1860s had already matured and becoming senior citizens.

[36] Kataev, 390-91.

[37] Nina Berberova, a 20th century memoirist, speaks of two intelligentsias: the first was apolitical and culturally oriented and dependent of the West, the other was politicized, revolutionary and tied to the Russian heritage. The latter succeeded in determining for the latter some of the criteria, with which they evaluated Russian history and contemporary reality. See N. Berberova, *Kursivointi minun*, Kursiv moi, Finnish edition (Juva: WSOY, 1990), 389.

[38] *Vekhi. Sbornik statei o russkoi intelligentsii* (SPb, 1909).

[39] For example, G.P. Fedotov, *Sud'ba i grekhi Rossii* Tom.1. (St Petersburg: "Sofia," 1991), 66-101.

[40] See Tibor Szamuely, *The Russian Tradition*.

[41] Ibid., 143-417.

[42] Ibid., 170-174.

[43] Ibid., 176; Isaiah Berlin for his part has pointed out that Bakunin's thinking in fact had a totalitarian strain in it. See Berlin, *Russian Thinkers* (London:The Hogarth Press, 1978), 82-114. This is also the view of Aileen Kelly. See A. Kelly, *Mikhail Bakunin. A Study in the Psychology and Politics of Utopianism* (New Haven and London: Yale University Press, 1987), 243-44.

[44] For example, Solzhenitsyn's article, "Obrazovanshchina," in *Russkaia intelligentsiia. Istoriia i sudb'a* (Moscow: 1999), 125-48.

[45] See,for example, Aleksandr Solzhenitsyn, *Lokakuu 1916* (October 1916 in Finnish).

The same point has been made by Viktor Leontowitsch, whose book "Geschichte des Liberalismus in Russland" was published in Russian in Solzhenitsyn's INRI (Issledovania noveishei russkoi istorii) series. The symbolism of the acronym of the series is evident. About the liberal nature of Solzhenitsyn's thinking see Leonard Schapiro, *Russian Studies* (London: Collins Harvill, 1986).

[46] Ibid., 112.

[47] Berlin 1978, p. 112

[48] K. Sokolov, "Mify ob intelligentsii i istoricheskaia realnost'," in *Russkaia intelligentsiia. Istoriia i sud'ba* (Moscow: 1999), 150.

[49] Szamuely, 327-28.

[50] Cit. by A. Kelly, *Toward Another Shore. Russian Thinkers Between Necessity and Chance* (Newhaven and London: Yale University Press, 1998).

[51] N. A. Gredeskul, "Perelom russkoi intelligentsii i yego deistvitelniy smysl'," in *Vekhi, Intelligentsiia v Rossii. Sborniki statei 1909-1910*, (1991), 239.

[52] Vinogradov,. 227.

[53] *Tolkovyi slovar' russkogo iazyka*, tom 1, pod. red. D.N. Ushakova (Moscow, 1935) stb. 1214.

[54] Kataev, 382.

[55] *Slovar' russkogo iazyka*, tom I (Moscow: "Russkii iazyk," 1981), s.v. "intelligentskii".

[56] Ibid.

[57] Iu. S. Stepanov, "Zhrets narekish', i zamenuisia: 'zhertva," in *Russkaia intelligentsiia. Istoriia i sud'ba* (Moscow, 1999), 39. Spectacles also give the stigma of an intelligent for some people in Isaac Babel's novel *Konarmiia* (Red Cavalry).

[58] See chapter 4 below.

[59] See S. Davies, " 'Us against them:' social identity in Soviet Russia, 1934-41," in *Stalinism. New Directions*, ed. S. Fitzpatrick (2000), 47-70.

[60] See chapter 2 below.

[61] Fitzpatrick, *Stalinism*, 24.

[62] Davies, *Us against Them*, 49.

[63] Bering, 94-147.

[64] Ibid., 32-51

[65] Ibid., 82-88,109-113.

[66] A term used in an anonymous letter, see Davies, *Us against Them*, 57.

[67] I.V. Stalin, "O nedostatkakh partiinoi raboty, 3.3.1937," in *Sochinenia*, tom 1(XIV), (Stanford: The Hoover Institution, 1967), 219.

[68] V. I. Lenin, *PSS*, tom 51: 48.

[69] See chapter 2 below.

[70] See for instance Lenin, "Proletarskaia revoliutsiia i renegat Kautskii," in V. I. Lenin, *Izbrannye proizvedeniia*, tom 3 (Moscow: Izdatel'stvo politicheskoi literatury, 1971), 1—83.

[71] E.f. Lenin, "Detskaia bolezn' 'levizny' v kommunizme," in V. I. Lenin, *Izbrannye proizvedeniia*, tom 3 (Moscow: Izdatel'stvo politicheskoi literatury, 1971), 295 and passim.

[72] See, for example, Viktor Deni, "Schastlivyi grazhdanin," 1932 and Viktor Deni, "Vragi pyatiletki," 1929, in V. Bonnell, *Iconography of Power. Soviet Political posters under Lenin and Stalin* (Berkeley: University of California Press,1997). See also Jeffrey Brooks, *Thank You Comrade Stalin!* (Princeton University Press, 2000), picture of a Soviet electric train driving over all kinds of enemies.

[73] Bering, 148-257.

[74] See *Sovetskaia istoricheskaia entsiklopediia*, tom 9, (Moscow: Sovetskaia entsiklopediia,1966), s.v."Meschane".

[75] *Malaia sovetskaia entsiklopediia*, tom 5, (Moscow: Sovetskaia entsiklopediia, 1930) s.v. "Meshchanstvo".

[76] *Slovar' russkogo jazyka*, tom 2, (Moscow: Russki jazyk, 1983), s.v. "meshchanskii".

[77] *Slovar' russkogo jazyka*, tom 2, (1983), s.v. "obyvatel'".

[78] See *Slovar' russkogo jazyka*, tom 4, (Moscow: Russki jazyk, 1984), s.v. "filister". Hypocrisy (obyvatel'skaia kosnost' i khanzhestvo) is also mentioned among the meanings.

[79] *Slovar' russkogo jazyka*, tom 3 (Moscow: Russkiy jazyk, 1983), s.v. "poshlyi."Maybe the concept is best understood to be referring to something, which is unworthy

from the point of view of human dignity; the level of distinguishing this depends on the moral and aesthetic level of the subject. So, anyone can shout at a deadly drunk person in a shop "kakaia poshlost'!" ("what a disgrace!") On the other hand, it takes a refined person to say the same about American bestsellers, as Nabokov does. I think that the alleged sexual dimension of poshlost' is not really a substantial one. Sex for its own sake just used to be considered unworthy and somehow degrading in all Western countries up to the cultural revolution of the 1960s.

[80] V. Nabokov, *Nikolai Gogol* (Norfolk: New Directions Books, 1944).

[81] S. Boym, *Common Places, Mythologies of Everyday life in Russia* (Cambridge, Mass and London: Harvard University Press,1994), 41.

[82] Ibid., 41-66.

[83] Ibid., 58.

[84] Ibid., 59.

[85] Ibid., 67.

[86] About this see Gertrude Himmelfarb, *One Nation, Two Cultures* (New York: Vintage Books, 2001).

[87] See,for example, N. Berdiaev, "Etika po siu storonu dobra i zla," in N. Berdiaev, *O naznachenii cheloveka* (Moscow: Respublika,1993), 158-60. For Berdiaev, poshlost' was "really this world, which has finally forgotten about the other world and rejoices it". Poshlost' may even "retain an eschatological character and become one possible end of human destiny. And one of the greatest ethical imperatives is to prevent this from happening." Ibid., 159.

[88] See,for example, Masha Gessen, *Dead Again. The Russian Intelligentsia after Communism* (London and New York: Verso, 1997), 28-34.

[89] "Byt" means also the way of life, which is characteristic for a certain group. For instance, *krestianskii byt* (peasant way of life) or *sotsialisticheskii byt* (socialist way of life). See *Slovar' russkogo jazyka*, tom 1, (Moscow: Russki jazyk, 1981).

[90] V. Mayakovsky, "O driani," cit. by Boym, 34. "Drian" means literally "canaille", a word, which was obviously awkward for any friend of the people (narod) and for a revolutionary .

[91] *Malaia sovetskaia entsiklopediia* (Moscow, 1930), s.v. "meshchanstvo," by S. Smidovich).

[92] Ibid.

[93] N. Riasanovsky, *Russia and the West in the Teaching of the Slavophiles* (Gloucester, Mass: Peter Smith, 1965), 120-27.

[94] Boym, 75-78.

[95] Steven Hoch, *Serfdom and Social Control in Russia* (Chicago and London: The University of Chicago Press, 1986).

[96] See, for example, Szamuely, 175.

[97] For example, Riasanovsky 1961, 109-110, 122, 125.

[98] Especially on the Slavophile side it was maintained that the Russians did not respect luxury, like the West-European nations, but rather were awed by the rags of a holy fool. The Russian virtue of heroism was confronted with the Western humdrum way of life and "soul-killing" mechanical work. Especially the Germans were dismissed as narrow-minded pedants, which compared very unfavourably with Russian spirituality. See Riasanovsky 1961, 122-25.

[99] About this see Michael Burleigh, *The Third Reich. A New History* (London: Pan books, 2001), 1-25.

[100] J. L. Talmon, *The Origins of Totalitarian Democracy* (London: Secker and Warburg, 1952).

[101] Berlin 1979, 128-29.

[102] J.G. Fichte, *Ueber das Wesen der Gelehrten und seine Erscheinungen im Gebiete der Freiheit.* Fichte, Gesamtausgabe I,8. Stuttgart 1995, Friedrich Frommann Vlg, 64.

[103] J.G. Fichte, *Die Anweisung zum seeligen Leben, oder auch die Religionslehre.* Fichte Gesamtausgabe I, 9, 55-59, 178.

[104] Kelly 1987, 32-45.

[105] I. Berlin, *Freedom and its Betrayal* (London: Chatto&Windus, 2002), 63-73.

[106] See Timothy Ware, *The Orthodox Church* (Penguin Books, 1997), 231.

[107] About the "de-moralization" of society as a major process, which has thoroughly changed the moral climate of the Western world see e.g. Gertrude Himmelfarb, *The De-Moralization of Society. From Victorian Virtues to Modern Values* (New York: Vintage Books, 1994).

[108] About Carlyle's spiritual crisis see Neff, 196; see also P.Gay, *Pleasure Wars* (New York, London: 1998), 35.

[109] See Manuel; and Neff.

[110] A. Gertsen, *Byloe i dumy.*

[111] Gay, *Pleasure Wars*, 26-30.

[112] Berlin 1978, 128-31.

[113] See T. Carlyle, *Sartor Resartus* (London: 1869), 60; T. Carlyle, *On Heroes, Hero-Worship and the Heroic in History* (London: 1896), 222, 275-76.

[114] ibid., 222.

[115] B.H. Lehman, *Carlyle's Theory of the Hero* (Durham NC, 1928), 116-17.

[116] See Carlyle, *Sartor Resartus*, 116.

[117] For example, Walicki, *Russian Thought*, 125.

[118] Isaiah Berlin discusses these topics in his book *Freedom and Its Betrayal*. London, Chatto and Windus 2002.

[119] "Denke daher bei jedem Bisse Brotes,... an den Gott... -an den Menschen. Aber vergiss nicht... die Dankbarkeit gegen die heilige Natur. ... So braucht man nur den gewöhnlichen, gemeinen Lauf der Dinge zu unterbrechen, um dem Gemeine ungemeines Bedeutung, dem leben als solchen ueberhaupt religiöse Bedeutung abzugewinnen. Heilig sei uns darum das Brot, heilig der Wein, aber auch heilig das Wasser! Amen." in: Ludwig Feuerbach, *Das Wesen des Christentums*, in *Gesammelte Werke*, (Berlin: Akademie Vlg, 1973), 454. About the psychology of the early hegelians see also Berlin 1979, 131-33.

[120] See W. James, *Varieties of Religious Experience* (Harvard University Press, 1985).

[121] Walicki 1979, 186-98.

[122] Szamuely, 257.

[123] Ibid., 258.

[124] Ibid., 258-71.

[125] See Hingley, 149-59.

[126] Ibid.

[127] I am conscious of the numerous various ways of interpreting Dostoevsky and

by no means do I pretend for any ultimate wisdom in this respect. My point is just to underline here the anti-philistine bias of Dostoevsky, who simultaneously also condemned revolutionary radicalism.

128 J.S. Mill, *Autobiography* (New York, 1948), 94, 113-14.

129 J. Symons, *Thomas Carlyle. The Life and Ideas of a Prophet* (London: Victor Gollancz, 1952), 228.

130 John S. Mill, *On Liberty. Representative Government* (Oxford: Basil Blackwell, 1948), 64.

131 Ibid.

132 A.I. Gertsen, "Kontsy i nachala," in *Intelligentsiia, vlast', narod,* (1993), 30-32.

133 A. Gertsen, "Dzhon-Stiuart Mill i jego kniga "On liberty," in *Sobranie sochinenii,* Tom. 11.(Moscow: 1957), 67-77.

134 David Remnick, *Lenin's Tomb. The Last Days of the Soviet Empire* (New York: Random House, 1993),332.

135 I. Turgenev, *Ottsy i deti.*

136 Kelly, *Toward another Shore,* 134-55.

Chapter 2

1 See J. Brooks, *When Russia Learned to Read* (Princeton: Princeton University Press, 1985).

2 See, for example, O.Figes, *A People"s Tragedy. The Russian Revolution 1891-1924* (London: Jonathan Cape, 1996), 159-62.

3 George Fischer, *Russian Liberalism. From Gentry to Intelligentsia* (Cambridge, Mass: Harvard University Press, 1958), 51-52.

4 Fischer, 45-48.

5 For example, Iurii I. Kirianov, "Mentality of Russian Workers at Turn of Twentieth Century," in *Workers and Intelligentsia in Late Imperial Russia: Realities, Representations, Reflections,* ed. Reginald Zelnik (Berkeley:University of California, 1999), 95-99 and passim. Kirianov refers to the chief of gendarmes, Sviatopolk-Mirskii, who described the new type of workers as "semiliterate" intelligents, who considered their duty to "deny religion and the family, scorn the law, disobey and mock authority."

6 See Theodor Shanin, *Russia as a "Developing Society"* (Houndmills Macmillan, 1985).

7 Figes, *People's Tragedy,* 182.

8 See Romanovski 2000, p. 177.

9 About this see A. Yanov, *The Russian Challenge and the Year 2000* (Oxford: Blackwell, 1987).

10 See Peter Gay, *The Cultivation of Hatred* (New York and London: W.W. Norton & Company, 1993).

11 See George L. Mosse, *The Crisis of German Ideology* (London: Weidenfeld and Nicolson, 1966), 149-237.

12 See I.K. Kirianov, "Vladimir Mitrofanovich Purishkevich: deputat -fraktsia," in *Konservatizm: idei i liudi,* (Perm: Izdatel'stvo permskogo universiteta, 1998), 105-122; Iu. I. Kiryanov, *Pravye partii v Rossii 1911-1917* (Moscow:Rosspen, 2001), passim.

[13] It is worth while noting that Purishkevich, had published a 11-volume book *Kniga russkoi skorbi* to commemorate the memory of the victims of revolutionary terrorists, which contained about a thousand biographies. In 1907 the duma honoured the memory of its member, G.B. Iollos, who had been killed by a representative of the Black hundreds. Purishkevich thereafter proposed an analogous homage to be paid to the victims of revolutionary terrorism. After a loudly scandal he was ousted from the duma session. No doubt, Purishkevich's proposal was provocative, but the reaction also tells something about the moods of the duma, which after all had a solid conservative representation. Kiryanov 1998, p. 106-07.

[14] See Abraham Ascher, *The Revolution of 1905* (Stanford, CA: Stanford University Press, 1988), 130, 257.

[15] Yet, B.H. Lehman, writing in the 1920s, still considered Carlyle's influence enormous. See Lehmann, Carlyle's *Theory*, 196.

[16] See Kelly, *Toward another Shore*, 134-55.

[17] I am referring to Mill's ideas about the danger of "conglomerated mediocrity", which causes stagnation in society and about the "Chinese" parallel as a warning example. See Gertsen, *Kontsy i nachala*, 26-44.

[18] For example, F. Nietzsche, *The Will to Power* (New York: Vintage Books, 1968),21, 489.

[19] See Kelly, *Toward another Shore*, 139-42.

[20] For example, F. Nietzsche, *Näin puhui Zarathustra* (*Thus Spake Zarathustra*, Finnish edition) paragraphs about the "superman" and the "last man", 1st chapter). The latter had "invented happiness" and people –the philistines- are more attracted by the prospect of becoming "last men" than by the idea of sacrifices in the name of the future higher being.

[21] L.N. Tolstoi, *Smert Ivana Ilicha* (Moscow: Khudozhestvannaia literatura, 1969).

[22] For example, L. Tolstoi, *Ylösnousemus* (Resurrection), Finnish edition; Walicki 1993, 326-46; L.N. Tolstoi, *Chto takoe iskusstvo?*

[23] Most clearly presented in Tolstoy's late essays. Walicki 1993, 339-43.

[24] See *Chto takoe iskusstvo?*

[25] See e.g. Pekka Pesonen, "Vallankumouksen henki hengen vallankumouksessa," *Slavica Helsingiensia*, Supplementum II, (Helsinki, 1987): 41-50; V. Erlich, *Modernism and Revolution. Russian Literature in Transition* (Cambridge,Mass and London: Harvard University Press, 1994), 14-31.

[26] See Walicki, *Russian Thought*, 371-405..

[27] Thus Spake Zarathustra was published in Russian in 1898 and many other works in the following few years.

[28] About parallelisms between Nietzsche and Dostoevsky see V.V. Dudkin, *Dostoevski – Nitsshe (problema cheloveka)* (Petrozavodzk: Izdatelstvo KGPI, 1994.

[29] V.F. Pustarnakov, "Byl li kogda-nibud Fridrikh Nitsshe '*samim russkim*' iz zapadnykh filosofov?" in *Fridrikh Nitsshe i filosofia Rossii. Sbornik statei*, (St Peterburg: Izdatelstvo Russkogo Khristianskogo gumanitarnogo institute, 1999), 105-07.

[30] See note 2 above.

[31] Nietzsche, *The Will To Power*, 19.

[32] About this see Mark D. Steinberg, "The Injured and Insurgent Self: The Moral Imagination of Russia's Lower-Class Writers," in *Workers and Intelligentsia in*

Late Imperial Russia: Realities, Representations, Reflections, ed. Zelnik. (Berkeley,1999), 309-29.

³³ See chapter 3.

³⁴ About this see Dieter Groh, *La Russia e l'autocoscienza d'Europa* (Piccola biblioteca Einaudi, 1980), 212; A. de Tocqueville, *Democracy in America,* Volume I (New York:Vintage Books, 1945), 452.

³⁵ Hannu Immonen has contested the common belief that the SR leadership would still, at the beginning of the XX century have been confident of the possibility of a non-capitalist way of development. Even so, the fact remains that the prospect of capitalism was understood as a threat to the fundamental values that made the human life worth living. See H.Immonen, *Agrarian Program of the Russian Socialist Revolutionary Party 1900-1914* (Helsinki: SHS,1988).

³⁶ C. Rougle, *Three Russians Consider America. America in the Works of Maksim Gorky, Aleksandr Blok and Vladimir Majakovsky,* Acta Universitatis Stockholmiensis. Stockholm Studies in Russian literature, 8 (Stockholm: Almqvist & Wiksell International, 1976), 40, 54.

³⁷ R. Sesterhenn, *Das Bogostroitelstvo bei Gorkij und Lunacharskij bis 1909. Zur ideologischen und literarischen Vorgeschichte der Parteischule von Capri* (Munich: Slavistische Beiträge Bd 158, Vlg Otto Sogner, 1982).

³⁸ Nietzsche"s general popularity among the symbolists and other contemporary literary movements, like futurism, probably helps to understand the apparent paradox of "Nietzschean social democrats".

³⁹ Ibid., 119-20.

⁴⁰ Ibid., 125-27.

⁴¹ Ibid., 138.

⁴² See Jutta Scherrer, "The Relationship between the Intelligentsia and Workers: The Case of the Party Schools in Capri and Bologna," in *Workers and Intelligentsia in Late Imperial Russia: Realities, Representations, Reflections,* ed. Zelnik. (1999), 172-85.

⁴³ See S.A. Smith, "Workers, The Intelligentsia and Social Democracy in St. Petersburg, 1985-1917," in *Workers and Intelligentsia in Late Imperial Russia: Realities, Representations, Reflections,*ed. Zelnik. (1999), 188- 205.

⁴⁴ M. Diondioshi, "K voprosu Blok i Nitsshe," *Studia Slavica Hungariensia* 43 (1998): 135-49.

⁴⁵ Ibid.,147.

⁴⁶ Ibid., 149.

⁴⁷ Lenin's very emotional but rather muddle-headed argumentation in "Materialism and Epirio-criticism" and his method of making citing of authority the criterion of truth see George H. Sabine, *A History of political Theory* (London: George G. Harrap,1964), 824-25.

⁴⁸ About the nature of Leninism in this respect see Alain Besancon, *The intellectual origins of Bolshevism.*

⁴⁹ Alain Besancon has said that Bolshevism was a prevalently ethical ideology, while Nazism was aesthetic. This may be due to an understatement of the aesthetic –anti-philistine- ethos of Bolshevism. See A. Besancon, *Le Malheur du siécle. Sur le communisme, le nazisme et l'unicité de la shoah* (Fayard, 1998), 54.

⁵⁰ See , for example, V.I. Lenin, Gosudarstvo i revoliutsiia, in *Izbrannye proizvedeniia,*

tom 2, (1971), 303-09.

[51] See,for example, Mosse, 13-25, 266-79 and passim.

[52] The "class" interpretation of Nazism seems unconvincing in the light of new research. See G. Steinmetz, "German exceptionalism and the origins of Nazism," in *Stalinism and Nazism, Dictatorships in Comparison,* eds. Ian Kershaw and Moshe Lewin (Cambridge University Press, 1997), 265-66.

[53] See e.g. George L. Mosse, *The Crisis of the German Ideology* (London: Weidenfeld and Nicolson, 1964), 13-25, 266-79 and passim.

[54] See Burleigh, 1-25.

[55] See e.g. Szamuely, 175.

[56] About this see e.g. John Carey, *The Intellectuals and the Masses: Pride and Prejudice Among the Literary Intelligentsia, 1880-1939* (London: St. Martin's, 1996); Peter Gay, *The Pleasure Wars* (W.W. Norton & Co).

[57] See Nils-Åke Nilsson, *Ibsen in Russland* (Stockholm: Almqvist& Wicksell, 1958.

[58] Max Nordau (Suedfeld), 1849-1923, German physician and writer of Jewish origin.

[59] For Nordau, not only were the Pre-Raphaelites, the French symbolists and decadents like Verlaine, Mallarmé, Baudelaire, Maeterlinck, Wilde and the like decadent –but also Tolstoy, Wagner, Ibsen and Nietzsche! See "T.," "Vyrozhdenie (entartung) Maksa Nordau," *Vestnik Evropy* 4 (Aprel 1894): 866-74.

[60] See Joachim Radkau, *Das Zeitalter der Nervosität* (Muenchen-Wien: Propyläen Taschenbuch. Casrö Hanser Vlg, 2000), 231-50.

[61] Ibid., 387-406.

[62] Gay, *Pleasure Wars*, 38.

[63] Pseudonym for Razumnik Ivanov (1878-1946). Razumnik was a well-known litterateur, who wrote monographs on literary history, e.g. Saltykov-Shchedrin and Blok. Razumnik was a friend of Blok, Esenin and Belyi and the ideologue of the "Scythian" movement. Politically, Razumnik was a left SR, who welcomed the October revolution and cooperated with the Bolsheviks. He was later arrested. See A. Lavrov, "Ivanov-Razumnik," in *Vozvrashchenie,*Vypusk I (Moscow: Sovetski pisatel', 1991), 303-05.

[64] See N.N. Smirnov, "Rossiiskaia intelligentsiia: k voprosu o definitsiiakh," *in Istorik i revoliutsiia* (Sankt-Peterburg: Dmitri Bulanin, 1999), 45.

[65] For example, L. Trotsky, "Ob intelligentsii," in *Intelligentsia, vlast', narod,* (1993), 105 and passim.

[66] V.G. Belous, "Ispytanie dukhovnym maksimalizmom," in *Ivanov-Razumnik. Pisatel'skie sudby. Tiurmy i ssylki* (Moscow: Novoe literaturnoe obozrenie, 2000), 5-11.

[67] L.I. Novikova and I.N. Sizemskaia, "Vvedenie," in *Intelligentsia, Vlast', narod,* (1993),12.

[68] Ivanov-Razumnik, *Istoriia russkoi obshchestvennoi mysli* (Spb, 1907).

[69] Ibid., 14.

[70] Ibid., 15.

[71] Ibid., 7. Here Ivanov-Razumnik refers to the authority of Petr Lavrov.

[72] Ibid., 7-9.

[73] Ibid., 20.

[74] Ibid., 21-22.

[75] Smirnov, *Rossiiskaia intelligentsiia*, 45.

[76] Trotsky, *"Ob intelligentsii,"* 258-73; B. Knei-Paz, *The Social and Political Thought of Leon Trotsky* (Oxford:Clarendon Press, 1978), 222.

[77] Trotsky, "Ob intelligentsii," 110.

[78] B.G. Rosenthal, *Dmitri Sergeevich Merezhkovsky and the Silver Age. The Development of a Revolutionary Mentality* (The Hague: Martinus Nijhoff, 1975), 163.

[79] D.S. Merezhkovski, *Griadushchii kham* (Sankt Petersburg, 1906), 3-4.

[80] Ibid., 7.

[81] Ibid.,8-9. On the topic of the oriental dimension in Russian culture and thought in the beginning of the XX century see Pesonen, *Vallankumouksen*, 75-79.

[82] Merezhkovskii, *Griadushchii kham*, 21.

[83] Ibid., 39

[84] See Rosenthal, *Merezhkovsky*, 163.

[85] See I.V. Kondakov, *Vvedenie v istoriiu russkoi kul'tury* (Moskva, 1997), 371.

[86] Ibid.

[87] See the *Vekhi*, for instance.

[88] See Kondakov, *Vvedenie i istoriiu*, 378-79; Merezhkovskii, 21.

[89] Discussed below in this book.

[90] N. Berdiaev, "Revolutsiia i kul'tura," in *Rossiiskie liberaly: kadety i oktobristy*, (Moscow: Rosspen, 1996), 102-08. Also Kondakov, 386.

[91] Ibid.

[92] N.A. Berdiaev, "Bunt i pokornost' v psikhologii mass," *in Intelligentsia, vlast', narod* (1993), 117-24.

[93] V.I. Lenin, *O partiinoi literature.*

[94] V.I. Lenin, "Chto delat'?" in, *Izbrannye proizvedeniia* tom 1, p. 83-229, especially 135-40.

[95] *Ocherki filosofii kollektivizma.* Sbornik 1, (Sankt-Peterburg: Znanie, 1909).

[96] Ibid., 394.

[97] Ibid., 396, 397.

[98] Ibid., 402.

[99] In 1905 Gorky did join the Bolsheviks, which weakened his authority among fellow-writers. See Mary Louise Loe, "Redefining the Intellectual's Role: Maksim Gorkiy and thre Sreda Circle," in *Between Tsar and People. Educated Society and the Quest for Public Identity in Late Imperial Russia*, eds. Edith W. Clowes, Samuel D. Kassow, and James L. West. (Princeton, New Jersey: Princeton University Press, 1991),198-307.

[100] See R. Pipes, *Struve, Liberal on Left , 1870-1905* (Cambridge, Mass: Harvard University Press, 1970).

[101] See M.A. Kolerov, *Ne mir, no mech'. Russkaia religiozno-filosofskaia pechat' ot "Problem idealizma" do "Vekh" 1902-1909* (St. Petersburg: Aleteia, 1996).

[102] Leonard Schapiro has pointed out that conservatism proper should be considered part of liberalism, while any kind of radicalism should not. The Vekhi-group, as well as Solzhenitsyn's thinking he considers conservative liberal -unlike the slavophiles. See his *Russian Studies* (London: 1986), 387.

[103] Iz-pod glyb. Parizh 1974.

[104] *Vekhi. Sbornik statei o russkoi intelligentsii* (Moscow 1909) (facsimile of the second 1909 edition), 3, 8.

[105] Ibid.

[106] Op. cit. p. 28, 36-37.

[107] Op. cit. p. 36-38.

[108] Op. cit. p. 41.

[109] Op. cit. p. 45-46.

[110] Op. cit. p. 90.

[111] Op. cit. p. 89.

[112] Op. cit. 97-124, esp. 116-117.

[113] Op, cit. p. 125-126, 130-131. Kistiakovsky defends the case of formal jurisprudence and its necessity for a free society. Leonard Schapiro has likewise considered the inimicity to formal law as one of the main criteria of totalitarian thinking. See his *Russian Studies*, p. 387.

[114] Vekhi, 160.

[115] Op., cit., p. 178-81. Frank uses here Nietzsche's expression "human, all too-human"(p. 181) *Vekhi: Pro et contra. Antologia* (Sankt-Peterburg: Izdatelstvo russkogo khristianskogo gumanitarnogo instituta, 1998), 121.

[116] V. Ilin (V.I.Lenin), O "Vekhakh," ibid., 488-95.

[117] Smirnov, *Rossiiskaia intelligentsiia*, 147.

[118] D.N. Ovsianiko-Kulikovskii, *Istoriia russkoi intelligentsii*, 1-2, (St. Petersburg, 1910-1911).

[119] I. I. Petrunkevich, "Intelligentsiia i "Vekhi"," in *Vekhi—Intelligentsiia v Rossii*, (1991), 210-220.

[120] P. N. Miliukov, "Intelligentsiia i istoricheskaia traditsiia," in *Vekhi—Intelligentsiia v Rossii* (1991), 294-300.

[121] Ibid., 380.

[122] Ibid., 377-81

[123] M. I. Tugan-Baranovsky, "Intelligentsiia i sotsializm," in *Intelligentsiia, vlast', narod*, (1993), 209-24.

[124] R. Vipper, *Dve intelligentsii i drugie ocherki* (Moscow, 1912).

[125] P. Novgorodtsev, "O putiakh i zadachakh russkoi intelligentsii," in *Vekhi, Iz glubiny*, (Moscow: Pravda, 1991), 424-442.

[126] Ibid.

[127] Ibid., 427. The author refers to a book of Edouard Berthe(?) Les méfaits des intellectuelles (1914) with a foreword by Georges Sorel.

[128] D. S. Merezhkovskiy, "Sem smirennykh," in *Vekhi: Pro et contra. Antologia* (Sankt Peterburg: Izdatelstvo Russkogo Khristianskogo gumanitarnogo instituta, 1998), 100-110.

[129] C. Read, *Religion, Revolution and the Russian intelligentsiia, 1900-1912: The Vekhi debate and its intellectual background* (London:1979), 139; True, Belyi remained a revolutionary, but for him, the "real" revolution was not about politics, but happened "in spirit." See Pesonen, 86-95.

[130] Trotsky, for example, stated in 1912 that "vekhism" had been the "nightmare" of the past few years." "The newspapers, the thick journals, collections of articles, speeches, indoor discussions –all has smelt of vekhism." Trotsky, "Ob intelligentsii," 105.

[131] See e.g. Viktor Leontowitsch, *Geschichte des Liberalismus in Russland* (Frankfurt am Main: Klostermann, 1974).

[132] V.M. Kruchkovskaia, "Politicheskie nastroeniia rossiiskogo studenchestva: 1905-1917 gg," in *Intelligentsiia i rossiiskoe oshchestvo v nachale XX veka*, (Sankt-Peterburg: Rossiiskaia akademiia nauk, institut rossiiskoi istorii, Sankt-peterburgskii filial, 1996) 109-110.

[133] Kelly, *Toward another Shore*, 135. The rhetorical question derives from Charles Moser.

[134] Cit by Kelly, *Toward another Shore* Cit. by Kelly, 143.

[135] Ibid. See also M.N. Stroeva, *Rezhisserskie iskaniia Stanislavskogo, 1898-1917* (Moscow: Nauka) 303-309. In his "open letter" Gorky—of all the people!—described Dostoevsky a nihilist, who had become disappointed in everything and developed a sado-masochist syndrome. In "the possessed" Gorky saw just a "pasquil with current political import" and "dark stains of a malicious misanthrope."

[136] See, for example, "Ellis", "V zashchitu dekadenstva. Po povodu stati N. Berdiaeva "Dekadentstvo i obshchestvennost'"," in *N.A. Berdiaev, Pro et contra, antologiia*, kniga 1 (Sankt-Peterburg: Izdatelstvo Russkogo khristianskogo gumanitarnogo instituta, 1994) 166-68.

[137] Nikolai Berdiaev, *Sudba Rossii. Opyty po psikhologii voiny i natsionalnosti* (Moscow, 1918. Reprint. Moscow: Izdatelstvo MGU, 1990).

[138] Berdiaev, *Sudba Rossii*, 12-14.

[139] Berdiaev, *Sudba Rossii*, 14-16.

[140] Berdiaev, *Sudba Rossii*, 156-59.

[141] C. Read, *Culture and Power in Revolutionary Russia* (Houndmills:Macmillan, 1990), 31.

[142] Maksim Gorkiy, Zametki o meshchanstve, in M. Gorkiy, *Sobranie sochinenii v 30 tomakh*, tom 23, (Moscow, 1953). 341.

[143] Ibid.

[144] Ibid., 342.

[145] Ibid., 343-34.

[146] Ibid., 352-54.

[147] Gorkii, "Zametki," 344.

[148] Maksim Gorkii, "Meshchanin," in *Polnoe sobranie sochinenii* tom 6, (Moscow, 1970), 383-84. This fragment was written in 1903 and was first published in 1938.

[149] H. Guenther, *Der sozialistische Uebermensch. Maxim Gorkij und der sowjetische Heldenmythos* (Stuttgart, Weimar, 1993), 40-41.

[150] Guenther, *Der Socialistische*, 56-57, 149; M. Banting, C. Kelly, and J. Riordan, "Sexuality," in *Russian Cultural Studies.An Introduction*, Eds. C. Kelly and D. Shepherd (Oxford University Press, 1998), 319.

[151] B. Groys, *Gesamtkunstwerk Stalin* (Muenchen/Wien, 1988), 53.

[152] Ibid., 47-48.

[153] Hans Guenther, *Der Sozialistische Uebermensch. Maxim Gorki und der sowjetische Heldenmythos* (Stuttgart/Weimar: J.B. Metzler, 1993), 128.

[154] Ibid., 121.

[155] Rufus W. Matthewson, *The Positive Hero in Russian Literature* (Stanford, California: Stanford University Press, 1975), 174.

[156] Guenther, *Der Sozialistische*, 122.

[157] M. Gorki, *Mat' (Sobranie sochinenii,* t.8 (Moscow: 1970),17.

[158] Ibid.,139.

[159] Ibid.,127.

[160] Ibid., 127-28.

[161] V. Desnitskii, "Istoricheskoe znachenie romana M. Gorkogo *Mat'*," *Literaturnaia ucheba* 2 (1933): 22-24, 29-30.

[162] Kornei Chukovsky tells about the "famous tears" of Gorky, which appeared for the slightest reason. See K. Chukovskiy, "Dnevnik 1918-1923," *Novyi mir* 7 (1990): 157.

[163] Maksim Gorkiy, *Foma Gordeev. Sobranie sochinenii,* tom 4 (Moscow: 1968),431.

[164] See, for instance, Kain and Artem or Makar Chudra. Of course, there may be literary influences for the idea of a lethal Gipsy pride, like Merimeé's Carmen etc.

[165] A bosiak means literally a barefooter. It refers to a group of people, which best could be defined *lumpenproletariat.*

[166] D. Merezhkovsky, "Chekhov i Gorkii," in *Griadushchii kham,* (St. Petersburg: 1906), 63-64.

[167] Maksim Gorky, *V Amerike. Sobranie sochinenii,* tom 6 (Moscow: 1970), 237-76.

[168] Ibid.

[169] Ibid.

[170] M. Reisner, *Proletariat i meshchanstvo. Dve dushi russkogo naroda v ucheniakh Leonida Andreeva i Maksima Gorkogo* (Petrograd: Knigoizdatel'stvo I.P.Belopolskogo, 1917), 1-7.

[171] Ibid.

[172] See B.G.Rosenthal, "A New World for a New Myth: Nietzsche and Russian Futurism," in *The European Foundation of Russian Modernism,* ed. Peter I. Barta. (Lewiston, New York: Edwin Mellen Press, 1991), 229 -33.

[173] About the Octobrist position see O.V. Volobuev, "Revoliutsiia 1905-07 v otsenke liberal-konservatorov," in *Liberalnyi   konservatizm. Istoriia i sovremennost',* (Moscow: Rosspen, 2001), 243-50.

[174] As a whole, however, the politics of the Kadet party were outspokenly radical. The banquets of the intelligentsia in 1904-05 presented so radical demands on the government (including general amnesty and immediate convocation of a constituent assembly) that fulfilling them would have amounted to a revolution. See G. Fischer, *Russian liberalism. From Gentry to Intelligentsia* (Cambridge, Mass: Harvard university Press, 1958), 191-95.

Chapter 3

[1] V. I. Lenin, "Chto delat?" . PSS, tom 6.,111-134.

[2] V. I. Lenin, "Ot kakogo nasledstva my otkazyvaemsia?" in *Izbrannye proizvdeniia,* tom 1 (1971), 61-62.

[3] op. cit. p. 63, 66, 74.

[4] Lenin, "Gosudarstvo i revoliutsiia," in *Izbrannye proizvedeniia,* tom 2 (1971), 227-324.

[5] K. Marx and F. Engels, *Manifesto of the Communist Party* (E.g. in Karl Marx, Friedrich Engels Valitut teokset kolmessa osassa. Edistys, Moskova s.a., part 1., 120).

[6] Lenin, "Gosudarstvo i revoliutsiia," 309.

[7] Ibid., 298-309.

[8] See, for example, K.Marx, *Class-Struggles in France in 1848-1850* (pp. 164-265 in Valitut, part 1.); K. Marx, "Der 18. Brumaire des Louis Bonaparte, in *MEGA*, Bd. 11 (Berlin: Dietz Vlg, 1985), 141-43.

[9] Lenin, "Gosudarstvo i revoliutsiia," 295-98.

[10] O. Figes and V Kolonitskii, *Interpreting the Russian Revolution: The Language and Symbols of 1917* (New Haven and London: 1999), 154-55.

[11] V. I. Lenin, "O nashei revoliutsii," in *Izbrannye*, tom 3, 720.

[12] For example,V.I.Lenin, "Karl Marx," in *Izbrannye*, (1971), 6-10.

[13] *Class Struggles in France* (Valitut, Vol. I, 198 and passim; *The Civil War in France*, MEGA Bd. 22 (Berlin: 1978), 142-44.

[14] K. Marx, Ber 18. *Brumaire*, MEGA Bd. 11, 141-42.

[15] Marx even concluded that the financial oligarchy, which embodied "unrestrained, abnormal and dissolute passions" was nothing else than a "lumpenproletariat, which had been reborn on the hills of the bourgeois society," see *Class Struggles in France*, Valitut Vol. 1, 183).

[16] Ibid., 193; *18th Brumaire*, MEGA Bd. 11, 141-43.

[17] Mark D. Steinberg, "Vanguard Workers and the Morality of Class," in *Making Workers Soviet. Power, Class and Identity,* ed. by Lewis H. Siegelbaum and Ronald Grigor Suny. (Ithaca and London: Cornell University Press,1994),66-84. See also Reginald D. Zelnik, "On the Eve: Life Histories and Identities of Some Revolutionary Workers, 1870-1905,"in *Making Workers Soviet. Power, Class and Identity,* ed. by Lewis H. Siegelbaum and Ronald Grigor Suny (Ithaca and London: Cornell University Press,1994), 48.

[18] Figes and Kolonitskii, *Interpreting the Russian Revolution,* 114-17.

[19] See Figes and Kolonitskii, picture 20.

[20] K. Marx, *Class Struggles in France* (Valitut, Vol. 1, 203).

[21] Ibid., 231.

[22] For example, Friedrich Engels, *Zur Wohnungsfrage,* MEGA, Bd. 24, (Berlin 1984), 26 and passim.

[23] K. Marx, *18th Brumaire of Louis Napoleon,* MEGA Bd. 11, 141-43.

[24] E. A. Iakovlev, "Predislovie," in *Chernaia kniga kommunizma,* (Moscow, 1999).

[25] V. I. Lenin, "Gosudarstvo i revoliutsiia," 298-99.

[26] Ibid., 265, 308.

[27] Ibid., 300-309.

[28] Ibid., 309.

[29] Ibid., 304.

[30] V. I. Lenin, "Uderzhat li bolsheviki gosudarstvennuiu vlast'?" in *Izbrannye proizvedeniia,* tom 2 (Moscow, 1971), 348-83.

[31] Ibid., 362-67.

[32] Ibid., 368-71.

[33] Ibid.

[34] Ibid., 376.

[35] V. I. Lenin, "Kak organizovat' sorevnovanie?" in *Izbrannye proizvedeniia,* tom 2, 468-76.

[36] Ibid., 470.

[37] Ibid., 473.

[38] Ibid. 474-75.

[39] Ibid., 470-71.

[40] V. I. Lenin, "Ocherednye zadachi sovetskoi vlasti," in *PSS*, tom 36., 165-208.

[41] Ibid. 202-03, 208.

[42] Variant stat'i "Ocherednye zadachi sovetskoi vlasti," in *PSS*, tom 36, 137-38.

[43] "Ocherednye zadachi sovetskoi vlasti," in *PSS* tom 36, 203.

[44] *PSS*, tom 36, 262.

[45] *PSS*, tom 36, 286.

[46] Ibid., 309.

[47] W. G. Rosenberg, "Labor Activism in Piter, 1918-1929," in *Piterskie rabochie i 'dik-tatura proletariata.' Oktiabr 1917-1929. Ekonomicheskie konflikty i politicheskii pro-test* (Sankt-Peterbug: Blits, 2000), 34.

[48] V. I. Lenin, "Ocherednye zadachi,"; See also V. I. Lenin, "O "levom" rebiatstve i o melkoburzhuaznosti," in *Izbrannye*, tom 2, 651-55.

[49] About the Kadets (Constitutional Democrats), which was the party of the intel-ligentsia par excellence, was quite radical. See, for example, W. Rosenberg, *Liberals in the Russian revolution. The Constitutional Democratic Party 1917-1921* (Princeton, NJ: Princeton University Press, 1974), 24 and passim.

[50] See O.N. Znamenski, *Intelligentsia nakanune velikogo oktiabria* (Leningrad: Nauka, 1988), 47-49.

[51] The members of the Provisional Government were about 40-60 years old. Miliukov had been born in 1859, Guchkov in 1862 and Kerensky in 1881. The authors of *Vekhi* had been born mostly in the first half of the 1870s.

[52] O. Figes in his book *A People's Tragedy. The Russian Revolution 1891-1924* (London: Jonathan Cape, 1996), considers 1891-1924 as one single period of revolution-ary crisis. However, the years of war and revolution are hard to compare with the more peaceful ones.

[53] Sheila Fitzpatrick has made a more sophisticated division. She divides three main groups of the intelligentsia of the 1920s–30s: the old intelligentsia, the cohort of the militants of the cultural revolution (1928-31) period and the vy-dvizhentsy, who were sent to study during the cultural revolution. See S. Fitz-patrick, *The Cultural Front* (1992), 14.

[54] This term was coined by Sheila Fitzpatrick, see her *Education and Social Mobility in the Soviet Union 1921-1934* (Cambridge: Cambridge University Press, 1979). The fifth generation of the Russian intelligentsia is what has been called the thaw generation. It consisted of those men and women, who were born in the late twenties and thirties. They had been too young for the war, but had ex-perienced it as children. They were the contemporaries of the West European "angry young men" and they supported the liberal initiatives of the late 50s and early 60s. The thaw generation survived to see the perestroika and the fall of the Soviet Union and its political system. They also were instrumental in breaking down the edifice of Soviet ideology. The next generation –the sixth one- grew up in the atmosphere of the perestroika. It had been born in the sixties and the seventies and it never really adopted Soviet ideology, but con-fronted it with varied information, which it received from home and abroad.

[55] For discussion about this generation see M.P.Zezina, *Sovetskaia khudozhestvennaia intelligentsiia i vlast'. V 1950-e – 60-e gody* (Moscow: Dialog-MGU, 1999).

[56] G. L. Smirnov, *Sovetskii chelovek. Formirovanie sotsialisticheskogo tipa lichnosti* (Moscow: Izdatel'stvo politicheskoi literatury, 1980.

[57] Not infrequently, the conduct of the intelligentsia has been considered the direct cause of the revolution. See, for example, Romanovskii, 189-204.

[58] Znamenskii, 100-101.

[59] About the dissolution of the army see Allan Wildman, *The End of the Russian Imperial Army.*

[60] T.A. Abrosimova, "Evoliutsiia nastroenii i pozitsiia intelligentsii nakanune oktiabria 1917 goda,"in *Istoriia i revoliutsiia*, (1999), 189-197.

[61] op. cit., 198.

[62] op. cit., 198.

[63] op. cit., 192-93.

[64] See, for, example, P.Kenez, *The Birth of the Propaganda State* (Cambridge:Cambridge University Press,1985), 35-44.

[65] Znamenskiy, 341.

[66] V. Brovkin, *Mensheviks after October. Socialist opposition and the Rise of the Bolshevik Dictatorship* (Ithaca and London: Cornell University Press, 1987).

[67] Contrary to what Kenez maintains (Kenez, 44), non-Bolshevik socialist newspapers appeared a couple of times even after June- August 1918.

[68] See M. Jansen, *A Show Trial under Lenin: The Trial of the Socialist Revolutionaries, Moscow 1922* (The Hague: Nijhoff, 1982).

[69] C. Rougle, "The Intelligentsia Debate in Russia 1917-1918," in *Art, Society, Revolution. Russia 1917-1921*, Acta Universitatis Stockholmiensis. Studies in Russian Literature 11, (Stockholm, 1979), 68-69.

[70] For example, R. Pipes, *Russia under the Old Regime.*

[71] N. Riasanovsky, *Russia and the West in the Teaching of the Slavophiles. A Study of Romantic Ideology* (Gloucester, Mass: 1965), 135-36.

[72] Ibid., 122.

[73] See Abbot Gleason, "Republic of Humbug: The Russian Nativist Critique of the United States 1830-1930," *American Quarterly* 44 (March 1992), 1-23.

[74] See A.N. Medushevski, "Demokratia i svoboda lichnosti (Pushkin i Tokvil)," in *Rossiia i mirovaia tsivilizatsiia. K 70-letiiu chlena-korrespondenta RAN A.N. Sakharova* (Moscow: Rossiiskaia Akademiia nauk, Institut Rossiiskoi istorii, 2000), 465-80, esp. 476-78.

[75] Katerina Clark, *Petersburg, Crucible of Cultural Revolution* (Cambridge, MA: Harvard University Press,1996), 2.

[76] Ibid.,16.

[77] Ibid., 20.

[78] Ibid., 21. See also Pekka Pesonen, "Vallankumouksen henki hengen vallankumouksessa," *Slavica helsingiensia*, Supplementum II, (Helsinki: 1987).

[79] See James von Geldern, *Bolshevik Festivals, 1917-1920* (Berkeley: University of California Press, 1993).

[80] See A. Nove, *An Economic History of the USSR 1917-1991* (London: Penguin Books, 1992), 62.

[81] For example, Figes, *A People's Tragedy*, 777-78.

[82] E.V. Basner, "My i zapad": ideiia missionerstva v russkom avangarde," in *Russkii avangard 1910-1920-kh gg v evropeiskom kontekste* (Moscow: Nauka, 2000), 27-34.

[83] Stites, *Revolutionary Dreams*, 88-100 and passim.

[84] Kenez 1985, 44-49.

[85] See Kornei Chukovsky, "Dnevnik 1918-1923," *Novyi mir* 7 (1990), 143.

[86] Op. cit., 153, 164, 149.

[87] Op. cit., 145, 156.

[88] Rougle, *The Intelligentsia Debate*, 89.

[89] Figes and Kolonitski, *Interpreting the Russian Revolution*, 168-69.

[90] M. McAuley, "Bread without the Bourgeoisie," in *Party, State and Society in the Russian Civil War*, ed. D.Koenker, W. Rosenberg, R.G. Suny (Bloomington and Indianapolis: Indiana University Press, 1989), 163.

[91] Ibid., 164-65.

[92] See Gleb Struve, *Russian Literature under Lenin and Stalin 1917-1953* (University of Oklahoma Press), 3.

[93] Ibid.

[94] Aleksandr Blok"s famous formulation. See A. Blok, *Rossiia i intelligentsiia* (Berlin: Skify, 1920), 23.

[95] *Skify. Sbornik* (Peterburg: 1917).

[96] Ivanov-Razumnik, *Rossiia i Inonia* (Berlin: Skify, 1920), 10.

[97] V. G. Belous, " Ispytanie dukhovnym maksimalizmom," in *Ivanov-Razumnik, Pisatel'skie sud'by. Tiurmy i ssylki* (Moscow: Novoe literaturnoe obozrenie, 2000), 11.

[98] Skoptsy: the sect of self-immolators. Self-castrators.

[99] "truth" denoted by the Russian word "istina."

[100] *Skify: Sbornik* (1917), VIII-IX.

[101] Ibid., XI.

[102] Ivanov-Razumnik, "Ispytanie ognem," ibid., 261-305.

[103] A. Belyi, *Revoliutsia i kul'tura* (Letchwort: Prideaux Press, 1971), 24. (First published in 1917).

[104] See Ivanov-Razumnik, *Ispytanie v groze i bure* (Berlin: Skify, 1920), 8.

[105] Ibid., 36-39; A. Belyi, *Na perevale i Krizis zhizni* (Peterburg: Alkonost, 1918), 90-97.

[106] Rosenthal, "A New World," 228.

[107] V. Markov, *Russian Futurism* (Berkeley and L.A: University of California Press, 1968), 384.

[108] See G. Struve, 14-17.

[109] Cit. in B.G. Rosenthal, "A New World for a New Myth: Nietzsche and Russian Futurism," in *The European Foundations of Russian modernism*, ed. Peter I. Barta (Lewiston, NY: Edwin Mellen Press, 1991), 229-31.

[110] Vasili Kamenski, one of the leading futurists, was, incidentally, one of the first pilots of Russia.

[111] Rosenthal, "A New World," 234.

[112] Anna Lawton and Herbert Eagle, eds., trs., *Words in Revolution: Russian Futurist Manifestoes 1912-1928* (Washington: New Academia Publishing, 2005), 51-52. Reprint of *Russian Futurism through Its Manifestoes, 1912-1928* (Ithaca and London: Cornell University Press, 1988).

[113] Ibid., 85-86, 87.

[114] Not necessarily so from the point of view of conventional thinking. "Long live darkness and black gods and their favorite pig" the chorus sang in *Victory over the Sun* (Rosenthal, "A New World," 230-31). The new barbarians, would be the precursors of the superman.

[115] G. Struve, 17

[116] Ibid., 20

[117] Ibid.

[118] For example, Leonard Schapiro, *The Russian Revolutions of 1917* (New York: Basic Books, 1984), 132-36.

[119] See Brovkin, *The Mensheviks After October*, 49-73.

[120] Jane Burbank, Intelligentsia and Revolution. Russian Views of Bolshevism 1917-1922 (New York, Oxford: Oxford University Press, 1986), 19-20.

[121] 39-40.

[122] 36, 44.

[123] 69-85.

[124] 128-30, 149.

[125] Cit. by Romanovskii, 213.

[126] Cit. by Burbank, 194.

[127] *Iz glubiny. Sbornik statei o russkoi revoliutsii*, Vtoroe izdanie (Paris: YMCA Press, 1967.

[128] Ibid., 25.

[129] Ibid.

[130] S. A. Askoldov, "Religioznyi smysl russkoi revolitsii," in *Iz glubiny. Sbornik statei o russkoi revoliutsii* (Paris:YMCA Press, 1967), 44-48.

[131] Op. cit., 60- 64.

[132] Nikolai Berdiaev, "Duhi russkoi revoliutsii," in *Iz glubiny. Sbornik statei o russkoi revoliutsii* (Paris:YMCA Press, 1967), 82.

[133] Op. cit., 74-79.

[134] Op. cit,. 82.

[135] Op. cit. p. 82-95. Also A.S. Izgoev pointed to Dostoevsky's Shigalev as a prophetical insight. Op. cit. p. 188. V.N. Muraviev also used the metaphor of Smerdiakov's parricide and Ivan's guilt to it. Op. cit. p. 241-42.

[136] Op.cit. , 95-102.

[137] S. L. Frank, *De profundis*, op. cit. p. 322. 326.

[138] Petr Struve, *Istoricheskii smysl russkoi revoliutsii i natsionalnye zadachi*, op. cit. p. 289-306.

[139] Op. cit., 289.

[140] Op. cit., 291-92.

[141] Op. cit. p. 299-300.

[142] Op. cit. p. 300-301.

[143] Op. cit., 305.

[144] A. S. Izgoev, *Sotsializm, kul'tura i bolshevizm*, op. cit., 204.

[145] See Romanovskii, 232.

[146] N. Poltoratskii, "Sbornik 'Iz glubiny' i ego znachenie," in *Iz glubiny. Sbornik statei o russkoi revolutsii* (Paris: YMCA Press, 1967), x.

[147] *Novaia zhizn'*, 9 (22) May 1917. Also in: M. Gorkij, *Obekväma tankar om oktoberrevolutionen* (Stockholm, 1983), 90.

148 *Novaia zhizn'* 23.12. (5.1.) 1917.

149 *Novaia zhizn'* 10 (23.) 11.1917.

150 *Novaia zhizn'* 19. 11. (2. 12. 1917).

151 *Novaia zhizn'* 1. 5. (18. 4.) 1918; See also NZh 30. (17. 7.)1918.

152 *Novaia zhizn'* 6. 6. (24. 5.).

153 Kondakov, 385.

154 B. D. Wolfe, *The Bridge and the Abyss. The Troubled Friendship of Maxim Gorky and V.I. Lenin* (London: Pall Mall Press, 1967), 36.

155 M. Gorki, *Revoliutsiia i kul'tura*, 3-e izdanie (Spb s.a., 1918), 2, 8.

156 Ibid., 9.

157 Ibid.

158 Ibid., 5-6.

159 Hans Guenther, *Der sozialistische Uebermensch. Maxim Gorkij und der sowjetische Heldenmythos* (Stuttgart-Weimar: J.B. Metzler, 1993), 75.

160 See V. Shentalinsky, *The KGB's Literary Archive* (London: The Harvill Press, 1995), 227.

161 Wolfe, 75-76.

162 Wolfe, 88.

163 Wolfe, 80.

164 M. Gorky, *Dve kul'tury. Kommunisticheskii Internatsional 1919*, Vol. 2, 172-73.

165 M. Gorky, *Internatsional intelligentsii. Kommunisticheskii Internatsional 1919*, Vol. 7-8.

166 Shentalinsky, 229.

167 Wolfe, 136, 145-49; Shentalinsky, 236-38.

168 M. Gorky, *O russkom krestianstve* (Berlin: 1923).

169 Shentalinsky, 238.

170 See Gorky, *O russkom krestianstve* (Berlin: 1923) ; Figes, A People"s Tragedy.

171 Shentalinsky, 241-44.

172 See *Programmy i ustavy KPSS*, (Moscow: Izdatel'stvo politicheskoi literatury, 1969), 19-28.

173 Ibid., 52.

174 Ibid., 51-61.

175 V. I. Lenin, "Detskaia bolezn' 'levizny' v kommunizme," in *Izbrannye*, tom 3, 285-301.

176 Ibid., 288, 307-15.

177 V. I. Lenin, "X s"ezd RKP(b)," in PSS, tom 43, 90. See also "Pervonachalnyi proekt rezoliutsii X s"ezda RKP o edinstve partii," in *Izbrannye*, tom 3, 528.

178 V. I. Lenin, "Gosudarstvo i revoliutsiia," in *Izbrannye*, tom 2, 260-61.

179 Programmy i ustavy KPSS, 52.

180 Lenin's speech at the 7th congress of the Moscow party organization, PSS, tom 44., 191-200.

181 For example, S.A. Pavliuchenkov, *Voennyi kommunizm v Rossii: Vlast' i massy* (Moscow: RKT-istoriia, 1997), 90-108.

182 M. S. Shatz, *Jan Waclaw Machajski. A Radical Critic of the Russian Intelligentsia and Socialism* (University of Pittsburgh Press, 1989), 150-51.

183 Cit. in Stites, *Revoultionary Dreams*, 74.

184 Shatz, 156-57.

[185] C. Read, *Religion, Revolution and the Russian Intelligentsia. 1900-1912. The Vekhi Debate and its Intellectual Background* (London: Macmillan, 1979), 160.

[186] Shatz, 174-75.

[187] "Obrashchenie tsentral'noi gruppy 'Rabochaia pravda'," in *Piterskie rabochie i "diktatura proletariata" Oktiabr' 1917-1929. Ekonomicheskie konflikty i politicheskii protest. Sbornik dokumentov* (St. Petersburg: Blitz, 2000), 305-12.

[188] Ibid., 311-12

[189] P. V. Alekseev, *Revoliutsiia i nauchnaia intelligentsiia* (Moscow: Izdatelstvo politicheskoy literatury, 1987), 44-45.

[190] Ibid., 49.

[191] See Taisia Osipova, "Peasant Rebellions: Origin, Scope, Dynamics and Consequences," in *The Bolsheviks in Russian Society. The Revolution and Civil Wars*, ed. Brovkin (1997), 154-73.

[192] See e.g. Evan Mawdsley, *The Russian Civil War* (Boston: Allen & Unwin, 1987), 272-78.

[193] Ibid., 278-85.

[194] Cit in. Lars T. Lih, *Bread and Authority in Russia 1814-1921* (Berkeley: University of California Press, 1990), 197.

[195] Ibid.

[196] S. Smith, "The Socialists-Revolutionaries and the Dilemma of Civil War," in *The Bolsheviks in Russian Society. The Revolution and Civil Wars*, ed. V. Brovkin (New Haven and London:Yale University Press, 1997), 83-100.

[197] V. I. Lenin, *O "levom" rebiatstve*. PSS t. 36,311.

[198] V. Dunham, *In Stalin's Time. Middleclass values in Soviet fiction* (Cambridge: Cambridge University Press, 1976), 21.

[199] See chapter 1.

[200] See James C. McClelland, "The Professoriate in the Russian Civil War," in *Party, State and Society*, 243-66, and Kendall E. Bailes,"Natural Scientists and the Soviet System," also in *Party, State and Society*, 267-95.

[201] I. V. Got'e, *Time of Troubles, The Diary of Iurii Vladimirovich Got'e*, Translated, Edited, and Introduced by Terence Emmons (London: I.B. Tauris Publishers, 1988), 319.

[202] Ibid., 157.

[203] M. McAuley, *Bread and Justice. State and Society in Petrograd 1917-1922* (Oxford: Clarendon Press, 1991), 373-75.

[204] Ibid.

[205] V. Buldakov, *Krasnaia smuta* (Moscow: Rosspen, 1997), 44.

Chapter 4

[1] V. I. Lenin, "XI s'ezd RKP(b)," in *Izbrannye*, tom 3, 633.

[2] Lenin PSS tom 43, 24.

[3] See Samuel Farber, *Before Stalinism. The Rise and Fall of Soviet Democracy* (Cambridge: Polity Press, 1990), 211.

[4] Lenin, "Proletarskaia revoliutsiia i renegat Kautskii," *Izbrannye*, tom 3, 17.

[5] Ibid., 41.

[6] See *Vlast' i oppozitsiia. Rossiiskii protsess XX stoletiia* (Moscow: Rosspen, 1995), 93-100.

[7] See A.Cherniaev, Finliandskiy sled v "Dele Tagantseva." *Rossiia i Finliandiia na XX veke* (Sankt-Peterburg: 1997), 180-200.

[8] See,for example, V. Brovkin, *The Mensheviks after October*, 105-25; D. Dallin, "Between the World War and the NEP," in *The Mensheviks*, ed. L.Haimson (Chicago: 1974), 192, 196-97.

[9] N. N. Primochkina, *Pisatel' i vlast'* (Moscow: Rosspen, 1998), 86-89.

[10] Aimermakher, 46.

[11] Ibid., 44.

[12] Primochkina, 86-89; Aimermakher, 52.

[13] L. Mally, "Intellectuals in the Proletkult: Problems of Authority and Expertise," in *Party, State and Society*, 296-311, 299.

[14] Ibid., 308.

[15] Ibid., 104-05.

[16] S. Fitzpatrick, *The Cultural Front. Power and Culture in Revolutionary Russia* (Ithaca and London: Cornell University Press, 1992), 1.

[17] Boym, 62.

[18] cit. by Stites, 168.

[19] Primochkina, 158.

[20] Fitzpatrick(1992), 2.

[21] Ibid.

[22] Ibid., 4.

[23] Ibid., 4-6.

[24] Dmitri N. Shalin, "Intellectual Culture," in *Russian Culture at the Crossroads. Paradoxes of Postcommunist Consciousness*, ed. Dmitri N. Shalin (Las Vegas: Westview Press, 1996), 68.

[25] V. S. Izmozik, *Glaza i ushi rezhima. Gosudarstvennyi politicheskii kontrol' za naseleniem Sovetskoi Rossii v 1918-1928 godakh* (Sankt-Peterburg: Izdatel'stvo Sanktpeterburgskogo universiteta ekonomiki i finansov, 1995), 134.

[26] Ibid.

[27] Aimermakher, 55.

[28] Aimermakher, 55-56.

[29] P.M. Kerzhentsev, *K novoi kul'ture* (Peterburg: Gosudarstvennoe izdatel'stvo, 1921), 68.

[30] See, for example, M. Slonim, *Soviet Russian Literature. Writers&Problems 1917-1967* (Oxford: Oxford University Press, 1967), 12.

[31] Aimermakher, 55-56.

[32] Aimermakher, 59-62.

[33] Protiv upadnichestvo, protiv "Eseninshchiny" (Moscow, 1926); Lunacharski, ed., *Upadochoe nastroenie sredi molodezhi. Eseninshchina* (Moscow: Izdatel'stvo kommunisticheskoi akademii,1927).

[34] V. I. Lenin, Uderzhat li bolsheviki godudarstvennuiu vlast'. In *PSS* tom 34., 287-339.

[35] See Nove, 62.

[36] Izmozik, 132.

[37] Nove 1992, 110.

[38] M. Lewin, *Making of the Soviet System* (New York: Parthenon Books, 1985), 19.

[39] See Fitzpatrick,(1992), 32; J.-P-Depretto, *Les ouvriers en URSS 1928-1941* (Paris: Publications de la Sorbonne, 1997), 359.

[40] See, for example, I. Getzler, *Kronshtadt 1921. Dokumenty* (Moscow: Demokratiia, 1997).

[41] V. I. Lenin, "XI s'ezd," in *Izbrannye*, tom 3, 647.

[42] Vlast i oppozitsia (1995), 107.

[43] Izmozik, 64.

[44] Fitzpatrick (1992), 18, 31. See also Izmozik, 108.

[45] Izmozik 1995, 109.

[46] Lenin, "Stranichki iz dnevnika 2.1.1923," in *Izbrannye*, tom 3, 707-08. Lenin mused that teachers especially should be given more bread and, besides, that he should be" lifted to such a high position, which he never could reach in a capitalist society." Ibid.

[47] V. I. Lenin, "Zadachi soiuzov molodezhi," in *Izbrannye*, tom 3, 423.

[48] See chapter 3 above.

[49] Fitzpatrick 1992, 26-27.

[50] See chapter 3 above.

[51] Cit. in Helga Schulze-Jung, *Ökonomie und Politik in Sowjetrussland 1920-24. Zum Prozess der Willensbildung in der KPR(b) in den ersten Jahren der neuen Ökonomischen Politik* (Marburg: Vlg Arbeitsbewegung und Gesellschaftwissenschaft, 1978), 174.

[52] Ibid., 219-21.

[53] S. Fitzpatrick, "The Myth of Class: Bolshevik Politics and the Idea of the Proletariat in the Early Soviet years," in *Il Mito dell'URSS. La Cultura occidentale e l"Unione Sovietica* (a cura di Marcello Flores e Francesca Gori), (Milano: Franco Angeli, 1990), 34-36.

[54] Fitzpatrick (1992), 27-29, 34.

[55] Ibid., 91 and passim.

[56] PSS, tom 54, 215-16.

[57] Iu. S. Borisov, *Proizvodstvennye kadry derevni 1917-1941* (Moscow: Nauka, 1991), 137.

[58] See Fitzpatrick (1992), 91-114.

[59] Vera Tolz-Zilitinkevich, *Russian Academicians under Soviet Rule* (Ph.D. dissertation., CREES, Birmingham: 1993), 256-59.

[60] Izmozik, 140.

[61] See, for example, P. Konecny, *Builders and Deserters. Students, State and Community in Leningrad, 1917-1941* (Montreal & Kingston: McGill-Queens University Press,1999),123-25; Borisov, 1991, 137-39.

[62] About the artists see Izmozik,. 64.

[63] See,for example, J. Burbank, *Intelligentsia and Revolution, Russian Views of Bolshevism 1917-1922* (Oxford: Oxford University Press, 1986).

[64] Mikhail Agurski, *Ideologiia natsional-bolshevizma* (Paris: YMCA Press, 1980).

[65] For example, J.Suomela, *Rajanatakainen Venäjä* (Helsinki: SKS, 2001).

[66] Hilde Hardeman, *Coming to Terms with the Soviet Regime. The "Changing Signposts" Movement among Russian Emigrés in the Early 1920s* (Northern Illinois University Press, 1994), 174 (the author refers to a poll made by Pravda and published in the autumn of 1922).

[67] A. E.Gorsuch, *Youth in Revolutionary Russia. Enthusiasts, Bohemians, Delinquents* (Bloomington and Indianapolis: Indiana University Press, 2000), 81.

[68] Hardeman, 158; About other smenavekhist newspapers see Suomela 2001, 130-33.

[69] S. S. Chakhonin, "V Kanossu!" in *Smena vekh* (1921), 166.

[70] Ibid., 150.

[71] Ibid., 156-63.

[72] S. Lukianov, "Revoliutsiia vlast'," in *Smena vekh*, 90.

[73] A.V. Bobrishev, "Pushkin i novaia vera," in *Smena vekh*, 148.

[74] Iu. Kluchnikov, "Smena vekh," in *Smena vekh*, 22.

[75] Hardeman, 154-55.

[76] Hardeman, 155, 158.

[77] N. Meshcheriakov, "Novye vekhi," *Krasnaia nov'* 3 (1923).

[78] A. Voronski, "O dvukh romanakh," *Krasnaia nov'* 2 (1921); "Iz sovremennykh nastroenii," *Krasnaia nov'* 3 (1921).

[79] P. Kogan, "Russkaia literatura v gody Oktiabrskoi revoliutsii," *Krasnaia nov'* 3 (1921).

[80] A. Voronski, "Literaturnye otkliki," *Krasnaia nov'* 2 (1922).

[81]M. Levidov, "Organizovannoe uproshchenie kul'tury," *Krasnaia nov'* 1 (1923). Levidov was criticized by V. Polonski in Krasnaia nov' 3 (1923).

[82] V. Polonski, "Zametki ob intelligentsii," *Krasnaia nov'* 1 (1924).

[83] M. A. Reisner, "Intelligentsiia, kak predmet izucheniia v plane nauchnoi raboty," *Krasnaia nov'* 1 (1922).

[84] A. Voronski, "O gruppe pisatelei 'Oktiabr" i 'Molodaia gvardia'," *Krasnaia nov'* 2 (1924).

[85] *Sud'by sovremennoi intelligentsii* (Moscow: Moskovskii rabochii, 1925).

[86] Ibid., 44-46.

[87] Lenin had already denounced this psychology in his booklet *What Is to Be Done* in 1902. See chapter 3 above.

[88] Ibid.

[89] See e.g. Veresaev's and Gladkov's works analyzed in this book.

[90] V. N. Brovkin, 54-63.

[91] See V. Brovkin, *Russia after Lenin. Politics, Culture and Society, 1921-1929* (London and New York: Routledge, 1998), 173-89.

[92] *"Sovershenno sekretno." Lubianka Stalinu o polozhenii v strane* (Moscow, 2001). This series, which will encompass the years 1922-34, contains reports of the workers' (and peasants') moods for every month.

Chapter 5

[1] V. I. Lenin, "Detskaia bolezn' "levizny" v kommunizme," in *Izbrannye proizvedeniia*, tom 3, 288.

[2] Ibid., 364.

[3] "X s'ezd RKP(b)," in *Izbrannye proizvedeniia*, tom 3, 528.

[4] V. I. Lenin, "O kooperatsii," ibid., 713.

[5] Ibid., 714, 715.

[6] M. Gorky, *Revoliutsiia i kul'tura, Kul'tura i svoboda* (Petrograd, 1917), 3.

[7] V. I. Lenin, O nashei revoliutsii, *Izbrannye proizvedeniia*, tom 3, 721-22.

[8] See below.

[9] V. I. Lenin, "Zadachi soiuzov molodezhi" (2.10.1920), in *Izbrannye proizvedeniia*, tom 3, 415-18.

[10] S. Plaggenborg, *Revolutionskultur. Menschenbilder und kulturelle Praxis in Sow-jetrussland zwischen Oktoberrevolution und Stalinismus* (Köln: Böhlau Verlag, 1996), 22-24.

[11] Ibid., 37.

[12] Ibid., 46-55; Stites, *Revolutionary Dreams*, 149-59, 200-204; V.I. Kasianenko, "Ob-shcestvennaia mysl' 20-kh godov o formirovanii sotsialisticheskogo byta v SSSR," *Voprosy istorii* 4 (1982): 35-36.

[13] L. Sosnovski, *O kul'ture i meshchanstve* (Leningrad, 1927), 13-14.

[14] Ibid., 106-07.

[15] T. Kostrov, "O kul'ture, meshchanstve i vospitanii molodezhi," *Komsomolskaia pravda* 1.4.1926.

[16] For example, L. Machikhin, "Sosnovskii mudrit," *Komsomolskaia pravda* 16.2.1927.

[17] For example, "My – ne meshchane!" *Komsomolskaia pravda* 12.5.1926.

[18] "O kulturnoi rabote Komsomola," *Komsomolskaia pravda* 9.3.1927.

[19] For example,G. Bergman, "Dve knigi o vrage," *Komsomolskaia pravda* 31.7.1928; Vl. K, "U poslednei cherty," *Komsomolskaia pravda* 22.01.1926.

[20] Plaggenborg, 86.

[21] Plaggenborg, 75.

[22] See chapter 4, above.

[23] See,for example A. Chistikov, "Gosudarstvo protiv kartochnoi igry," in *Normy i tsennosti povsednevnoi zhizni, 1920-e 1930-e gody* (St. Petersburg: Neva, 2000), 299- 316.

[24] M. Gorky, "Ot "vragov obshchestva"—k geroiam truda," Pravda, 26.1.1936.

[25] N.B. Lebina, *Povsednevnaia zhizhn sovetskogo goroda. 1920-e – 1930-e gody* (St. Petersburg: Neva, 1999), 84.

[26] Lebina 1999, 53, 58, 63. In 1926 ¾ of the hooligans in St. Petersburg were worker youths.

[27] The term referred to a certain Bykov, who, in Leningrad, had tried to kill the master of his workshop.

[28] The so called Chubarov-alley case, see Naiman.

[29] Peredovik= one who surpassed the records of others at work.

[30] Lebina, 75.

[31] V. I. Lenin, "Zadachi soiuzov molodezhi (speech on 2 October 1920)," in *Izbran-nye proizvedeniia*, tom 3, 422 -23.

[32] See, for example, Gabor T. Rittersporn, "Formy obshcestvennogo obikhoda molodezhi I ustanovki sovetskogo rezhima v predvoennom desiatiletii," in *Normy i tsennosti*, 347-64.

[33] See Lebina, *Povsednevnaia zhizn'*, 58.

[34] Ibid., 25.

[35] See I. Takala, " "Veselie Rusi": iz istorii alkogol'noi problemy v Rossii (1900-1930-e gody)," in *Normy i tsennosti*, 269-77.

[36] Trotsky, *Voprosy*, 65-69, 70-75, 140-47.

[37] Ibid., 65-66.

[38] Naiman, *Sex in Public*, 137.

[39] Ibid., 138.

[40] Ibid., 183.

[41] Lebina, *Povsednevnaia zhizn'*, 34.

[42] J. Obertreis, " "Byvshee" i "izlishnee"," in *Normy i tsennosti*, 90.

[43] A. Slepkov, *Byt molodezhi* (Moscow, 1926), 6-9.

[44] See N. Lebina, "O pol'ze igry v bizer," in *Normy i tsennosti*, 21- 25.

[45] Obertreis op. cit., 86.

[46] Lebina, *Povsednevnaia zhizn'*, 207.

[47] Ibid., 211.

[48] Ibid., 215.

[49] Ibid., 216.

[50] Ibid., 217-18.

[51] See N. Edmunds, "Music and Politics: The Case of the Russian Association of Proletarian musicians," *Slavonic and East European Review*, 78, no. 1 (January 2000) : 74-76.

[52] R. Rothstein, "The Quiet Rehabilitation of the Brick Factory: Early Soviet Popular Music and its Critics," *Slavic Review* 39, no. 3 (September 1980), 374.

[53] Doklad deyatelnosti 2-go otdela OPK OGPU za 1924 g. Archive of the FSB, fond 2,. Op. 3., delo 679, 47

[54] OGPU vsem gublitam, oblitam 2.7.1924, Archive of the FSB, fond 2, op. 2, delo 884, 32

[55] Doklad o deiatelnosti 2-go otdelenia OPK OGPU za 1923 g., Archive of FSB, fond 2, opis 3, delo 679, 3.

[56] Ibid., 15.

[57] OGPU, vsem gublitam, oblitam 2.7.1924, Archive of the FSB, fond 2, opis 2, delo 884, 44

[58] Doklad o deiatelnosti za 1924, 8.

[59] OPK OGPU, svodka za mart 1925, fond 2, opus 3, delo 679, 63.

[60] Ibid., 63 ob, 64.

[61] Brovkin, 150.

[62] The files are being published in the series *"Sovershenno sekretno". Lubianka Stalinu o polozhenii v strane (1922-1934 gg.).* (Moscow, 2001) Volumes 1-7 (covering the years 1922-1929) exist by 2005.

[63] For example, *Sovershenno sekretno*, tom 4, 423-30.

[64] *Sovershenno sekretno*, tom 4, chast 2, 821-22, 881-90 etc.

[65] See about this also S. Fitzpatrick, *Stalin's Peasants*, (Oxford: Oxford University Press, 1994.

[66] *Sovershenno sekretno*, tom 2, 305-319, 387-96.

[67] Ibid., 95 etc.

[68] *KPSS v rezoliutsiiakh i resheniiakh s'ezdov, konferentsii i plenumov TsK* (Moscow, 1984), tom 4, 9.

[69] *Sovershenno sekretno*, tom 4., chast 2, 783.

[70] *Sovershenno sekretno*, tom 2, 389; tom 4., chast 2, 720-21.

[71] Fitzpatrick 1992, 91-114.

[72] Ibid., 55-56.

[73] Ibid., 55-58, 98.

[74] Fitzpatrick 1992, 94.

[75] Fitzpatrick 1992, 102-103.

[76] I. I. Shitts (Schütz) was born in 1874. A historian by education he taught in a lyceum, wrote articles for the Granat encyclopeadia and worked in other comparable jobs. He sent his diary to France, probably through diplomatic mail. It was found and published in 1991 by Vladimir Berelowitch. See Berelowitch's "posleslovie" in Dnevnik 'velikogo pereloma' (Paris: YMCA-Press, 1991), 321-23.

[77] Ibid., 10-11.

[78] Ibid.

[79] See T.M. Goriaeva, Politicheskaia tsenzura v SSSR 1917-1991 (Moscow: Rosspen, 2002), 227-28.

[80] Fitzpatrick 1992, 104-09.

[81] Ibid., 110.

[82] A. Lunacharski, "Intelligentsiia i ee mesto v sotsialisticheskom stroite'lstve," Revoliutsiia i kul'tura, Vol. 1, 1927, 23-35.

[83] The analogy comes from the countryside, where the "seredniaks" (middle-peasants) had to be drawn to the Bolsheviks" side.

[84] N. Bukharin, "O starinnykh traditsiiakh v sovremennom kul'turnom stroitel'stve (mysli vslukh)," Revoliutsiia i kul'tura, Vol. 1, 1927 (15. November).

[85] M.A. Reisner (1868-1928) was one of the most remarkable Bolshevik scholars, whose interests encompassed many fields, from justice, sociology and history to psychoneurology. He was an active Bolshevik, one of the founders of the Communist Academy.

[86] M. Reisner, "Meshchanstvo, (sotsiologicheskii ocherk)," Krasnaia nov' 1 (1927): 149-63.

[87] See chapters 1 and 3, above.

[88] Taras Kostrov, pseudonym of Aleksandr Martynovskii (1901-1930).

[89] T. Kostrov, "Kul'tura i meshchanstvo," Krasnaia nov' 3-4 (1927): 21-33.

[90] F. B. Gladkov, Tsement. Sobranie socinenii, tom 1., 277-517 (Moscow 1983). See also, K. Clarke, The Soviet Novel. History as Ritual (Chicago, London, 1981), 69-80.

[91] Pervyi vsesoiuzhnyi s'ezd sovetskikh pisatelei 1934. Prilozheniia (Moskva: Sovetskii pisatel', 1990), 24.

[92] N. Ostrovski, Kak zakalialas' stal' (Moscow 1977).

[93] Ibid., 368.

[94] Ibid., 170-71.

[95] Ibid., 255.

[96] Ibid., 364-66.

[97] Ibid., 234,323.

[98] Ibid., 285.

[99] G. I. Petrovskii, "Kak khorosha zhizn'!" Molodaia gvardiia no. 1 (1936): 178-81.

[100] M. Kolosov, "V chem sila Nikolaia Ostrovskogo?" Molodaia gvardiia 1 (1936): 182- 83.

[101] L. Rub, "Nikolai Ostrovsky i ego chitateli," Molodaia gvardiia 4 (1935): 143 46.

[102] N. Zhdanov, "Smysl zhizni," Znamia 3 (1937): 269-76.

[103] A. Platonov, "Pavel Korchagin," Literaturnyi kritik 10-11 (1937): 242.

[104] See R. Stites, Revolutionary Dreams, 133.

105 R. Stites, *The Women's Liberation Movement in Russia: Feminism, Anarchism and Bolshevism 1860-190* (Princeton, NJ: Princeton University Press, 1978).

106 E. Naiman, *Sex in Public. The Incarnation of Early Soviet Ideology* (Princeton, NJ: Princeton University Press, 1997).

107 See the examples in Ostrovsky's, Veresaev's and Gladkov's books, for instance,

108 A. Kollontay, *Novyi moral i rabochii klass* (Moscow: Izdatelstvo TsIK, 1919.

109 *Sotsializatsiia zhenshshin*. s.l., s.a. (Petrograd, 1918?). This booklet was obviously a Bolshevik mystification, which was done in order to compromise the anarchists.

110 Discussed, for example, by Walter Laqueur, *The Fate of the Revolution* (MacMillan, 1967).

111 F. Engels, *Der Ursprung der Familie, des Privateigentum und des Staats* (Berlin: MEGA Bd. 29, 1990). In fact, here Engels is quite vague about the possible liquidation of the family.

112 I. Utekhin, *Ocherki kommunal'nogo byta* (Moscow: OGI, 2001), 123-29 and passim.

113 See V. V. Grishaev, *Selskokhoziaistvennye kommuny Sovetskoi Rossii 1917-1929* (Moscow: Mysl', 1976), 92, 143. About the communes see also Robert Wesson, *Soviet Communes* (New Brunswick, NJ: Rutgers University Press, 1963).

114 See L. Viola, *Peasant Rebels under Stalin* (New York and Oxford: Oxford University Press, 1996), 49-59.

115 P. M. Kerzhentsev, *K novoi kul'ture* (Peterburg: Gosudarstvennoe izdatel'stvo, 1921), 82-84.

116 Trotsky 1923, 55-58.

Chapter 6

1 Nove, 1992, 157.

2 Brovkin,1999, 222.

3 I. Stalin, Results of the July Plenum of the CC, CPSU(b). in: *Works*, Volume 11 (Moscow: Foreign Languages Publishing House, 1954), 206-13.

4 Ibid.

5 I. Stalin, The Right Deviation in the CPSU (b). *Works*, Vol. 12, 22-29.

6 M. Lewin, 1985, 221.

7 For the extremely dire economic situation, see Elena Osokina, *Za fasadom stalinskogo "izobilia"* (Moscow: Rosspen, 1998) and S. Fitzpatrick, *Stalin's Peasants*, 48-67 and passim.

8 S. Fitzpatrick, *The Russian Revolution*, (Oxford: Oxford University Press, 1982), 8 passim.

9 M. E. Glavatsky and V.F. Chufarov, "O formirovanii nauchno-pedagogicheskoi intelligentsii v SSSR," in *Iz istorii sovetskoi intelligentsii* (Novosibirsk: Nauka, 1974), 42.

10 Ibid., 43.

11 I. Stalin, Work of April Joint Plenum of CC and CCC. *Works*, Vol. 11, 57-68.

12 Ibid., 60-72.

[13] Lynne Viola, *The Best Sons of the Faherland: Workers in the Vanguard of Soviet Collectivization,* (Oxford: Oxford University Press, 1987), 210-18.

[14] I. Stalin, Speech at the Eigth Congress of the All-Union Leninist Young Communist League 16th May 1928, *Works,* Vol. 11, 79-82.

[15] Fitzpatrick, 1992, 149-62.

[16] Ibid., 161.

[17] Ibid., 142.

[18] Fitzpatrick, 1992, 129-48.

[19] R.W. Davies, *The Industrialization of Soviet Russia,* Vol. 3, *The Soviet Economy in Turmoil* (Basingstoke: Macmillan, 1989), 261-67.

[20] Fitzpatrick, 1992, pp. 139-40; L. Sabsovich, *SSSR cherez 10 let.* (Moscow: Moskovskii rabochii, 1930).

[21] A new journal, *Trezvost' i kul'tura,* first published in 1928 pointed the way. See 1(1928): 3 and passim.

[22] *Trezvost' i kul'tura* 1 (1928): p. 10 describes the situation in Dneprostroi, where everybody was drinking hard. Strangely enough, the hardest drinkers were the workers, who drank until they became unconscious.

[23] "Nashi zadachi," *Trezvost' i kul'tura*; "Kul'turnaia revolutsia," *Trezvost' i kul'tura* 1 (1928).

[24] "Ot redaktsii," *Revoliutsiia i kul'tura* 1(1927): 5-7 (The journal was started at the end of the year.

[25] A.Deborin,"Marksizm i kul'tura," *Revoliutsiia i kul'tura* 1 (27).

[26] N. Bukharin, "O starinnykh traditsiiakh i sovremennom kul'turnom stroitel'stve," Revoliutsiia i kul'tura 1 (1927): 22-23.

[27] P. Kerzhentsev, "Chelovek novoi epokhi," *Revoliutsiia i kul'tura,* 3-4 (1927):19- 21.

[28] Fitzpatrick, 1992,113.

[29] I. Stalin, Grain Procurements and Prospects for the Development of Agricultural Development in *Works,* Vol. 11, 6.

[30] Hiroaki Kuromiya, "The Commander and the Rank and File. Managing the Soviet Coal-mining Industry, 1928-33," in *Social Dimensions of Soviet Industrialization,* ed. William G. Rosenberg and Lewis H. Siegelbaum, (Bloomington and Indianapolis: 1993).

[31] According to a contemporary foreign observer. See V.A. Shishkin, *Rossiia v gody "velikogo pereloma" v vospriiatii inostrannogo diplomata (1925-1931 gg.)* (Sankt Petersburg: Dmitrii Bulanin, 1999), 263-64.

[32] See Fitzpatrick, 1992, 115-41 and passim.

[33] For example, T. Vihavainen, "Sovjetpressens syn på officerskretserna i Finland omkring 1930," *Historisk tidskrift för Finland* 2 (1980): 150-64.

[34] See Shitts, 260 and passim.

[35] For example Fitzpatrick (Ed.) 1978 .

[36] Fitzpatrick 1992, 143.

[37] *Programmy i ustavy KPSS* (Moscow: Izdatel'stvo politicheskoi literatury, 1969), 19-62.

[38] I. Stalin, *Works,* Vol. 12, 197-205.

[39] Ibid.

[40] *Istoriia vsesoiuznoi kommunisticheskoi partii (bol'shevikov). Kratkii kurs* (Moscow: Gosudarstvennoe izdatel'stvo politicheskoi literatury, 1953) 294-95.

[41] I. Stalin, *Works,* Vol. 3, 40-43.

[42] I. Stalin, *Works*, Vol. 13, 53-82.

[43] I. V. Stalin, conversation with the German Writer Emil Ludwig. 13 December 1931, *Works*, Vol. 13, 106-25.

[44] I. Stalin, Report to the Seventeenth Party Congress. 26 January 1934. *Works*, Vol. 13, 288-388.

[45] Ibid., 358-69.

[46] Ibid.,362-64.

[47] Ibid., 361.

[48] See Fitzpatrick, 1992, 127.

[49] Fitzpatrick, 1992, 145-48; Lewin, 236.

[50] Fitzpatrick, 1992, 145-48.

[51] Lewin, 237.

[52] See Lewin, 236.

[53] Primochkina, 1998, 116-41.

[54] N.Slomova, "S kem zhe my, Serapionovye brat'ia?," *Revue des etudes slaves*, tome 71, Fasc. 3-4, 541-553.

[55] Aimermakher, 125-27.

[56] Ibid., 131.

[57] Aimermakher, 124-25.

[58] K. Clark, "Engineers of Human Souls in an Age of Industrialization: Changing Cultural Models, 1929-41," in W. Rosenberg and L. Siegelbaum (Eds.), 252.

[59] Ibid.

[60] Ibid., 253.

[61] Primochkina, 1998, 222-27, 29.

[62] Literaturno-osvedomitel'naia svodka 5-go otdela SOOGPU 24.5.1930, TsA FSB, D. no PF-410, l. 24-28; Vsevolod Sakharov, *Mikhail Bulgakov: Pisatel' i vlast'* (Moscow: Olma-Press,2000), 161-71.

[63] *Vlast' i khudozhestvennaia*, 29-31, 138, 142, 144.

[64] Gorky to Stalin on 8 January 1930. *Vlast' i khudozhdestvennaia*, 124-25.

[65] Gorky to Stalin on 2 November 1930, *Vlast' i khudozhestvennaia,* 130-31.

[66] *Vlast' i khudozhestvennaia*, 143-44.

[67] Shentalinsky, 257.

[68] M. Gorky, "O tsinizme. Otvet korrespondentu," *Pravda*, 30 January 1931.

[69] Ibid.

[70] "Romain Rolland i Gorkii," *Pravda*, 30 January 1931.

[71] Ibid.

[72] "Ruki proch ot M. Gorkogo!" *Pravda,* 15 January 1931.

[73] M. Gorky, "Otvet intelligentu," *Pravda*, 21-22. May 1931.

[74] M. Gorky, *S kem vy, "mastera kultury"? (Otvet amerikanskim korrespondentam).* Moscow, 1932.

[75] Ibid., 26-27.

[76] Ibid., 16-17.

[77] Ibid., 24.

[78] Ibid.

[79] Ibid., 30-31.

[80] V. Friche, "M. Gorkii i proletarskaia literatura," *Krasnaia nov'* 3 (1928): 230.

[81] Ibid.

[82] Friche, "M. Gorki i proletarskaia literatura," *Krasnaia nov'* 3 (1928): 229.

[83] Ibid., p. 230. See also L. Kleinbort, "Maksim Gorkii i chitatel' nashikh dnei," *Krasnaia nov'* 10 (1928): 158- 85.

[84] Ibid. See also M. Shaginian's opinion in *Vlast' i khudozhestvennaia*, 239.

[85] Postanovlenie politbiuro TsK VKP(b) "O vystupleniakh chasti sibirskikh lite-ratorov i literaturnykh organizatsii protiv Maksima Gorkogo" 15 December 1929, in, *Vlast' i khudozhestvennaia*, 123-24. Gorky seemed embarrassed about this support and asked Stalin to stop these kinds of measures. Ibid., 124-25.

[86] V. V. Veresaev (1867-1945, pseudonym for V.V. Smidovich) had both a philologi-cal and a medical education. He published books, which described the Rus-sian intelligentsia from the 19th Century to the 1940s. He received the Stalin prize in 1943.

[87] V. V. Veresajev, *Sestry (Sisarukset* Finnish edition. Hämeenlinna, 1935).

[88] Istoriia sovetskoi politicheskoi tsenzury: Dokumenty i kommentarii. (Moscow: 1997), 294

[89] The "light cavalry" refers to raids by Komsomol activists, which purported to exercise moral—and other—pressure against petty bourgeois bureaucrats and other non-proletarian phenomena.

[90] Ibid. 315-16

[91] We are told that only 400-500 of the 6000 workers were in the movement,Veresajev, 1935, 286.

[92] Ibid., 112, 327-28.

[93] Ibid., 318.

[94] Ibid.,248.

[95] Ibid., 175-78.

[96] Ibid., 183-84, 208-10.

[97] Ibid., 358.

[98] Ibid., 286, 364.

[99] K. Polonskaia, " 'Sestry' Veresaeva," *Literaturnyi kritik* 3 (1933): 135-39. *Komso-molskaia pravda* in its turn had doubts about the author's familiarity with his subject: he might have known some Komsomols, but that did not mean that he knew the Komsomol in general. See Z.Vitenzon, "Chei grekh?" *Komsomol-skaia pravda* 137, (1933).

[100] V. Veresaev, *Literaturnye portrety* (Moscow: Respublika, 2000), 485-92. Veresaev's text was written in 1938.

[101] I. Ilf., E. Petrov, *Dvenadtsat' stul'ev. Zolotoi telenok* (Moscow, 1948).

[102] E. Troshchenko, "Poslednie prikliucheniia anarkhicheskogo individuuma," *Krasnaia nov'*, 9 (1933): 169-76.

[103] Evg. Zhurbina, "Ob Il'fe i Petrove," *Oktiabr'* 10 (1937), 172.

[104] V. Mayakovskii, "Klop", "O Klope" (essays) in *V. V. Mayakovskii, teatr i kino*, tom 2 (Moscow: Gosudarstvennoe izdatel'stvo Iskusstvo, 1955), 443- 448.

[105] Konst. Shuvalov: Elektrotekhnik "Bob," *Komsomolskaia pravda* 27 August 1927.

[106] V. Mayakovskii, Klop. *Sobranie sochinenii v odnom tome* (Moscow: 1958), 404-21.

[107] Ibid., 422-442.

[108] V. Mayakovskii, 1955, 455.

[109] See, for example, *The God that Failed. Six Studies in Communism* (London: Hamish Hamilton, 1950).

[110] E.G. Nello Aiello, *Il lungo addio. Intellettuali e PCI dal 1958-1991* (Roma-Bari: Editori Laterza, 1997).

[111] Especially successful was Willy Muenzenberg, who, according to Marcello Flores, involved practically "the whole intelligentsia of the world" in his pro-Soviet actions. See M. Flores, *L'immagine dell ÚRSS. L'occidente e la Russia di Stalin (1927-1956)* (Milano: Il Saggiatore, 1990), 19.

[112] V. Shlapentokh, 105-48.

[113] P. Hollander, *Political Pilgrims. The Travels of Western Intellectuals to the Soviet Union, China and Cuba 1928-1978* (Oxford and New York: Oxford University Press, 1981).

[114] Ibid., 48-49.

[115] Ibid., 57.

[116] Ibid., 53, 57, 62.

[117] See, for example, Flores 1990, 95.

[118] Hollander, 74-101.

[119] Ibid., 106, 135.

[120] Hollander, 160-67. See also L. Feuchtwanger, *Moscow 1937. My Visit Described for my Friends* (New York: The Viking Press, 1937).

[121] See Sylvia R. Margulies, *The Pilgrimage to Russia. The Soviet Union and the Treatment of Foreigners, 1924, 1937* (Madison: The University of Wisconsin Press, 1968).

[122] See, for example, *The Rationalization of Russia by Bernard Shaw*. Edited with and introduction by Harry M. Geduld (Bloomington: Indiana University Press, 1963 (originally 1933)), 76-79, 80-82.

[123] Michela Nacci, Il "Communismo borghese." La Russia e l'America viste dall'Europa. In: *Il mito dell'URSS* 1990, 365-73. Also the emigrated Menshevik, F. I. Dan believed that Russia was "Americanizing." See Andrea Panaccione, "L'Immagine dell'URSS nell'emigrazione menscevica: F.I.Dan," in *Il mito* 1990, 61-86.

[124] Flores, 90, 65-67 and passim.

[125] Nacci 1990, 377; Francesco Cataluccio, :"Joseph Roth e i miti dell'America," in *Il mito* 1990, 335-42.

[126] See the list of books by the year in Flores 1990.

[127] See Andrea Graziosi, "La conoscenza della realtà sovietica in occidente negli anni '30. Uno sguardo panoramico," in *Il mito* 1990, 157-71.

[128] Bernard Shaw, for instance, called the plan "the only hope of the world." Flores, 1990, in *Il mito* 1990, 120.

[129] See L. Kopelev, *Und schuf mir einen Götzen. Lehrjahre eines Kommunisten* (Hamburg: Hoffman und Campe, 1979), 289-337.

[130] *Glazami inostrantsev* (Moscow: Gos. izdatelstvo khudozhestvennoi literatury, 1932).

[131] Depretto, 1997, 356.

[132] "Konservatiivi Bellairsin kysely ulkoministeri Hendersonille," *Helsingin Sanomat*, 3.1.1930.

[133] See the reports of the Finnish envoy in Geneve. Archive of the Finnish Foreign Ministry. Reports of the London Mission. UM 73 A. Joensuun maakunta-arkisto.

[134] Ibid., Reports of the Finnish envoy in London.

[135] Ibid., The Committee's letter to the Finnish Envoy, 20 January 1923.

[136] See the leading articles of *The Times, Daily Telegraph, Morning Post* and *Manchester Guardian* of 5 June 1931.

[137] "The Unclean Thing," *The Morning Post*, 20 July 1931.

[138] "A Mad Policy," *The Morning Post*, 23 July 1931.

[139] S. Chapman, *The Metro-Vickers Trial in Context* (Master of Social Sciences Dissertation., CREES, Birmingham 1996), 36.

[140] See e.g. Stalin's letter to Gorky on 15 December 1930. *Vlast' i khudozhestvennaia*, p. 138. This explanation was repeated in countless slogans on the front pages of the press. The same ideas were still expressed in the histories of Soviet foreign policy up until the end of the Soviet era.

[141] See Iz doklada Pravitelstva SSSR VI S'ezdu Sovetov, 8 March 1931, *Dokumenty vneshnei politiki SSSR*, tom XIV (Moscow, 1968), 135- 45.

[142] Ibid.

[143] The topic has been treated by A. Solzhenitsyn in his GULAG-Archipelago, especially tom III, Finnish edition *Vankileirien saaristo*. Kustannuspiste. (Tampere, 1976). Good official documents are in I. Chukhin, *Kanaloarmeitsy Karelii* (Petrozavodsk, 1990).

[144] Solzhenitsyn, 1976, 67.

[145] *Belomorsko-baltiiskii kanal imeni Stalina. Istoria stroitel'stva 1931-1934*, Pod. red. M. Gorkogo, L. Averbakha, S. Firina (Moscow: 1998) (Reprint from 1934), 68.

[146] All the canals were presented on the book's inner cover for comparison. See *Belomorsko...* 1998.

[147] *Belomorsko-baltiiskii...* 1998, 608-13.

[148] Ibid., pp. 48-64. The idea of the "fascist" nature of Finland was the invention of the Finnish red refugees, who were living in Soviet Karelia, where they had a leading role until the mid-30s, after which they were destroyed *en masse*. About this see e.g. M. Kangaspuro, *Neuvosto-Karjalan taistelu itsehallinnosta* (Helsinki: SKS, 2000) (an English summary).

[149] *Belomorsko-baltiiskii*, 2.

[150] Ibid., 12.

[151] Ibid.

[152] Ibid., 15.

[153] Ibid., 17.

[154] Ibid., 18.

[155] Ibid., 19.

[156] Ibid., 19-20.

[157] B. Studer, B. Unfried, *Der stalinistische Parteikader. Identitätsstiftende Praktiken und Diskurse in der Sowjetunion der dreissiger Jahre* (Köln: Böhlau Vlg, 2001), 45.

[158] See S. Zhuravlev, *"Malenkie liudi" i "bol'shaia istoriia". Inostrantsy moskovskogo elektrozavoda v sovetskom obshchestve 1920-kh – 1930-kh gg.*

[159] See I.R. Takala, Natsional'nye operatsii OGPU/NKVD v Karelii in *V sem'e edinoi, Natsional'naia politika partii bol'shevikov i ee osushchestvlenie na Severo-Zapade Rossii v 1920-1950-e gody*, pod redaktsiei Timo Vikhavainena i Iriny Takala (Petrozavodsk: Izdatel'stvo petrozavodskogo universiteta, 1998), 161-206.

[160] See A. Kostiainen, *Loikkarit* (Helsinki: Otava, 1988).

[161] See Takala, 1998.

[162] Studer-Unfried 2001, 15. See also Bertold Unfried, *Selbstkritik im Stalinismus. Erziehungsmittel und Form des Terrors*, In: Wladislaw Hedeler (Hg.) *Stalinscher Terror 1934-41* (Berlin: BasisDruck, 2002), 161, 170-73.

[163] Studer-Unfried, 21.

[164] Ibid., 154.

[165] Ibid., 289.

[166] Ibid., 214.

[167] Ibid., 159.

[168] Ibid., 294.

[169] See Jens-Fietje Dwars, Deutungsmuster des stalinschen Terrors, in Hedeler (Hg.), 299-309.

Chapter 7

[1] See, for example, Lewin, 254-56.

[2] Dunham, 3-23.

[3] Lewin, 251-57.

[4] The classic presentation of this principle may be found in the notorious *Short Course of the History of the CPSU*. See *Istoriia vsesoiuznoi kommunisticheskoi partii (bol'shevikov). Kratkii kurs* (Moscow: Gospolitizdat, 1953), 309-15, 343-46.

[5] Ibid., 278-86, 290-98.

[6] J.V. Stalin, Works, Vol. 13., 362-66.

[7] Lewin, 235.

[8] A. Avdeenko, "Ob intelligente," Pravda, 9 December 1934.

[9] See, for example, Vikhavainen-Takala 1998, 26-30.

[10] About this see T. Vihavainen, "How did the Bolsheviks Cope With National Sentiments?" in *The Fall of an Empire, the Birth of a Nation*, ed. Chris J. Chulos and Timo Piirainen (Ashgate: Aldershot, 2000), 75-98.

[11] Stalin, "Speech delivered at the First All-Union Congress of Collective-Farm Shock Brigaders," in *Works*, Vol. 13. 254-56. All the kolkhozniks would be well off in 2-3 years, Stalin promised.

[12] Stalin, "Speech at the First All-Union Meeting of the Stakhanovites 17.10.1935," in *Works*, Vol. 14. 89 In fact, the abolition of rationing meant increasing difficulties for many, who could not afford the now free prices.

[13] S. Davies, "The Crime of 'Anti-Soviet Agitation" in the Soviet Union in the 1930s," *Cahiers du monde russe*, 39 (1.2) (Janvier-Juin 1998), 155.

[14] Ibid.

[15] For example, S. Fitzpatrick, *Everyday Stalinism. Ordinary Life in Extraordinary times: Soviet Russia in the 1930s* (New York and Oxford: Oxford University Press, 1999), 156-63.

[16] See, for example, D. Beyrau, *Intelligenz und Dissens. Die Russischen Bildungsschichten in de Sowjetunion 1917 bis 1985* (Goettingen:Vandenhoeck & Ruprecht, 1993), 122-24.

[17] I. Golomsshtok, *Totalitarnoe iskusstvo* (Moscow: Galart, 1994), 106-07.

[18] Public opinion seems to have been quite freely interpreted by the powers that be. See Fitzpatrick, *Everyday Stalinism*, 152-54.

[19] Stalin, "Report for the XVII Party Congress," in *Works*, Vol. 13. 381.

[20] For example, Fitzpatrick 1992, 230-35.

[21] Confidential letter of the CC on 18 January 1935, cited by Stalin in his report "About the Defects of Party Work, on 3 March 1937," in *Works*, Vol. 14. 191-92.

[22] Stalin, "About the Project of the Constitution of the USSR," in *Works*, Vol. 14. 136-83.

[23] "Izmenilsia sostav nashei intelligentsii," *Pradva*, 13 December 1936.

[24] Lewin, 234-36, 247.

[25] See I.Kaplan, "O polnoi pobede sotsializma v oblasti kul'tury," *Komsomolskaia pravda*, 5 March 1939.

[26] In practice, the vast majority of the new workers were of peasant origin. See Lewin, 218-21. Lewin speaks about a "deculturation" of the new workers on page 304.

[27] H. Guenther, *Die Verstaatlichung der Literatur. Entstehung und Funktionsweise des sozialistisch-realistischen Kanons in der sowjetischen Literatur der 30er Jahre* (Stuttgart: J.B. Metzlersche Verlagsbuchhandlung, 1984), 10-12.

[28] Ibid., 11.

[29] Ibid., 11, 13.

[30] Ibid., 11.

[31] Ibid., 13.

[32] Ibid., 16.

[33] Ibid., 14. See also this book , chapter 8.

[34] See below in this chapter.

[35] Hans Guenther, *Die kompensatorische Funktion der sozialistisch-realistischen Literatur der 1930-er Jahren,"in: Stalinismus. Probleme der Sowjetgesellschaft zwischen Kollektivierung und Weltkrieg* (Frankfurt am Main and New York: Hrsg. Gernt Erler und Walter Suess, Campus Verlag, 1982), 261, 270.

[36] See Vera Dunham's classic, *In Stalin's Time. Middle-Class Values in Soviet Fiction* (Durham and London, 1990).

[37] See Katerina Clark, *The Soviet Novel. History as Ritual* (Chicago and London: The University of Chicago Press).

[38] V. I. Lenin, "Zadachi soiuzov molodezhi," in *Izbrannye proizvedeniia*, tom 3, 411-12.

[39] About this slogan see A.I. Morozov, *Konets utopii. Iz istorii iskusstva v SSSR 1930kh godov* (Moscow: Galart, 1995), 61-62.

[40] See J. Brooks, "Socialist Realism in Pravda: Read All about It?" *Slavic Review*, 53, no. 4 (Winter 1994): 989.

[41] See Groys, *Gesamtkunstwerk*, 56.

[42] Dmitri Furmanov, *Tshapajev*, Finnish edition (Moscow: Progress, 1979), 117-19.

[43] Ibid., 157.

[44] Ibid.,206.

[45] For example, A. Volkov, "Kniga o tvorchestve Dmitriia Furmanova," *Literaturnyi kritik*, 8 (1936); M. Serebrianski, "Dmitrii Furmanov," *Literaturnaiia ucheba*, 2 (1936); A. Makarenko, "'Chapaev" D. Furmanova," *Literaturnyi kritik*, 10-11(1937), 102-119.

[46] See Elena Osokina, *Za fasadom "stalinskogo izobiliia."* (Moscow: Rosspen, Moscow 1998), 75-80, 173-83.

[47] *Pervyi vsesoiuznyi s'ezd sovetskikh pisatelei 1934. Stenograficheskii otchet* (Moscow: Khudozhestvennaia literatura, 1934), reprint edition (Moscow: Sovetskii pisatel', 1990), prilozheniia iii, iv,v.

[48] "Gorky's letter to Stalin on 2 August 1934," in *Vlast' i khudozhestvennaia intelligentsiia*, 220-223.
[49] *Pervyi vsesoiuzhnyi* 1934, 1.
[50] *Pervyi vsesoiuznyi* 1990, 2-5.
[51] Ibid., 3.
[52] Ibid., 7.
[53] Ibid.
[54] Ibid., 8-9.
[55] Ibid., 11-12.
[56] Ibid.,13-14.
[57] Ibid., 16-18.
[58] Ibid., 675-81.
[59] *Pervyi vsesoiuzhnyi*, 479-503.
[60] *Vlast' i khudozhestvennaia*, 234-35.
[61] *Pervyi vsesoiuznyi*, 499-500.
[62] *Pervyi vsesoiuznyi*, 491.
[63] *Pervyi vsesoiuznyi*, 573-78, 671.
[64] *Vlast' i khudozhestvennaia intelligentsiia*, 230-31.
[65] *Vlast' i khudozhestvennaia*, 227-28.
[66] Berberova, 256 (*Poslednie novosti*, 10.7.1927; « refutation » *Pravda*, 23.8.1927).
[67] *Vlast' i khudozhestvennaia*, 232-36.
[68] *Vlast' i khudozhestvennaia*, 227-28.
[69] *Vlast' i khudozhestvennaia*, 420-21.
[70] Ibid., 316-17.
[71] *Pervyi vsesoiuznyi*, 286-87.
[72] *Vlast' i khudozhestvennaia*, 229-30.
[73] Ibid., 232-33.
[74] Isaac Babel in ibid.
[75] Semeiko in ibid.
[76] Spravka ob otnoshenii pisatelei k proshedshemu S'ezdu, TsA FSB, fond 3, opus 7, por. 56, ll. 70-93
[77] See B. Groys, *Gesamtkunstwerk Stalin* (Muenchen, Wien, 1988).
[78] About such intellectuals see, for example, *Vlast' i khudozhestvennaia*, 257-64, 487-99.
[79] Cited in Brandon Taylor, *Art and Literature under the Bolsheviks*, Vol 1 (London and Concord, Mass: Pluto Press,1991), 17.
[80] Ibid., 42.
[81] Bukharin in a discussion about art and revolution on 13 March 1925, cited in *Marxismus und Formalismus. Dokumente einer Literaturteoretischen Kontroverse* (Muenchen: Hrsg. und uebersetzt von Hans Guenther und Karl Hielscher, Carl Hauser Vlg, 1973), 67-68.
[82] Lunacharsky in a debate in *Pechat' i revolutsiia* in 1924, cited in *Formalismus*, 83-95.
[83] I. Golomshtok, *Totalitarnoe iskusstvo* (Moscow, 1994), 247, 109-110.
[84] Golomshstok, pictures.
[85] Groys, *Gesamtkunstwerk*, 47-48.
[86] *Bol'shaia sovetskaia entsiklopediia*, tom 24, (Moscow, 1953) s.v. "Klassitsizm."
[87] K. Clark, *The Soviet Novel. History as Ritual* (Chicago and London: University of Chicago Press).

[88] Hubertus Gassner and Echkhart Gillen, "Vom utopischen Ordnungsentwurf zur Versöhnungsideologie in aestetischen Schein. Beispiele sowjetischer Kunst zwischen den 1. Fuenfjahrplan und der Verfassungskampagne 1936-37," in *Stalinismus*, 304, 334.

[89] Guenther, *Maxim Gorkij*, 136-37.

[90] Groys, 47.

[91] See Hans Guenther, *Maxim Gorkij*,184-97.

[92] "Spetssoobshchenie sekretno-politiceskogo otdela glavnogo upravleniia gos-bezopasnosti o tvorcheskoi konferentsii moskovskihk khudozhnikov, 2.12.1935" in *Istoriia sovetskoi politicheskoi tsenzury* (Moscow: Rosspen,1997), 477-80.

[93] M. Gorky, "O formalizme," *Pravda*, 9 April 1936.

[94] "Stat'i 'Pravdy' ob iskusstve i ikh znachenie," *Literaturnyi kritik*, 3 (1936): 3-11.

[95] The struggle against "vulgar sociologism," or explaining the essence of an artistic product by the class-origin of the author became one of the topics of the day. See, for example, M. Rozental, "Protiv vulgarnoi sotsiologii v literaturnoi teorii," *Literaturnaia gazeta*, 10 September 1936.

[96] P. Kerzhentsev, "Chuzhoi teatr," *Pravda*, 17 December 1937.

[97] See above chapter 1.

[98] See Leonid Maksimenkov, *Sumbur vmesto muzyki. Stalinskaia kul'turnaia revoliutsiia 1936-38* (Moscow: Iuridicheskaia literatura, 1997).

[99] Sobraniia moskovskikh pisatelei po voprosu o formalizme 10.3., 13.3., 16.3.1936 TsA FSB RF (Archive of the FSB), fond 3, opus 3, por. 1216, ll. 1–16.

[100] B. Guber, "...odin smelyi chelovek, kotoryi skazal otkryto to, chto dumaet bol'shinstvo ob etikh lakeiakh iz 'Pravdy'" ; Zamochkin, "Pasternak fakticheski vyrazil nastroeniia bol'shinstva pisatelei, kotorye boiatsia tolko priamo govorit'," ibid.

[101] *Vlast' i khudozhestvannaia*, 302-04.

[102] Otkliki literatorov i rabotnikov iskusstv g. Moskvy v sviazi s opublikovaniem v "Pravde" stati o kompozitore Shostakoviche. TsA FSB RF, fond 3, op. 3, por. 121, ll. 31-38.

[103] Sobranie moskovskikh pisatelei po voprosu o formalizme. TsA FSB, f.3, op. 3, por. 1216, ll. 9-16.

[104] It was observed that, for example, Susanna Mar and L. Nikulin considered Pasternak's speech as "anti-Soviet" and "reactionary." Ibid.

[105] *Vlast' i khudozhestvennaia*, 220-23.

[106] In 1985 Mikhail Geller, with some credibility wrote that Soviet newspeak was no longer a Soviet phenomenon, but had already, in fact, become the "Esperanto of the second half of the twentieth century." See M. Geller, *Mashina i vintiki* (London: Overseas Publications Interchange Ltd, 1985), 286.

[107] Sinyavsky, *Soviet Civilization*, 195.

[108] Ibid.,196.

[109] Geller,1980,275.

[110] Ibid.

[111] *Programmy i ustavy*, 39.

[112] Geller, 274.

[113] The program of the VKP(b) of 1919, in *Programmy i ustavy*, 38.

114 See, for example, A.V. Blium, *Za kulisami "ministerstva pravdy"*. *Tainaia istoriia sovetskoi tsenzury 1917-1929* (Sankt Peterburg: Akademicheskii proiekt, 1994), 82-93.

115 See, for example, *Vlast' i khudozhestvennaia*, Stalin's letters, 126-27, 134-37, 141-42 and others.

116 Ibid., 99-100.

117 Ibid., 100-101.

118 See Goriaeva, 213-17.

119 Blium, 47.

120 "Privivat' shkolnikam liubov' k klassicheskoi literature," *Pravda*, 8 August 1936.

121 A.V. Blium, *Sovetskaia tsenzura v epokhu total'nogo terrora 1929-1953* (Saint Petersburg: Akademicheskii proekt, 2000), 150.

122 Ibid., 164.

123 Ibid., 149-50, 168.

124 Ibid., 158.

125 *Istoriia sovetskoi politiceskoi tsenzury*, 278-81.

126 Ibid., 181.

127 Ibid., 225-26.

128 Ibid., 109.

129 *Pervyi vsesoiuznyi*, 1990, sodoklad S.Ia Marshaka, 20-38.

130 Blium, 212.

131 Ibid., 212, 222.

132 Ibid., 94-123.

133 Ibid., 108.

134 *Istoriia sovetskoi politicheskoi tsenzury*, 284-85.

135 Blium, 140.

136 *Istoriia sovetskoi politiceskoi tsenzury*, 323.

137 Ibid., 21.

138 Ibid., 170-72.

139 *Istoriia sovetskoi politicekskoi tsenzury*, 430-31.

140 Blium, 49.

141 Blium, 202-203.

142 Ibid., 202-09.

143 A model case is that of the Finn Raoul Palmgren. See T. Vihavainen, *Stalin i finny* (Saint Petersburg: "Neva," 2000), 96-97.

144 See for instance Gorky's letter to A. A. Andreev 8.12.1935 in *Shchast'e literatury*, 201.

145 For instance, in 1936 it was decreed that Moscow writers would have 100 cars for their use. *Shchast'e literatury. Gosudarstvo i pisateli 1925-1938* (Moscow: Rosspen, 1997), 226.

146 D. Beyrau, *Intelligenz und Dissens. Die russischen Bildungsschichten in der Sowjetunion 1917 bis 1985* (Goettingen: Vandenhoeck &Ruprecht, 1993), 99.

147 Ibid., 100.

Chapter 8

[1] See *Vlast' i khudozhestvennaia intelligentsiia*, 487-99. ("Spetssoobshtshenie upravleniia kontrrazvedki NKGB SSSR "Ob antisovetskikh proiavleniiakh i otritsatelnykh politicheskikh nastroeniiakh sredi pisatelei i zhurnalistov") and passim.

[2] As many as 420 persons of the total of 2524 of the personnel of the Academy of Sciences in Moscow were arrested by the beginning of 1938. *Obshchestvo i vlast'. 1930-e gody. Povestvovanie v dokumentakh* (Moscow: Rosspen, 1998), 182.

[3] *Istoriia vsesoiuznoi kommunisticheskoi partii (bol'shevikov), Kratkii kurs*, 3-4.

[4] Stalin, "O nedostatkakh partiinoi raboty." Doklad na plenume TsK VKP(b) 3 marta 1937, *Sochineniia*, tom XIV, 219-24.

[5] Ibid., 202, 211.

[6] Stalin, Zakliuchitel'noe slovo na plenume tsentralnogo komiteta VKP(b), 5.3.1937, *Sochineniia*, tom XIV, 225-47.

[7] *Istoriia kommunisticheskoi partii. Kratkii kurs*, 309-313,331-32.

[8] Ibid., 337-46.

[9] This meant for instance criminal and other asocial elements, who were destroyed by the thousand in the "Mass operations" of the NKVD. See G. Rittersporn, "'Vrednye elementy,' 'opasnye menshinstva,' i bolshevistskie trevogi," In *V sem'e edinoi: Natsionalnaia politika partii bol'shevikov i ee osushchestvlenie na Severo-zapade Rossii v 1920e-1950-e gody*. Pod red. Timo Vikhavainena i I. Takala. (Petrozavodsk: Kikimora Publications and Izdatel'stvo PGU, 1998), 99-122.

[10] About the "historical front" in general, see, for example, *K izucheniiu istorii* (Moscow: Ogiz, 1938).

[11] Self-criticism as such was not a new invention. It had been the standard method of party purges since 1933 if not earlier. See Unfried 2002, 159-78.

[12] M. Serebrianski, "Sovetskaia khudozhestvennaia literatura za piat' let", *Pravda*, 23.4.1937.

[13] I. Lezhnev, "O Literature i ee kadrakh," *Pravda*, 23.4.1937.

[14] P. Iudin, "Pochemu RAPP nado bylo likvidirovat'," *Pravda*, 23.4.1937.

[15] "Zaiavlenie P. F. Iudina sekretariam TsK VKP(b) I. V. Stalinu I L. M. Kaganovichu o dramaturge V. M. Kirshone, 23.4.1937," in *Vlast' i khudozhestvennaia*, 359-60. Iudin named other people, like the historian I. I. Mints, who was not repressed.

[16] "Pis'mo B. Iasenskogo I. V. Stalinu, 25.4.1937," in *Vlast' i khudozhestvennaia*, 360-62.

[17] Stalin had used in in his speeches in the February-March plenum of 1937 and later it was a key concept of the *Short Course*. The term had also been used also in orthodox theology.

[18] For example, "Vykorchevat' bez ostatka," Leader, *Literaturnaia gazeta*, 15.5.1937.

[19] *Vlast' i khudozhestvennaia*, 404-11 and passim.

[20] "Za bolshevistskuiu bditelnost' v literature," *Novyi mir* 6 (1937): 195-209.

[21] Ibid., 196, 205.

[22] M. Rozental, "Partiia i literatura," *Literaturnyi kritik*, 10-11(1937): 9-36.

[23] Ibid., 31.

[24] See e.g. Babel's case in Shentalinskii 1995, 22-71 and Pilnyak's case, 139-57.

[25] Shentalinskii, 58.

[26] Ibid., 56.

[27] Ibid., 56.

[28] Ibid., 58-60.

[29] Ibid., 156.

[30] *Vlast' i khudozhestvennaia*, 413-14.

[31] Ibid., 415-21.

[32] *Vlast' i khudozhestvennaia*, 354-55.

[33] Shentalinskii 1995, 41.

[34] *Vlast' i khudozhestvennaia*, p. 420-21.

[35] Flores, 270-74.

[36] Hollander, 163-64

[37] L. Feuchtwanger, Moskau 1937; D. Pike, *Deutsche Schriftsteller im Sowjetischen Exil 1933-45* (Frankfurt am Main: Suhrkamp Verlag, 1981), 240-42. Feuchtwanger's pose was widely deprecated in the West. For instance "almost all" Norwegian writers sent him a letter of indignation. See Pike, 241.

[38] Cit. in Hollander, 161.

[39] Dwars 2002, p. 304 In German: "Man kann nicht sagen: in dem Arbeitersstaat Russland herrscht Freiheit. Aber man kann sagen: dort herrscht die Befreiung".

[40] A. Gide, *Retouches à mon retour de l'URSS* (Gallimard, 1937).

[41] "Romen Rollan ob Andre Zhide," *Pravda*, 11.1.1937. Some Soviet writers, like Pasternak, were bold enough to support Gide, which did not escape the attention of the NKVD. See *Vlast' i khudozhestvennaia*, 348.

[42] L. Feikhtvanger, "Estet o Sovetskom Soiuze," *Pravda*, 30.12.1936.

[43] "Smekh i sliozy Andre Zhida," *Pravda*, 3 12.1936.

[44] I. Gruzdev, "Chetvertyi tom 'Klima Samgina'," *Literaturnyi sovremennik*, 6 (1937), 36.

[45] S. Coeure, *La grande lueur a l'est* (Paris: Seuil, 1999), 277.

[46] Ibid., 279.

[47] Ibid., 281.

[48] Pike, 223-24.

[49] Ibid., 231.

[50] Ibid., 233-40.

[51] Ibid., 236-37.

[52] J. Suomela, *Rajantakainen Venäjä. Venäläisten emigranttien aatteelliset ja poliittiset mielipiteet Euroopan venäläisissä sanomalehdissä 1918-1940* (Helsinki: SKS, Bibliotheca historica 67, 2001), 225-32.

[53] Ibid., 234-37.

[54] *Novaia Rossiia*, 24.1.1937 and 12.1.1938 ; cited by Suomela, 237-38.

[55] Bertoni was an Italian fascist journalist, who spent a year in Moscow. The first issue of his book, *Russia: trionfo del fascismo* (Milano: La prora, 1937), was published in 1934, in the aftermath of an Italo-Soviet pact of 1933, which had greatly warmed the relations of the two countries.

[56] Bertoni , 6, 184, 201, 239.

Chapter 9

[1] K. Marks, F. Engels, "Manifest kommunisticheskoi partii," in *Sochineniia*, tom 4, 419-59.

[2] See chapter 4. above.

[3] See, for example, L. Holmes, *The Kremlin and the Schoolhouse. Reforming Education in Soviet Russia, 1917-1931* (Bloomington and Indianapolis: Indiana University Press, 1991), 3 -6.

[4] See A. N. Artizov, "To Suit the Views of the Leader. The 1936 Competition for the best textbook on the History of the USSR," *Russian Social Science Review*, 34, no. 3 (May-June 1993), 73-93.

[5] See K. Petrone, *Life has Become More Joyous, Comrades. Celebrations in the Time of Stalin* (Bloomington and Indianapolis: Indiana University Press, 2000), 116-26.

[6] Dunham, 1976, 22.

[7] Ibid.

[8] See chapter 5 above.

[9] See, for example, V. Brovkin, "Mobilization, Utilization and the Rhetoric of Liberation: Bolshevik Policy Toward Women," in *The Bolsheviks in Russian Society*, ed. V. Brovkin. (1997), 212-34.

[10] A. S. Barsenkov, A. I.Vdovin, V. A. Koretski, *Russkii vopros v natsional'noi politike, XX veka* (Moscow, 1993), 88-108.

[11] Stalin, "Report for the XVII Congress of the VKP(b), Speech in the 1st meeting of the kolkhoz udarniks," in *Works*, Vol. 13, 266-71; 365-66.

[12] See, for example, Dokladnaia zapiska Leningradskogo oblastnogo komiteta o kul'turnoi rabote obkoma ot 11 noiabria 1936 goda. TsGAIPD (Leningrad Party Archive), Fond 24, opis 2B, Delo 1612.

[13] Stalin, "Rech' na pervom vsesoiuznom soveshchanii stakhanovtsev, 17.11.1935," in *Works* XIV, 79-101, esp. 83.

[14] V. Volkov, "The Concept of Kulturnost' in Stalinism," in *Stalinism, New Directions*, ed. Sheila Fitzpatrick. (London and New York: 2000), 218-19.

[15] Ibid., 220.

[16] Ibid., 221.

[17] Ibid., 222-227.

[18] Ibid., 227; Catriona Kelly, "Kulturnost and Consumption" in *Constructing Russian Culture in the Age of Revolution: 1881-1940*, ed. C. Kelly and D. Shepherd (Oxford and New York: Oxford University Press, 1998), 303. Kelly sees the campaign a little longer, beginning in 1934 and ending in 1938.

[19] C. Kelly,"Kulturnost in the Soviet Union," in *Reinterpreting Russia*, ed. Geoffrey Hosking and Robert Service (London: Arnold Publishers, 1999), 203.

[20] S. Fitzpatrick, *Everyday Stalinism* (1999), 83.

[21] L. Siegelbaum, *Stakhanovism and the Politics of Productivity in the USSR, 1935-1941* (Cambridge: Cambridge University Press, 1988), 185.

[22] Fitzpatrick, *Everyday Stalinism*, 90.

[23] Ibid., 90-93.

[24] E. Osokina, *Za fasadom "stalinskogo izobilia"* (Moscow: 1998), 167.

[25] See J. Gronow, *Caviar with Champagne. Common Luxury and the Ideals of the Good Life in Stalin's Russia* (Oxford and New York: Berg), 25 and passim.

[26] J. Hessler, "Cultured Trade. The Stalinist Turn Towards Consumerism," in *Stalinism, New Directions*, ed. Fitzpatrick (2000), 182-209.

[27] Petrone, *Life Has Become More Joyous*, 120-26.

[28] Ibid., 120.

[29] "Lichnaia obshchestvennaia zhizn'," *Komsomolskaia pravda*, 192. 1937; "Byt—eto politika," Leader, *Komsomolskaia pravda*, 2.9.1937; "Byt neotdelim ot politiki," Leader, *Komsomolskaia pravda*, 22.7.1939.

[30] The reports in *Sovershenno sekretno: Lubianka Stalinu o polozhenii v strane* (Moscow, 2001) confirmed this every month.

[31] See chapter 6 above.

[32] "U bolshevika slovo ne raskhoditsia s delom!" *Pravda*, 18 July 1937.

[33] Ibid.

[34] Ibid.

[35] G. Lukach, "Velikoe nasledstvo A. M. Gorkogo," *Literaturnyi kritik*, 9 (1936): 22-23.

[36] An. Linin, "Zametki na poliakh 'Zhizni Klima Samgina'," *Na pod'eme*, 9-10 (1932): 129; B. Valbe, "O 'Klime Samgine.' Samginovshchina, individualizm i meshchanstvo,"*Oktiabr'*, 2 (1933).

[37] V. Arkhangelski, "O "Klime Samgine" M. Gorkogo," *Leningrad*, 9 (1932): 75.

[38] I. Gruzdev, "Obraz Klima Samgina," *Pravda*, 22.12.1936.

[39] T. Khmelnitskaia, "Konets 'Lishnego cheloveka'," *Literaturnyi sovremennik*, 3 (1937): 256.

[40] I. Luppol, "Chetvertyi tom 'Klima Samgina'," *Pravda*, 13.4.1937.

[41] M. Gorky, "Literaturnye zabavy," *Pravda*, 24.1.1935.

[42] M. Gorky, "Proletarskaia nenavist'," *Komsomolskaia pravda*, 29.3.1935.

[43] "Ko vsem ravnodushnym, lentiaiam, poshliakam i prochim urodam, kotorye eshche zhivut i melkaiut v nashei strane."

[44] "Bolshoe tvorcheskoe chuvstvo," *Komsomolskaia pravda*, 15.10.1935.

[45] "Nasha nenavist'," Leader, *Komsomolskaia pravda*, 23.9.1935; "Razoblachat' chuzhdye nravy," Leader, 22.6.1935.

[46] Davies, *Popular Opinion*, 131-32.

[47] *Istoriia vsesoiuznoi (Kratkii kurs)*, 312.

[48] D. Osipov, "Iudushkiny priemy," *Pravda*, 10.12.1936.

[49] "A. M. Gorkii o Shchedrine," *Pravda*, 10.12.1936.

[50] D. Zaslavskii, "Sviataia nenavist'," *Pravda*, 10.12.1936

[51] Ibid.

[52] It is worth noting that also the *Short Course* in its final conclusions singles out those "feeble in faith" among the enemies. (*Istoriia...*), 344.

[53] A. Sinyavsky, *Soviet Civilization. A Cultural History* (New York: Arcade Publishing (New York: 1988), 125-42.

[54] The "central organ" *Pravda* had a quite special role in the Soviet Union. Whatever it published, could safely be considered exemplary and worth emulation for all the other papers. In ideologically important matters the lesser papers used to delay the publication of their own opinion until *Pravda* had expressed its view. Campaigns like that about the struggle against the formalists or for Bolshevik vigilance, were launched and orchestrated by *Pravda*, which would

attack minor papers, if their line did not adequately remind that of *Pravda*.

[55] For example, "Konstitutsiia geroicheskogo naroda," *Pravda*, 16.1.1937; 15.7. "Slava stalinskim bogatyriam!" *Pravda*, 15.7.1937; "Narod vstrechaet svoikh geroev," *Pravda*, 26.7.1937; "Geroicheskie zhenshchiny geroicheskogo naroda," *Pravda*, 3.7.1938; "Slavnaia epopeiia zavershena," *Pravda*, 20.2.1938; "Slava geroiam!" *Pravda*, 21.2. 1938; "Geroiny–letchitsy," *Pravda*, 7.10.1938; "Slava Sovetskim geroiam!" *Pravda*, 8.10.1938.

[56] For instance the feat of the polar flyer Chkalov was the subject matter of 4 pages of *Pravda* in 26.7.1937 and also of 3 pages the following day. S. Levanevski's flight to America was given 2 pages on 13.8.1937. Ivan Papanin, who, with his equipment, had been drifting in the Polar Sea became a super-hero. Papanin's rescue was described on 4 pages on 20.2.1938 and on 3 pages the following day. His arrival in Leningrad was described on three pages in four issues of *Pravda* (16.-19.3.1938).

[57] Of course, there were and had been the same kind of heroes also in the West, including Charles Lindbergh, but their deeds and personalities were understood to be exceptional—and hence sensational.

[58] A. A. Zhdanov, "Leninskie prednachertaniia voploshchenii v zhizn'," *Pravda* 28.1.1938.

[59] "Geroicheskie zhenshchiny nashei rodiny," *Pravda*, 9.10.1938 and others.

[60] Al. Dunaevskii, "Otvazhnye devushki," *Pravda*, 2.3.1937 and others.

[61] "Zhenskie pokhody na shliupkakh," *Pravda*, 10.9.1937.

[62] "Zhenskii avtomobil'nyi probeg," *Pravda*, 25.3.1938.

[63] "Sorevnovanie voroshilovskikh vsadnits," *Pravda*, 5.8.1938.

[64] "30800 kilometrov na velosipedakh," *Pravda*, 5.2.1937.

[65] A. Sharov, "Pozadi 7500 kilometrov," *Pravda*, 2.3.1937; "500 Poletov v den'," *Pravda*, 8.8.1937; "Moskva-Stokgol'm-Moskva. Skorostnyi perelet letchika-ordenonostsa, tov. Novikova," *Pravda*, 21.6.1938; "Patriotizm i geroizm," *Pravda*, 29.6.1938; "Vysotnyi polet letchika N. Fedoseeva," *Pravda*, 3.8.1938; "Vysotnyi polet kapitana F. Zherebchienko," *Pravda*, 26.8.1938 and many, many others.

[66] N. Voronov, "Parashutnyi pryzhok s vysoty 9800 metrov," *Pravda*, 29.7.1937; N. Voronov, "Pryzhok s vysoty 11037 metrov," *Pravda*, 26.8.1937.

[67] "Iz Moskvy v Khabarovsk za 20 chasov 58 minut," *Pravda*, 18.9.1938.

[68] "Nachalsia perelet po 11 respublikam," *Pravda*, 30.9.1938.

[69] K. Clark, "Utopian Anthropology as a Context for Stalinist Literature," in *Stalinism. Essays in Historical Interpretation*. Ed. By Robert Tucker (New York: 1977), 185-91.

[70] F. Vinogradov, "Brat za brata," *Pravda*, 6.2.1937; "Geroi Khasana," *Pravda*, 14.10.; 19.10; 20.10.1938; etc.

[71] "Sovetskii geroizm," *Literaturnyi kritik*, 8 (1937): 3-12.

[72] About this see J. Brooks, *Thank You Comrade Stalin!.Soviet Public Culture from Revolution to Cold War* (Princeton NJ: Princeton University Press, 2000).

[73] See chapter 6 above.

[74] V. Solov'ev, N. Mikhailovskii, "Otkrytie parka im. S. M. Kirova," *Pravda*, 19.5.1938.

[75] "120-tysiachnii miting v Baku," *Pravda*, 13.1.1938.

[76] "Narodnye gulian'ia v Leningrade," *Pravda*, 25.7.1938.

[77] "Schastlivyi den'," *Pravda*, 13.1.1938.

[78] O. F. Leonova, "Chuvstvo ogromnogo shchast'ia," *Pravda*, 14.1.1938.

[79] *Pravda*, 27.4.1938.

[80] "Zhit' stalo khorosho," *Pravda*, 14.5.1938.

[81] "Prazdnik Shchastlivoi molodezhi," *Pravda*, 13.7.1938.

[82] "Fizkul'turnyi parad v Leningrade," *Pravda*, 31.7.1938.

[83] "Narodnoe gulian'e v Leningrade," *Pravda*, 31.8.1938.

[84] "Shchastlivye deti stalinskoi epokhi," *Pravda*, 23.9.1938 (editorial); "Shchastlivaia zhizn' sovetskikh detei," *Pravda*, 23.9.1938; "Milliony detei veselo otdykhaiut v pionerskikh lagerakh," *Pravda*, 9.7.1938.

[85] P. Angelina, "Radostnyi, shchastlivyi trud," *Pravda*, 9.1.1938.

[86] For example, Melik-Pashaev, "Radostno rabotat'," *Pravda*, 5.1.1937.

[87] "Solntse-sovety," *Pravda*, 12.2.1937.

[88] For example, G. Simon, *Nationalism and Policy Toward the Nationalities in the Soviet Union* (Westview Press, 1991), 58-61.

[89] E. Sitkovskii, "O sovetskom patriotizme," *Pod znamenem marksizma*, 9 (1938): 39-57.

[90] F. Konstantinov, "Rastsvet lichnosti v SSSR," *Pod znamenem marksizma*, 2 (1938):42-46.

[91] Ibid. p. 48

[92] V. Berestnev," O preodolenii perezhitkov kapitalizma," *Pod znamenem marksizma*, 3 (1938): 42-44.

[93] Ibid., 44.

[94] For example, "Intelligentsia–sol' zemli sovetskoi," Leader, *Komsomolskaia pravda*, 20.10.1938; "Revoliutsionnuiu nauku – sovetskoi intelligentsii," Leader, *Komsomolskaia pravda*, 30.9.38; "Intelligentsiia strany sotsializma," Leader, *Komsomolskaia pravda*, 4.4.1939; "Molodaia intelligentsiia strany sotsializma,"Leader, *Komsomolskaia pravda*, 14.2.1939.

[95] See, for example, the leaders of *Pravda* on 24.9.1938, "Intelligentsiia strany sotsializma"; 12.10.1938, "Pochetnye zadachi sovetskikh inzhenerov"; 15.10.1938, "Smelee ovladevat' teoriei marksizma-leninizma"; 17.10.1938, "Okruzhim vnimaniem sovetskuiu intelligentsiiu"; 21.10.1938, "Pomoch' tekhnicheskoi intelligentsii ovladet' bolshevizmom"; 23.10.1938, "Sovetskie gosudarstvennye sluzhashchie"; 25.10.1938, "Vooruzhit' bolshevizmom sovetskoe uchitel'stvo."

[96] "Intelligentsiia strany sotsializma," Leader, *Pravda*, 24.9.1938.

[97] "Sovetskie gosudarstvennye sluzhashchie," Leader, *Pravda*, 23.10.1938.

[98] "Smelee ovladevat' teoriei marksizma-leninizma," Leader, *Pravda*, 15.10.1938.

[99] "Pechat' – moguchee oruzhie propagandy." Leader, *Pravda*, 14.10.1938.

[100] Kershaw, 88-106.

[101] I. V. Stalin, "Otchetnyi doklad na XVIII s'ezde partii, 10.3.1939," in *Sochineniia*, tom 1 (XIV), (Stanford, 1967), 398-99.

[102] Ibid.

[103] See E. Iaroslavskii, *O roli intelligentsii v SSSR* (Moscow: OGIZ, 1939), 28.

[104] Ibid., 35, 39-40.

[105] Ibid., 32. See also . "Makhaevskoe otnoshenie k intelligentsii," *Komsomolskaia pravda*, 15.6.1939 and "Khuliganskoe otnoshenie k intelligentsii," *Komsomolskaia pravda*, 16.1.1939.

[106] Cit. in V. A. Nevezhin, "Stalin's 5 May 1941 Addresses: The Experience of Interpretation," *The Journal of Slavic Military Studies,* 11, no. 1 (March 1998): 140.

[107] Robert V. Daniels, "Stalinist Ideology as False Consciousness," in *Il mito* (1990), 233.

[108] Ibid., 235. For a good example about the hostility of a representative of an outstanding member of the technical intelligentsia towards the free-thinking and dissident creative intelligentsia ("kruzhkovaia" or "kukhonnaia" "intelligentshchina") see N. Moiseev, (2000), 133, and passim.

www.ingramcontent.com/pod-product-compliance
Lightning Source LLC
Chambersburg PA
CBHW020602270326
41927CB00005B/144